D0261381

# Quiet Revolutions

on Taiwan, Republic of China

# Quiet Revolutions

## on Taiwan, Republic of China

### Edited by Jason C. Hu

Publisher: Jason C. Hu
Published by Kwang Hwa Publishing Company
2 Tientsin Street, Taipei, Taiwan, ROC

Printed by China Art Printing Works Yu Tai Industrial Corp., Ltd.
6 Pao Chiang Road, Hsintien, Taipei County, Taiwan, ROC

Collator: Chang Hui-chen
Photographers: Yeah Ming-yuan       Huang Chung-hsin
Design and Layout: Chen Su-ling

1st edition, D5     July 1994
Catalog Card No.: GIO-EN-BO-83-045-I

Printed in the Republic of China on Taiwan
Price: US$ 12.00   NT$300

# Contents

# Preface

Previous page: A dazzling fireworks display lights
up the skies over the Chiang Kai-
shek Memorial Plaza in celebra-
tion of the Republic of China's
Double Tenth National Day.

# Preface

The Government Information Office often selects and publishes speeches and important writings by government leaders, on both a periodical and occasional basis, to foster understanding at home and abroad of governmental administrative thinking and social conditions. However, the compilation process for this pioneer undertaking, *Quiet Revolutions on Taiwan, Republic of China*, differed considerably from that of previous GIO publications. Most compilations of speeches by government leaders are arranged chronologically and generally published once a year, thus primarily serving as sources of reference. But we felt a collection of important articles and monographs focusing on timely topics would be even more effective publicity about what has taken place in Taiwan recently and would heighten awareness of its significance. Thus, the plan for selecting and soliciting articles for this work was thematic, and its compilation process was particularly exacting.

Why then, are we publishing *Quiet Revolutions on Taiwan, Republic of China*? The reason is simple: to bear witness to our times. Over the past four decades, the Republic of China has created the world-acclaimed "Taiwan experience" or "Taiwan miracle" which has been analyzed in many publications. However, the ROC has not ceased creating new "miracles" following the "Taiwan experience." In recent years, the Taiwan area has witnessed significant reform and progress in its political, social, cultural and media sectors. The momentous fact that some of these changes are unprecedented in China's five-thousand year history would call for regarding them as "the dawning of a new era." However, perhaps because these reforms were not achieved at the cost of bloodshed or social turmoil, they have, sadly to say, not gotten sufficient press or attention.

The Government Information Office is responsible for changing this situation. We hope the world will take better note of and more deeply understand the efforts and achievements of the Republic of China in the Taiwan area. Although Sir Winston Churchill once said that momentous change is rarely achieved without the shedding of a great deal of blood, sweat and tears, we want the world to know that the significant reforms of the ROC throughout the Taiwan area have mostly been implemented through a quiet, rational, and peaceful process. The people in Taiwan have certainly shed plenty of sweat and tears, but never a drop of blood in attaining all they have achieved. Our record is there for all the world to see.

Democracy in Taiwan has taken root and is growing vigorously. Every crucial moment of power transference has taken place in accordance with our constitution, a far cry from what has happened in other developing nations. Democratic reforms in other such countries often entail social turmoil and bloodshed, but in the Republic of China they have been carried out steadily, peacefully and progressively. The driving force behind our successful reforms has come from the perseverance and vision of our statesmen and the understanding and acceptance of the entire citizenry. Thus, in the long run, we have been able to achieve miraculous results with ballots rather than bullets, with debates instead of battles. Since the scope and significance of these changes is no less than a revolution and the process has been rational and peaceful, we call them "quiet revolutions," also implying the Chinese expectation of "progress in tranquillity."

The term "quiet revolutions" appeared in an *Asian Wall Street Journal* editorial entitled "Taiwan's Quiet Revolution." It declared our "quiet revolution" model for democratic reform, based on economic know-how and step-by-step progress, to be poles apart from the bloody revolutions of the Balkan nations. Our example has proven, the paper said, that not all revolutions require firing bullets.

Most of the forty-five articles included in this book have been selected from internationally known newspapers and academic periodicals; others were written specifically for this publication. The time period involved dates from President Lee's inauguration on May 20, 1990 to the present. Special consideration was given to selecting objective and representative articles. Nevertheless, these works do not necessarily reflect the positions of the ROC government. The contents are divided into eight categories; namely, general policies, politics, the economy, agriculture and the environment, mainland affairs policy, foreign relations, culture and miscellany. To uphold their credibility, all articles in this book are essentially unaltered.

To enable ROC policy makers themselves to bear witness to these "quiet revolutions," we have also included monographs or articles, some of which have appeared in international publications, written by President Lee Teng-hui; Premier Lien Chan; Koo Chen-fu, senior advisor to the president; Fredrick F. Chien, minister of foreign affairs; Huang Kun-huei, chairman of the Mainland Affairs Council; James Soong, governor of the Taiwan Provincial Government, and other government leaders.

A look back at how far we have come bears testimony to how arduous a task it has been for the ROC to accomplish in just five years so much reform and progress—the "quiet revolutions" of which President Lee Teng-hui has been the very architect. The publication of this book coincides with the fourth anniversary of President Lee's inauguration as the Eighth-term President of the ROC. We would therefore like to express our sincere congratulations on this occasion.

Jason C. Hu
Director-General
Government Information Office

# Taiwan's Quiet Revolution

An editorial in the *Asian Wall Street Journal*
November 11, 1992

Not all revolutions are waged with mortars and violence. The bloody Balkans are not the only model of change. From Taiwan comes the example of the "quiet revolution," based on economic know-how and the gradual introduction or reworking of democratic institutions.

Jason Hu, spokesman for the government of Taiwan, stressed this point in a recent speech to the Carnegie Council on Ethics and International Affairs in New York. "Quietly, but surely," he said, "Taiwan and a couple of the other so-called tigers of East Asia, namely Singapore and South Korea, have now traversed far along the path to democracy, but in a much different way from those who have taken the path of violence." Whether it be Confucian culture, which seeks harmony and consensus building, or just plain good economic sense, Taiwan has performed a peaceful miracle.

The extent of the well-known economic miracle can be gleaned from the facts: Taiwan is now the world's 14th-largest economy. Its per-capita income is $8,813, compared with $350 per-capita for mainland China. Long ostracized from regional organizations, it is now active in the Asian Development Bank and has joined the Asia-Pacific Economic Cooperation forum. And it has observer status to the GATT talks, a welcome move though, as we've said before, Taiwan deserves to be a full member.

And then there is the political revolution. The National Assembly has been overhauled, and the legislature is due to come under similar restructuring next month. The elderly incumbent legislators who were elected on the mainland in the late '40s have been retired gracefully. The country now has a stable two-party system, with the Democratic Progressive Party challenging the Kuomintang. There is a mostly free press. Some street demonstrations have briefly jolted social stability, but nothing like the violence that shook Peru or continues to batter what was once Yugoslavia.

Yet another sign of Taiwan's political liberalization came over the weekend, with the end of 43 years of martial law on Quemoy and Matsu, two tiny islands off the coast of southeastern China. Quemoy and Matsu are two names that will go down in the history of the Cold War. In 1958 the U.S. deployed the 7th Fleet when they were bombarded by the Communists on the mainland. As recently as the early '80s, there were occasional hostilities across the waters. The Defense Ministry announced on Friday that next year residents will elect their own lawmakers. Citizens of the nearby mainland cities of Xiamen and Mawei have no such privilege, of course.

In his New York speech, Mr. Hu said Taiwan deserves more credit for its achievements — not just its economic ones but its political ones. "Please don't forget or ignore our quiet revolutions," he pleaded. "In terms of the peace and prosperity we enjoy today, we've shown that the quiet way to democratic development is the admirable way to go." Indeed, a powerhouse economy is not the only model Taiwan has to offer the world's developing democracies.

Reprinted by permission of the
*Asian Wall Street Journal*

# I.
# General Policies

Previous page:President Lee Teng-hui and Premier Lien Chan applaud the athletes competing in the 1993 Taiwan Regional Games.

# The Beginning of a New Era[1]

Lee Teng-hui

Major changes have occurred in the international and domestic situations since 1988. Internationally, the tides of freedom and democracy have swept the whole world. The tattered communism are pushed to the dead end. The collapse of Eastern Europe, the unification of Germany, the disintegration of the Soviet Union, and the end of the Cold War have changed the face of the world. Domestically, we have upheld the ideals upon which this nation was founded, the Three Principles of the People. We have pushed ahead with development based upon political democracy, economic freedom, and the equitable distribution of wealth. We have terminated the Period of National Mobilization for Suppression of the Communist Rebellion, done away with the temporary provisions of the Constitution, mapped out the *Guidelines for National Unification* and, stage by stage, amended the Constitution. These political innovations can be characterized as a set of reasonable and peaceful constitutional reforms that have not only given full expression to the will of the people and but have also adapted the basic law of the nation to realities and requirements prior to national unification. In contrast to the gory suppression of the democracy movement by the Chinese communist regime, the economic recession in industrially advanced nations, and the turbulence in the third world, we have been able to gradually accomplish political democratization, under the preconditions of maintaining social stability and

*Lee Teng-hui is President of the Republic of China.*

3

economic development. This outstanding achievement fills us with incomparable confidence.

Today we stand at a turning point in history. Over two thousand years ago, the Chinese had such democratic thoughts as "the people rank higher than the nobility" and "the people are the foundation of the state." In recent years, we in Taiwan have successfully adopted the Western political philosophy of government of the people, for the people and by the people, and created on Chinese soil the first ever democratic society based on party politics. This achievement, unprecedented in Chinese history, marks the beginning of a new historic era.

Historically, the Chinese have had a traditional caste mentality, ranking people as "intellectuals, peasants, artisans, or merchants." Yet, after more than forty years of propagating education and increasing wealth, we have established a democratic system that is highly concerned for humanity and respects the free will of all people. The social reforms and mental development that we have achieved today in Taiwan have shattered a feudalistic mentality and system that was thousands of years old. This marks the beginning of a new historic era.

Midway through the Ching dynasty, the Manchu court adopted a closed-door policy, resulting in the decline of the nation, the impoverishment of the people, the stagnation of production, and the backwardness of science and technology. The Republic of China on Taiwan, after forty years of determined effort aimed primarily at improving the people's livelihood, has proudly created an economic miracle, which has seen the average per capita GNP rise from a little more than one hundred U.S. dollars to over ten thousand U.S. dollars—a feat unprecedented in Chinese history. This too marks the beginning of a new historic era.

4

While the materialistic nature of communism and its illusions were once in vogue and once swept the Chinese mainland, our late president, Chiang Kai-shek, had the prescience to first point out that communism was doomed to failure. Over the last forty-odd years, our fellow members and compatriots, irrespective of geographic origins, have come together to form a strongly knit "organismic community" on the bastion of national revival that is dedicated to the great undertaking of eliminating communism and unifying China with democracy, freedom, and equitable prosperity. This task is unprecedented in China's history. We are, at this very moment, participating in the creation of a new historic era.

In terms of national development, we are the creator of the "Taiwan experience" and the source of China's hope. One small contribution to the development of Taiwan means a proportionate increase in the hope for the modernization of all of China. Consequently, in addition to political innovation, cultural enrichment, and diplomatic breakthrough, we have also emphasized the realization of the Six-Year National Development Plan to stimulate the economy and improve the quality of the people's livelihood. We hope that by "reconstructing the economic social order and achieving completely balanced development" we can make the Republic of China into a modern nation characterized by democracy, freedom and equitable prosperity by the end of this century.

In conclusion, I must emphasize that the final goal of all of our efforts is still the unification of China. When I took office as the eighth-term president of the Republic of China, I solemnly declared:

"...if the Chinese communist authorities can recognize the overall world trend and the common hope of all Chinese, implement political democracy and a free economic system, renounce the use of military force in the Taiwan Straits and not interfere with our development of foreign relations on the basis of a one-China policy, we would be willing, on a basis of equality, to establish channels of communication, and completely open up academic, cultural, economic, trade, scientific, and technological exchange, to lay a foundation of mutual respect, peace, and prosperity. We hope then, when objective conditions are ripe, we will be able to discuss the matter of our national reunification, based on the common will of the Chinese people on both sides of the Taiwan Straits."

Based on this declaration, we drew up the *Guidelines for National Unification* and renounced the use of force for national unification. It is regrettable, however, that the Chinese communists still choose to overlook increasingly obvious developments in the world and refuse to give up the "one China, two systems" mentality. This had caused the great undertaking of national unification to be stalled in the short-term phase—something no Chinese person wants to see. Here again, we would like to sincerely call upon the Chinese communists to recognize the major trends, to measure public opinion, and to make a positive response.

We must join our hands, link our hearts, and step farther forward in the march towards democratic reform as we strive together to carry out our sacred mission to develop Taiwan and reconstruct China.

NOTES
1. An excerpted address delivered by Lee Teng-hui, President of the Republic of China, at the opening of the 14th National Congress of the Kuomingtang on August 16, 1993 in his capacity as the party's chairman.

# Innovation through Pragmatism[1]

Lien Chan

Since 1988, we have experienced a historic five years filled with changes. During this period we have undergone the tests of legal reform and party politics in the process of democratic development; we have faced the challenges of industrial upgrading and economic transition in an environment of increasing international economic competition. We have at the same time witnessed the collapse of the communist blocs, the dissolution of the Soviet Union, the emergence of a new international order, and the threat of diplomatic blockade and military expansionism by the Chinese communists. Nevertheless, we have been able to achieve the following key administrative objectives:

*Lien Chan is Premier of the Republic of China.*

—Constitutional democratic reform: Under the premise of preserving the original text of the ROC Constitution and maintaining the framework of the division of power among the five yuan, articles have been added to the Constitution in response to the pre-reunification needs of our nation: The Period of National Mobilization for Suppression of the Communist Rebellion has been terminated and the *Temporary Provisions Effective During the Period of National Mobilization for Suppression of the Communist Rebellion* have been abolished in order to promote the further development of constitutional democracy. In conjunction with constitutional reform, the *Public Officials Election and Recall Law* has been amended, and elections were held for the second National

Assembly and second Legislative Yuan, in order to give full voice to the will of the people, and lay a foundation for party politics and local council and assembly politics; new members to the Control Yuan have also been appointed to office, based on constitutional revisions and with the approval of the Second National Assembly; 135 laws and orders relating to the Period of National Mobilization for Suppression of the Communist Rebellion have been reviewed, thus further ensuring the protection of civil and human rights.

—Economic development: Major achievements include increasing public investment, setting up an equitable and reasonable tax system, placing our financial system on a sounder footing, privatizing national corporations, accelerating the upgrading of industry, providing developmental assistance to small and medium-sized enterprises, ensuring fair trade practices, balancing foreign trade, and stabilizing the energy supply. These have all become major forces in the nation's economic development.

Over the past five years, we have experienced outstanding performance in the areas of economics and trade. Our GNP currently stands at more than US$200 billion, ranking 20th in the world; per capita GNP now exceeds US$10,000, ranking 25th in the world; our total value of foreign trade is over US$150 billion, ranking 14th in the world; and of this, exports account for US$81.5 billion, ranking 12th in the world. At the same time, we have amassed US$85.6 billion in foreign exchange reserves, the highest in the world. And the ROC has received high rankings in competitiveness and investment climate annual reports published by authoritative international organizations. Moreover, the ROC is one of the few nations in the world that has been able to achieve high growth under conditions of stability. Annual economic growth has averaged 6.69 percent over the past five years, and the consumer price index increase has remained at approximately 4.38 percent.

In the process of economic development, we have also placed great importance on environmental and ecological protection, and effectively controlled and reduced environmental hazards. Key measures include actively working to reduce waste output, promoting recycling and reuse of resources, constructing waste disposal sites and incinerators, and strictly controlling sources of industrial pollution, while bringing our domestic production structure into compliance with the demands of environmental protection.

—Diplomacy: The achievements of democratic reform and increased economic power have contributed to the development of our external relations. In this period, the number of countries having formal diplomatic relations with the Republic of China grew from 22 to 29. Five years ago, we had 60 representative offices in 40 countries with which the ROC had no formal diplomatic relations. Today we have 90 representative offices in 60 countries with which we do not have formal diplomatic relations, and our official national designation, the Republic of China, is used in the names of 17 of these agencies. The level of contact with other countries has also been greatly upgraded. Many countries with which the ROC has no formal diplomatic relations have sent important government officials to the ROC for visits to express their strong desire to improve relations with the ROC. Furthermore, we are actively working to give something back to the international community. Every year, the ROC allots a budget of US$5.76 million in humanitarian aid to assist countries experiencing natural disasters. The ROC has also established an International Economic Cooperation and Development Fund with a budget of

US$1.1538 billion. Through a package loan program encompassing investment, credit extensions, technical assistance, and participation in international financial organizations, the ROC assists friendly countries in their development. It is our hope that people in the rest of the world will stand up and take note of the ROC's sincerity and efforts to repay the international community.

—Relations with mainland China:Currently there is a National Unification Council under the Office of the President of the ROC; the Executive Yuan has established the Mainland Affairs Council, and helped to set up the private Straits Exchange Foundation. All of these organizations work together to carry out matters concerning the two sides of the Taiwan Straits, and to implement the ROC's policies on mainland China.

In order to achieve its long-term objectives of national unification and to safeguard the rights of the more than 20 million Chinese who live in the Taiwan area, the *Guidelines for National Unification* have been drawn up, to serve as the highest guiding principle in the making of policies concerning mainland China. The legislative process has also been completed for the *Statute Governing Relations Between People of the Taiwan Area and the Mainland Area*, so as to provide a legal framework for the growing exchanges taking place between the two sides. The Executive Yuan has also requested that its agencies draft related laws and regulations as quickly as possible to guide in the development of relations between the two sides. In order to discuss the solution of a number of non-official, functional matters, groundbreaking talks between responsible people of non-official intermdiary groups were held in Singapore in April of this year, and four agreements were signed on a basis of equality. This has made a substantive contribution to future institutionalization of channels of communication between the two sides.

## Face New Issues; Accept New Challenges

Over the past forty-some years, we have on this piece of earth successfully prevented invasion by communist forces and broken through economic backwardness to create the world-renowned "Taiwan experience." But at the same time, it is undeniable that we also face many new issues and challenges.

A matter we find most alarming is the confusion in national identification. An advocacy for "Taiwan independence" has cropped up in our society in recent years. This advocacy is perhaps an emotional reaction of a minority of people out of their detest of Chinese communism and to the threat of interference in our affairs posed by Chinese communists forces. Such people may end up expressing these feelings in the form of a narrow-minded regionalism. We understand this line of thinking, but can in no way accept it. This kind of thinking deliberately pushes aside our common history and ethnic heritage as well as realities. It is against the principles of nationalism, restricts our future developmental space, and could raise the level of tension between the two sides of the Taiwan Straits and result in irreparable injury to both the country and individuals. President Lee Teng-hui once said: "Identification with the Republic of China is a basic premise of any responsible political advocacy." The people of our country must give this matter careful thought and reach a consensus on it.

Our greatest cause for concern is lack of respect for the rule of law. Democratic government means government by the law; this is basic common sense, but is also a truth that is easy to disregard. Our people speak out their support for democracy and fight for rights; but at the same time they are unwilling to accept the controls of law and justice, and the burden of their responsibilities to society. There is an increasing tendency to make any and every issue into a political issue, leading to widespread skirting of the law, playing with the law, and violation of the law. This is not a phenomenon that should occur in a modern society.

Another trend demanding our attention is the slowing down of economic growth. Although the economic growth rate in the ROC is still among the highest in the world, a number of warning signals have been appearing recently, including the difficulty of acquiring land, the labor shortage, rapidly rising wage levels, and an increase of irrational environmental protests. These all have both direct and indirect effects on private and foreign investment; the ROC's favorable balance of trade is also greatly diminishing. Other external factors include the steadily growing economic power of the Asian-Pacific region; pressures of readjustment due to the ROC's future admission into the General Agreement on Tariffs and Trade(GATT); and economic reform and liberalization in mainland China; all of these will erode the relatively favorable position that the ROC previously held and relied on. In the future we will have to make even greater efforts to ensure stable economic growth.

Another matter that demands our attention is losses in economic efficiency and fairness in society. We realize that in a democratic society there will naturally be more demands for greater equality and justice; farmers, labor, and various minority interest groups in particular will demand better welfare and support. Any democratic society, however, must place a premium on hard work and efficiency, build up a tax base and tax sources, maintain a liberal economic system and respect private property ownership if it is to motivate its people to work, and thus move towards progress and prosperity. Only in this way will it be able to bear the burden of providing greater equality and justice to its members. So as a responsible government, we must both be productive and provide welfare. We must not only strike a reasonable balance between economic efficiency and fairness in society; we must also try to attain a higher degree of fairness by doing our best to raise economic efficiency.

## Key Administrative Efforts: innovation through pragmatism

The key points of current administrative work are as follows:

### (1) Pursuing national unification

President Lee once said: "Taiwan and mainland China are both inseparable parts of the territory of China, and all Chinese are our countrymen and brothers. In this time in which the entire human race is seeking peace and reconciliation, all Chinese should also work, in a peaceful and democratic manner, toward our common goal of national unification." In this statement he clearly elucidated our firm stand on pursuing national unification. The manner in which it is done should be rational, peaceful, and on a basis of equality and reciprocity. It will proceed gradually and in a predetermined order from the short-term phase of "exchange and reciprocity", to the medium-term phase of "mutual trust and cooperation", to the long-term phase of "consultations on unification," ultimately resulting, based on a consensus of the Chinese on both sides of the Taiwan Straits, in the establishment of a democratic, free, and prosperous China. In other words, we persist in the ideal of "one China." We are aware of the reality that Taiwan and the mainland are currently ruled by two different political entities. While we hope that we will be able to attain our goal of national unification at an early date, we must at the same time fully respect the wishes and protect the rights of the more than 20 million people who live in the Taiwan area. The government is now actively working to institutionalize exchanges between the two sides of the Taiwan Straits, promoting cultural and educational exchange so as to increase mutual understanding, reduce hostility between the two sides, and gradually establish on both sides a consensus of China as one cultural entity. At the same time we have authorized the Straits Exchange Foundation to discuss various matters with the Chinese communist Association for Relations Across the Taiwan Straits such as how to combat maritime crime, and smuggling of goods and people; how to solve legal incidents involving fishing vessels, and various legal suits. The Chinese communists have thus far not, however, recognized us as a political entity, and make overt efforts to belittle our international standing. They are not even willing to renounce the use of force against Taiwan, thus keeping relations between the two sides in a stalemate, restricted to the short-term phase of the *Guidelines for National Unification*. It is our hope that the Chinese communists will act pragmatically and recognize the direction in which world trends are heading, that they give up their outdated theory of sovereignty, and that they act wisely and give us a favorable response at an early date. It is also our hope that all people of our society understand clearly that our policy of unification is the most advantageous to all the people of our country, and is in fact our only viable policy option. We must therefore improve communication on this matter, and establish a consensus that we all share the same destiny. Only in this way can we assume the initiative in the process of interactive relations between the two sides of the Taiwan Straits, and open up new paths and horizons for the Chinese people.

## (2) Thoroughly implementing constitutional democracy

Democracy is the most effective way for us to bring together the strength of the people, and it is our strongest claim for joining the ranks of the democracies of the world. Over the past three years we resolutely and determinedly overcame all manner of obstacles to succeed in completing a series of rational and peaceful constitutional democratic reforms, thus writing a valuable new chapter in the history of the Taiwan experience. We are, however, well aware that having completed constitutional amendment and revision, much still remains to be done in order to carry the content of these amendments and revisions a step further, so that our constitutional system and the democratic spirit can be fully incorporated into the everyday life of the people. For this reason, it is our hope that before the end of this year, the legislative process can be completed for the *Self-governance Law for Porvinces and Counties*, and *Self-governance Law for Special Municipalities*, and the *Redistricting Law for Administrative Areas*; and also that revisions in the *Public Officials Election and Recall Law*, and the *Law on Civic Organizations* can be made, so that popular elections for provincial governor and special municipality mayors can be held as soon as possible, bringing us a step closer to our goal of implementing local autonomy. We will also review and draft legislation to regulate lobbying and political contributions and related matters to prevent the improper intervention of money in politics.

We are also aware that we cannot depend solely on government administration to fully implement constitutional democracy. Improving coordination between the executive and legislative branches of the government and raising the level of the people's concept of democracy and the rule of law in a short amount of time are also areas in which we should concentrate future efforts.

## (3) Establishing clean and effective government

Accompanying the rapid pace of changes in the social environment over the past several years has been a corresponding rise in the demand for a high quality of government administration. In order to meet the increased expectations of the people and improve our service to the people, the Executive Yuan is currently advancing a number of administrative innovations, with the goal of establishing an administration that is "based on the people, and practiced according to the law." This will set our administration on the track towards an orientation of "serving the people," so as to realize the concrete goals of "institutionalized government agencies, a streamlined organization, efficient staffing of agencies, and modernized administrative management." The Executive Yuan expects to complete a comprehensive review of central and local government agencies and organizations in one year and, within three years, to institute related measures to reduce the budget and staff of the Executive Yuan and its agencies by five percent; as part of this plan, the 1994 annual budget will be reduced by two percent. In addition, the government has also resolved to strictly implement a system of reporting personal wealth by public servants, to address the concerns of the people regarding the intrusion of big money interests and bribery in the political process. We will, based on the "administrative innovation program," strictly require government disciplinary agencies to step up their anti-corruption work, under the premise of protecting the dignity and honor of the vast majority of public servants, so that the handful wrongdoers will have no place to hide and be brought to justice. We will work towards the goal of ensuring that government agencies at every level conduct their business in full accordance with the law and ethics of good behavior, and that they maintain an attitude of fairness, actively aim for high efficiency in their work, and exhibit full competence in whatever duties they must perform; thus establishing a clean and effective government that has the trust and support of the people.

## (4) Accelerating national development

A nation should base its development on a comprehensive plan, and should aim for a balanced development. The main task of the government is to break through developmental bottlenecks and accelerate the pace of the nation toward modernization by strengthening the infrastructure and improving basic facilities. The Six-Year National Development Plan is now in its third year. Overall, the plan can be considered successful both in planning and execution. Of the 64 projects under the plan budgeted at more than NT$20 billion, 19 are currently in the planning stages, and 45 have entered the construction stages. Due to the huge budget required by the Six-Year National Development Plan, the government, in order to find ways to bring in new income while cutting costs where it can and amass needed capital, is stepping up its monitoring of spending to reduce waste, and is also planning methods of rewarding participation by private interests so as to push forward large scale public construction projects. Regulations have been drafted regarding participation by private interests in transportation-related construction projects, and are currently under review in the Legislative Yuan. In addition, the government has recently completed a mid-point assessment regarding the financial burden exacted by the plan, and the government's ability to execute the plan, in which some priorities have been readjusted. The plan is continuing to be actively pushed forward.

Regarding military preparedness, we are actively working towards putting together a national defense force that stresses quality over quantity. We are, on the one hand, making careful assessments on how to gradually streamline military personnel. We hope to reduce the number of our troops to below 400,000 within one decade. On the other hand, we aim to improve our capability for battle by thoroughly modernizing the weaponry of the three branches of the ROC's armed forces, both through domestic development and foreign imports. We are also making efforts to improve the working environment of military agencies, sending out a call to young people to serve their country in the military, and encouraging our armed forces to engage in social service. These are all key efforts we are making in the area of national defense towards the objective of ensuring peace in the Taiwan Straits area and strengthening our national security.

Regarding transportation development projects, our objectives are to integrate and connect international, inter-city, regional and metropolitan transportation systems, and to develop Taiwan into a transportation hub of the Pacific region. The mass rapid transit system, the second freeway, the Taipei-Ilan highway, and the high-speed railway are now either under construction or in the planning stage. The aim of these projects is to effectively raise the capacity of our transportation system. In the area of communications, we place great stress on raising quality and efficiency. We especially need to improve communication facilities in and to remote areas.

As regards improving the investment climate, the government has recently drafted an Economic Stimulus Package to encourage and promote private investment and to open up new economic horizons. We are at the same time placing great stress on effective use of resources, promoting economic and trade development with mainland China and raising government administrative efficiency. We have drafted 22 concrete measures in these areas which can be put into effect immediately. In addition, we are establishing an Asia-Pacific Regional Operations Center, in response to long-term developmental trends, to help private investment over the coming three years reach a growth rate of 10 to 15 percent, while at the same time helping maintain 6 to 7 percent economic growth. This plan is certain to make a major contribution to effectively raising productivity, improving the economic system, and laying a foundation for sustained economic development.

In the area of agricultural development, we maintain a policy of "developing agriculture, improving rural villages, and taking care of farmers," and are pushing forward a comprehensive program for adjusting the agricultural structure and an agricultural development plan for the Taiwan area. The program includes the following eight key measures: training agricultural personnel, planning agricultural land use, improving the agricultural product distribution system, introducing innovations in agricultural technology, strengthening agricultural organizations, adjusting the structure of the fishery industry, increasing farmer welfare, and stepping up ecological protection work. Our aim is the institution of modern business management techniques in agricultural production, modernization of agricultural life, and a "naturalization" of rural village ecology, so as to promote sustainable development for agriculture.

In the area of overseas Chinese work, we are taking the initiative and playing a more active role to achieve breakthroughs wherever possible. We need to improve communication and understanding to unite and build a consensus among all overseas Chinese. We are all one people, descendants of the same great progenitors; all have a contribution to make to the nation, and all are a source of inexhaustible hope for our people.

## (5) Developing pragmatic diplomacy

The political, economic, and social progress and development in the ROC have given us a strong desire and adequate strength to give something back to the international community. And full participation in international organizations and activities by the ROC would certainly make positive contributions to the world community. The ROC is currently a member of the Asian Development Bank and the Asian-Pacific Economic Cooperation forum. The ROC is also an observer in GATT, and the ROC's application for full membership in GATT is currently being processed.

In the post-Cold War period, nations of the world have generally turned to international organizations and multilateral cooperation to handle international problems, and the influence of international organizations today is growing by the day. The ROC has faced many barriers in its efforts to participate in multilateral international organizations and activities since its withdrawal from the United Nations in 1971. Our government is now sending out a call to the international community to take the existence and development of the Republic of China on Taiwan seriously. Continuing to exclude the ROC from international organizations is unfair, immoral, and unpragmatical. We hope through our active participation to make an even greater contribution to world peace and prosperity. In addition to working toward re-entry into the United Nations, another key task of our future diplomatic work is to insist that the ROC be accorded a reasonable international position prior to China's unification.

The path to United Nations membership will be an arduous one, one that is certain to be undermined and thwarted by the Chinese communists. Only by working together in harmony, building up a consensus, rallying the strength of all our people, and looking to the international community for support will we be able to attain our goal at an early date.

## (6) Cultural, educational, scientific and technological development

The government has always made cultural and educational work a high priority, reflecting our deep awareness of the fact that cultural and educational enrichment and improvement are the foundation of all development, and that scientific and technological research and development are the most effective means for advancing national development. In addition to supporting and working together with private investors, the government will continue to push forward cultural development, protect our cultural resources, promote activities in the arts, work to establish ethical concepts for modern times, and cultivate the notion of serving others, while also making active efforts to improve the quality of education, ensure a society that is sound and healthy for body and mind, strengthen extension and adult education programs, and realize the ideal of whole life learning. We will also work to train scientific and technological personnel, establish a good research environment, accelerate the widespread application of scientific and technical knowledge, and develop high-tech and technology-intensive industries, so that the ROC's scholarly achievements and industrial technology can reach the level of the advanced countries at an early date. The government has now, in the drafting of its educational budget, fulfilled the constitutional requirement that educational expenses shall account for 15 percent of the total central government budget. In the area of public education, we are working towards making life education primary, and academic education secondary, and towards achieving a balanced distribution of educational resources in conjunction with overall regional development by establishing universities in remote areas. Other areas of concentration will be

*21*

enriching the content of vocational education and improving graduate schools both in quality and quantity in response to the needs of our future national development.

### (7) Establishing a harmonious society

The government's ultimate administrative goal is to establish a harmonious society that provides our people with a fair, just, peaceful, and pleasant living and developmental environment in which everybody enjoys freedom from want and fear, and in which everybody is united under our system of constitutional democracy, able to enjoy the rights it offers while also fulfilling the responsibilities it demands of each citizen. To work towards the realization of this ideal, the government will strengthen social welfare programs, taking into account such factors as the overall distribution of the nation's resources, social fairness and justice, and the government's financial ability; it will assign a priority to each item, then actively work to carry out each program. In the area of the social welfare system, special legislation has already been passed regarding the welfare of the elderly, children, youth, and the handicapped, and legislation concerning women's welfare is currently being proposed and drafted. National health insurance will be made available to every person in our country by late 1994, as originally planned, and an annuity system for citizens is currently being planned. According to statistics, the portion of the central budget allotted to social welfare and services has risen from over NT$1.9 billion in 1989 to NT$26.7 billion in the 1994 fiscal year, an approximately 14-fold increase. We will continue to increase this amount to improve social welfare measures. The government must at the same time make a comprehensive effort to deal with gangsterism and crime, stamp out illegal drug use, step up its "war on drugs," increase police beat duties, conduct a thorough overhaul of public safety measures, and work to nip crime in the bud through various channels, including education, guidance campaigns, and the home.

In addition, the government has drafted a Public Safety Protection Program covering matters concerning public safety, such as improving and strengthening fire and building safety regulations, registration of businesses, school safety, workplace safety, food safety and sanitation, traffic management, and tourist facility management, to protect the safety of human life and property. Other areas of concentration include: instituting reasonable environmental protection standards, improving the quality of drinking water, setting up methods for proper disposal of waste, improving environmental sanitation, providing protection from flooding and air and noise pollution; also, ensuring fair trade practices, protecting consumer rights, protecting intellectual property rights, protecting endangered species and wildlife, building up a positive international image; paying particular attention to labor, farmer, fisherman, aborigine, and veteran rights and concerns, and improving their living conditions and environment; and finally, advancing the development of new towns and communities, and increasing construction of public housing.

## Gear Government Policy to the People's will for the Lasting Glory of the Chinese Nation

We are all eager to work together to complete our great future mission and contribute our wisdom. President Lee once declared: "Stability can be maintained only through strength, and stability is a necessary prerequisite to prosperity." All of you involved in government administration, myself included, should adhere to this principle. We must, with a broad-minded work spirit and the abundant fruits of our administrative work, increase confidence in our government among all our countrymen, win over even greater support, and cultivate a feeling that the people and our government are together in weal or woe and that we should always be closely united as passengers of a boat in a storm.

We are confident that the 1990s will be a key decade in the Republic of China's bid to enter the ranks of the developed nations, and will be a decade in which we make historic advances. We must follow the will of the people, and we must make these the key motive force in the development of a modern nation and thoroughly implement the ideals of the Three Principles of the People, so that our efforts and contributions will become the everlasting pride of the entire Chinese nation.

NOTES
1. An excerpted administrative report by Lien Chan, Premier of the Republic of China, to the 14th National Congress of the Kuomingtang held in August 1993.

# Quiet Revolutions: A New Beginning for an Ancient History[1]

Jason C. Hu

Today is July 16. Nine hundred and eleven years ago this evening, a great Chinese poet, Su Tung-po, invited several of his close friends for a river cruise. They drank and sang aboard the boat. After enjoying the natural beauty of the bright moonshine and caressing breeze, the poet wrote an ode that has enthralled lovers of Chinese poetry for nearly a thousand years. Today, as guest of my Dutch friends, also on a boat with such great ambiance, the rapture I feel enjoying wonderful food and drink with you all reminds me of that special moment in ancient times captured in Su Tung-po's ode.

*Jason C. Hu is director-general of the Government Information Office, Executive Yuan.*

As an expression of gratitude for all this hospitality, I would also like to tell a story of events that have gone largely unnoticed. Admittedly, my story is not as romantic and touching as Su Tung-po's ode, but it is, I hope, equally poignant and evocative. The story is about the 21 million upwardly mobile people in the Republic of China on Taiwan struggling for a change in their historical destiny. After you hear this story, I hope you will remember that its main characters—the Chinese living in the Taiwan area—will always be your friends.

I'm sure many of you have heard a great deal about what has been termed the Taiwan economic miracle. But beyond achieving a miracle in purely economic terms, the people of Taiwan have also brought

25

about profound and remarkable political, social, cultural, scientific, and technological reforms over the last few years. Some of the reforms have been praised as innovations unknown during the 5,000 years of Chinese history, leading President Lee Teng-hui to refer to these years as the "beginning of history."

Perhaps because these reforms are taking place without loss of life or bloodshed, they have drawn less worldwide attention than have other more dramatic international events. There is a Chinese saying, "wearing fancy clothing and walking at night," that summarizes the situation. It means that when a man of great success returns to his hometown triumphantly, no one can see his fancy clothing and thus learn of his success if he walks about only at night. In similar fashion, the Republic of China's success story has remained enshrouded in relative darkness. Perhaps because it is not very sensational, it has not grabbed the front-page headlines. In fact, the outstanding accomplishments of my nation have been attained so quietly that they have largely gone unnoticed.

In sharp contrast, we find that during the same period of time as these unheralded momentous events have been taking place in our country, ethnic war in the former Yugoslavia, explosive standoffs among the republics of the Commonwealth of Independent States, conflict between warlord militias and the U.N. peacekeeping forces in Somalia, and the insurgency of leftist guerrillas in Peru have received more attention. As one cynical journalist once told me, "Gory news is good news, and the gorier the better." He also declared, "the worse the bruise, the better the news."

However, in this world of turmoil, democracy does not necessarily have to be achieved by violence, and quiet reforms are not necessarily less valuable or meaningful than those achieved through bloodshed.

Shouldn't we take a closer look at East Asian Confucian cultures for models of political change and ask ourselves, "What really works?"

Quietly, but surely, the Republic of China on Taiwan has traveled a long way toward democracy, but unlike other countries, it has never taken the path of violence. Instead, it has relied on consensus building and the pursuit of harmonious progress. The lack of dramatic clashes in our societies isn't always what they seem, because behind the scenes, social pacts and other forms of acceptable behavior have already been established by consensus building. Frankly, it's a much more peaceful way to transform a society.

Sir Winston Churchill once said that enormous change rarely comes without the shedding of much blood, sweat and tears. Looking at the various armed conflicts around the globe today—be they in Yugoslavia, Peru, the new CIS republics, or even Northern Ireland—Churchill's words appear to ring as true as ever.

But what about the quiet revolutions in the Republic of China on Taiwan? What about the emerging models of East Asian democracy? Why should violent revolutions monopolize the headlines while no less profound change is occurring peacefully elsewhere? Why do we accentuate the negative, when we could certainly learn much more from the positive? If I sound as though I am complaining, well in a way, I am. I think our quiet revolutions merit more attention. And yes, I think we deserve more credit for what we have achieved socially and politically, as well as economically.

Over the past forty years on Taiwan, we have shed much sweat, a few tears, but almost no blood to get to where we are today. Our record exists for all to examine. Grassroots democracy has grown steadily, and we have experienced peaceful, constitutional changes of leadership at every juncture of the transfer of power. The occurrence of not one single coup d'etat already sets us apart from most of our peers in the developing world. Healthy pluralism, a viable opposition movement, and the rise of an independent fourth estate all point to a record of progress that is unprecedented for its peaceful and stable evolution.

In the Seventies, former President Chiang Ching-kuo gave an excellent description of our formula for developmental success, especially political development. He said the Taiwan experience reflected strict adherence to a policy of seeking "stability with progress, and progress with stability." If the ROC model means anything, it is that these two factors of development should be inextricably linked to the success of a nation-state's pursuit of democracy and developed status.

In coming here today, I want to trumpet forth the news about the quiet revolutions on Taiwan. It is time that we shared our experience with those who need answers to the endless cycles of war, revolution, poverty, and disease. While our experience may not always be the most appropriate model for others, I can say with certainty that our way at least works for the absolute majority of Chinese. Please permit me to tell you a little about the path to democracy and a new historical beginning that we have chosen.

The Republic of China on Taiwan is actually undergoing a number of simultaneous mini-revolutions. Visitors to our shores can't miss the fact that our society is in the midst of great flux, with traditional Chinese culture undergoing the ultimate test of adaptability and fusion with modern Western culture. The result is a composite of old and new. This is a brand-new beginning for our venerable history, and our nation and people are full of vitality and hope.

28

## Political Revolution

The first of these "quiet revolutions" is political. It has followed on the heels of our economic success.

Scholars are paying more attention to Taiwan because we present one of the rare cases in the post-World War II era where political development has evolved peacefully. If you think about it, where else has democracy matured with so much peace and stability? If Taiwan is not a model of democracy, then what is?

Our critics, many of whom say we have moved too slowly toward democracy over the years, should pause to think again. Our path of democratization is gradual, to be sure. It was carefully laid out, based on the principles set forth at the turn of the century by our nation's Founding Father, Sun Yat-sen. The Taiwan experience clearly demonstrates that slow, well-considered steps toward democracy make more sense than rash actions that wreck the economy and ruin millions of lives along the way.

If more countries are going to achieve democracy, I think it is imperative that our experience on Taiwan be better understood in world political circles. Of course, it may be true that a certain set of factors has to be present for democracy to take root and flourish as it has on Taiwan, such as emphasis on education, an enlightened and strong leadership, solid grassroots development of democracy, a strong work ethic and firm family values. Different cultures and countries may have different constellations of such factors.

Today, our process of democratic maturity has brought us very near our primary goals. Last year, we began putting the final touches on our political reforms. The makeup of the National Assembly was overhauled during the first "all Taiwan area" elections, and in December last year, the legislature underwent a similar transformation. During the campaign period, candidates of the ruling party, opposition parties and independent candidates all aired their political views and took part in vigorous debates. The whole election was completed peacefully amidst heated competition. The ruling party won 64 percent and the major opposition party, the Democratic Progressive Party, garnered 35 percent of the vote.

Allow me to add a footnote here. In any Western nation, a 65 percent vote is described as a landslide. Yet, all newspapers in Taiwan described the ruling party's performance as "a major setback" and made it the top story on their front page. This indicates that people in Taiwan are still getting accustomed to the nature of Western democracy, which takes for granted a divergence of views and the existence of many political parties. Undeniably, the check-and-balance system of bipartisan politics is taking shape in the Republic of China, and through trial and error, we are gradually finding our own way.

A democratic and pluralistic society is emerging in the Republic of China as the political environment matures. Although many people in my country hold various views and democracy there is still a bit rough around the edges, we can see the clear outlines of a consensus: the Republic of China's move toward democracy has passed the point of no return. The democratic reform in the Republic of China is characterized by peace and stability, unlike that of most other countries, where it is often marked by violence and bloodshed.

This difference mainly comes from the wisdom and dedication of our foresighted leadership of today and yesterday. Since our central government moved from the Chinese mainland to Taiwan in 1949, we have dedicated a large portion of our budget to education, and have worked incessantly to promote local self-government. We want to promote the concept of democracy through education and strengthen our democratic system through elections. Since the lifting of martial law, President Lee Teng-hui has been the architect of our "quiet revolutions," leading us in carrying out a substantial democratic reform without having to resort to the use of guns.

## A Technological and Quality-control Revolution

Another area affected by rapid changes on Taiwan is our technology base and the quality of our products. Economically, we are engaged in a do-or-die effort to shift the majority of our products from the low-end to the more sophisticated, more value-added high-end. We can no longer compete at the low-end, because mainland China, Malaysia, Thailand, Indonesia, and the Philippines are nipping at our heels in the race toward development. Thus, we must compete more effectively against the economic giants, and to do so, we must improve the quality of our products and our technology. Toward this end, a mini-revolution is occurring here. We have decided to earmark large amounts of money for R&D in order to turn out more high value-added products to be marketed under our own brand names. According to a *Time* magazine survey made in Europe this year, European entrepreneurs and experts graded Japan and Taiwan as the top two nations that had undervalued their products in terms of quality. Taiwan ranked seventh for product quality alone, ahead of Denmark and Norway. This indicates Taiwan has improved the quality of its products in recent years and almost shaken off the low-end stigma.

There is much talk at home about turning Taiwan into a regional center for high-tech manufacturing, finance, and other services. A major step in this direction is the implementation of the US$315 billion Six-Year National Development Plan. It provides a bonanza of opportunities for foreign firms to land major contracts, especially in aerospace projects, environmental control, and mass transportation. The gigantic plan not only reflects that the Republic of China is fortunate to have the national wealth to undertake such projects, but also indicates our determination to modernize our infrastructure and improve our quality of life.

Another mini-revolution concerns the environment. An environmentalist awakening is sweeping the island. For decades, the environment was sacrificed on the altar of economic growth, and so was our quality of life! However, we have no intention of shirking our responsibility in this regard. The US$315 billion Six-Year National Development Plan calls for public and private sector investment of US$26.5 billion for pollution control and environmental cleanup. While economic growth used to be put ahead of the quality of life, both have now been put in proper perspective. Economic development must not be achieved at the cost of environmental degradation.

Some international media have termed Taiwan "Asia's Ugly Duckling," but the island is improving its environment so quickly and thoroughly that it won't be long before the media can rightly describe it once again as "Ilha Formosa," the name given by Portuguese mariners 500 years ago when they first saw Taiwan's beautiful coastline. I know this may sound optimistic, but at least we are on the right track environmentally.

## The Mainland Policy Revolution

One of our most important areas of change concerns our policies toward the Chinese mainland. The relationship has changed dramatically, from the tense vilification and military conflict of the Cold War era to the increased mutual understanding of today. Interestingly enough, this warming of relations across the Taiwan Straits has come about without outside prodding or interference. We Chinese are working out our differences by ourselves. We are reaching out to foster mutual understanding as a foundation for the peaceful reunification of our country. We are letting private contacts pave the way, be they through family reunions, exchanges of information, or other forms of cultural interaction.

Nevertheless, our optimism is restrained by some objective factors. The Chinese communists have never renounced the use of force as a means for reunifying the two sides of the Taiwan Straits. They have reminded us once and again that if we move in directions that they do not like, they "reserve the right to invade Taiwan."

Naturally, we must be mindful of this threat. We cannot turn a blind eye to their deployment of thousands of jet fighters at bases ten minutes away from our shores, hence our insistence on acquiring advanced jet fighters to boost our defense capability. Despite an improvement in cross-Straits relations, we absolutely need to maintain a credible force of deterrence in the face of such belligerent statements that all too often come from the other side.

It is frankly still too early to foresee exactly how relations will develop between the two sides. We have said over and over that further improvement of cross-Straits relations hinges on Peking's attitude, not Taipei's. We have become a model of successful development, so future relations between the two sides depend on what and how the mainland authorities do. Meanwhile, we will continue our careful and responsible move toward national reunification, provided our democracy, security and development are ensured.

## A Diplomatic Revolution

In the realm of diplomacy, the decade of the Seventies was an especially low period for my country. In 1971, we lost our seat in the United Nations, and on January 1, 1979, the United States established diplomatic ties with Peking. For the next decade or so, the ROC admittedly had a very difficult time of it.

However, we have not let ourselves be orphaned. For several years, our government has pursued a program of what we call "pragmatic diplomacy." This is a highly flexible approach to the way we conduct relations with the rest of the world. Our aim is to play an active role in the international community and to strive for the dignified treatment due a sovereign state. Because of our economic strength—as well as our long-term commitment to democracy—I believe we are faring quite well.

For example, although we have only 29 embassies and 5 consulates-general abroad, we now have quasi-official trade, cultural, or representative offices with another 60 countries. This number is steadily increasing. In September last year, for example, Russia announced that it would open an office in Taipei to facilitate trade and other contacts. Our representative office in Moscow has already been inaugurated and begun its operations.

We have also become more integrated into international organizations. We are active in the Asian Development Bank (ADB), were invited to join the Asia-Pacific Economic Cooperation (APEC) forum three years ago, and now have observer status at GATT. These substantive successes demonstrate our resolve to participate more fully in regional and world organizations.

Admittedly, we have to make continuing adjustments to our approaches and to be painfully flexible with our name. As with our participation in the Olympics, we have permitted various representative offices and international organizations to use names other than the Republic of China. We believe that this will be a temporary phenomenon. For now, this is an acceptable level of pragmatism. By being flexible on the issue of our name, we can participate more in the international community and make a greater contribution to it. This is absolutely necessary, for we have a responsibility as the world's fourteenth largest trading power to support and be a part of a healthy international marketplace to make it function more reasonably and effectively.

Here, I must emphasize that despite the Chinese communist attempts to restrict our international room for maneuver and downgrade our stature, no one including the Chinese communists, can deny the fact that Republic of China on Taiwan exists. The Chinese communists may control the Chinese mainland, but in the international community they do not and cannot represent the 21 million people of the Republic of China.

Our average annual income tops US$10,000 and we possess the world's largest foreign exchange reserves, including US$85.6 billion in foreign currencies and US$5.1 billion in gold bullion as of May 1993. If these factors were taken into account, the Republic of China would rank at least among the top 30 of all 183 U.N. members. It is a matter of record that we have been working consistently to become a constructive member of the international community.

ROC President Lee Teng-hui's words suffice to express the determination of ROC citizens. On the 12th of last month, the president said: "The existence of the Republic of China on Taiwan is a fact that no one should overlook. As a member of the world community, we have for a long time vigorously tried to repay the world community for what it has given us. Nevertheless, the Republic of China is excluded from international organizations despite its strength. This is immoral and unjust. At a time when the Cold War is over and a new world order is about to be established, the Republic of China's vigorous bid for joining the international community and becoming a member of international organizations not only is a common aspiration of its people but also exemplifies its eagerness to fulfill its international responsibilities."

The point is, the Republic of China is a member of the international community and can't be overlooked. In this fast-shrinking and highly interdependent world, we will not and should not shun the international arena. Conversely, the United Nations should not ignore the existence of an important, peaceful and friendly country that is willing and able to cooperate, like the Republic of China.

## A Cultural Renaissance

In Taiwan today , traditional values and concepts are being interwoven with contemporary values. Anywhere you look, the old and new coexist. Is this a Chinese society, or a brand-new world of mixed cultures and values?

I think most Chinese have a deep feeling about this modern day paradox. Our culture, a legacy of over five thousand years, is important to us. But the test of any generation is how to preserve the culture that defines who we are while infusing it with new vitality.

I like to assert that our contemporary culture is truly profound and full of vitality. On the Chinese mainland, for instance, Chinese culture is treated as a museum piece, a tourist attraction designed to earn hard currency. Not on our side of the Taiwan Straits. Chinese culture not only thrives in Taiwan in both its ancient and contemporary forms through its endurance and resilience, but has become more attractive in the course of rejuvenation, a process even more majestic than a revolution. All around us, the arts are in bloom, with modern nuances constantly being added to the traditional. And in those areas where the arts have fallen on hard times, such as our movie industry, we are exerting ourselves to revitalize them. Our motion picture industry has been in a bit of a slump lately, so as one measure to rejuvenate it, we have designated 1993 as National Motion Picture Year. The government provides the incentives, but it's up to the artists themselves to create their own new horizons.

Our television industry is also on the verge of a mini-revolution. The agency I head, the Government Information Office, is laying the groundwork for the introduction of cable TV in Taiwan, and is also supporting the establishment of a more viable public broadcasting system. Both cable and public television will spur the existing three commercial networks to improve their programming.

Such changes are not limited to the electronics media. Indeed, our thriving newspapers and magazines have blossomed in an era of free speech, so much so that the number of dailies has increased from 31 to 294, and the number of journals and magazines has shot up to 4,586. All of them have become independent and outspoken. As government spokesman, no one is more qualified than I to attest to the vitality and critical views of our rapidly emerging fourth estate.

37

Culture is what distinguishes us from others as we all try to get along better in this ever-shrinking world. And for increasing mutual understanding among all people, we are striving to internationalize Chinese culture. We have established a first-class medium for this in our Chinese Information and Culture Center in New York City. The success of this Center in bringing Chinese culture to Americans has led us to plan for more such centers in other world capitals.

Of course, the story I have just told is not inherently sensational, so I don't expect my journalist friends among us to carry it on the first page tomorrow. As in the past, these revolutions will go on quietly. It will neither be reported beneath sensational headlines nor receive lengthy coverage. But I hope our achievements will receive the understanding and recognition in the world that they deserve. Please never overlook or forget our "quiet revolutions." The peace and prosperity we enjoy today come from a series of quiet pluralistic changes much like a colorful and beautiful butterfly is produced through the process of metamorphosis. It grows from a larva to a pupa before it flutters beautifully before our eyes. Without bloodshed, without violence, the process is certainly a commendable choice.

To return to the story of our famous Sung poet, after enjoying the natural beauty and finishing many rounds of toasts, Su Tung-po and his friends fell into a sound and content sleep amidst the banquet fare, not waking until dawn. Of course, I don't have the luxury to expect that reaction from you to my story. It is late now. I appreciate your patience in allowing me tell this important but seldom heard story. It is the most glorious moment in the modern forty-year chapter of history written by the Chinese in Taiwan in their quest for freedom, democracy and prosperity. While it exemplifies their happiness, it also reflects their sweat and tears. This indeed constitutes a new beginning for an ancient history. Thank you for letting me share this story of success with you. Good night!

NOTES
1. A speech delivered by Jason C. Hu, director-general of the Government Information Office, the Executive Yuan, the Republic of China, in Rotterdam, the Netherlands on July 16, 1993.

# II.
# Politics

Previous page: President Lee receives Huang Hsin-chieh, then chairman of the Democratic Progressive Party, prior to the National Affairs Conference in mid-1990.

# Building the First Chinese Democracy: the Crises and Leadership of President Lee Teng-hui

Ramon H. Myers

On March 29-31, 1986, President Chiang Ching-kuo of the Republic of China (ROC) on Taiwan informed his ruling party, the Kuomintang (KMT), that he wanted political reforms. Over the next few years the KMT lifted martial law, allowed a free press to form, permitted political parties to compete, and began amending the nation's constitution. By 1994 these momentous political reforms had created China's first democracy.[1] For some forty years a strong man and a powerful party had held enormous power. Few had believed the KMT would move so rapidly to create a new political marketplace in which opposition parties could compete. In fact, the transition to democratization easily could have been derailed if three severe challenges had not been overcome.

*Ramon H. Myers is a senior fellow of the Hoover Institution, Stanford University, California.*

First, the People's Republic of China (PRC) had always threatened the ROC from without by military invasion and from within by subversion. In the early 1980s the communist party had proposed to the ROC government that the KMT should begin to negotiate so that Taiwan could eventually enjoy a special administrative district status under the PRC's control, or else Beijing's leaders might have to use force to achieve that same goal. The ROC's leaders replied by advocating no contacts with the PRC, and its ruling party still regarded a state of war to have existed between the two regimes. Until the present, the threat of a PRC military takeover or naval blockade of Taiwan is very real.

Second, ever since the February 28, 1947 uprising, a Taiwanese national independence movement had operated overseas, committed to destroying the ROC government and creating in its place a Republic of Taiwan with a new constitution.[2] Associated with that overseas threat was an incipient political movement within Taiwan challenging the KMT's authority to govern. More and more younger politicians first became active in the 1970s by challenging KMT candidates in elections, publishing journals strongly critical of the KMT and government, and trying to form political associations that eventually might become an opposition party.

Finally, KMT membership always had consisted of a mixture of mainlander Chinese and island-born Taiwanese whose ancestors had come from southeast China in previous centuries. Mainlanders had dominated the party since its rebuilding in 1950-52.[3] In March 1986, the 77-year-old Chiang Ching-kuo suffered severe diabetes. He only had slightly less than two more years to live. Several years earlier, in February 1984, Chiang had picked a Taiwanese technocrat named Lee Teng-hui to serve as his vice-presidential running mate. Could Lee continue to carry out Chiang's reforms and lead the nation according to Chiang's grand vision of establishing a workable democracy on Taiwan and transfer that to the mainland to pave the way for the unification of China? Powerful mainlander leaders in the KMT deeply resented and feared a newcomer in their ranks, especially a Taiwanese they did not trust. To bring the KMT under the full control of strong man Chiang's successor would be no easy task if Chiang suddenly died as the reforms just began. In fact, on January 13, 1988 Chiang abruptly passed away, and Lee Teng-hui now found himself the new president with the difficult task of continuing Chiang Ching-kuo's political reforms and confronting three challenges that could split his party, create powerful opposition that might divide society, and goad the communist leadership to take reckless action toward Taiwan. Because of President Lee's unique leadership abilities, none of these events ever took place; instead, the nation's political development continued to evolve peacefully toward democracy.

## Lee's Ascendancy to Power

On March 22, 1984 Lee Teng-hui became the seventh vice-president of the ROC. He never had participated in an election. His rise to power had been more swift than that of any politician since 1949. Hand-picked by Chiang Ching-kuo, many only could wonder why Lee had ascended so rapidly and so high. Lee's extraordinary childhood, his education, and his outstanding personal achievements as a public servant and scholar partially explain the riddle; finally, Chiang Ching-kuo's unique leadership style provides a clue to how he picked the nation's leaders.

Born on January 15, 1923 in the village of P'u P'ing in San Chih township northwest of Taipei city, Lee Teng-hui grew up in a small landowning family that farmed and rented various plots to tenants. Lee's ancestors, of Hakka origin, had once lived in Fukien. They had migrated to Taiwan and settled near Tamsui city in San Chih township. Lee's father, Li Ching-jung, had three sons, of whom Lee was the second.[4] The family was not impoverished, but everyone worked hard. As a child, Lee often accompanied his grandfather to the Taipei produce market early in the morning to sell their farm's products. Lee excelled in the Japanese education system, which only began to develop from primary school to university education track in the 1920s. From 1929 to 1935, Lee had attended three primary schools and then graduated from a Japanese middle school in Tamsui city. In 1939 he was one of four Chinese students in his school to attend Taipei city's elite high school.[5] By now Lee's father served in the Tamsui Farmer's Union first as director of sales and supply, and later as its Executive Director. In 1943 Lee was selected to attend Kyoto Imperial University to study agricultural economics; he graduated in 1946 and returned to Taiwan in that same year, an outstanding achievement for a Chinese youth during World War II. As the son of a father who had expanded the family's wealth and moved upward to a high-status service occupation, Lee greatly admired Japan's achievements and the qualities of its leaders, who had produced the Meiji Restoration, modernized Japan, and made that small country powerful, respected, and feared: such qualities were a spirit of teamwork, a strong sense of wanting to achieve, a long-term perspective to accomplish one's goals, and a deep respect for the values of personal loyalty and duty. These qualities greatly helped endear Lee to Chiang Ching-kuo, who admired similar qualities.

Upon returning to Taipei at the age of twenty-three, Lee first taught as an instructor at National Taiwan University, the country's finest university, and then won a scholarship to attend Iowa State University in 1951 to continue his study of agricultural economics. Returning in 1953, he became an instructor in National Taiwan University's department of economics. Already regarded as an outstanding young agricultural economist, the Joint Commission on Rural Reconstruction (JCRR) employed him as an economic analyst and assigned him to conduct feasibility studies for their pilot projects in the countryside, which at that time suffered great underemployment and rapid rural population growth. In the next few years Lee published several outstanding articles explaining the cause of Taiwan's agricultural transformation and the contribution of irrigation and other forms of investment to that remarkable green revolution. In 1965 Lee won another scholarship to go to Cornell University, and at the age of forty-two in 1968 he had completed his course work and written a Ph.D. thesis that won the prize given by the American Agricultural Economist Association for the most outstanding doctoral thesis in the United States. Lee's work had focused on how increased agricultural productivity and the surplus extracted from agriculture through taxation and other means had contributed to capital formation and Taiwan's industrialization in the twentieth century, a period covering Japanese colonial rule and the establishment of the ROC on Taiwan. Developing an ingenious accounting method to measure the annual surplus contribution to Taiwan's new capital formation, Lee was able to make imaginative use of Taiwan's excellent statistics and produce an impressive quantitative and analytical work that was highly praised by professional economists. With his new degree in hand, Lee returned to Taiwan as full professor at National Taiwan University and an adviser to the JCRR.

Lee's exceptional educational and professional career now put him at the pinnacle of academic prestige in Taiwan and won him international acclaim. On June 2, 1972 while attending a conference in New Zealand, the Executive Yuan requested he become a minister without portfolio.[6] In his new position, the government assigned Lee to visit many African states to study aid projects that the ROC tried to offer as a means of expanding their diplomatic contacts in that region to compete with similar PRC efforts there. Lee also had the opportunity to visit all areas of Taiwan, where he increased his personal ties of friendship. Then in June 1978 President Chiang Ching-kuo, without any prior announcement, appointed Dr. Lee to become the mayor of Taipei city, one of Taiwan's two cities where the government appointed, rather than allowed an elected person, to serve as governor. The appointment stunned many in political circles and made many extremely jealous of the young technocrat, who was only fifty-five years old. President Chiang had long been observing Lee Teng-hui's performance in the Executive Yuan. He liked this technocrat, who pursued his work wih a singlemindedness, thoroughness, and analytical acumen that could scarcely be found in any of the other bureaucrats in government. Chiang also was pleased that Lee had no political base and cared little to establish one. Lee had often proven his capabilities to handle committee assignments, because with penetrating logic and care he compelled his committees to do their homework and present careful, reasoned recommendations for the government.[7]

In 1979 Chiang saw to it that Lee Teng-hui was selected to the prestigious, powerful standing committee of the KMT, which ruled over the central committee. A group of thirty-odd persons, chaired by Chiang Ching-kuo, the KMT's standing committee often met to decide and agree upon key policy decisions for the party and government to adopt. As Lee only had been a KMT member for around a decade, his sudden appointment to this august body again surprised many inside and outside the KMT.[8] Then in 1981 Chiang picked Lee to become governor of Taiwan. While fortunate in his personal and public life to enjoy a meteoric political career, tragedy suddenly befell him in 1983 when he lost his only son to cancer. This tragedy perhaps became a key factor for making Chiang believe for the first time that Lee might really become his successor. In the Chinese way of thinking, a leader without a son was far more inclined to use the power given to him by another power-holder to carry out his legacy rather than to cultivate such power for himself and his family members.[9] One year after the death of his son, Chiang decided Lee should serve as his vice-presidential running mate. He had now arrived at the pinnacle of political power.[10]

## Using Power: The First Two Years

For nearly forty years the Chiang family had dominated Taiwan's politics. When Chiang Ching-kuo passed away on January 13, 1988, one commentator exclaimed that "no one can believe a president could serve and not have the name of Chiang."[11] The transfer of power to a Taiwanese was unprecedented, and the atmosphere remained tense as the nation's elite waited. The newly confirmed president quickly took the reins of power and began a series of personal visits: first to members of the Chiang family to express his regrets and promise to uphold the late president's legacy; next, he called on KMT elders and sought their advice; then he conferred with government advisers and evaluation commissioners; he then met with top military leaders and asked for their support; promising in return his respect and help; finally, he paid a visit to the nation's front lines on the offshore islands and praised them for their fighting spirit.[12] One month already had passed. Lee then undertook a series of quick trips to cities and towns to call on local leaders and ask them for their support. In this ritualistic way, Lee conveyed the image of a leader who not only cared for the nation's leaders and ordinary people but expressed deep veneration for a dead leader and his promise to carry on his policies.

But numerous difficulties now intruded and needed attention: Taiwan was in the grip of a "mainland China fever" with new demands to loosen the government's "no contact" policy with the PRC; the nation had to decide whether to participate in the upcoming Asian Games and how to be represented; the Thirteenth KMT Congress was to be held in the summer of 1988; the national representatives, elected in 1948 on the mainland, still controlled the government, and the new opposition party, the Democratic Progressive Party (DPP), continually used that issue to mobilize popular anger toward the government. Throughout 1988-89 President Lee cleverly maneuvered and dealt with his problems by the tactic of delay while planning and implementing a longer-term strategy of political reform. On June 1, 1989 he replaced an unpopular premier, Yu Kuo-hua, with Li Huan, promising more decisive action from the Executive Yuan. He extended General Hao Pei-tsun's term for another year to serve as head of the Chiefs of Staff. In late 1988 he announced that a newly developed fighter aircraft would be named after Chiang Ching-kuo.[13] Meanwhile, he began planning how to expand national elections to replace the old senior representatives. His first step was to support a new law mandating handsome retirement stipends for all national representatives who voluntarily retired from their offices. He defeated a tactic at the summer Thirteenth KMT Congress to deny him the chairmanship of the party, with the support of Deputy Secretary-General Sung Ch'u-yu, who campaigned on his behalf.[14] At the first year's commemoration of Chiang's passing, Lee extolled the late president's achievements and vowed to carry on his mission of unifying China under the Three Principles of the People as set forth in Sun Yat-sen's doctrine. By early 1988 most KMT members scored his performance as commendable, and it appeared that even a majority of the old national representatives making up the powerful First National Assembly might even vote for him as the eighth president of the ROC in March 1990.[15]

The only group of politicians who expressed serious criticism of President Lee were members of the DPP who were contemptuous of his appointment of new cabinet members, calling them "amateurs leading the experts" who continually made the wrong decisions.[16] In late 1989, the KMT suffered its first serious election setback since 1949 when the DPP captured six of the county seats and greatly improved their election standing to win around 30 percent of the popular vote. As the year 1990 loomed, leading KMT standing committee members began planning their move to select a vice president who could counsel and possibly control Lee Teng-hui should his leadership become dubious.

Could Lee effectively assert his new leadership in the KMT and still deal with the grave problems that faced the nation: the new threat from the PRC and the challenge of a group of an incipient overseas, nationalistic Taiwanese movement calling for a separatist course of political development for Taiwan?

## The First Major Crises and
## Their Resolution

On February 11, 1990 President Lee shocked his party by announcing his vice-presidential running mate to be Li Yuan-ts'u, a lawyer, former president of National Chengchih University, a military judge, and a constitutional expert.[17] Lee had picked him primarily because of his constitutional legal skills and the strong support he could expect Li to give him. The president had consulted no one and had checkmated that small group of KMT powerholders expecting to have one of their own serve as vice president. The KMT began to split over the president's choice of vice president, one group denouncing the president's dictatorial ways, and the other group defending the president's right to select his vice president. These two nebulous groups became known in political circles as the "mainstream faction," who were supportive of Lee Teng-hui, and the "non-mainstream faction," who opposed Lee's political actions. The free press, meanwhile, fanned the flames of speculation, intrigue, and rumors swirling about Taipei.

Soon a group of National Assembly representatives began campaigning for another presidential ticket: they proposed the Taiwanese Lin Yang-kang for president and Chiang Wei-kuo, a mainlander, as vice president. Both men agreed to run. This new development further divided the National Assembly and KMT. The political atmosphere became even more intense at the opening of the National Assembly, in which the DPP-elected members, a distinct minority in that body, *51* created pandemonium at the opening day's meeting by upsetting numerous dining tables for the lunch. One aging representative later died from a heart attack suffered at the opening day's outbursts.

President Lee immediately took decisive action. He called upon eight KMT elders to serve as a negotiating team to bring the two sides together and achieve a consensus as to which ticket the National Assembly should vote to approve. Between March 3 and March 10, the group of elders, led by Chiang Yen-shih, a colleague of Lee's from their days with the JCRR, met with top KMT leaders and mounted pressure on the Lin-Chiang ticket to withdraw. On March 10, Lin and Chiang did withdraw, leaving the field free for Lee and Li. Immediately, Lee and Li began paying courtesy calls on the 800-odd National Assembly persons who were to vote on March 21-22 for the new president and vice president.

The crisis was far from over. For more than a decade the predecessors of the DPP, politicians who had opposed the KMT and called themselves "outside the ruling party" (tang-wai) had published their vitriolic attacks in periodicals of alleged corruption and abuse of power practiced by those national representatives who governed in the Legislative Yuan or Parliament, the National Assembly, and other branches of government. In the new climate of free speech, public passions mounted, and many openly vented their resentment toward those National Assembly representatives who alone elected the ROC's leaders, received a high salary, and often lived abroad. In mid-March the DPP had mounted a series of demonstrations outside the building where the National Assembly met to hold its election for the eighth ROC president. These were often violent, noisy altercations. On March 14 several events converged to focus national press attention on the activities of the National Assembly: the judiciary upheld the Assembly's refusal to allow eleven DPP representatives to participate because they had refused to take the national oath at the opening day's ceremony; second, a National Assembly committee advocated expanding the Assembly's power. Public indignation quickly mounted, and soon students began protesting on the major campuses throughout the island, calling a massive, island-wide student demonstration at the Chiang Kai-shek Memorial. By March 14, some 22,000 students had camped out in downtown Taipei to create a movement resembling the great student demonstrations at T'ien-an-men in Beijing in the spring of 1989. The ROC government did not relish the international attention this new incident might attract.

On March 17, President Lee appeared on all three national television channels to appeal for calm and patience. By March 18 the number of student protesters had increased to 30,000. Meanwhile, President Lee privately urged the National Assembly to reject their recommendations for greater power, and publicly promised the government would hold a National Affairs Conference in June to examine the nation's problems and their solutions. President Lee also began negotiating with student leaders. Through these multiple efforts the president convinced the students to disband and return to their home and classrooms. A national crisis had been averted. President Lee's idea for the June National Affairs Conference had been brewing in his mind for some time. He especially wanted a high-visibility meeting to represent the full spectrum of society and discuss the problems facing the nation.

The years 1988 through spring of 1990 had been marked by numerous violent street demonstrations, which Taiwan had never experienced. The DPP and its supporters mobilized many of these activities, but they had been joined by labor unions, discontented farmers, and angry citizens resentful of growing pollution and intervention in their lives by local city councils. Similarly, a spate of murders, robberies, and kidnappings had erupted to create new public fears and uncertainty that public order was fast disintegrating. On May 20, 1990, President Lee replaced Premier Li Huan with former general Hao Pei-tsun, an appointment that elicited shock, criticism, and several public demonstrations in Taipei protesting the ascendancy of the military in the government. Lee's brilliant choice for new premier defused his KMT critics and later won him considerable public support because the new premier immediately took decisive, strong action to mobilize the nation's police to clean up crime and improve urban traffic flow.

Although crime greatly declined in late 1990 after Lee's election as the eighth ROC president on March 21, 1990, the government still faced the serious problem of how to accommodate the DPP and, more particularly, the overseas Taiwanese nationalist movement. The KMT and DPP had no formal contact with each other after the DPP illegally formed in September 1986, and the previous KMT liaison with former tang-wai leaders had only occurred earlier in the spring of 1986, when Chiang Ching-kuo had initiated several meetings with political opposition leaders in an effort to deter them from forming their political party. Finally, the long shadow cast over the island by the tragic February 28, 1947 uprising still stirred bitter memories in the public toward the ruling party and government. Ever since the anniversary of that uprising in 1987, each year afterward on February 28, countless peaceful demonstrations were held throughout the island to commemorate the victims of that uprising. The challenge now facing President Lee was how to achieve political reconciliation and develop a peaceful political marketplace in which political parties could compete without violence and hatred. This was the single most pressing problem that the new president hoped to resolve when he proposed his astonishing idea of a June 1990 National Affairs Conference [Kuo-shih hui-i].[18]

President Lee appointed his old friend Chiang Yen-shih to organize the National Affairs Conference, and Chiang quickly convened a committee to design the conference, select invitees, and arrange the affair. During April and May 1990, the elite looked upon this conference with great skepticism; many even believed the president had some hidden agenda that he hoped to achieve for his personal ends. This public cynicism toward the Office of the President and his June national conference has been referred to as representative of a "culture of miscreance," in which those outside the political center are convinced their leaders lack any sincere commitment to the well-being of society. This severe way the Chinese public, particularly the elite, always judged their leaders had been a stumbling block for Chinese leaders to develop a political marketplace based on the rule of law; President Lee had to overcome public cynicism to develop support and participation for a conference he hoped would initiate political reconciliation of those who had long hated and opposed the ROC government and the ruling party. At first few supported President Lee's proposal, and the press greeted his idea with great suspicion.

But the new president was ingenious, and he used Chinese-style negotiation to break the logjam threatening to ruin the affair. He resorted to political brokering. On April 2, 1990, President Lee invited DPP chairman Huang Hsin-chieh to the Office of the President for tea and conversation. This event shook Taipei's political world, and overnight Huang became a news celebrity. Huang praised President Lee's move, and in subsequent weeks he even managed to convince leading members of the DPP to participate in the June conference. Meanwhile, Lee worked hard on his party and obtained its support for the June conference.

Chiang Yen-shih's committee also approached leading intellectuals and won their backing. President Lee personally wrote some overseas dissidents like P'eng Ming-min to invite their participation; a number accepted, but P'eng imposed unrealistic conditions that the government in the end could not accept, and so he did not attend.

On June 28, 1990 the conference convened at the Grand Hotel in Taipei, with President Lee speaking to the group on two themes. First he stressed that the ROC "will have a healthy, complete, and all-round constitutional system" and, second, he emphasized that "there will be a unified China." True to the spirit of the political reforms launched by Chiang Ching-kuo, President Lee had still not deviated from the political reform mission initiated by the late president.

Of the 150 participants invited, only 136 had shown. The conference ended on July 4, and what an event it was. At the evening banquets, television cameras viewed bitter political rivals toasting each other and smiling. KMT leaders like Premier Hao and former overseas dissident and later DPP chairman Hsu Hsin-liang even toasted each other. Sung Ch'u-yu met with DPP leaders during the conference behind closed doors to discuss how a future ROC president might be directly elected by the people. The conference ended with considerable disagreement but a spirit of willingness to agree to disagree. DPP and KMT delegates worked out procedures to maintain normal contact thereafter. In some areas, important consensus was even achieved. A majority agreed that a new National Assembly should be elected and that the Constitution should be moderately revised. President Lee announced at the end of the conference his willingness to establish a KMT committee to recommend procedures for completing constitutional reform. Most members also agreed on the need to eliminate the provisional articles added in 1948 to the 1947 Constitution, which gave the Office of the President enormous power and maintained a state of virtual war with the Communist regime. A majority also agreed the ROC government should develop a new negotiating strategy for dealing with the PRC. Most important of all, the ROC government pledged to allow overseas dissidents to return home and take up a normal political life as long as they abided by the new rules of the political marketplace. A strong spirit of reconciliation emerged from this remarkable conference. The conference most certainly elevated the status of the DPP; the press now took that party to be a serious opposition party, and DPP members for the first time spoke with greater moderation about future political reform.

Some three months later, on October 7, 1990, President Lee established a National Unification Council [Kuo-t'ung-hui] made up of thirty individuals and chaired by the president.[19] The president hand-picked this group, carefully selecting outstanding individuals from different sectors of government, political parties, public media, National Assembly, business, labor, Taipei-Kaohsiung city councils, and national defense agencies and the National Security Council. This council was served by twelve research groups and four committees, which prepared information and recommendations to the council. On October 8, President Lee announced to the new council that "Taiwan independence can never be achieved. From now on, we will always insist never to abandon our claim of sovereignty over mainland China nor give up our dream of freedom, democracy, and an equal distribution of wealth for all the Chinese people."[20] Again President Lee emphasized that the ROC government's mission was to pursue the eventual unification of China but on conditions acceptable to those that now existed in Taiwan. Just as Chiang Ching-kuo before him had advocated, President Lee again reiterated that someday the

Republic of China must represent all of China because that meant the "creation of a new age in which the ROC stood upright with pride in the world."[21]

The Council recommended in February 1991 the government set up a private organization empowered by the government to handle relations with the government, to be called the Straits Exchange Foundation (SEF). Financed by both the private and public sectors, the SEF's task was to expand communication channels with the PRC. On February 23, 1991 the Council unveiled its Guidelines for National Unification, which the government quickly approved and became the basis for a new ROC policy toward the PRC. For the first time, the ROC government implicitly acknowledged that two different geographical areas existed but under the jurisdiction of two different political entities. ROC policy henceforth was to be based on preserving the rights and interests of the Taiwan people and to protect their security and welfare. Yet the ROC welcomed unification with the mainland people as long as human rights, democracy, and the rule of law existed and could be maintained for all of the Chinese people after unification. The guidelines stipulated three stages must take place to build the firm cooperative efforts that could make unification a reality. A public opinion poll taken by a government agency in that same month showed that half of the 3,022 people sampled agreed with the current pace at which ROC-PRC relations were evolving through trade and peoples' exchanges, whereas nearly a quarter believed the trend was too slow.[22]

As the year 1991 began, a new mood of confidence and stability for the first time prevailed. The president had successfully achieved a political reconciliation that few had believed possible more than six months before. As the next section will argue, his strategy for amending the Constitution and speeding up the retirement of senior representatives who ran the government was on course. The nation had a new foreign policy toward the PRC based on diverse opinion and expertise, which attested to this new leader's strong preference to establish national policies by broad consensus rather than by autocratic rule. The power struggle crisis within the KMT had receded as a strong premier took charge and earned high opinion poll ratings. President Lee's own opinion poll ranking showed him having nearly 80 percent of the public strongly approving his performance. The three major challenges facing the ROC had not entirely been overcome, but this new leader had shown great innovative ability, strong conviction, remarkable political skill, and enormous patience to deal with his opponents, win most of them over to his way of thinking, and build a new political consensus in which it seemed that none had existed before.

**New Triumphs and More Crises**
Working quietly behind the scenes with younger party leaders like Sung Ch'u-yu, Ma Ying-chiu, and others, President Lee moved ahead in early 1990 to amend the Constitution, retire the senior national representatives, and plan for the new national elections that must replace them. The president realized that only this bold political reform could win popular support for him and the KMT, although many high-ranking party members would not approve. By undertaking such actions, the president also realized that the KMT eventually had to become a new party capable of winning massive voter support. The KMT indeed could buy votes as it had in the past to guarantee victory, but in the new, open polity that now prevailed, the party had to offer voters a real alternative and obtain their support to prove that it alone had the moral mandate to govern Taiwan and unite China under a new Republic of China. President Lee realized this great challenge, and so he worked patiently to achieve these

59

goals while knowing full well that he would be opposed by leading KMT officials who preferred the status quo and retaining their current hold on power.

President Lee approved the following strategy and implemented it.[23] The party would cooperate with the DPP in the Legislative Yuan to obtain from the judiciary a ruling to set a date when the senior representatives must retire. At the same time, top party leaders including the president would informally meet with every senior representative and urge their speedy, voluntary retirement to hasten that process. Finally, the president planned to convene the First National Assembly sometime in the spring of 1991 to amend the Constitution to pave the way for new elections. To win these elections, however, President Lee realized the KMT must begin party reform immediately in order to obtain the majority of votes required to control the new National Assembly, Legislative Yuan, and Control Yuan, the three key government organs which the senior representatives now held. Without that control the KMT could not expect to govern in the new political marketplace and carry out its historic mission of achieving national unification.

Little known to the public, President Lee's plan began unfolding as soon as he was elected as the eighth president of the ROC on March 21, 1990. On April 4, 1990 the Legislative Yuan approved a resolution requesting the Council of Grand Justices in the Judicial Yuan to interpret the role of the senior representatives according to existing law.[24] On June 21, 1990 the Council of Grand Justices decided in court case 261 that on December 31, 1991 all senior representatives of the First National Assembly must step down as defined by the existing law, and that ruling applied to all other sectors of government where senior representatives held office. Meanwhile, President Lee and other KMT officials continued to informally meet with senior representatives throughout 1990 and early 1991 to use moral suasion to urge their speedy retirement. A small group of senior representatives, however, vowed never to retire, and they received some moral support from outspoken, aged KMT members. By early 1991, President Lee, assisted by his legal expert, Vice President Li, had worked out a strategy for constitutional amendment.

On February 26, 1991, President Lee ordered the First National Assembly to convene a provisional meeting in April 1991 to pave the way for electing a new National Assembly. But more was at stake. Before the Assembly convened on April 8, 1991, the senior representatives had been informed that the president wanted them to approve his request to terminate the Temporary Articles and end the state of insurgency with the PRC. Second, he wanted the delegates to approve new articles to regulate the election of a Second National Assembly and a new Legislative Yuan.[25] On April 22 the president's requests had been approved, although considerable violence had been perpetrated at the meetings by several DPP delegates. The KMT now had slightly more than half a year to prepare for the December 21, 1991 election of the Second National Assembly, an election that was the most important the party had ever faced on Taiwan. If the party failed to win a majority of seats in that new body, it could not expect to control the constitutional amendment process as it would like. The pace of democratization would then be determined by political forces that President Lee might not be able to handle.

Meanwhile, as chairman of the KMT, Lee and his secretary-general, Sung Ch'u-yu, began pushing party reform. This reform, beginning in early 1991, called for mandatory retirement of older middle- and lower-level cadres, consolidating departments to cut waste, and expanding consultation between party headquarters and local party leaders. By late summer 1991 this painful restructuring had been accomplished, but many complaints resounded for months after from members who argued that veteran cadres should never had been forcibly retired. Lee's bold move had revitalized the party by fall of 1991 to prepare for the critical December 21 election of the Second National Assembly. Although the DPP opposed this political body, that party willingly competed because they eventually hoped to abolish the National Assembly.

The late fall election was waged with furious words and heated campaigning by all competing candidates. The DPP abandoned its moderate message of the past and projected a radical political message calling for a new constitution and a Republic of Taiwan. President Lee personally campaigned around the island and called on voters to support a party that had provided prosperity, peace, and stability. The president's appeal was enormous, and the party's new message resonated favorably among voters, who voted overwhelmingly for KMT delegates. On December 25, President Lee attended a ceremony honoring the members of the First National Assembly who were retiring by December 31. He presented 469 senior representatives with silver medals to reward them for their long-term services to the ROC.[26] Less than two years after being elected president, Lee Teng-hui had removed all senior representatives from the ROC government and established national elections for their replacement. His party had been trimmed and had successfully won the majority of seats in the Second National Assembly, which would continue constitutional reform. The president's popularity with the voters was enormous. Facing great adversity more than eighteen months earlier, Lee had overcome those difficulties and taken the ROC a huge step forward toward complete democratization without violence and instability.

By thoroughly beating the DPP in the December 21, 1991 election and normalizing relations between the KMT and overseas dissidents and the DPP itself, President Lee had helped to institutionalize pluralistic party competition according to the law. The December 21, 1991 election had been widely criticized for massive vote-buying, but that charge had been frequently made in previous elections. Most important, that election had been peaceful, and candidates had complied with the law. Moreover, the president had taken the unprecedented step to ask the Executive Yuan on January 17, 1991 to set up an eight-person study group to gather information about the origins and outcome of the famous February 28, 1947 uprising and recommend to the government appropriate action to assuage the bitter memories associated with that event. In early 1992 the commission published its report, which blamed the government for partly causing the uprising and for using excessive force to suppress the uprising.[27] On behalf of the government, President Lee later apologized, and his government pledged to spend US$71 million as compensation for the victims and build several shrines to commemorate that tragedy. These actions by a Taiwanese president finally put that tragic affair to rest and was a healing measure to build a bridge of goodwill between a small segment of the Taiwan people and the ROC government.

By terminating the Period of National Mobilization for Suppression of the Communist Rebellion, President Lee had ended the state of war between the ROC and PRC and established peaceful negotiations as the new approach his government would take toward that communist regime. Lee would continue to upgrade ROC defense capabilities, but true to the spirit of his new guideline for the unification of China, he still persevered to fulfill the mission of the KMT and its late chairman, Chiang Ching-kuo. At his international press conference of April 30, 1991, President Lee emphasized that "the most important thing about democratic reform is the actualization of democratization of our political system."[28] Lee's desire for the "actualization of democratization," however, soon triggered a new crisis in his party that continued until its Fourteenth Party Congress of August 1993.

In January 1992 most observers believed the KMT intended to push for a new method of presidential and vice presidential indirect election adopted by the new Second National Assembly, whereas the DPP wanted a direct popular election for these leaders. On March 4, President Lee met with high-level government and KMT officials and stated that the KMT must give strong consideration to approving the direct election method for future leaders. His statement stunned the party. At the March 14-15 Third Plenum of the KMT, a great debate erupted in the central committee over which election procedure the party should adopt. The split was deep, again along the old "mainstream" versus "non-mainstream" groupings, but this time with considerable crossover of party members. Why had the president suddenly changed his mind on an issue on which it had appeared the party had long agreed?

The president had learned from his island-wide campaigning in previous months that popular sentiment for direct presidential election was widespread. But Lee realized that many powerful KMT leaders opposed the direct election of future leaders, because they feared this trend toward democratization would favor Taiwanese nationalist separatism. Moreover, Lee also knew that he probably had the votes in the central committee to ram through a party resolution to endorse direct election and reform the constitution accordingly. Such a move, however, would only worsen KMT factionalism and impair the party's guidance of future democratization as well as imperil the long-run unification of China.

The Third Plenum debate was heated, and only secret meetings between Lee and top party leaders resolved the crisis. They agreed to a compromise plan that no action on selecting the presidential election procedure be taken until 1995, at which time the Third National Assembly would then discuss and decide the matter. President Lee realized that time was on his side. Popular support would become manifest both in the KMT and outside to support direct election. With patience and tact he managed to restore, if only temporarily, party harmony and, most important, to avoid amending the Constitution in a way that only might severely discredit the KMT in the future and damage its ability to win voter support.

The meeting of the Second National Assembly in the spring of 1992 was a tempestuous affair, marked by periodic violence and constant vituperative behavior by most of the groups in that body. By mid-May the Assembly had done its work and approved eight new articles for amending the Constitution: several of these specified the procedures for future appointments of the Judicial Yuan, Examination Yuan, and Control Yuan. The public media had carefully reported the antics of Assembly persons, and the Assembly's accomplishments did not elicit great praise from Taiwan society. The DPP strongly criticized the Assembly's work, and several radical groups attempted to gather petitions demanding the Assembly be abolished. The KMT and government praised the Assembly's work and urged the country to prepare for the new Legislative Yuan's election in late December 1992.

Meanwhile, various KMT members and academics began criticizing and scolding President Lee for his mishandling of constitutional revision. A new faction in the KMT, calling themselves the New Wave Group, now joined the fray and publicly criticized the president for not addressing such issues as political corruption. Criticism from these same political groups intensified and came to a head in February 1993 when President Lee made clear that the recent election of a new Legislative Yuan in late December 1992 required its confirmation of a new Executive Yuan; he called for everyone in the cabinet to present their resignations. This created a dilemma for Premier Hao.

For many months, rumors had circulated about the growing tension and enmity between the president and his popular premier. In the area of personal appointments, especially regarding the armed forces, the premier had often expressed his displeasure with the president's appointments, and these had become public knowledge. Many also perceived the premier as championing those elements in the KMT who did not hide their displeasure at the president's governance of the country and the party. Many believed that when Premier Hao submitted his resignation he would not be reappointed, and indeed that was the case. In March, President Lee appointed a new premier, Dr. Lien Chan, an old colleague from National Taiwan University days and a career bureaucrat who had served with distinction but was not particularly popular. The forced retirement of Hao set off more opposition to the president.

On February 11, 1992 a vitriolic letter written by the politician Chu Kao-cheng, a former DPP member who later bolted that party and established his own party, appeared in the Taipei press. Chu charged Lee with "treating other people as tools," "playing golf with businessmen and surrounding [himself] with the bosses of large financial groups and enterprises," and "arbitrarily destroying the foundations of Taiwan."[28] A week later, various people tried to collect petitions among the overseas Chinese to protest President Lee's abusive use of power. Some even drew up plans for public demonstrations against the president. None of these efforts bore fruit. Then in August 1993 a small group of KMT members angrily left their party and established a new party to protest the nation's growing political corruption and the government's failure to improve economic growth and prevent the increasingly unequal distribution of wealth and income. Having reconciled many angry and bitter Taiwanese with the KMT and the ROC government who now peacefully participated in the new political marketplace, President Lee now had to deal with the anger and fear of many mainlanders who worried that the president had become a political strongman who no longer cared about their interests.

### Steering the Course

At the Fourteenth Congress of the KMT in mid-August 1993, President Lee admitted the KMT's heavy historical burden of unifying the Chinese nation had made its task of governing Taiwan difficult. He appealed to the party membership to "beat the long list of odds," "win support from our fellow members and compatriots at home and abroad, continue to lead the whole people, realize our party's ideals envisioned in the Three Principles of the People, and carry out our party's goal of bringing happiness to the country and the people."[29] Lee urged the membership to realize that their party stood at a "turning point of history." Lee reminded his audience that democracy was now a reality in Taiwan but its quality had to be improved and the process deeply imbedded in society. He appealed to party members' sense of moral standards, to work hard, to "hang together," promote excellence, and tackle "all of our problems democratically." He concluded that only by making Taiwan a solid model of economic and democratic progress could China be unified. He again referred to the salient guidelines for unification his council had hammered out in early 1991 by stressing peaceful negotiations with the communist regime and his hope that leadership would renounce using force to achieve national reunification. Like Chiang Ching-kuo before him, Chairman Lee emphasized that only the KMT had "constructed the Republic of China" and it was "also the political party that will reconstruct the Republic of China; it is not only a political party that always can withstand the test, but also a political party that can always lead in the march of the times."

With these fighting words echoing in party members' ears, the KMT then voted by secret ballot for the first time, to elect Lee Teng-hui to a new four-year term as chairman. The newly elected standing and central committees' members represented more young Taiwanese in the party's leadership than in the past.

Chiang Ching-kuo's successor had steered the ship of state through rough and sometimes stormy seas for nearly six years. Formidable and still casting a dark shadow over Taiwan's future, the PRC's leaders still threaten to use force if the ROC does not ultimately agree to a new arrangement with the PRC. President Lee and a bipartisan group have produced the guiding principles for the ROC to negotiate with the PRC, and if historical conditions properly evolve, Taiwan might be unified with the mainland sometime in the distant future.

The long-standing Taiwanese nationalist movement always has been a dangerous threat to the KMT and the ROC government and a possible cause of political instability and international pressure from the West. In a series of masterful moves, President Lee had legitimated the DPP in the political marketplace. That party never commanded more than a quarter to one-third of the popular votes in any election. Whenever that party displayed its true, radical image, the voters strongly rejected their candidates and votes over-whelmingly for the KMT. President Lee understood

Taiwanese sentiment toward that tragic rebellion of 1947, and his government had offered a remarkable apology to the victims. Yet the president never endorsed Taiwanese independence and vigorously criticized any politician supporting that goal.

Finally, as the first Taiwanese chairman of the KMT and president of the ROC, Lee Teng-hui had moved cautiously to deal with the political heavyweights inside the KMT. He gradually built a network of loyal supporters in the party and government. As that network expanded, Lee's political influence grew. He displayed remarkable skill at making key personnel appointments to eliminate his rivals and selecting outstanding candidates to represent the KMT in recent national elections. He treated the party elders with respect and displayed a veneration for Chiang Ching-kuo and the Chiang family that reflected the broad civilizational values of this leader.

Lee's unusual schooling in the Japanese educational system, his brilliant career as an academic and technocrat, and his Western education gave him unusual skills and a multicultural experience unique in Chinese political history. But there were other qualities about this man that enabled him to persevere through the difficulties of the past six years. He could endure humiliating attacks by enemies without displaying rancor and anger. His long-term planning of the ROC's democratization process reflects his rational and incisive thinking. Finally, his deep sense of loyalty to the man who valued him so highly, Chiang Ching-kuo, suggests a rare virtue in the political world, in which expediency all too often seems more appropriate than adhering to convictions based on solid, core values.

As the winds of democracy blow more strongly in the ROC on Taiwan, a popular election for a president will probably be held in late 1995 or 1996. The future of the ROC seems more certain and hopeful if a leader like Lee Teng-hui decides to throw his hat into the ring and compete to become the nation's first democratically elected president.

## NOTES

1. To be sure, democratization is not complete: government still controls the electronic media; constitutional reform to permit the popular election of a president, vice president, and governor of Taiwan province will not take place until 1995-96; and so forth. Even so, national elections are now institutionalized and political party competition is a reality.

2. See Lai Tse-han, Ramon H. Myers, and Wei Wou, *A Tragic Beginning: The February 28, 1947 Uprising* (Stanford, Calif.: Stanford University Press, 1991).

3. See Ramon H. Myers and Ts'ai Ling, "Out of the Ashes of Defeat: Revitalizing the Kuomintang in Taiwan, 1950-1952," in Compilation Committee for the Conference on Eighty Years of Building the Republic of China, comp., *Proceedings of Conference on Eighty Years' History of the Republic of China, 1912-1991* (Taipei: Chin-tai Chung-kuo ch'u-pan-she, 1991), vol. 1, pp. 89-120. See also Bruce J. Dickson, "The Lessons of Defeat: The Reorganization of the Kuomintang on Taiwan, 1950-52," *China Quarterly*, no. 133 (March 1993), pp. 56-84.

4. Hsu Han, *Li Teng-hui ti ch'i-shih-nien* [The Seventy Years of Lee Teng-hui] (Taipei: K'ai-chin wen-hua ch'u-pan-she, 1993), pp. 25-26. Li Ching-jung's first son joined the imperial Japanese army in World War II and disappeared while serving in the Philippines. His third son, named Li Ping-nan, today works as a general manager in a business enterprise.

5. Ibid., p. 37.

6. Li Ta, *Li Teng-hui chuan* [Biography of Li Teng-hui] (Taipei: Kuang-chiao-ching, 1988), p. 44.

7. Ibid., p. 45.

8. Hsu Han, op. cit., p. 76.

9. Li Ta, op. cit., pp. 49-50.

10. Some observers like Hsu Han (p. 83) argue that Chiang Ching-kuo selected Lee because he had no political supporters, was morally upright, and not obligated to anyone; he had no son to promote; as a Christian, Lee's close ties with the Presbyterian Church in northern Taiwan could serve to check

the radical Presbyterian Church in the south; he wanted an able Taiwanese to deal with the Taiwan nationalist movement, both overseas and at home. Finally, Chiang could demonstrate to the U.S. authorities that mainlanders and Taiwanese could get along and that equality and justice existed for everyone in Taiwan, irrespective of ethnicity.

11. Ssu-ma Wen-wu, "Li Teng-hui ti 100 t'ien" [The First Hundred Days of Lee Teng-hui], *Hsin-hsin-wen* [The Journalist], no. 58 (April 18-24, 1988), p. 21.
12. Ibid., pp. 21-22.
13. Nan Fang-ssu, "Li Teng-hui ti-i-nien ti ch'eng-chi-tan" [A One-Year Report Card on Lee Teng-hui], *Hsin-hsin-wen*, no. 96 (January 9-15, 1989), pp. 22-23.
14. For a good description of this event, see *Tzu-li tsao-pao*, January 2, 1988, p. 2.
15. Kuo Hung-chih, "Tsung-t'ung nien chung k'ao-chi, minchung kei-t'a chi-fen" [How Did the People Score the President in Terms of Their Year-End Evaluation?], *Hsin-hsin-wen*, no. 96 (January 9-15, 1989), pp. 26-32.
16. Ch'en Ming-feng, Wei Hung-yu, Liao Fu-hsun, "Ni tsen-yang k'an che i-wen T'ai-wan jen yuan-shou?" [What Do You Think About the Taiwanese Leader?], *Hsin-hsin-wen*, no. 96, (January 9-15, 1989), p. 35.
17. This discussion of the March 1990 election is based on Ts'ai Ling and Ramon H. Myers, "Emerging Democracy: The 1990 Election in the Republic of China on Taiwan," *China Quarterly*, no. 129 (March 1992), pp. 123-148.
18. The discussion below about the National Affairs Conference is based on Ts'ai Ling and Ramon H. Myers, "Manichaean Suspicions and the Spirit of Reconciliation: Currents of Public Opinion in Taiwan on the Eve of the 1990 Conference on the Republic of China's Destiny," *American Asian Review* 9:2 (summer 1991), pp. 1-41; see also Ts'ai Ling and Ramon H. Myers, "Achieving Consensus Amidst Adversity: The Conference to Decide the Republic of China's Future (June 28-July 4, 1990), *American Asian Review* 9:3 (fall 1991), pp. 1-40. A more appropriate translation of Kuo-shih hui-i (National Affairs Conference) is the Conference to Decide the Destiny of the Country.
19. *Chung-kuo shih-pao*, October 2, 1990, p. 1 for lead article describing the composition of the important national council.
20. *Chung-kuo shih-pao*, October 8, 1990, p. 1.
21. Ibid., p. 2.

22. Government Information Office, ROC, *The Republic of China Yearbook, 1993* (Taipei: Government Information Office, 1993), p. 149.

23. For a long discussion of the strategy, readers can refer to an unpublished paper by Ts'ai Ling and Ramon H. Myers titled "On the Road to Political Reform: Electing the First National Assembly. Its Evolution and Demise, and the December 21, 1991 Election of the Second National Assembly in the Republic of China."

24. "Shih-hsien shih tsui-chia ti pi-t'ui' fang-an" [To Interpret the Constitution Is the Best Proposal to Force Retirement], *Tzu-yu shih-pao*, April 4, 1990, p. 2.

25. For the ten new articles added to the Constitution see *Republic of China Yearbook, 1991-92*, pp. 580-581.

26. "Chih-shen kuo-tai kung-ch'eng sheng-t'ui; Li tsung-t'ung ch'in-sung chiang-chiang tai-kuo-jen chih-hsieh" [All Senior Representatives of the National Assembly Have Made Their Contributions and Now They Retire; President Lee Personally Grants Awards to Them on Behalf of the Country], *Chung-kuo shih-pao*, December 26, 1991, p. 2.

27. Hsing-cheng-yüan, yen-chiu erh-erh-pa shih-chien hsiao-tsu [The Executive Yuan, the Team Examining the February 28, 1947 Incident], *Erh-erh-pa shih-chien yen-chiu pao-kao* [Research Report on the February 28, 1947 Incident] (Taipei: Executive Yuan, 1992), v. 1-2.

28. Lee Teng-hui, *Creating the Future: Toward a New Era for the Chinese People* (Taipei: Government Information Office, 1992), pp. 41-42.

29. Lee Teng-hui, "Address at the Opening Ceremony of the Fourteenth National Congress of the Kuomintang of China on August 16, 1993," p. 2.

Reprinted by Permission of Ramon H. Myers

# Political Development in the Republic of China on Taiwan, 1985-1992: An Insider's View

James C.Y. Soong

*World Affairs*
Fall 1992

The basic facts are beyond dispute. Since the beginning of its export-oriented economic growth in the mid-1960s, the real gross national product of the Republic of China (ROC) on Taiwan grew at an average rate of nearly 9 percent a year. In fact, Taiwan has successfully transformed its socioeconomic structure from predominantly rural and agrarian to one of urban and industrial. More impressively, this growth has been accompanied by a favorable pattern of income distribution, low unemployment, universal literacy, and the near elimination of poverty that usually alienates the poorest social strata in other less developed countries (LDCs). It is little wonder that scholars of development often speak of the "economic miracle" in Taiwan (Gold, 1986).

*James C.Y. Soong is governor of the Taiwan Provincial Government.*

Following its impressive economic growth, there has been increasing demand in Taiwan for more political openness (Scalapino, 1987:77). Rules upon which social and political activities were sanctioned can no longer address the population's near-feverish demand for political participation. Overseeing the society's rapid transformation and the appropriate management of this new-found vitality and enthusiasm is a matter of critical importance for the ruling Kuomintang (KMT). Simply stated, the KMT's goal is to institutionalize political processes and to strengthen the rule of law operating under a democratic, constitutional framework.

In analyzing the relationship between socioeconomic growth and political development, the most commonly assumed paradigm is that the likelihood of political democracy increases as the level of socioeconomic development improves (Lipset, 1959). Indeed, Taiwan's rapid socioeconomic progress has brought democratic inclinations and has produced an environment conducive to full democracy. Mass education, urbanization, and internationalization have all contributed to the emergence of a democratic political system in Taiwan. However, because democracy is a foreign import and it needs to operate under Taiwan's Chinese socio-cultural traditions, there are inevitable contradictions and tensions that would affect its structural underpinnings and effectiveness.

## Democracy and Chinese Cultural Traditions

In spite of ethnic and religious diversity, there is a background culture that binds people together in Taiwan, a culture deeply rooted in Confucianism. Unlike others, Confucianism is a code of ethics and standard of conduct, developed to guide the relationships between people (Han, 1984). It emphasizes mutual respect and common acknowledgement of mutual obligations. Within these relationships, a common understanding of what is mutually expected reduces the need for much forthright, direct communication.

In politics, Confucianism views government as an extended family, with individuals knowing their place and responsibility (Hicks and Redding, 1984). As Lucian Pye explains, "Just as the Confucian concept of the ideal government was an extension of the ideal family, so the prime tasks of government were the same as those of the family: to provide security, continuity, cohesion, and solidarity" (1985:63).

Against such an inherent cultural backdrop, the notion of a participatory pluralist society where an actively involved citizenry compete for favorable policy outcomes by open, frequently hostile confrontation appears peculiar to most Chinese on Taiwan. In particular, Confucian emphasis on group harmony rather than individualism sets the socio-political context in stark contrast with many of the early-industrialized, parliamentarian democracies in Western Europe and North America. Using the United States as a case in contrast, Samuel Huntington explains the difference succinctly:

> In such a society, the critical need is to avoid competition and disharmony, and hence elaborate consultation within the group is required before a decision can be reached. Americans, on the other hand, are comfortable with open conflict, majority votes, and a more individualistic, "lone ranger" style of leadership [Huntington, 1981:56].

Therefore, importation of concepts such as democracy must first be grafted onto traditional values and developed into an acceptable version before becoming part of the code of conduct, and it remains important to reconcile policy measures with traditional Chinese values of deference to seniority, maintenance of networks, and preference for mediation over confrontation. While features of paternalism might have gradually been phased out and replaced by participation and competition in today's Taiwan, a complete elimination of Confucian ideals that have had profound impact on Chinese social ethos and political structure for thousands of years is unlikely.

## Process of Democratization in the ROC

The probable political consequences of modernization, according to Karl W. Deutsch, are the continuous "expansion of the politically relevant strata" and the increasing demand by the people for expansion and improvement of government services to satisfy their needs (Deutsch, 1961:497-98). Under these conditions, a political system must seek means to enhance its capabilities and maintain stability at the same time.

In view of the changes brought on by Taiwan's rapid socioeconomic progress, the late president and KMT chairman, Chiang Ching-kuo, courageously initiated a series of far-sighted reforms. Most significantly, the ROC government lifted martial law (*Chieyen*) and began granting citizens permission to vistit their Mainland relatives in 1987. During the past five years, socio-political activities and organizations blossomed in Taiwan, as evidenced by the increased numbers of registered political parties (from 3 during martial law to 69 in mid-1992), daily newspapers (from 31 in 1986 to 246 in mid-1992), and magazines (from 3354 before lifting martial law to 4356 by mid-1992). Although President Chiang Ching-kuo passed away unexpectedly in January 1988, he had already set into motion the locomotive for further efforts at democratization in Taiwan. Moreover, through these historical reforms, President Chiang made certain that the ruling Kuomintang would remain an adaptable political entity capable of continuously absorbing and managing the demands generated by modernization "with relatively few eruptions and breakdowns" (Eisenstadt, 1964:347).

## President Lee Teng-hui's Policy Agenda

Political reforms continued in the post-Chiang Taiwan. Prior to his inauguration in May 1990, President Lee Teng-hui (Ph.D. in agricultural economics from Cornell University) met with his top advisors to formulate a blueprint for Taiwan's continued growth and development in the next six years. In view of the constraints as well as opportunities that might confront the ROC, President Lee outlined the following policy agenda for his presidency:

## Democratization

As Taiwan readies itself for the twenty-first century, the existing socio-political institutions and structures must be overhauled to accommodate the population's rising demand for more openness and greater participation. Foremost, the ROC Constitution needs to be amended to reflect Taiwan's political realities. The ruling Kuomintang undertook such a challenge with a "two-year, three-phase" approach, beginning with the voluntary retirement of the Mainland-elected members in the ROC's three branches of Parliament.

Despite the fact that they had not been subject to re-election since 1947, these senior parliamentarians were responsible for promulgating programs and legislation that propelled Taiwan's economic take-off. In appreciation of their past contributions, the ruling party put forth a retirement plan that included a handsome pension at preferential interest rates and the formation of a civic organization with advisory function on national unification. Although some members resisted initially, they all eventually relinquished their position and retired from active duty by the end of 1991, thus marking a significant step in constitutional reform.

This peaceful, bloodless transfer of power not only was history-making in itself, it also accelerated the pace of constitutional reform in the ROC. Elections for the Second National Assembly were held in December 1991. With a campaign platform of "Progress and Prosperity amidst Stability," the Kuomintang won close to 72 percent of the popular vote, with nearly 79 percent of the National Assembly seats. Based upon such solid support, the ruling Kuomintang was entrusted with the popular mandate to institute the necessary Constitutional reforms.

During the Second National Assembly Conference on Constitutional Revision in March-May 1992, amendments were passed that clearly defined the authority and responsibilities of the different branches of the government. Furthermore, more than one hundred pieces of legislation that were promulgated during the "Period of Communist Rebellion" were repealed and replaced with new legislative provisions by mid-July 1992. Since constitutional reform is an on-going process, the Second National Assembly plans to reconvene in the next four years to thoroughly examine issues such as the presidential election system and the term of office for members of the Legislative Yuan, a branch of the Parliament.

On the other hand, the ruling Kuomintang has been trying to develop a modus operandi with the ROC's largest opposition force—the Democratic Progressive Party (DPP). Although the political beliefs and ideals of the two major parties differ significantly, the ruling party has demonstrated sincerity and goodwill in legislative consultation with the DPP. The biggest obstacle to the formation of a well-structured two-party system, however, remains with the DPP's internal factional strife.

Since its inception in September 1986, the DPP has embroiled itself in an ideological struggle over the issue of Taiwanese independence and has subsequently split into two distinct factions: the "Formosa Faction" and the "New Tide Faction." In particular, the New Tide Faction has openly advocated a de jure independent Taiwanese nation and successfully incorporated pro-independence provisions into the DPP Constitution in October 1991. However, the DPP suffered a severe blow in the December 1991 elections when voters shunned its separatist tendency and shied away from its candidates, resulting in the DPP capturing only 23 percent of the popular vote and 75 seats in the

Second National Assembly. Thus, while the DPP may attract the support of a disenchanted minority on Taiwan, it has not matured into a loyal opposition that is accountable for its rhetoric or actions. In the future, the ruling KMT will continue its goodwill toward the DPP. However, unless the DPP corrects its ideological orientation, bipartisan relations will likely remain unpredictable.

## Modernization

In many ways, modernization is not an elusive goal that developing countries strive for. It is a continuous process whereby a society improves its resource allocation, productive capability, and cultural assets. While the ROC has achieved and maintained enviable socioeconomic growth rates, modernity as a way of life has not yet been widely entrenched in Taiwan's society.

President Lee fully realizes the importance of modernizing the Taiwanese society, not just technologically and materialistically, but culturally as well. With the goal of bringing the ROC into the ranks of developed nations, the government has launched the ambitious Six-Year National Development Plan to upgrade the island's infrastructure and technological base. With a total budget of US$303 billion allocated for over one hundred projects, the ROC government seeks to: raise national income; provide sufficient resources for continued industrial growth; promote balanced regional development; and upgrade the national quality of life, through implementation of the Six-Year Plan.

On the other hand, President Lee decided to head the National Cultural Association himself to cultivate the appreciation for arts and other cultural activities. Today, at Taipei's National Theatre, National Concert Hall, and other cultural centers throughout the island, one can regularly experience cultural entertainment from ballet to Taiwanese opera. This concerted effort to promote arts and cultural development is designed to make the ROC on Taiwan known not only for its material wealth and technological prowess, but also for its cultural richness and diversity.

## Unification

Since Deng Xiao-ping's "open-door" policy of the early 1980s, the Chinese Communist Party (CCP) has implemented successive policies to revitalize its stagnant economy. However, it has become increasingly clear that reforms and changes cannot be confined to the economic realm only. Indeed, the CCP cannot continue to encourage economic initiatives while commanding that its citizens remain fully subservient to the party-state. Concentration of power in the hands of a few thus remains a major obstacle for reforms on the Mainland.

Another more serious problem lies in the unpredictability of the CCP regime, its leadership, and its policies. In many ways, the CCP lacks the institutional measures that would assure the peaceful transfer of power or the continuation of policies. With the "rule of men" by fiat firmly entrenched in its policymaking process, changes in leadership makeup may well mean an abrupt termination of its current reforms. Lack of political institutionalization thus constitutes the biggest handicap to the CCP's reform efforts.

Over the years, the ruling Kuomintang formulated its Mainland policy by strictly adhering to the "one China" principle and by putting the welfare and security of Taiwan's 20 million inhabitants ahead of all other considerations. From the "recovery of the Mainland through military campaign" of the 1950s to "unification of China under the Three Principles of the People" in the 1980s, there has been a decidedly clear

shift from past dogmatism to today's pragmatic considerations. Being the ruling party, the Kuomintang's
Mainland policy is founded upon a long-range perspective and consists of incremental steps that do not
carry adverse consequences that would threaten the
island's continued prosperity or security. While ROC
citizens as of mid-1992 have visited the Mainland in
excess of 3.7 million times (with the total number of
persons exceeding 1 million) since 1987, the ROC government will not hastily accelerate the pace of cross-
straits contacts for the sake of nationalism.

The *Guidelines for National Unification* drafted by
the National Unification Council (NUC) in 1991 now
serves as the highest directive governing ROC Mainland policy. The guidelines call for China's unification
under the principles of democracy, freedom, and equitable distribution of wealth through peaceful means.
Although no definite timetable was set in the guidelines, the pace of improved relations is closely linked
with measurable progress in relations between the two
sides. This further demonstrates the ROC's current
pragmatic approach in managing its Mainland
relations.

In a fundamental way, the Taiwan-Mainland
confrontation has gradually evolved from an ideological struggle between the KMT and CCP to a choice of
lifestyles. It is now a choice that our Mainland compatriots, not the Peking regime, must make, not only for
themselves, but for future generations of the Chinese
people as well.

## Concluding Remarks

As a near-universal goal, modernization is what
every developing society strives to achieve, but the
process of modernization can be quite volatile; and it
usually creates tensions. For a society undergoing
modernization, there are inevitable tensions between

calls for equitable sharing of the fruits of an enlarged national wealth and requirements of continual growth and stability; between the heightened aspirations for greater political participation and the limited availability of public offices; and between the fast-rising demand for more public goods and services and the government's slow-growing capacity to meet them.

To any political system these dichotomous developments present challenges. To the Republic of China on Taiwan, it is no exception. In recent years, the KMT has demonstrated its willingness to bring about changes, to accommodate diverse views, and to confront future challenges with courage and conviction. In fact, 51,731 new members joined the Kuomintang during April-June 1992. Of these new members, 76.8 percent were under age 35 and nearly 81 percent were, at least, college graduates. Success in recruitment indicates that today's Kuomintang embodies a vision and political beliefs that are shared by most people on Taiwan. More importantly, ROC citizens are acutely aware that today's Kuomintang is a force of stability not only for their welfare but also for the hope and aspirations of their Mainland compatriots.

On balance, an assessment of the key variables that will determine Taiwan's future strongly suggests that prospects for its continued economic prosperity, social stability, and political development appear optimistic. Although rough roads lie ahead, the ruling Kuomintang is certain that a prosperous, democratic, and socially just Taiwan can truly serve as a model for the Chinese Mainland and other developing countries to emulate.

## REFERENCES

Deutsch, Karl W., "Social Mobilization and Political Development," *American Political Science Review*, 55 (September 1961): 493-514.

Eisenstadt, Shmuel, "Breakdowns of Modernization," *Economic Development and Cultural Change*, 12 (July 1964).

Gold, Thomas, *State and Society in the Taiwan Miracle* (Armonk, N.Y.: M.E. Sharpe, 1986).

Han, S. S., "Of Economic Success and Confucianism," *Far Eastern Economic Review*, 126 (1984): 104-6.

Hicks, G.L., and S.G. Redding, "The Story of the East Asian 'Economic Miracle'; Part Two: The Cultural Connection," *Euro-Asia Business Review*, 2 (1984): 18-22.

Huntington, Samuel P., *American Politics: the Promise of Disharmony* (Cambridge: Belknap Press, 1981).

Kahn, Harold L., *Monarchy in the Emperor's Eyes: Image and Reality in the Chien-lung Reign* (Cambridge, Mass.: Harvard University Press, 1971).

Lipset, Seymour Martin, "Some Social Requisites of Democracy," *American Political Science Review*, 53 (1959): 69-105.

Scalapino, Robert A., "Asia's future," *Foreign Affairs*, 66 (Fall 1987): 77-108.

Reprinted by Permission of *World Affairs*

# Constitutional Reform and Democracy

Chu Yun-han

*Chu Yun-han is a professor of political science at National Taiwan University.*

## Introduction: the Scope and Process of Constitutional Reform

■ Constitutional reform is a general term referring to adjustment of the legal system during democratization. It is essential to the success of democratization and can determine the quality of future representative government. Throughout Taiwan's political transition, disputes between the ruling party and the opposition over the pace, scope, and direction of political liberalization and democratization have centered on the issue of constitutional reform. Political appeals of the opposition, including the early demands for lifting the ban on new political parties, rescinding the *Emergency Decree*, re-electing parliament, terminating the Period of Mobilization or Suppression of the Communist Rebellion, and restoring constitutional rule, along with the latest calls for Taiwan independence and rewriting of the Constitution, have been invariably related to the adjustment of the constitutional system. The power succession and integration of the ruling elite, elections, social mobilization of the opposition movement, and consultations between the ruling party and the opposition have been the four primary factors of political transition in Taiwan. In the end, the progression of phased democratization must rely upon structural and legal reform.

In a broad sense, constitutional reform and democratization are two sides of the same coin. Formerly, people in Taiwan were inclined to consider

84

constitutional reform in its narrow sense. Constitutional reform was seen mainly as constitutional amendment plus the concomitant adjustments in the electoral system aimed at keeping the two in line with the constitutional standards of democratic countries. This idea of placing the emphasis of constitutional reform on the constitution itself has greatly narrowed the scope of constitutional reform. If we were to use this yardstick to measure the progress of Taiwan's democratization, we could fall into the narrow track of electoralism[1], which could lead to only partial democratic reform.

The original sense of constitutionalism includes the establishment of constitutional authority and the principle of the rule of law, as well as thorough application of the principle of sovereignty of the people. In the transformation from an authoritarian system to a democratic system, the following should be emphasized:

- preservation of basic human rights;
- protection of independent social movements;
- guarantee of fair competition among political parties; and
- restructuring of power relationships among national organizations, especially normal fulfillment of the legislative and supervisory functions, command and control of military and intelligence organizations by the civilian government, and independence of the judicial branch.

In a broad sense, the aims of constitutional reform and democratization are almost identical. Constitutional reform should include the various changes in the legal system required for carrying out these aims. Besides the Constitution, the reform should include all political laws related to the effective functioning of constitutional government, such as the *Freedom of Information Act*, the *Organic Law of National Defense*, the *Electoral Law*, the *Law of Assembly and Parades*, and the *National Security Law*. Constitutional reform does not end with constitutional amendment.

Another question about constitutional reform is whether it should involve the restructuring of national organizations. In Taiwan, constitutional reform, for historical reasons, does involve the defining of national structures. Today, opposing positions on the definition of the national structures are intertwined with the constitutional reform process. Advocates of a new constitution call for Taiwan independence, while champions of the Republic of China invariably advocate constitutional amendment. There is no middle ground. This intractable situation has made the path to constitutional reform more difficult.

The problem of which road should be chosen for constitutional reform should be considered alongside of the question of democratization. Building a consensus among the major factions on the new democratic order is very important. Judging from the latest instances of successful democratization, amending the present constitution, rewriting a new constitution, or restoring an old constitution all are feasible approaches, and there is no definite relationship between successful democratization and the writing of a new constitution. Few authoritarian regimes that are facing disintegration have succeeded in establishing completely new democratic systems. Of these countries, Spain and Turkey have written new constitutions, while Greece and Argentina have restored their old constitutions. In most Eastern European nations and in the former Soviet Union, democratic systems are either pending establishment or are still very weak and, therefore, cannot be taken as models.

All nations that have successfully carried out constitutional reforms have their specific backgrounds and conditions and thus cannot be stereotyped. But generally speaking, the option chosen should be based on two factors: (1) whether the present or the old constitution is democratically legitimate, including whether the basic design can meet constitutional criteria, and whether the process of its writing met minimum standards of democratic legitimacy. If no old constitution can be restored or if the present constitution is seen by the public as a tool for maintaining the old authoritarian system, the writing of a new constitution is probably the only choice; otherwise, the old constitution would have to be restored. The second factor to be noted is the transitional process of the political entity. If the ruling body of the original authoritarian political entity has won a certain degree of support in society and has succeeded in guiding the transition, then constitutional amendment or restoring the old constitution might be more advisable. Since in such a situation there are no major differences between the government and the opposition over the design of the future constitutional system, and there is a close connection between the old system and the new one, the writing of a new constitution should not be adopted, because it would entail the social cost of creating contention in society. This is because writing a new constitution inevitably leads to adjustments in the whole political structure and a reallocation of political resources. If, however, rulers of the political entity have lost support in society and are unable to guide the political transition, the old political design will disappear as the authoritarian system disintegrates, making the writing of a new constitution the only choice.

Based on this analysis, constitutional reform in the Republic of China should not be cast simply as a controversy between advocates of national unification and proponents of Taiwan independence. The issue is, rather, choosing between amendment of the present constitution and writing a new constitution according to the country's specific background and its conditions of transition. This crucial consideration should not be based on which path to constitutional reform is beneficial to either national unification or Taiwan independence. The real question is which path can best meet the demands of democratization and build a majority consensus.

To better answer this question, we must understand whether the present constitution is democratically legitimate. Undoubtedly, the *Constitution of the Republic of China* was designed according to the basic criteria of constitutionalism.[2] In the past, authoritarian rulers counted on an extraordinary system that froze and gutted some major provisions of the normal constitution. In other words, the present constitution is not considered by the public as a tool for maintaining the old authoritarian system. Rather, it has been an effective weapon employed by liberal intellectuals and oppositionists in their challenge against the authoritarian system. In terms of adjustments in the legal system, it is not difficult to sort out the entanglement between the extraordinary system and the normal system, particularly since the passage of the *Additional Articles of the Constitution*. These additional articles in a sense have completed the design of the legal system required in the transitional period, and the link between the old legal system and the new one is no longer a problem. The question whether the constitution met the minimum conditions of democratic legitimacy when it was written cannot be answered through reasoned debates, because it is linked to the question of determining the scope of national sovereignty, which, in turn, is related to the controversy over national unification and Taiwan independence.

Judging by the unique features of Taiwan's transition from authoritarianism, the argument for constitutional amendment still enjoys considerable support in society mainly because the Kuomintang still enjoys some degree of ruling legitimacy and it has played an effective and leading role during transition. In particular, the Kuomintang has, under a "nativist" policy, recruited native elite who believe that reform from within can complement political nativization, and that the results of writing a new constitution would be unpredictable.

Most voters are now worried about the huge social costs that the writing of a new constitution would incur. This is because of a lack of consensus regarding the design of a future constitutional system, and the impact of the new constitution on the current political order. Such worries also come from the realization that the writing of a new constitution would inevitably be entangled with the question of national structure, and that the move would coincide with advocacy of Taiwan independence. Therefore, the writing of a new constitution would certainly cause heated struggle between the proponents of national unification and the advocates of Taiwan independence, and could also sour relations between the two sides of the Taiwan Straits. Amendment to the constitution could be limited to the level of political structure[3], but we must understand that support for constitutional amendment by many politicians and common people does not necessarily mean support for a one-China policy that would cancel out the various possibilities for political development between Taiwan and the Chinese mainland. Many people believe that Taiwan should not be eager to solve the issue of unification or independence and change the one-China policy on the constitutional level. They also believe that constitutional amendment is a sine qua non for guiding cross-Straits relations toward constructive development.

# Electing a National Assembly for Constitutional Amendment: Breakthroughs in Current Constitutional Reform

Whether current constitutional reform can be carried out smoothly through constitutional amendment depends, theoretically, on whether the amendment package dominated by the Kuomintang can win majority support in society. In practice, however, the success of constitutional reform hinges on whether the major political forces in society are willing to accept common procedural criteria in political competition and whether a consensus can be reached on the range of issues to be discussed in electoral competition. Coordination is particularly required from powerful political bodies that are motivated by a strong desire for changing the status quo. In other words, extensive consultations between the major political parties are indispensable to the reconstruction of a democratic order.

Judged from this angle, the prospects for constitutional reform in Taiwan are not rosy. Developments after the National Affairs Conference have shown that the two parties are increasingly antagonistic to each other's stands and are inclined to institutionalize their positions. The Kuomintang dominated the formulation of the *Additional Articles of the Constitution* and asserted that the articles were designed for the transitional period before the country is reunited. After that, the Democratic Progressive Party (DPP) announced their draft *Constitution of the Republic of Taiwan* and formally included the term "Taiwan independence" in its charter. The two parties seem unwilling to leave a room for future maneuvering. Under such circumstances, whether the year-end election of the National Assembly that will amend the constitution can break this stalemate forms the core of our concerns. What role will the year-end elections play in Taiwan's democratization? Will it be favorable or unfavorable to the consultation model of democratic transition?

To answer these questions, we must look back at the model of interaction followed by the ruling and opposition parties during various turning points in constitutional reform. We should also examine the negotiating experience of the two parties and assess the role of elections at each crucial point in Taiwan's democratization. The negotiating experience of the two parties in dealing with the issue of structural reform is very limited. They are still feeling their way and are far from their goals.

Interaction between the two parties on the issue of adjusting the constitutional system has followed a model in which the Kuomintang dominates the adjustment and design of the legal system, including the substance and the timetable. Before any major changes in the legal system, the two parties either held no consultations or just went through the motions. Consultations thus far have yet to yield any results. Often legal restructuring has provided the opposition party with more room for maneuvering and more opportunity for political mobilization or reallocation of political resources. Yet, each consultation has provided the opposition with a new issue and planted seeds for future disputes.

The Kuomintang has dominated the most crucial legal changes in the transformation of the political system. These changes have included lifting the *Emergency Decree*, setting a timetable for parliamentary elections, and promising to abrogate the *Temporary Provisions Effective During the Period of Mobilization for Suppression of the Communist Rebellion* and the period of communist rebellion itself. The lifting of the *Emergency Decree* opened the door to further political liberalization. These last two moves have put Taiwan's political transition on the track to democratization; but at each stage, the Kuomintang has set the limits for the scope and speed of political transition. These limits are reflected in the *Law of Assembly and Parades*, the *Civic Organizations Law*, and the *National Security Law* enacted just before the abrogation of the *Emergency Decree*. On the eve of terminating the Period of Mobilization for the Suppression of the Communist Rebellion, the Kuomintang, by drawing up the *Additional Articles of the Constitution*, decided the procedure and timetable for parliamentary reelections, established the president's emergency powers, extended the period for adjusting laws held over from the Period of Mobilization for Suppression of the Communist Rebellion, and set up a policy framework for the period leading to national unification. These moves have their preestablished limits, which could trigger severe conflicts between the two parties. Such conflicts would goad the two parties to move toward consultations to keep the conflict under control. Nevertheless, there were few substantive consultations, and DPP contentions have seldom swayed the Kuomintang's decisions. Fruitless conflicts seem only to harden the opposition's determination to put up bigger challenges.

The Kuomintang's political position relies on three pillars of support. These are: its dominant power in the elective bodies on the central level, its massive influence in the media and society, and its firm control of the national administration. By comparison, elections are not the Kuomintang's major political recourse. But pressure from the DPP in elections has become an invisible, indirect pressure on the Kuomintang in matters of legal adjustment. If the scope and pace of democratic reform fall too far behind the public's expectations, this disparity will become a political millstone on the KMT's neck in elections. The Kuomintang has never before capitalized on elections to strengthen its ability for dominating constitutional reform.

In contrast, the DPP has been able to hasten the disintegration of the old authoritarian system. The DPP and major social activists have mainly objected to the various legal designs of the old authoritarian system that have unjustly restricted political freedom and limited the scope and progress of democratization. To challenge such restrictions and limitations, the DPP counts on parliamentary struggle, mass movements, and elections. Of the three, elections receive precedence. The DPP often uses electoral pressure to choose its time to challenge the limits of KMT positions, and counts on voter support to consolidate its breakthroughs. This was reflected in the DPP's timing for the insertion of the "Taiwan independence" phrase in its charter. Under this model of interaction, the DPP uses elections to counter any possible reactions from the KMT. For the DPP, election outcomes can strengthen its opposition vis-a-vis the KMT and increase its political capital for challenging other KMT limitations; but they have done little good in interparty consultations. Strictly speaking, the real dialogue between the two parties on the issue of constitutional reform began with the holding of the National Affairs Conference, which was intended to facilitate broad discussion with the opposition on political and social integration. The holding of the conference meant recognition of the DPP's indispensable role in effective constitutional reform. On the eve of the conference, the two parties expected to reach a certain degree of consensus. The KMT showed its sincerity by committing itself to the abolition of the *Temporary Provisions Effective During the Period of Mobilization for Suppression of the Communist Rebellion*, by terminating the period of communist rebellion, by giving presidential audience to the DPP chairman, and by announcing a series of political amnesties. In return, the DPP earnestly joined in the preparations for the conference. Although the DPP declared its "Grand Charter of Democracy," it pointedly avoided sensitive questions involving national structure, such as the extent of sovereignty, citizenship, and national designation. In preparing the agenda for the conference, the KMT also intentionally downplayed the issue of national unification. In other words, both parties tried to stereotype their positions. Apparently, they tacitly agreed to leave some room for maneuvering by temporarily setting aside the controversy over the issues of unification and independence.

The National Affairs Conference was the beginning of consultations between the two parties. They expected to build a consensus, but failed to arrive at any concrete agreements. The only conclusion reached at the conference, if any, concerned parliamentary re-election, and this was turned into empty words by an interpretation of the Council of Grand Justices. The National Affairs Conference led to the dialogue between the two parties, but failed to pave the way for a process of interpartisan consultations because of dissension in both parties. For the Kuomintang's part, there was no consensus on such basic issues as the advisability of holding such a conference, its status, and a formula for constitutional reform. In terms of *Realpolitik*, consensus within the Kuomintang would have been a necessary prerequisite for entering into interpartisan consultations; otherwise, the conference could not possibly come to anything. Soon after the conference, the Kuomintang leadership came to realize that the conditions for carrying out constitutional reform outside the present system simply did not exist and, therefore, it scrapped the idea of organizing an independent constitutional reform group. As the bubble of expectations burst, the two parties parted company. The Kuomintang organized a small internal group for constitutional amendment, quickly catalyzed the establishment of the National Unification Council, formulated the *Guidelines for National Unification*, and decided to convene a provisional National

Assembly to write the *Additional Articles of the Constitution*. The DPP interpreted these measures as an intention on the part of the KMT to railroad constitutional reform through singlehandedly, and as the beginning of institutionalization of its position on national unification. Since then, the DPP has all but abandoned any hopes for interpartisan consultation, and has turned to all-out boycotts and countermeasures.

Just before the *Additional Articles of the Constitution* were passed by the provisional National Assembly, the DPP mobilized the masses for a large-scale protest, which prompted interpartisan consultations to solve the crisis. The crisis was defused when the KMT accepted a proposal for formulating sunset articles to relegate the question of legalizing the National Personnel Administration and the National Security Bureau to the constitution-amending National Assembly for decision. The minor concessions of the KMT, however, failed to reduce surging DPP opposition to the KMT's manipulation of constitutional amendment. To counter the year-end National Assembly election, the DPP called a "people's constituent conference" to write the "Constitution of the Republic of Taiwan" to highlight its diametrically opposed positions on such issues as the scope of sovereignty, citizenship, and national designation. Simultaneously, the DPP amended its charter to include the words "Taiwan independence" to institutionalize its conflict with the KMT over the issue of national unification and Taiwan independence. By that time, the consultation model had been pursued during several previous crises before there was a realization that it could not be continued. The model's inapplicability became clear when Article 100 of the *Criminal Code* was being revised. Agreements reached under the pressure of crises could not be approved by either party. Backlash within the parties doomed the brinkmanship.

At a time when the DPP has pushed the issue of "Taiwan independence" to the showdown stage and two-party consultations are close to rupture, can the year-end National Assembly election fulfill its function of political integration? Or will the outcome of the election be used by both parties, as in the past, to consolidate positions that will further erode the possibility of reconciliation? This question is hard to answer. Nevertheless, we can sort out the favorable and unfavorable factors of political consultations before making a comprehensive assessment.

For the first time, the KMT strengthened its position by guiding the constitutional reform through popular elections. Unlike in the past when the KMT depended on old members of the National Assembly who lacked any mandate at all to dominate constitutional reform, the KMT can now count on an overwhelming number of seats elected by the 21 million people of Taiwan. The election also marked the first time that the Kuomintang, freed from much of its traditional political burden, used constitutional reform to appeal to voters and challenge the DPP's advocacy of Taiwan independence. If the KMT can maintain the upper hand, the DPP would lose its public support should it continue to reply on confrontation in parliament. On the other hand, the current provisions for constitutional amendment favor the establishment of two-party or multiparty consultations. Since the KMT cannot obtain the support of three-quarters of the parliament, it must enter into consultations with other parties; otherwise, it has no way to pass its proposals.

There are also two unfavorable factors. First, there is little hope for the two parties to reach a consensus on presidential elections, a central issue for the DPP, and the one that was once most likely to lead to a consensus. Within the Kuomintang there is general agreement on the proposal for electing the president by "commissioned delegates." This agreement coincides with the KMT's interests because under such a design, the KMT can fully capitalize on its grassroots electoral mechanism by mobilizing the support of local factions. Therefore the KMT is unlikely to budge on this point. Second, the KMT seems fully prepared for a breakdown in consultations. When the provisional National Assembly was in session, it amended all the articles of the constitution that might not work under present conditions. In other words, even if the KMT cannot garner support from three-quarters of the constitutional National Assembly to be convened in 1994, and if the two-party consultations should rupture before bearing any fruit, there would be no constitutional crisis under the current constitutional system. With this in mind, the KMT tends to hang tough and is unwilling to make concessions.

## Conclusion: Prospects for Constitutional Consultations and Consolidation of Democracy

If constitutional reform is limited to legal adjustment on the constitutional level, it is not very likely that all problems can be resolved once and for all through the convocation of a constitution-amending National Assembly after the year-end elections. On the surface, this involves irreconcilable difference between the two parties over the issue of national identification. Under the surface, there is the conflict of power allocation. It would be unimaginable for the Kuomintang to accept loss of ruling power, however temporarily, and let the nation be governed alternately with the Democratic Progressive Party. It is also unimaginable for the DPP to accept the loss of all possibility of winning ruling party status because of KMT-dominated structural reforms. Therefore, the DPP has shifted its goals to reforms outside the system. Under such circumstances, it would be a luxury to expect that the two parties could reach a consensus soon on the issue of constitutional reform.

The Democratic Progressive Party believes that social mobilization for Taiwan independence has not been exploited to its full potential, and that reforms outside the present structure have not passed the test of popular support. The DPP is convinced that the goals of its current struggle should be an opportunity for increased competition and mobilization, and that a comprehensive agreement with the Kuomintang is impossible and unnecessary. The DPP has focused its efforts on changing the way the president is elected. It has learned from recent elections for county chiefs and city mayors that high-level one-to-one elections can weaken the Kuomintang's capability for grassroots mobilization and magnify the importance of publicity. It also believes that as the power and position of the president have been strengthened, the nomination of a presidential candidate could sharpen the struggle within the Kuomintang and even lead to its division. This is certainly wishful thinking on the part of the DPP. At the same time, the KMT cannot but immerse itself in the pursuit of its short-term interests. It will put its interests in continuing to rule above its interests in democratic consultations.

Judging from this assessment, democratization in Taiwan is still far from being consolidated. An environment for full-range consultations will not emerge until several more nationwide elections have been held, various political views are tested by vote, and the heat of excessive mobilization in society can cool down. This is true particularly because political development on the island cannot extricate itself from outside influences in view of Taiwan's particular international status. In fact, the feasibility of both the KMT policy of national unification and the DPP advocacy of Taiwan independence depend on the evolution of the international order, the formation of the Chinese economic sphere, and the different perceptions and expectations of internal changes on the Chinese mainland. Before the dust of these uncontrollable and unpredictable outside factors settles, the two parties will not abandon their policies or platforms. The consolidation of a democratic order lies in the willingness of all political forces to subject their interests to the criteria of democratic competition and to accept the uncertainty of the democratic process. A favorable environment for establishing a foundation of sincerity has not appeared.

The showdown on the unification-independence issue is still far off. The two parties have wasted too many resources on their disputes over the high-level agenda, for which the public has had to pay huge costs. At the moment, both parties have ignored the detailed design of a democratic system and the question of how to ensure a fair reallocation of economic resources in society through a democratic process, and how to nurture the development of a pluralistic culture. They should not let parliamentary politics be swept away by money politics before the dispute on national unification and Taiwan independence is settled. The public has paid the price for democratization before it could enjoy its power and rights through full participation in the democratic process.

(Postscript: This essay was delivered at the Symposium on Current Questions of Constitutional Reform, sponsored by the Democracy Foundation, in November 1991. Although written one-and-a-half years ago, the essay is still valid, except for one major policy change made by the Kuomintang leadership in March 1992: it seems that direct presidential elections are now certain.)

NOTES
1. "Electoralism" means to reduce the establishment of democracy to nothing more than nationwide elections without concern for whether or not the structure of the political society and civic society is fully liberalized or whether the elected government can really supervise and command the various

parts of the national strucutre. See Terry Lynn Karl, "Dilemmas of Democratization in Latin America," *Com-parative
Politics*, October 1991, pp.1-21.
2. See "Constitutional Reform" by Hu Fu and others, *Center of
National Policy Studies*, 1990, Taipei.
3. This writer has discussed in a previous article the issues that
should be treated first when the National Assembly convenes
next year to amend the ROC constitution and, therefore, no
repetition is necessary. See "The Jurisprudential Basis for and
Draft of Constitutional Amendment," by Hu Fu, Lu Ya-li and
Chu Yun-han, *Society of Constitutional Reform*, 1990.

# Political Reform Movements in the ROC: History and Prospects

Hsu Ching-fu

## Background

The Kuomintang, or Nationalist Party of China, has been in power for forty-some years since the ROC government retreated to Taiwan in 1949. During this period, sporadic political reforms have been implemented. However, reforms that led to real structural changes did not begin until the last years of the late President Chiang Ching-kuo's tenure in office.

Before the structural political reforms were instituted, three features characterized ROC politics:

First, the *Temporary Provisions Effective During the Period of National Mobilization for Suppression of the Communist Rebellion* and the *Emergency Decree* dictated the operation of the whole political system and restricted people's freedoms of speech, assembly, association, publication, and exchange of information.

Second, under the pretext of maintaining the former legal system, the government continued parliamentary operations and supported top-down governance by ruling party elite.

Third, the government allowed limited local self-government in order to meet popular demands for political participation.

Subjectively, this political arrangement did not live up to the spirit of democracy. Objectively, how-

*Hsu Chin-fu is chairman of the political science department at National Taiwan University.*

ever, the Nationalist Party was able to maintain it for quite a long period of time. During this Cold War period, the East and West blocs were diametrically opposed to each other, and the U.S. and mainland China were unable to normalize relations.

Nonetheless, the situation changed along with developments at home and abroad. The aforementioned political arrangement not only required the support of the police and military systems; it also required the backing of the people. However, due to antagonism between the two sides of the Taiwan Straits, the people gradually lost their confidence and patience in the ruling party's political ideals, and in slogans such as "Oppose communism and recover the mainland," "Tyranny will eventually perish," and "Respect the legal system."

The ROC faced serious challenges internationally in the 1970s when it was forced to withdraw from the United Nations, and diplomatic relations with Japan and the U.S. were severed. Diplomatically, these were hard times for the ROC.

In view of the situation at home and abroad, people in the ROC began to question the legitimacy of the political structure. At this crucial historic moment, the Nationalist Party had two options. The first was to suppress the people's dissatisfaction and doubt with strong military and police powers. The second was to revamp the political structure.

The first option could have achieved temporary results, but would eventually be opposed and resisted internationally and domestically. In addition, pent-up opposition emotions, vented either through street demonstrations or underground armed revolutions, were serious threats to Taiwan, which then as now relied heavily on a robust international economy and stable domestic politics. The final result would be even more disadvantageous to the Nationalist Party's continued rule.

By choosing the second option, the Nationalist Party would lose the political resources it had long possessed as the only party in the country. This would be resisted by the conservative faction and would intensify intraparty struggles and conflicts. It would be more favorable to the Nationalist Party over the long run, however, if their political reforms could meet the expectations of the people and restore the legitimacy of the political structure.

Weighing the long- and short-term gains and drawbacks of the two options, the Nationalist Party, led by the late President Chiang Ching-kuo, chose the second and launched political reform. This was a wise and forward-looking decision. It not only temporarily resolved the domestic political crisis, but also won unanimous affirmation in the international community.

## Political Reforms during President Chiang Ching-kuo's Later Years

Political reform in the ROC can be divided into two stages. The first stage began during President Chiang Ching-kuo's later years, and the second, during President Lee Teng-hui's tenure in office.

As president, Chiang launched such political reforms as electing additional parliamentary representatives, consolidating parliamentary function in accordance with public opinion, promoting "nativization", and recruiting eminent Taiwanese to the cabinet, the central committee of the ruling party, and to major posts such as governor of Taiwan. Strictly speaking, these moves could not be called structural reforms.

The real structural reforms began during the last two years of President Chiang's presidency.

The major reforms launching during Chiang's later years as president included lifting the *Emergency Decree* as well as the ban on establishing new newspapers and political parties, protecting the people's freedom of assembly and association, and allowing residents of Taiwan to visit relatives in mainland China.

Although an *Emergency Decree* was nominally in force, the ROC government did not implement strict military control, and most of the population was governed under a regular legal system. This was the origin of the statement, "Only three percent of the Taiwan area was ruled under the *Emergency Decree*." Although this arrangement imposed very few practical restrictions on the population, it drew criticism for creating a double legal standard. Thus, lifting the *Emergency Decree* was the government's first step towards a normal constitutional government.

Newspapers are an important medium in a democratic society. During the period of the *Emergency Decree*, the establishment of newspaper offices and the content and number of pages of newspapers were monitored and restricted by administrative organs. This certainly is not a normal state of affairs for a democratic society. Lifting the ban on new newspapers resulted in the establishment of new newspaper offices and newspapers. From that time on, administrative monitoring and control were replaced with judicial procedure. The people's freedom to acquire information, their 'right to know', were thus protected.

"Democracy" could be defined as "multiparty politics." A democratic government should protect the people's freedom to establish and participate in political parties. Parties should be able to win the right to rule through competition with other parties, then to work hard to attain their political ideals. However, according to the old *Law on Civic Organizations* enforced during the days of the *Emergency Decree*, the establishment of political parties was restricted, and only one civic organization of its kind could be set up in one area. These restrictions on the establishment of political parties and civic organizations certainly did not accord with the concept of democracy.

To promote greater democracy, the government allowed the establishment of the Democratic Progressive Party before it revised the *Law on Civic Organizations*. The *Law on Civic Organizations* was subsequently amended to protect the people's freedom of founding political and civic organizations. Thus, the general public was granted more freedom. The only requirement was that newly established political parties had to be reported to the government in advance.

Under the *Emergency Decree*, the people's rights of assembly and presenting petitions were protected by the ROC Constitution; however, people were not protected by the law when they attempted to exercise such rights, and were to the contrary severely restricted. In order to better protect people's basic rights, the *Law on Assembly and Parades* was passed in 1988 to allow indoor gatherings and registered outdoor gatherings. The law also has a penalty clause for those who impede others from gathering and conducting parade activities. Since the passing of this law, the people's right of assembly and parade has been protected by law, indirectly promoting the development of social movements, and allowing minority groups to voice their opinions freely.

Opening up visits to mainland China was another structural reform. During the period of the

Cold War and National Mobilization for Suppression of the Communist Rebellion, anyone who visited the Chinese mainland would be accused of colluding with the enemy. This was another form of restricting people's freedom of movement. The division of the two sides of the Taiwan Straits, however, had long ago stabilized, and if the government had continued to prohibit contacts between people on the two sides, it would have lost their trust. Based on humanitarian considerations, the government decided to allow Taiwan residents to visit their relatives on mainland China. Tourism to the Chinese mainland has also thrived, since the government has not strictly limited travel to family visits only. Thus began extensive exchanges between the two sides of the Taiwan Straits.

These exchanges have had a major political impact. That is, the ideology established by the ROC government during the Cold War period has been totally dismantled. The statements that "the Chinese communists are our enemies" and "The senior parliamentarians represent the legal system" were shaken. This change was very significant for the political reform of the next stage.

## President Lee Teng-hui's Political Reforms

President Lee Teng-hui introduced a second stage of political reform after succeeding Chiang as president of the Republic of China. This reform covered the following seven areas.

(1) A wider scope of constitutional freedoms were granted: During the later years of Chiang Ching-kuo's presidency, some of the people's basic rights and freedoms were well protected. President Lee greatly reduced the number of people blacklisted and thus not allowed to enter and exit the country freely, and protected political dissidents' constitutional freedom of movement. In order to better protect the

people's freedom of speech and prevent individuals from being baselessly accused of sedition, the government amended Article 100 of the *Criminal Code* and deleted the clause on verbal sedition.

(2) Parliamentary re-elections: According to Article 6, Paragraph 2 of the *Temporary Provisions Effective During the Period of National Mobilization for Suppression of the Communist Rebellion*, should areas in the Chinese mainland be recovered, parliamentary representatives of said areas to the central government shall be elected area by area. Thus pending reunification, parliamentary representatives of the Chinese mainland area cannot be re-elected. Interpretation No. 31 rendered by the Council of Grand Justices stipulated that before members to the second parliamentary organizations can be elected, members to the first National Assembly, Legislative Yuan and Control Yuan shall continue to exercise their functions and powers. This was the origin of the ROC's "senior parliamentarians."

When a parliamentary vacancy opened up due to natural attrition, the government appointed a runner-up in the 1947 election or someone else from the same province as the previous incumbent to fill his place. However, the people of Taiwan did not recognize the validity of these "new" delegates. If the government had at this time abruptly dissolved the parliamentary organizations, a constitutional crisis would have arisen. Therefore, the government passed a set of voluntary retirement measures and encouraged senior representatives to step down. In line with current trends, the Council of Grand Justices also made Interpretation No. 261, which set December 31, 1991 as the expiration date for the term of office of delegates to the first parliamentary organs. Through this administrative and judicial maneuvering, the issue of the "ten thousand-year-old parliament" was finally resolved in a democratic spirit.

(3) Implementation of democratic and constitutional government: The *Temporary Provisions Effective During the Period of National Mobilization for Suppression of the Communist Rebellion* altered the structure of the central government as stipulated in the ROC Constitution. Since the issue of China's reunification could not be resolved within a short time, the government could not have obtained support from the public if it had continued to invoke the Temporary Provisions rather than return to constitutional rule. Therefore, President Lee Teng-hui announced the termination of the Period of National Mobilization for Suppression of the Communist Rebellion, abolished the Temporary Provisions, and reactivated the ROC Constitution.

More importantly, the termination of the Period of National Mobilization for Suppression of the Communist Rebellion occasioned a fundamental change in the relationship between the two sides of the Taiwan Straits. The Chinese communists were no longer an object of suppression. The ROC government no longer labeled them as "enemies" or a "rebellious group", but as a political entity. This change led to a series of major modifications in the ROC's domestic and foreign affairs. Simply stated, these events signaled the official end of the Chinese Cold War in domestic political ideology.

(4) Launching of constitutional reform: With the termination of the Period of National Mobilization for Suppression of the Communist Rebellion, the ROC has returned to normal constitutional operation. Nonetheless, practical application of a constitution written on the Chinese mainland decades ago to the Taiwan area was another problem. Opinion at this point was polarized: one side maintained that the government should

write a new constitution and proclaim a new republic. The other side held that the constitution should be revised for application in Taiwan. After considering the legal and political realities involved, the ruling party decided to revise the Constitution. This was the origin of the two-stage constitutional reform.

Three tasks would need to be accomplished in the first stage of the reform. First, members of the first National Assembly had to establish a legal basis for electing delegates to the second National Assembly. Second, the organization of the central government had to be adjusted: the Constitution had to be revised to create a legal basis for the establishment of the National Security Council, the National Security Bureau, and the Central Personnel Administration. Third, in view of the division of the two sides of the Taiwan Straits, a *Statute Governing Relations Between the People of the Taiwan Area and the Mainland Area* needed to be drafted.

The second stage of constitutional reform had four additional outcomes. First, in response to the wishes of the people in the Taiwan area, the ROC president was to be elected by popular vote. Second, the functions and powers of the National Assembly were to be expanded in order to facilitate the advancement of constitutional reform. Third, the Control Yuan was to be reorganized as a quasi-judicial organization so as to prevent the intervention of money politics in the exercise of supervisory powers. Fourth, the Legislative Yuan would, based on the Constitution, draft the *Local Self-government Law* and the *Local Self-government Organic Law* in order to speed up the implementation of local self-government.

(5) Institutionalization of multiparty politics: The first stage of constitutional reform for the first time provided a number of seats to parliamentarians

representing the nationwide constituency and overseas Chinese under a proportional representative system based on political party membership. Furthermore, in order to make political parties financially viable, donations to political parties were made tax-exempt. Moreover, political parties were allowed to broadcast election campaign commercials on TV to propagate their political ideals.

(6) Healing the wounds of history: The February 28 Incident (referring to the 1947 riots of Taiwanese against mainlanders) and the entry and exit blacklist that restricted the movement of opposition elements have long been sources of political instability in Taiwan. It would be very difficult to develop harmonious politics if these destabilizing factors were not eliminated. To address the situation, President Lee Teng-hui personally received family members of victims of the February 28 Incident and instructed the government to conduct research on the history of this event.

(7) The fight against money politics: The government plays an important role in national economic development. The economic strength of a country in turn affects the formulation of government policies. Due to dishonesty in elections, the power of money has gradually invaded the political realm. As a result, some people receive special privileges, and officials collude with businessmen.

In order to check the deterioration caused by money politics, the government has recently passed the *Public Functionary Assets Disclosure Law* and asked public officials with a number ten ranking or above, as well as parliamentarians at all levels, to declare all their assets. At the same time, the government has resolved to eradicate bribery. All administrative departments are expected to rid themselves of all corrupt practices.

## Assessment and Prospects
## of Political Reform

Four features can be identified in the political reforms advanced by the late President Chiang Ching-kuo in his later years and by President Lee.

(1) They are gradual and orderly reforms. The late President Chiang Ching-kuo focused the political reforms of his later years on lifting the restrictions imposed on people's basic rights and freedoms by the *Emergency Decree* and the *Temporary Provisions Effective During the Period of National Mobilization for Suppression of the Communist Rebellion*. Therefore, the people's freedoms of assembly, association, information exchange, and speech were better protected.

President Lee's political reforms can be subdivided into an earlier and later stage. During the earlier stage, in addition to further safeguarding the people's basic rights provided for in the ROC Constitution, President Lee attached much importance to political reforms, including amending the Constitution, readjusting the powers of the central government, and setting up standards for multiparty politics. The emphasis of the later stage of political reform shifted to rectifying political practices and culture.

(2) They are moderate reforms. Although resisting political reform is considered a conservative and backward behavior, overly radical movements could potentially cause social instability. Theoretically speaking, the reformers are members of the old society, not omnipotent gods; therefore they are unable to ignore the burden of the history. The ROC's political reforms, however, have been moderate in approach. For example, the government provided large pensions to encourage senior parliamentarians to retire voluntarily, and amended the Constitution

instead of replacing it with a new one. These are evidence of moderation.

(3) They are "nativized" reforms. After two stages of political reform, Taiwan politics are about to become fully nativized; and the political structure built upon assumptions rooted in the old legal system no longer exists. All political parties must undergo the test of public opinion, and elections are what determine who the final victor will be. This is totally different in significance from the employment of Taiwanese in government before political reforms. Before political reforms, the decision to hire Taiwanese was made by a handful of people. Since implementation of the political reforms, the future of all political powers must be decided by the whole populace of Taiwan. In other words, the public has the final say.

(4) They are peaceful and stable reforms. During the two stages of political reform, political struggles and storms surfaced from time to time. All considered, however, the political reforms progressed in a peaceful and stable environment. During the process of political reform, military and police personnel, who were responsible for social control before the reforms, fully accepted the leadership of civil officials and did not launch an armed rebellion. Harmony was maintained, the economy continued to develop, and national income grew.

Although the ROC has achieved notable results in its political reform efforts in the past, it must still address the following issues:

(1) Fighting against money power: The two-pronged tactic of money politics is to obtain political power through vote buying in elections, and then to acquire economic benefits with political powers. The pivot point in the process is acceptance of graft by

government officials. Although the *Public Functionary Assets Disclosure Law* is now in place, monitoring of assets is only one way of fighting money politics. In the future, regulations concerning political donations and influence-peddling should be formulated in order to thoroughly eliminate the rampant practice of money politics.

(2) Opposing violence: At present, gangster involvement in politics is very common, especially at the local level. Underworld figures obtain profits by running "special" types of businesses or through other illegal means, and then profess to be public-spirited candidates running for office. In other words, when the underworld uses small favors to bribe and establish a common-interest relationship with the public, it does great harm to the whole society. Therefore, getting rid of underworld influence in politics and encouraging good people to come forward and work for the public good has become an important issue since the "nativization" of politics in Taiwan.

(3) Launching administrative reforms: Politics and administration are inseparable. All political reforms need to be carried out by administrative procedures. Administrative reforms include eliminating corruption to establish an honest government, enhancing administrative efficiency to increase the government's effectiveness, and promoting neutrality among officials as a basis for government operations and to win over the trust of the populace.

(4) Building the concept of an interdependent community: Although the ROC has chalked up some initial achievements in establishing a democratic system, the operation of a democratic government must be based on a consensus of all the people. Currently, the ROC must reach a consensus regarding national identity and the concept of an interdependent

community. Without agreement on these issues, political successes will not be able to make up for cultural losses. Therefore, the ROC should end emotional disputes regarding provincialism, unification and independence.

Generally speaking, reformed politics in the ROC will be more democratic and pluralistic. Minorities and public opinion will receive greater respect, thus transforming Taiwan into an interdependent community that functions as an organic whole. However, reform is a never-ending task. Although some initial results have been reaped from past reforms, the ROC must continue to devote itself to improving the local political environment and culture in order to consolidate its foundation for democracy.

# III.
# The Economy

Previous page: The Republic of China on Taiwan
is one of the most dynamic commercial centers in Asia.

# On Becoming an Economic Power

Koo Chen-fu

## Facing a Crossroads in Historical Development

"How to become an economic power" is an important historical as well as contemporary issue.

Koo Chen-fu is chairman of the Chinese National Association of Industry & Commerce.

Historically, achieving national wealth and power has long been a cherished hope of the Chinese. It was the goal our forebears Tseng Kuo-fan, Chang Chih-tung, K'ang Yu-wei, and others pursued over the last hundred years. It was the target resolutely sought by the revolutionary martyrs who overthrew the Ch'ing dynasty to establish the Republic of China. The Principle of the People's Welfare, the Plan for National Reconstruction, and the Fundamentals of National Reconstruction were the historical symbols of our Founding Father's drive for national wealth and strength. From the 1911 Revolution through the Northern Expedition, the May Fourth Movement, and the Sino-Japanese War, up through the ROC government's withdrawal to Taiwan to institute national modernization and development—all represent the Chinese people's trials, gropings, and struggles in their search for wealth and power. The history of this period is full of the aspirations, frustrations, and blood and tears of the Chinese people.

After more than forty years of development and cultivation, our country has today become what is known as a "newly industrialized country (NIC)." The

117

"Taiwan miracle" or "Taiwan experience" has become a model for developing countries in their search for wealth and power. We have gradually realized, however, that our country now faces a bottleneck that is holding back further development. As our economy upgrades toward higher industrialized status, we have encountered varying degrees of stagnancy in investment, science and technology, management, labor, and the social arena. We now face the threat of "stagflation." If we cannot break through the bottlenecks and dilemmas of these economic developments, economic sluggishness and regression will ensue.

From both historical and contemporary perspectives, what must the Republic of China become aware of and do in its drive to become an economic power?

The rise and fall of a country are subject to internal laws of historical development. This law encompasses its own inherent truths and additional external factors. The loss of Spanish oceanic supremacy, the decline of British imperialism, and the dimming of the Egyptian and Indian cultures are all examples of a natural rise-and-fall cycle. Argentina and the Philippines both underwent periods of economic development that were the envy of other developing countries, but yet both are now mired in economic stagnation. Apparently, the wealth and power of a country also follow the rule that "not to advance is to retreat."

Taiwan has won world recognition for its "Taiwan miracle." One by-product of this "miracle" was a turn toward self-centeredness and selfishness. Actually, we are now at a crossroads of historical development: one road leads to wealth and power, and the other to decline. If we are insensitive to warnings and unable to maintain the diligence and frugality of the past four decades to solve current problems, we are certain to go the same way as Argentina and the

Philippines, and lose in the competition among the Four Little Asian Dragons. In such a situation, how to become an economic power would become a moot issue.

So before proceeding with this discussion on how to become an economic power, I will first issue an appeal to those at all levels of government to carefully monitor the present economic crunch, the political turmoil, the social disorder and instability, the increasingly uneven distribution of wealth, and the sense of uncertainty that the middle class has about its future.

## Breaking out of the Cycle of Poverty; Becoming a Newly Industrialized Country

In the process of industrialization, the biggest difficulty for developing countries is to break out of the poverty cycle. The "poverty cycle" means simply poverty producing poverty and being poor for poverty's sake. That is, social productivity cannot exceed certain productivity levels. Consequently, people consume all they produce. Unable to accumulate capital and increase production, the economy sinks into an endless struggle with poverty. This also applies to the Chinese traditional agricultural society.

The reasons for the "poverty cycle" in the former feudal agricultural society mainly were (1) totalitarianism, (2) land confiscation and concentration in the hands of a few, (3) insufficient education and (4) destruction due to war and disorder.

Due to these factors, traditional agricultural society could not release social capital frozen in land for industrial and commercial production, raise productivity, protect people's legal rights, and develop the people's potential creativity. The investment environment, lacking fair competition, could not establish appropriate norms. This in turn resulted in an absence of investment incentives and business opportunities. The ravages of war and its ensuing chaos seriously damaged social productivity.

If the political, economic, and social development in the 40-some years after the retrocession of Taiwan Province have truly created a "miracle," it is because we broke the thousand-year-old poverty cycle tradition of agricultural China and became a newly industrialized country. We went through the stages of launching land reform, implementing local self-government, encouraging private investment, fostering private enterprises, initiating compulsory education, developing an export-oriented free economy, and promoting constitutional reform. It would be difficult to convey the full extent of tangible and intangible progress accumulated over four decades of peace and stability. What I want to emphasize here is that we must stick to the principles developed during our breaking out of the "poverty cycle" to a newly industrialized country, and resolutely march forward in order to avoid the so-called "boom-bust cycle." That is to say, we must maintain the existing developmental foundations and advance. We must move from the present stage of industrial development to a higher level.

But what were the principles of development used to break out of the "poverty cycle" and become a newly industrialized country? I would group them into the following five categories:

The first was land reform, breaking the traditional production patterns of land use, (1) by encouraging increased agricultural production and raising farmer morale, and (2) by releasing capital invested in land for reinvestment in industrial production, thus supplying the capital needed for industrial operations.

The second was to implement democracy, to stimulate the people to participate in the rebuilding of society, and thus to establish fair standards for the people's rights and duties, and a legal foundation for fair competition.

The third was to institute a free economic system, with the government adding developmental guidance in policies to improve the investment environment and to encourage private investment.

The fourth was to implement compulsory education, to raise the quality of our human resources and to enhance the concept of developing pluralistic values.

The fifth was to promote the opening of social pluralism, to incubate the rise of multiple social forces, to effectively carry out the utilization of social resources.

The five factors grouped together can be called the "Taiwan Experience." Although the listing of the principles involved do not exactly replicate what actually happened, grasping these principles can certainly help us to understand what a country should know and do to become an economic power.

In the process of breaking out of the "poverty cycle," the Republic of China accumulated experience in economic growth, political maturity, and social liberalization, while building up a framework for national industrialization. But to truly become an economic power, we must make further structural breakthroughs. Otherwise, running in the old ruts and sticking to the present developmental routines, management scales and economic modes, the Republic of China will, at best, remain in the ranks of the newly industrialized countries. The most important thing to keep in mind is that the "Taiwan Miracle" does not guarantee that we will automatically and naturally develop into an economic power. If we delude ourselves with past achievements and pay no attention to our current problems—the political disorder, the erosion of social values and the sense of uncertainty our fellow countrymen have for the future, even the accomplishments we have made thus far will disappear.

Therefore, at this particular time, becoming an economic power can mean to carry on passively as in the past to open a way for the future, or it can mean to actively try to catch up. With this understanding, we can use the "Taiwan Experience," gained through liberalization and internationalization, to construct a "Taiwan Model" for becoming an economic power.

## What Is an Economic Power?

I have spent some time elaborating on the historical and contemporary background, foundation, and conditions of our becoming an economic power. My purpose in doing so is to illuminate the road we have followed in the past and the direction that we must take in the future. We are now poised to set off on the road to become an economic power under the above conditions. But before we advance, we must define just what an "economic power" is.

Generally speaking, a country is deemed to be a power or superpower in terms of its military or economic strength. Very seldom is culture taken into consideration. The strength of the present-day superpowers of the world—the United States, Germany, the Soviet Union and Japan—is based on their economic and military power rather than their population, geography or culture. In fact, the 19th century "Gunboat Policy," which symbolized the might of a country, was closely related to the rise of mercantilism. The superpowers' overseas colonialism and later imperialism were mixtures of military and economic strength.

Professor Paul Kennedy of Yale University in the United States says in his book, *The Rise and Fall of the Great Powers*, that a characteristic of the new international system established gradually after the downfall of Napoleon was the appearance in an already very stable global economy of a transoceanic, transcontinental trading and financial network centered in Britain. Professor Kennedy said that the manufacturing power, which was stimulated by the growth of the international economy and the Industrial Revolution, was displayed in the modernization of military and naval technology during this period.

From this, we can see that the essential nature of a "World Power" lies both in its military and economic structure. But Kennedy also points out that economic growth is the basis of a world power. And the military power of a strong nation is, in effect, the manifestation of that economic strength. Paul Kennedy pinpoints very concisely in his book the reason why Japan became a strong Asian power: it was due to simultaneous economic growth and military development.

If a "World Power" is defined in terms of its economy, then the nature of a strong economic power should be evaluated on the basis of its productivity. The amount of productive power is seen in a nation's GNP and per capita income. The following are the GNP and per capital incomes of the four world powers—the United States, Japan, (West) Germany and the United Kingdom—in 1988:

| | Per Capita GNP | Per Capita Income (in US dollars) |
|---|---|---|
| United States | 28,520 | 21,100 |
| Japan | 21,020 | 23,730 |
| West Germany | 19,480 | 19,410 |
| United Kingdom | 14,560 | 14,500 |

These simple statistics tell us that a fundamental requisite for an economic power is a per capita GNP and per capita national income between US$14,000 and US$28,000. (Per capita GNP and per capita national income normally vary only slightly). The ROC's per capita GNP in 1991 was US$7,512. (In 1990 it was US$6,050, so there was an increase of US$1,459 in just one year's time.) This figure, however, is still far behind those of other economically advanced nations. According to an optimistic estimate, the ROC's per capita GNP will reach US$20,000 in the year 2000. Considering our present economic foundation and social conditions, however, this does not mean that we will automatically become an economic power on a par with the United States, Britain, Japan and Germany.

We must squarely face two problems to avoid remaining only a "peripheral country among the economically advanced nations": (1) "What should we do to become an economic power within a set period of time?" and (2) "What type of economy should we establish to catch up with the economically advanced nations?" In other words, we must build ourselves into Asia's second economic power after Japan. We should therefore not rest on the laurels of our current status as leader of the Asia's "newly developed countries."

How does a nation come to be an economic power? Why is it that the United States, Britain, Japan and Germany are economic powers when the Soviet Union, whose military strength can counter that of the United States and whose per capita GNP stands at US$7,510, is not regarded as an economic power? It is because the economy is not an isolated factor. Although economic development encompasses a wide array of complex conditions including political, cultural, social, and educational ones, plus availability of sufficient resources, a more important factor involves the renouncement of communism. Unless the

124

Soviet Union does that, it can never become a world economic power.

Generally speaking, I believe an economic power must possess the following five prerequisites: (1) the principle of free competition in a market economy; (2) a social environment that helps create business profits and safeguards private property; (3) an investment environment that spurs production and brings out the potential of its citizenry; (4) a technological and educational basis to raise social productivity; and (5) a national consensus and identification with the goals of national development.

Economist Arnold C. Harberger once said that economic development manifests itself in many different ways because each country has unique and diverse conditions. The factors that help usher in economic development, however, do not differ from country to country; they are the prerequisites of every nation if it is to develop economically. Therefore, I believe the factors that helped the United States, Britain, Japan and Germany to develop into economically strong nations are equally applicable and indispensable to the development of our country. In fact, our process of development in becoming one of Asia's newly developed nations is similar in many ways to the early and mid-term development of these economic powers. For instance, political democracy and a free economy are yardsticks of development worldwide.

## Moves to Become an Economic Power

I have elaborated in the foregoing paragraphs on our developmental process in moving toward becoming an economic power. I have also examined the essential nature of an "economic power." Now, I would like to discuss the steps we must take to reach this objective.

I must clarify at this point that our emphasis is on examining long-term economic development. Short-term development will be left to market functions and to effective resource distribution. Therefore, I want to discuss here a developmental strategy for becoming an economic power, as well as the type of economic development necessary to become such a power. I will not go into concrete measures and details.

## Establishing the "Technological Culture" of an Economic Power

I must emphasize that to become an economic power, we must first break out of the confines of "the developmental mode of underdeveloped nations." This means that if we, being an export-oriented economy, are to move a rung higher in economic development, we must break away from the present state of "relying on an economic system dominated by advanced nations." If we cannot move away from our long-term dependence on imports from Japan and exports to the U.S., we cannot improve our manufacturing structure for scientific and technological advancement. We will always be a step behind the advanced nations. All that will be left for us are the crumbs that fall from the table of the advanced nations.

Economist R.O. Norton once warned the United States that it must maintain a position of leadership in the sciences, or it would be overtaken by developing nations in the post-1950s period. The only way for the U.S. to promote production growth was to be at the forefront of scientific knowledge, to keep pushing ahead, and not merely adopt or introduce technology from other countries. This warning is also applicable to the ROC. Simply put, we must catch up to the scientific and technological level of the U.S. and Japan if we are to become an economic power. We must not merely accept outdated technologies supplied by the U.S. and Japan. Furthermore, we cannot rely on patchwork technology cobbled together by multinationals.

I use "technology" in a broad sense that encompasses "upgraded productivity." It covers the collective systemic and organizational effects of upgraded quality of manpower, improved management and production facilities, efforts by scientific and technological personnel, venture enterprises, and educational reform. Therefore, as we move toward becoming an economic power, we must first establish this broad interpretation of a "technological culture" to avoid being defeated by the protectionism of advanced nations and the developing nations which are close on our heels.

More importantly, the former strategy of using imports to stimulate industrial development has encountered formidable restrictions and difficulties. Currently, manufacturing stands at about 40 percent of the ROC's GNP. This figure is about the same as certain Western European nations in the 1950s. This proves that if the manufacturing sector cannot speed up technological innovation, it can no longer be the major force in promoting economic growth. Nonetheless, reforms in the manufacturing sector or the development of new products cannot be separated from the premise of "technological progress." Manufacturing must also bring about technological progress through liberalization and internationalization.

## Establishing the "Political Culture" of an Economic Power

Economic development and political maturity are inseparable. The Industrial Revolution and political democracy developed side by side in Western Europe. Japan's industrialization was rooted in the Meiji Restoration. Many Third World countries and developing nations were plunged into vicious cycles after the Second World War: it was either periodic economic factors that hampered political progress or periodic political upheaval and authoritarianism that restricted economic development. The examples of

Argentina and the Philippines mentioned earlier are proofs. I have also pointed out that the "Taiwan Miracle" is a product of promoting democracy.

Political science Professor Robert A. Dahl has said that economic and political modernization complement economic growth and political stability. We must equip ourselves with the magnitude and standards of a political power if we are to become an economic power. A political power is one with a high degree of constitutional democracy. The constitutional reform stressed by both the ruling and opposition parties is in fact the force that propels us toward becoming an economic power. The model of partisan politics that has emerged since the lifting of the ban on new political parties must be regularized, so that the legislation of the 1940s through the 1970s aimed at supporting economic development is able, through the checks and balances and progress of partisan politics, to enhance the ability of 1980s legislation to stimulate economic development.

Although political democracy is not an ideal system, it is nonetheless universally acknowledged as the best political system. In economic terms, political democracy safeguards the profit and market principles of a free economy. It moreover safeguards the freedom and rights of its citizenry to invest in and set up businesses, while at the same time providing a stable investment environment and the basis for fair competition. These are fundamental prerequisites for becoming an economic power.

In April 1992, President Lee Teng-hui convened a National Affairs Conference which discussed constitutional reform extensively and arrived at a consensus on a number of important reforms. I believe when these various reform measures are implemented, they will help us realize and raise our level of constitutional democracy. This will make the ROC a highly democratic nation and will help lay the political foundation for becoming an economic power. I advocated convening a national economic conference following the National Affairs Conference to link constitutional reform with economic reform. In other words, we must gear the massive engineering for building an economic power to our political power. Only in this way can we join the ranks of developed nations. Economic development and political reform are interrelated. When economic development reaches a certain level, demand for political reform will follow. Moreover, political reform will provide an environment conducive to sustained economic growth. Thus establishing the political culture of an economic power is both a political and economic necessity.

## Establishing the "Social Culture"
## of an Economic Power

Politics and economics are social institutions. Political and economic development can create the content and conditions of society. Social science scholar W. Weber has said that political and economic development must be derived from a certain "social atmosphere." Economist W.T. Rostow refers to it as "social conditions." Simply put, it is the citizenry that shapes politics and the economy. It is no wonder that many scholars have in recent years advocated the formation of a "civil society" to replace our "individual society." This means establishing a healthy society that is hardworking, upwardly mobile, pluralistic, liberal and made up of a responsible citizenry. It is a fair, mutually caring welfare society that respects public interest as well as the interests of the whole.

Our economy is currently in the industrialization stage, and we have a democratic political system. But most of our society is still stuck in the backward, feudalistic stages, characterized by selfishness, materialism, cold-heartedness, aloofness and individualism. The general public shows disdain for the public interest, and our country is ridiculed by others as an "island of greed." This kind of society is definitely not the society of an economic power, not can it in its current state meet the demands of being an economic power. It must therefore be restructured. We must establish the social culture of an economic power. It must be a civil society, a fair welfare society—a society made up primarily of a healthy and hardworking middle class, a pluralistic yet integrated society. Our society should be one in which all social powers are affirmed, a fair society in which minority groups are respected and helped.

An economic power can neither be founded on a feudalistic agricultural society nor based on a utilitarian society in which commercial investment is disorganized and speculative. This is why I stress that we must establish the social culture of an economic power.

## Conclusion

The foregoing discussion of economic development combines the developmental experiences of Europe, the United States, Japan and Germany with our own to give a global perspective that points the way to becoming an economic power. I have not listed concrete financial and economic measures. Ex-Premier Hau Pei-tsun in his administrative report to the Legislative Yuan on the Six-Year National Development Plan has elaborated on such measures. In closing, I attempt to briefly describe the new look of an economic power.

I believe that the economically strong ROC of the future will be a high-tech manufacturing structure established on a system of constitutional democracy. It will have a high GNP, a high quality lifestyle, a rich educational culture and an effective social welfare system. It will actively participate in the world economy and international affairs, especially with regard to the regional economy (like Asia-Pacific economic organizations) and will make significant contributions to them.

Finally, I would like to stress that creating the political, economic and social conditions for an economic power calls for the participation and creativity of the citizenry. It demands a can-do government and the cooperation of the whole, upwardly mobile citizenry. A saying goes: "With hard work, everything is possible." The United States, Japan, and Germany have done it. So can the Republic of China. This is the kind of faith that we should all have.

In this 80th year of the Republic of China's founding, let us adhere to this belief and strive to become a true economic power!

# Productivity—A Strategy for the Century of the Pacific

Casper Shih

*Casper Shih is general manager of the China Productivity Center.*

Editor's Note: This article was originally a speech made by Dr. Casper Shih at the monthly Dr. Sun Yat-sen Memorial Meeting of the Presidential Office in July. Part of the content was published in Taipei newspapers. A number of readers concerned about the future of Taiwan's industry later asked for the full text of the speech, which analyzes from a global point of view the strategies used to upgrade Taiwan industry, and calls for government adoption of more forward-looking economic and trade policies toward the mainland.

At the close of the 19th century, U.S. Secretary of State John Hay once said the Mediterranean was the sea of the past, the Atlantic, the sea of the present, and the Pacific, the sea of the future. This statement appears to have become true today. Countries surrounding the Pacific Ocean have been growing amazingly fast. In the 60s, the gross national products of Pacific rim nations were only half that of the United States and one third that of Europe. But by the year 2000, their GNPs will equal those of all North America, and will surpass those of Western Europe. This is why observers believe there will be three key economic centers in the future—the Pacific rim area, Europe plus the Commonwealth of Independent States, and North America. Judging from their growth rates and market potentials, we can safely say that the 20th century will be the "Century of the Pacific."

It has been said that the "Century of the Pacific" would be a "Century of Japan." But others have noted that Japan will be able to dominate only the first 30 years, and that the last 70 years would belong to the Chinese. I totally agree with this. But let us first examine whether the strategies employed in Taiwan can help bring about this "Century of the Chinese."

Despite shortages of capital, technology, natural resources and other economic elements needed to expand our market, we created a trade value of US$118.5 billion in 1989 and became the world's 13th largest trading nation. This is because we adopted appropriate policies, employed suitable people, and put in over 40 years of plain hard work.

Taiwan is one of the prime movers that have turned the Pacific into a world economic and trade center. Whether we can go one step further and continue to play the role of a little economic giant in the Pacific area and become an economic heavyweight in the world depends on how forward-looking and practical the economic development strategies we adopt are.

In the past year, a democratic movement brought about the collapse of the totalitarian communist system in Eastern Europe. Reforms made by former Soviet Union leader Gorbachev played an important role in this. After Gorbachev took power in 1985, he boldly pushed through a series of economic reforms in the Soviet Union in an attempt to save their ailing economy. But he soon discovered that without political reforms, it would be impossible to carry out any economic reforms. The measures he adopted were aimed at cutting the political umbilical cord between the Soviet Union and the Eastern European nations. What he did, however, has greatly promoted world peace and led to reconciliation between the Soviet Union and the United States. The cold war was thus ended.

The North Atlantic Treaty Organization later turned a potential enemy—the Soviet Union—into a potential friend. The entire world began moving towards devoting itself to the development of peace and democracy. Investment in armaments has shifted instead to economic development, which has resulted in keener economic competition. Obviously, the economy will play a major role in world development.

## From OEM to ODM and OBM

Taiwan adopted an export-oriented strategy in its economic development in the early period, but over the past several years, such a strategy has been undermined by stiff international competition. Trade protectionist measures adopted by advanced nations have limited our exports, and pressure by these nations to open our markets has reduced government protection of domestic industries. Developing countries in the meantime have begun to pose strong competition to us. These countries on the one hand imitate the economic development policies of Taiwan, offering incentives to encourage their firms to increase exports; on the other hand, they use their relatively richer resources and cheaper labor to enter the world market, in hope of supplanting us in the competitive role we now play.

Strictly speaking, we became one of the large trading countries in the world because of the contributions made by thousands of small but highly flexible manufacturing firms in Taiwan. For a long time, OEM (original equipment manufacturing) had been the main production model of companies here, that is, the buyer provides the order, specifications, design and even technology, and the manufacturer charges for production costs to earn a small profit. However, in the past several years (1985-89), statistics have showed that average pay for workers in the manufacturing sector has increased 8.3 percent per year, while productivity has risen only 7.04 percent. Labor in Taiwan is no longer cheap. Thus, it is necessary for ROC industries to upgrade in order to produce more value-added products and increase productivity. We must therefore work to introduce ODM (original design manufacturing) and OBM (original brand manufacturing) in Taiwan.

As to how we can promote the added value of our products, I think it is necessary to invest major efforts in the research and development (R&D) of new products. Only when we can actually increase the added value of our products through R&D will we be able to increase the overall productivity of our industries. In fact, this is our only strategy for survival in the Century of the Pacific.

Taking Japan as an example: after the Second World War, which left Japan a war-torn land, the Japanese government and industries actively imported foreign technologies and worked tirelessly to study, digest, absorb and improve these technologies to make them their own. Step by step, through the production of daily necessity items, shipbuilding, steel, automobiles, CNC machine tools, electronics and VLSI (very large size integrated circuits), they established a "Japan is No. 1; Japanese technology is the best" image in industry in various areas of the world. They are now working to develop their aerospace and aviation industry.

It is clear that R&D in industrial technology was the key to Japanese national economic growth, and an R&D strategy aimed at developing new products is what we should emulate to promote the overall productivity of our industries. I personally think this can be done in the following ways.

- Strengthening R&D and management. Taiwan's overall technological level is fairly high, because the ROC has many engineers or technicians who have received a university or graduate school level education, are engaged in R&D, and are willing to absorb new knowledge. What we lack are those who can manage such people. We could use U.S.-educated talent as executives to guide our technicians and engineers to conduct R&D for certain special programs. In fact, the subjects to be chosen for R&D, the foreign technologies to be mastered, the methods of using our limited resources for developing products acceptable to others, and the evaluation of the results of the R&D—all require a set of management techniques. We should step up our efforts in this area.

People tend to think that R&D in high-tech industries requires a great deal of money and time, and therefore many consider R&D impossible for small and medium-size enterprises in Taiwan. But I think this is a serious misunderstanding that keeps our small and medium-size enterprises from engaging in R&D. In fact, what small and medium-size enterprises should do at the present stage is to conduct R&D, making use of well-developed technologies to explore the market and to create new products to meet demand. This applies not only to high-tech industries, but also to traditional and conventional industries, since through R&D they also can develop value-added products.

Several years ago, for example, in order to counter the pressures of a rapidly appreciating NT dollar, the China Productivity Center, while helping many small and medium-size enterprises, worked with the Institute of Technology and Industrial Research to assist a badminton production company to use the softwood waste materials of the badminton butt to develop a car engine pad. This enabled the company to turn waste from their badminton production, which was worth NT$40 million annually, to produce various kinds of high-class pads worth NT$80 million per year. This company was also assisted in selling their new product to Japan, where Toyota Motors expressed great interest in it.

■ Promotion of design management ability. Design must be in line with marketing trends, and good designers must be sensitive to marketing. Through their designs and packaging, the stern look of a high-tech product can be successfully marketed and a customer demand created. Unfortunately, we don't have many such designers here. This is due to an education system which emphasizes science and technology, but overlooks the importance of creativity and initiative.

In junior high schools here, there are certain to be a number of students who are talented in design and marketing but are ignored by the school authorities and placed in classes for students with poorer academic performance. As a long-term goal, we must restructure our current education system and stop trying to make all students conform to the same standards. In fact, cultivating talent is like cultivating a seed. Different seeds must be germinated and cultivated in different ways. For the time being, I suggest that the government recruit more foreign designers and allow them to stay here for a short time to engage in design work and in educating the younger generation. This could be one solution. Student designs could be given to local manufacturers for production.

Over the past three years, the China Productivity Center has widely introduced CAD/CAM technology to encourage manufacturers to create their own designs, and made samples in order to produce higher value-added sports, leisure, and men's shoes. Two years ago, manufacturers exported US$3.8 billion worth of shoes, with unit price of only US$5; but today shoes produced with CAD/CAM design can be sold for as much as US$16 or more per pair. The most expensive pair sells for US$380.

■ Overall guarantee of quality. Quality is a state of mind and way of life. We must establish an enterprise culture centered on quality in order to ensure consistency of quality. As it introduced modern management techniques, Taiwan, in its haste to advance from its old pattern of technological development to industrial engineering, neglected to first lay a solid foundation of good quality concepts. Therefore, quality has been the Achilles heel of our products, and has diminished our competitiveness in the international market. If we use our own brand names to enter the international market but fail to actively promote a quality culture and establish a sound quality system, all our efforts will be in vain.

Quality must be top-down. If an employer is committed to developing quality, all problems concerning quality can be easily solved.

■ Overall promotion of industrial automation. Automation is the only path for upgrading traditional industries. On the one hand, it reduces reliance on labor, and on the other, it ensures consistent quality. Over the past eight years, the production automation program implemented by the Executive Yuan and the Automation Technology Advisory Committee set up by the Ministry of Economic Affairs have helped reduce the impact on traditional industries of the rapid appreciation of the NT dollar in the past three years. Therefore, we must continue to introduce production and merchandise technologies from advanced countries in order to upgrade our industrial structure and produce better and higher value-added products n Taiwan.

The National Science Council, along with the Ministry of Economic Affairs and the Science and Technology Advisory Office, the Industrial Development Bureau, and the Board of Foreign Trade under the Ministry, have been working to promote automation and upgrading of the industrial structure in recent years. I hope this can congeal into a consensus in all production, government and academic sectors so that everybody can be aware of its importance and can spend more resources and time to help ROC industry complete its transitional development within a short time and move from developing nation status to become an advanced economy.

## Keeping Our Roots in Taiwan

Moving industries abroad is an issue of great concern in the process of economic transformation. When an industry loses its comparative edge, it will eventually have to face either moving to a developing country or failure. Many labor-intensive industries in Taiwan, such as textiles, footwear, and umbrellas have gradually moved production to Southeast Asian nations and mainland China.

Moving industries abroad can be very positive, since it can help eliminate industries with lower economic efficiency, and thus open up room for production of more competitive products. But this "industrial migration" does not necessarily mean that production of a certain product, including its marketing, development, and component and spare parts manufacturing will all be moved abroad. What should be moved is only the part which is less economical when produced here. If the migration leads to an uprooting of the industry, it will result in a "hollowing out of industry." This is a potential crisis which must not be overlooked.

What exactly are the "roots" of an industry? I think it is its R&D capability. When the government helps local firms establish their R&D ability through various policies and measures, it is necessary that these firms leave their "roots" in Taiwan.

Some enterprises think investing in mainland China is the only option in such a migration. But I think this is a rather dangerous tendency. Investing in mainland China must be only one part of an overall strategy of economic development of Taiwan, not the rash act of an individual enterprise. Investment in mainland China must take into consideration any future impact on Taiwan.

Today, the strongest weapon for survival is our economic strength, and this is the only weapon we can use in competing with mainland China. We must therefore be cautious in using our economic edge to strive for the largest space for survival we can manage. There are two goals in our economic strategy towards mainland China: first, striving for recognition from our mainland countrymen, and second, safeguarding our national security.

Some people think that these two goals are mutually exclusive. If the mainland economy becomes stronger, it will pose a great threat to the security of Taiwan. But I think otherwise, because communism cannot survive in a wealthy society, and the promotion of a higher standard of living in mainland China is the best protection for Taiwan's security. Conversely, a poor and backward mainland is the greatest threat to our safety.

## Current Mainland Economic and Trade Policy

We must develop a long-term economic development policy towards mainland China. We can help the mainland liberalize its economy from coastal areas to inland areas, stage by stage. This strategy should include:

■ Training and educating high-ranking mainland businessmen. Thought is the foundation of all actions. Only with a concept of free enterprise will people be able to accept the actual operations of free enterprise. High-ranking business executives of mainland China, which currently functions under a planned economy, often lack the concept of a market economy, and this is the major obstacle to the development of a free economy there. We could systematically invite large numbers of these people to Taiwan for two weeks to one month of training in market economy theory and practical business management to increase their knowledge and hence familiarize them with the operation of free enterprise in Taiwan.

■ Transfer of experience to small and medium-size enterprises in mainland China. Developing small and medium-size enterprises is the fastest way to get an economy on its feet. The creation and management of small and medium-size enterprises in Taiwan are the most valuable economic development experience of the island. We can encourage such Taiwan firms to set up plants in mainland China, and cooperate with mainland enterprises. We can also help businessmen to gradually develop small and medium-size enterprises and form non-governmental organizations. We can offer experience, training and management techniques to employees and businessmen, and possibly set up a career development fund to help them found their own businesses.

■ Orchestrating the policies of Taiwan enterprises investing in mainland China. In unity is strength. Individual Taiwanese firms investing in mainland China often suffer losses as a result either of being cheated or due to mismanagement. The government can assign semiofficial agencies to help these firms work together and make diversified investments in a systematic way. This should encourage Taiwan firms to develop themselves into respectable organizations in mainland China that are welcomed there. In this way, the enterprises will gain a certain degree of influence on the mainland, and will help spread the word of the "Taiwan experience" there.

From a long-term point of view, investment in mainland China provides a chance for a small Taiwan business to become large, and it can help compensate for two deficiencies in Taiwan's economic development—lack of resources and a large market. Mainland China could become Taiwan's largest production base, and its largest market, too. It is our mission and responsibility to promote a higher standard of living in mainland China. If we can work in this direction, the Chinese people will pin their hopes on Taiwan.

The China Productivity Center has been in existence for 35 years. In the early period when Taiwan's economy was just beginning to get off the ground, the Center played a role of helping small and medium-size enterprises strengthen their management structure and raise the level of their technology. We have taken part in the creation of the first "economic miracle" here, and assisted local firms in surviving the oil crisis and the appreciation of the NT dollar.

The World Bank recently cited the Center as a model for similar organizations in developing countries, and has invited us to Colombia and the Philippines to help found organizations there. Today, in witnessing another transformation of Taiwan's economy, we are confident that the Center will be able to be part of the creation of a second "economic miracle" here at home.

142

# The ROC's Role in the World Economy

Cheng Chu-yuan
*Issues & Studies*
November 1992

*The Republic of China (ROC) on Taiwan has achieved an impressive economic record over the past four decades, developing from a backward agricultural economy into a modern industrial society. Export-oriented policies have enabled Taiwan to become the world's fourteenth largest trading country with the world's largest reserves of foreign exchange. Over the past decade, Taiwan has also emerged as a major exporter of capital, with growing investments in mainland China and Southeast Asia.*

*One result of this phenomenal achievement is that Taiwan has become a model for other developing countries. Mainland China, in particular, has drawn from the Taiwan experience in devising its open-door policy on foreign investment and its foreign trade development measures, as well as its rural and urban reforms.*

*Taiwan's role in the world economy is likely to become more discernible in the future as the ROC develops into a foreign aid donor, a new regional financial center, and chief investor in mainland China.*

*Cheng Chu-yuan is a professor of economics at Ball State University, Indiana.*

The Republic of China (ROC) on Taiwan has achieved an economic record rivaled by few other developing nations in the post-World War II period. As Taiwan has been transformed from a backward agrarian economy to a modern industrial society, its per capita income has risen sixty-fold in four decades. In 1952, the ROC's per capita GNP was only one-thirtieth that of the United States, but by 1990 it had advanced to one-third.[1] The ROC now ranks as the world's fourteenth major trading country with the world's largest foreign exchange reserves,[2] and it plays an important role in the international economy. In the past decade, the ROC has changed its financial position from a capital importer to a major capital exporter, investing extensively in mainland China and Southeast Asia. At the same time, it has promulgated a series of regulations to promote the liberalization and internationalization of the economy with the goal of building Taipei into a regional financial center by the end of this century.[3] The success story of the ROC has attracted worldwide attention. Many components of the Taiwan model are now being followed by other less developed countries.

The purpose of this paper is to assess the role played by the ROC in the world economy. The study focuses on three major aspects: the place of the ROC in the world's commodity and capital markets; the effects of Taiwan's experience on mainland China and other developing countries, and the ROC's potential influence in the world economy in the years ahead.

## Phenomenal Economic Growth

The initial conditions of the ROC on Taiwan were no better than those of other underdeveloped countries. In terms of natural endowment, Taiwan's land area of 36,000 square kilometers (13,885 square miles) is 7 percent that of Thailand, 11 percent that of Malaysia, and less than 2 percent that of Indonesia. It is less than 0.004 percent of the area of mainland China. A mountainous island with very meager mineral resources, Taiwan's best natural endowment is its arable land, which accounts for only one-fourth of the total land area.[4]

In 1949, when the Nationalist government retreated from the mainland to Taiwan, the island's economy faced two serious problems: the sudden increase in population and heavy military expenditures. Per capita GNP in 1952 was only US$50 (US$150 in 1980s terms) and inflation was rampant. These difficulties, however, did not deter the ROC government. Between 1950 and 1960, a host of reform and developmental policies were implemented. Notable among these policies were the establishment of a mixed economic system under which state and private enterprises coexisted, and an "indicative" national plan which operated together with the market mechanism. Other major measures included a peaceful land reform in rural areas, an export expansion development strategy and an open-door policy to attract foreign capital and technology.

The pursuit of these policies has successfully transformed the island from an agriculture-based economy into a dynamic modern society. Taiwan's economic achievements are displayed in growth, stability, equity, standards of living, and change in the economic structure.

Taiwan's real GNP growth rate was 7.5 percent between 1952 and 1960, 9.7 percent between 1960 and 1970, 9.6 percent between 1970 and 1980, and 7.8 percent between 1980 and 1990. The long-term growth rate of 8.8 percent between 1952 and 1990 was one of the world's highest.[5]

Not only has the ROC achieved high rates of growth but it has also demonstrated a consistent and steady growth pattern. Throughout the entire forty years, Taiwan's per capita GNP rose every year with the exception of 1974 when the island suffered a brief recession caused by a worldwide energy crisis. But the short recession was soon followed by a rapid recovery in subsequent years.[6]

145

With a steady growth in per capita income, and the increasing abundance of consumer goods, living standards in Taiwan have been the highest ever attained in Chinese history. Economic prosperity brought considerable changes in people's consumption patterns. In 1964, 59.7 percent of a family's consumption expenditures in Taiwan went on food, beverages, and tobacco. The percentage dropped to 39.4 percent in 1981 and 33.7 percent in 1989. As people spent relatively less on food, they enjoyed better housing, education, and recreation. Consumption expenditures for housing rose from 17.2 percent in 1964 to 23.8 percent in 1989; and for education and recreation from 1.2 percent in 1964 to 12 percent in 1989.[7]

The most remarkable achievement in Taiwan's industrialization, however, has been its income distribution. Despite the very high rates of growth and capital formation, income distribution has become much more equal over the past four decades. Improvements in income distribution in Taiwan stem from two important factors: the successful land reform program, which substantially improved the lot of the rural population, and the rapid rise in demand for nonagricultural labor, which lifted the real wages of urban workers. In 1953, family income among the top 20 percent was estimated at twenty times that of the bottom 20 percent. By 1972, the gap was narrowed to 4.5 times and in 1980, it was further reduced to 4.2 times. In recent years, as stock and real estate speculations flourished, the trend has reversed somewhat. By 1990 the gap widened to 4.9, but is still one of the best among the developing nations.[8]

Dramatic changes have also been effected in economic structure. In 1952, when the ROC embarked on industrialization, agriculture accounted for 32.2 percent of the gross domestic product (GDP). The share dropped steadily to 20.6 percent in 1964, 15.5 percent in 1970, and 4.2 percent in 1990. Concomitantly, the share of industry (including mining, manufacturing, public utilities, and construction) rose from 19.7 percent in 1952 to 42.3 percent in 1990, surpassing the 35 percent attained by advanced industrial countries.[9]

Taiwan's outstanding economic performance greatly elevated the ROC's role in the world economy. In 1952, on the eve of Taiwan's First Four-Year Economic Development Plan, the island's total foreign trade was only US$326 million. By 1991, it had reached US$139 billion, ranking it the fourteenth largest trading country in the world.[10]

## A Rising World Trade Power

One component of Taiwan's developmental model is the pursuit of an export promotion scheme. Aware of the limited size of the domestic market, Taiwan has, since the 1960s, employed export expansion as its guiding policy.

As early as the 1950s when import substitution was the main objective of industrial development, a series of export promotion schemes were instituted. One of the most important measures was the devaluation of Taiwan's currency, an act that contributed to reducing the cost of exporting commodities. Another major measure was a tax rebate on exportable industrial products. These two measures markedly enhanced the competitive power of Taiwan's products in international markets. The third major measure was the creation of three export processing zones in the coastal exporting centers to attract foreign capital and technology.[11] Under these new policies, Taiwan's foreign trade soared. Between 1952 and 1962, prior to the new policy, foreign trade rose at an annual rate of only 6.1 percent, lower than the GNP growth rate. But between 1962 and 1974, Taiwan's total trade increased twenty-two times, with an annual growth rate of 29.4

**Table 1**
**Foreign Trade as Percentage of Taiwan's GNP (1961-90)**

|  | 1961 | 1966 | 1971 | 1976 | 1981 | 1986 | 1990 |
|---|---|---|---|---|---|---|---|
| Exports |  |  |  |  |  |  |  |
| (US$ millions) | 195 | 536 | 2,060 | 8,166 | 22,611 | 38,849 | 67,214 |
| As % of GNP | (11.2) | (17.0) | (31.3) | (44.2) | (47.2) | (51.6) | (41.6) |
| Imports |  |  |  |  |  |  |  |
| (US$ millons) | 322 | 622 | 1,844 | 7,599 | 21,200 | 24,165 | 54,719 |
| As % of GNP | (18.4) | (19.8) | (28.0) | (41.1) | (44.2) | (31.3) | (33.8) |
| Dependency Ratio |  |  |  |  |  |  |  |
| (Trade/GNP) | 29.6 | 36.8 | 59.3 | 85.3 | 91.4 | 82.9 | 75.4 |

Source: *Industry of Free China* (Taipei) 76, no. 5 (November 1991): 6

percent. The highest growth rate was reached in 1970-74, when the annual rate was 41.5 percent, surpassing Japanese postwar records. In the last decade, Taiwan's foreign trade has accounted for about 80 percent of GNP and has become the island's engine of growth (see table 1).

Between 1961 and 1990, Taiwan's total foreign trade increased 233-fold, from US$517 million to US$121.9 billion. During these three decades, the annual growth rate of foreign trade was about three times the GNP growth rate. Consequently, Taiwan's dependency ratio (trade/GNP) rose from 29.6 percent in 1961 to a high of 91.4 percent in 1981 before declining to 75.4 percent in 1990. The high dependency ratios indicate that the economy of the ROC has been closely integrated into the world economy.

The staggering rise of foreign trade catapulted the ROC to the position of one of the world's major trading countries (see table 2). It is officially projected that by 1996 when the ROC completes its six-year plan, Taiwan will be among the top ten exporting countries in the world.[12]

The role of the ROC in world trade can be further evaluated by two other indicators: its share of the

## Table 2
## Taiwan's Changing Rank among the World's Major Trading Countries

| Year | Total Trade | Exports | Imports |
|------|-------------|---------|---------|
| 1979 | 24 | 21 | 25 |
| 1980 | 22 | 24 | 21 |
| 1981 | 22 | 16 | 22 |
| 1982 | 22 | 15 | 23 |
| 1983 | 18 | 14 | 20 |
| 1984 | 19 | 12 | 21 |
| 1985 | 18 | 11 | 22 |
| 1986 | 16 | 11 | 20 |
| 1987 | 13 | 11 | 17 |
| 1988 | 13 | 13 | 16 |
| 1989 | 15 | 12 | 16 |
| 1990 | 14 | 11 | 16 |

Source: *Monthly Bulletin of Statistics* (New York, United Nations), various issues.

world's total trade and its ability to earn foreign exchange.

In the 1950s and 1960s, the ROC's share of world trade was minuscule, and in 1979, it still accounted for less than 1 percent of the world's total. The share rose phenomenally in the 1980s. By 1989, ROC trade accounted for almost 2 percent of the world's total trade and 2.2 percent of the world's total exports (see table 3). But in terms of population, the ROC accounted for only 0.4 percent of the world's total. In 1990, Taiwan's total trade of US$121.9 billion was 2.15 times that of Thailand and 2.56 times that of Indonesia. Although India has a population forty times as large as Taiwan's, its foreign trade is only one-third that of Taiwan.[13]

The strength of the ROC in the world's commodity markets is also illustrated by its capacity to maintain a huge trade surplus. Taiwan suffered a trade deficit in the years 1952-77. Since then, the island has continuously enjoyed a trade surplus. The surplus for the years 1982-91 added up to US$106.8 billion. By the end of 1991, foreign exchange reserves held by the Central Bank of China totaled US$82 billion, the largest in the world.[14]

The rapid growth of ROC trade and its ability to produce a surplus stems primarily from changes in its industrial structure and the composition of its exports.

In 1961, 32 percent of Taiwan's GNP came from agriculture and 17 percent from manufacturing. By 1990, the share of agriculture dropped to only 4.9 percent while the share of manufacturing rose to 34 percent. The drastic change in the industrial structure led to an alteration in export composition. In 1960, 68 percent of exports were raw and processed agricultural products; industrial products accounted for only 32 percent. By 1990, 95.5 percent of Taiwan's exports were industrial products.[15]

**Table 3**
**The Share of the ROC's Trade in Total World Trade (1979-90)**

US$100 million

| Year | Total Trade | | | Exports | | | Imports | | |
|------|------|------|------|------|------|------|------|------|------|
| | World Total | Taiwan's Total | % | World Exports | Taiwan's Exports | % | World Imports | Taiwan's Imports | % |
| 1979 | 33,259 | 309 | 0.96 | 16,391 | 161 | 1.0 | 16,868 | 148 | 0.88 |
| 1980 | 40,404 | 395 | 0.98 | 19,906 | 198 | 1.0 | 20,498 | 197 | 0.96 |
| 1981 | 40,088 | 438 | 1.1 | 19,718 | 226 | 1.1 | 20,370 | 212 | 1.0 |
| 1982 | 37,354 | 411 | 1.1 | 18,335 | 222 | 1.2 | 19,019 | 189 | 1.0 |
| 1983 | 36,843 | 454 | 1.2 | 18,125 | 251 | 1.4 | 18,718 | 203 | 1.1 |
| 1984 | 38,878 | 524 | 1.4 | 19,097 | 304 | 1.6 | 19,781 | 220 | 1.1 |
| 1985 | 39,303 | 508 | 1.3 | 21,221 | 307 | 1.6 | 20,082 | 201 | 1.0 |
| 1986 | 43,089 | 641 | 1.5 | 21,169 | 399 | 1.9 | 21,920 | 242 | 1.1 |
| 1987 | 50,327 | 887 | 1.8 | 24,803 | 537 | 2.2 | 25,524 | 350 | 1.4 |
| 1988 | 57,348 | 1,103 | 1.9 | 28,228 | 606 | 2.1 | 29,120 | 497 | 1.7 |
| 1989 | 61,517 | 1,186 | 1.9 | 30,205 | 663 | 2.2 | 31,312 | 523 | 1.7 |
| 1990 | 69,048 | 1,219 | 1.8 | 33,817 | 672 | 2.0 | 35,231 | 547 | 1.6 |

**Source:** United Nations, *Monthly Bulletin of Statistics,* various issues.
**Note:** Trade data are reported on a F.O.B. basis for exports, and a C.I.F. basis for imports.

**Table 4**
**Taiwan's Trade Surplus (1981-91)**

(US$ million)

| Year | Exports | Imports | Balance |
|------|---------|---------|---------|
| 1981 | 21,261 | 21,441 | (-) 180 |
| 1982 | 22,659 | 19,624 | 3,035 |
| 1983 | 22,810 | 18,311 | 4,499 |
| 1984 | 28,562 | 21,834 | 6,728 |
| 1985 | 30,612 | 21,480 | 9,132 |
| 1986 | 33,698 | 21,053 | 12,645 |
| 1987 | 46,890 | 28,968 | 17,922 |
| 1988 | 57,887 | 43,750 | 14,137 |
| 1989 | 63,559 | 50,903 | 12,656 |
| 1990 | 66,013 | 53,256 | 12,757 |
| 1991 | 76,160 | 62,860 | 12,300 |

Source: *Taiwan Statistical Data Book 1991* (Taipei: Council for Economic Planning and Development, 1991), 208.

In 1966, of the five most important exported commodities and services, 23.4 percent were processed food products; 13.1 percent were transport services, 8.8 percent were plywood, and 6.2 percent were animal products. By 1986, the five exported commodities generating the largest revenues were electronics products (15.7 percent), garments (13 percent), textile products (10.2 percent), metal and articles (5.3 percent), and other manufactures (10.8 percent).[16] The change from low value-added products to high value-added products is one of the major factors contributing to the sharp rise in Taiwan's export value.

## An Emerging Capital Exporter

Prior to 1977, the ROC was basically a foreign capital recipient. Most foreign capital came from the United States, Japan, and Western Europe (see table 5). Although total foreign investment between 1952 and 1990 amounted to only US$11.3 billion (a figure less than Taiwan's trade surplus in one year in the

**Table 5**
**Foreign Investment in Taiwan (1952-90)**

(US$1000)

| Year | Total | | United States | | Japan | | Europe | | Others | |
|---|---|---|---|---|---|---|---|---|---|---|
| | Cases | Amount | Cases | Amount | Cases | Amount | Cases | Amount | Cases | Amount |
| 1952-1979 | 1,191 | 1,510,336 | 314 | 666,192 | 721 | 371,575 | 50 | 246,112 | 105 | 226,457 |
| 1980 | 71 | 243,380 | 15 | 110,093 | 35 | 86,081 | 11 | 14,428 | 10 | 32,778 |
| 1981 | 73 | 356,294 | 25 | 203,213 | 27 | 64,623 | 9 | 13,196 | 13 | 75,262 |
| 1982 | 82 | 320,286 | 33 | 79,606 | 24 | 152,164 | 11 | 46,570 | 14 | 41,946 |
| 1983 | 100 | 375,382 | 35 | 93,294 | 33 | 196,770 | 7 | 20,746 | 25 | 64,572 |
| 1984 | 100 | 518,971 | 41 | 231,175 | 28 | 113,978 | 15 | 92,242 | 16 | 81,576 |
| 1985 | 107 | 660,703 | 42 | 332,760 | 32 | 145,236 | 15 | 100,011 | 21 | 82,696 |
| 1986 | 206 | 705,574 | 56 | 138,428 | 88 | 253,596 | 24 | 139,642 | 38 | 173,908 |
| 1987 | 363 | 1,223,069 | 74 | 414,061 | 207 | 399,240 | 38 | 234,332 | 44 | 175,436 |
| 1988 | 438 | 1,061,161 | 60 | 134,726 | 212 | 431,867 | 75 | 206,236 | 92 | 288,332 |
| 1989 | 478 | 2,241,026 | 54 | 343,002 | 233 | 640,552 | 85 | 531,420 | 106 | 726,052 |
| 1990 | 376 | 2,081,657 | 61 | 540,367 | 179 | 826,800 | 66 | 348,350 | 70 | 366,140 |
| Total | 3,586 | 11,297,839 | 811 | 3,291,669 | 1,819 | 3,682,482 | 408 | 2,010,671 | 548 | 2,313,017 |

Source:Investment Commission, Ministry of Economic Affairs, ROC, *Hua-ch'iao chi wai-jen t'ou-tzu tui wo-kuo ching-chi fa-chan te kung-hsien* (Statistics on overseas Chinese and foreign investments, and their contributions to our economic development)(Taipei), various issues.

1980s), the contribution made by foreign capital to the island's economy was far-reaching and profound.

Of all the contributions to Taiwan's economy made by overseas Chinese and foreign investments, the effect on export promotion was the most conspicuous. In the three years 1977-79, when Taiwan's exports grew extremely rapidly, the share of overseas Chinese and foreign-invested firms in Taiwan's exports was as high as 29 percent. Even as late as 1982, their share still stood at 25 percent of Taiwan's exports. Of Taiwan's major export commodities in 1982, 65.2 percent of electronics and electrical appliances, 63.5 percent of chemicals, and 38 percent of textiles were produced by overseas Chinese and foreign invested firms.[17] As Taiwan's economic base expanded, the share of these firms shrank. It was 16.7 percent in 1986, 15.52 percent in 1987, and 15.61 percent in 1988, still representing quite a respectable share.[18]

After four decades of phenomenal growth, Taiwan's economy was by the mid-1980s confronting many formidable problems. Among them were labor shortages, soaring labor costs, sky-high land prices, mounting concerns about pollution, and the sharp appreciation of Taiwan's currency relative to the U.S. dollar. Under growing pressure from the United States, the Taiwan dollar was allowed to appreciate by 20 percent in 1987, 28 percent in 1988, and another 9 percent in 1989. In January 1989, the U.S. government suspended the benefits of its general system of preference to Taiwan. The ROC no longer enjoys most-favored-nation trade status. All these developments substantially increased production costs and affected Taiwan's competitive edge in the international market. Many Taiwan enterprises began to transplant their operations overseas.[19]

The outflow of capital started in 1984, but accelerated after 1987. Prior to 1987, the ROC government

**Table 6**
**Taiwan's Capital Flow (1961-90)**

(US$ million)

| Year | Balance | Direct Investment and Other Long-term Capital | Short-term Capital |
|------|---------|-----------------------------------------------|--------------------|
| 1961-70 | 915 | 588 | 327 |
| 1971-80 | 4,091 | 4,266 | -175 |
| 1981 | 995 | 886 | 109 |
| 1982 | 739 | 1,268 | -529 |
| 1983 | 645 | 1,043 | -398 |
| 1984 | -828 | -738 | -89 |
| 1985 | -439 | -777 | 284 |
| 1986 | 13 | -1,408 | 1,421 |
| 1987 | 1,627 | -2,386 | 4,013 |
| 1988 | -7,512 | -6,031 | -1,481 |
| 1989 | -8,303 | -7,432 | -871 |
| 1990 | -10,725 | -6,402 | -4,323 |

Source: *Chung-hua min-kuo T'ai-wan ti-ch'u chin-jung t'ung-chi yueh-pao* (*Financial Statistics Monthly*, Taiwan District, the Republic of China)(Taipei), various issues.
Note: Minus sign denotes capital outflow.

strictly controlled foreign exchange, prohibiting the outflow of capital and requiring government approval for foreign investment. In 1987, its huge foreign exchange reserves enabled the government to relax exchange controls. Residents in Taiwan are now allowed to transfer overseas a maximum of US$3 million per person per year, so a family of four can now transfer a total of US$12 million, adequate for a medium-sized operation outside the island. As a result, capital outflow began to surge, with more than US$30 billion reportedly leaving the island in the 1987-91 period.[20]

During the first stage of capital outflow, the prime destination was the United States. Private investment in the United States with government approval rose from US$107 million in 1985 to US$620 million in 1989. But actual investment is widely believed to be many times the official figure.

In the past, most of Taiwan's private investment in the United States was concentrated in restaurants, motels, and real estate. In recent years, as Taiwan entered the era of high-tech, many companies in the fields of computers, petrochemicals, and banking have begun to take over American firms. In 1988, the Pacific Wire and Cable Company in Taiwan purchased thirty-eight American savings and loan associations for a total cost of US$37.5 million. In 1989, the Taiwan Continental Engineering Company acquired American Bridge Co. of Pittsburgh for US$100 million. In 1990, the Chinese Petroleum Corporation purchased Huffco Petroleum. In May 1990, Taiwan President Enterprise acquired Wyndham Foods, the United States' third largest biscuit maker, for US$335 million. In the field of computers, Taiwan Acer Incorporated acquired Altas Computer System in California and Taiwan Wyse Company acquired its U.S. parent company.[21] All of these new ventures are a part of the shift in Taiwan's overseas investment from services to manufacturing, especially in high-tech industries. Last November, an aerospace company in Taiwan engaged in negotiations with McDonnell Douglas to buy up to 40 percent of its commercial aircraft business for US$2 billion. Although the deal has not been consummated, it further reflects the well-known acquisition power of Taiwanese capital.

The injection of Taiwan capital had a significant impact on many sections of the American business community. In the past few years, when the U.S. computer industry was experiencing a slump, Taiwan electronics firms invested US$692 million in Silicon Valley, California, creating 13,545 new jobs.[22] In southern Texas, the building of a US$1.5 billion petrochemical complex by the Formosa Plastics group also helped to ward off economic woes. However, the most dramatic development has been the ROC's investment in Southeast Asia and the coastal areas of the Chinese mainland.

## Table 7
## Taiwan's Direct Investment in Four
## Southeast Asian Countries (1986-90)

| Country | Year | Host Government Data | | ROC Government Data | |
|---|---|---|---|---|---|
| | | Amount (US$ million) | No. of Cases | Amount (US$ million) | No. of Cases |
| Thailand | 1986 | 70 | 21 | 5.81 | 3 |
| | 1987 | 300 | 102 | 5.36 | 5 |
| | 1988 | 842 | 308 | 11.88 | 15 |
| | 1989 | 871 | 214 | 51.60 | 23 |
| | 1990 | 761 | 144 | 149.39 | 39 |
| Malaysia | 1986 | 4 | 15 | 0 | 0 |
| | 1987 | 91 | 37 | 5.83 | 5 |
| | 1988 | 313 | 111 | 2.70 | 5 |
| | 1989 | 815 | 191 | 158.64 | 25 |
| | 1990 | 2,383 | 270 | 184.88 | 36 |
| Philippines | 1986 | 0.35 | 8 | 0.07 | 1 |
| | 1987 | 9.04 | 43 | 2.64 | 3 |
| | 1988 | 109.87 | 86 | 36.20 | 7 |
| | 1989 | 148.69 | 190 | 66.31 | 13 |
| | 1990 | 140.65 | 158 | 123.00 | 16 |
| Indonesia | 1986 | 18 | N.A. | 0 | 0 |
| | 1987 | 8 | 3 | 0 | 0 |
| | 1988 | 913 | 17 | 1.92 | 3 |
| | 1989 | 158 | 50 | 0.31 | 1 |
| | 1990 | 618 | 94 | 61.87 | 18 |

Source: *Lien-ho pao* (*United Daily News*) (Taipei), March 30, 1991, 11.

Between 1986 and 1990, Taiwan businesses went on an investment spree in Thailand, Malaysia, the Philippines, and Indonesia. Although official statistics on approved investments indicated a total of only US$869 million, data supplied by the host countries added up to US$8.57 billion, almost ten times the official figure (see table 7). Recent ROC official sources reveal that during the past six years more than US$13 billion has been poured into Southeast Asia.[23]

In 1990, Taiwan's investment in Malaysia reached a record high of US$2.4 billion, ranking it the number one foreign investor in that country. In 1989, Taiwan's investment in the Philippines ranked second after Japan, but higher than the United States. There are now more than 5,000 Taiwanese firms operating in Thailand, Malaysia, Indonesia, and the Philippines and they have become a formidable economic force in Southeast Asia.

Taiwan's investment in mainland China has gained momentum in recent years. Prior to 1987, there was virtually no Taiwanese investment on the mainland. Then, after the lifting of martial law in July 1987 and the subsequent relaxation of foreign exchange controls, some adventurous businessmen began investing in the coastal cities, especially in Amoy (Xiamen), directly across the Taiwan Straits. Initial investments were rather moderate, consisting primarily of small and medium-sized enterprises which would yield a quick return. Mainland Chinese government statistics show that average contracted capital per project was around US$1.6 million in 1988.

Before 1990, 90 percent of Taiwan's investments on the mainland were in manufacturing, with export as their goal. Total investment in 1987 was only US$100 million. The pace accelerated in the following years, partially because of the deterioration of the investment environment in Taiwan and partially because of the preferential treatment offered by the mainland authorities. This "push and pull" effect combined to trigger a "mainland fever" in 1990 when more than US$1.5 billion in Taiwan capital was committed to new ventures in mainland China. By the end of 1991, accumulated Taiwan investment on the mainland exceeded US$3 billion. A recent Japanese study indicates that in the past five years, more than US$15 billion of Taiwan capital entered Hong Kong, of which a substantial amount has been channeled into the mainland.[24]

Extensive investment in Southeast Asia and mainland China brought about a rapid increase in intraregional trade. When Taiwan businesses set up new firms in these areas, almost 55 percent of raw materials and 60-70 percent of machinery were imported from Taiwan, making them Taiwan's fastest growing export markets. In the five-year period 1985-90, Taiwan's exports to Indonesia increased three times; to Thailand, 5 times; to Malaysia, 4.7 times; to the Philippines, 2.4 times; and exports to mainland China went up 2.3 times.[25] By 1991, the ROC had become the second most influential economic power in Southeast Asia after Japan and the second largest investor in mainland China after Hong Kong.

Compared with other industrial powers, Taiwan's net overseas assets of US$100 billion at the end of 1991 were still relatively small. Japan's overseas net assets in the same period were US$383 billion, about four times those of Taiwan. But since Japan has a population six times as big, Taiwan ranks higher on a per capita basis. When compared with most debt-ridden Third World countries, debt-free, cash-rich Taiwan undoubtedly represents a triumphant example of postwar economic development.

# A Model for Third World Countries

In the 1960s and 1970s, the ROC's achievements drew little attention from the West, or from within Asia. Since the late 1970s, however, the Taiwan success story has gained recognition among the world's top economists. Four Nobel laureates, Simon Kuznets, Frederick Hayek, Milton Friedman, and Lawrence Klein, have written articles praising Taiwan.[26] Even the Chinese Communist leaders in Peking (Beijing) have admitted that in the contest of economic growth between the two parts of China, Taiwan appears to be the winner.[27] The experience of Taiwan has since become a model not only for mainland China but also for other developing countries.

Before 1979, the two sides of the Taiwan Straits experimented with two completely different models of industrialization and modernization. While Taiwan pursued a balanced growth and export expansion strategy under a mixed economic system, mainland China followed the Stalinist model of lopsided developmental policies and a highly centralized planned system. The wide gap between these two economies in terms of per capita income and standard of living prompted the Peking leadership to launch a wholesale reform in 1979. Many of Peking's new policies appear to be quite similar to those implemented in Taiwan.

One major impact of the Taiwan model on mainland China's development has been the abandonment of Mao's self-reliance doctrine and the adoption of an open-door policy. In 1979, four special economic zones similar to the export processing zones in Taiwan were set up in Kwangtung (Guangdong) and Fukien (Fujian) provinces. In a novel move in April 1984, the Peking authorities announced that an additional fourteen coastal cities would be opened to the outside world. From Dairen (Dalian) in the north to Peihai (Beihai) in the south, almost all major ports are now open to foreign investors. The government went a step further in early 1985 by opening three more prosperous regions. These are the Yangtze River Delta, the Pearl River Delta, and the Amoy-Changchow-Chuanchow Triangle in Southern Fukien Province. After the CCP's Thirteenth National Congress in October 1987, a new guideline was put forward calling for the opening-up of the entire coast to outside investment.[28] In recent years, the Pearl River Delta has in essence followed the Taiwan model and is designated by the mainland Chinese leaders to become the fifth of Asia's "little dragons" after Taiwan, Hong Kong, Singapore, and South Korea.

Second, in contrast to the previous three decades (1949-78), when foreign trade played only a minor role, the new leadership in Peking has given a leading role to foreign trade. Between 1979 and 1991, mainland China's foreign trade rose 3.6-fold. In 1978, foreign trade accounted for only 9 percent of the country's GNP. By 1990, it accounted for 27.3 percent.[29] Attracting foreign capital has now become an overriding policy goal for Chinese economic planners. From 1979 to August 1991, mainland China absorbed US$21.3 billion-worth of foreign investment and incurred foreign debts of US$52 billion. The Chinese economy has rapidly moved from isolation toward internationalization, a policy Taiwan has vigorously implemented since the 1970s.

Third, in rural areas, the ill-conceived commune system was abolished in the early 1980s and replaced by a household contract system. The new system, although not exactly the same as the land-to-the-tiller program in Taiwan, is a total rejection of Mao's collective farming program and a return to individual operation. It has led to the diversification and commercialization of the Chinese rural economy and the emergence of millions of village enterprises which now account for one-third of mainland China's gross industrial output value.

Fourth, radical reforms are under way in the urban economy to enlarge the decision-making power of individual enterprises, to separate government administration from business units, and to combine the market mechanism with central planning. An embryonic stock market and a real estate market have also developed in recent years. The economy is moving toward privatization, another significant departure from the original Stalinist model and a new step in the direction of the Taiwan model.

In Southeast Asia, Taiwan's export promotion and open-door policies have also been widely imitated in the last decade. Most countries have shifted from import substitution to export expansion. The development process in this area has defied the dependency theory advanced by many Latin American economists in the 1960s which contended that trade between developed capitalist nations and developing nations is a zero-sum game, and that the trade network via the capitalist system and the multinational corporations historically exploited the underdeveloped countries and had harmful social and political ramifications.[30] This anti-trade sentiment has led many Third World nations to pursue an import subsitution policy rather than expand exports. The experience of Taiwan and the Southeast Asian countries testifies that trade with advanced capitalist countries is not necessarily a zero-sum game. Insofar as the developing countries can improve technology, control product quality, and fully utilize their comparative advantages, they can penetrate into the capitalist markets. For countries with limited resources, small domestic markets, and a dense population like Taiwan, export expansion proves to be the best way to escape the "low-level equilibrium trap." Expansion of foreign trade and the inflow of foreign capital help to shift the country's production possibilities frontier outward and enable small countries to enjoy economies of scale. By following an outward-looking strategy, both mainland China and Thailand have escaped from stagnation and achieved a high rate of growth in the last decade. Between 1980 and 1989, mainland China's GNP grew at 9.7 percent per year, while Thailand achieved 7 percent annual growth.[31] In recent years, even countries in Latin America and now the republics of the former Soviet Union have gained insights from the Taiwan experience. The role of the ROC as a development model for Third World nations has gradually taken root in international society.

## The ROC in the Twenty-first Century

Looking ahead into the twenty-first century, the ROC on Taiwan will have a more mature economy and assume a more discernible role in the international community.

First, the ROC has, since last year, embarked on an ambitious medium-term plan for national development, the goals of which are to upgrade the industrial structure, promote balanced regional development, and improve the quality of life. Under the new six-year plan (1991-96), the ROC government has committed a total of US$303 billion for 775 projects. Key projects in the plan include a high-speed railway, rapid transit systems in major cities, highway expansion, petrochemical plants, the island's fourth nuclear power plant, infrastructure for heavy industries, pollution control facilities, housing projects, and the development of science and technology. It is anticipated that by 1996, exports will reach US$122.8 billion and imports US$120.7 billion, placing Taiwan among the top ten trading countries in the world.[32]

Second, as Taiwan's overseas assets continue to

grow and income from outward investment increases, the ROC may perform a new role as a foreign aid contributor to less developed nations. In 1988, an International Economic Cooperation and Development Fund was set up with a modest initial capital of US$400 million. By the end of June 1991, it had granted a total of US$127 million to fifteen countries. A new International Aid Fund is also under consideration. The ROC government is now actively seeking the opportunity to participate in both the "Paris Club" and the European Bank for Reconstruction and Development. In February 1992, at the request of the two governments, Taiwan donated US$15 million-worth of medicines to Ukraine and shipped 100,000 tons of rice to Russia. The ROC government recently decided that in the coming decade, foreign aid will account for 0.17 percent of GNP, slightly higher than the 0.15 percent level attained by most donor countries in recent years.

Third, as Taiwan's investment in Southeast Asia grows by leaps and bounds, and as the island's foreign exchange reserves continue to rise, Taiwan may emerge as a new regional financial center. This goal has been incorporated into the current six-year plan, and both the Central Bank and the Ministry of Finance have set timetables for its realization.[33] Although Taiwan's own domestic market is limited, its financial power in the Far East stands second only to Japan. The island can be regarded and used as a gateway to a much larger East and Southeast Asian regional market by American and West European multinational corporations. Taiwan's expanding supply of skilled technical manpower and its long-standing connections with ethnic Chinese distributors in this region are assets that could make the ROC an Asian economic power in the twenty-first century.

Fourth, as the political atmosphere between the two sides of the Taiwan Straits improves, economic cooperation between Taiwan and the mainland will increase. Mainland China is now Taiwan's fifth largest export market and Taiwan is the mainland's second largest investor. Trade between Hong Kong and Taiwan has also increased tremendously. Hong Kong is now Taiwan's third largest export market and the principal source of its trade surplus.[34] As interdependency among these three Chinese communities continues to rise, by the end of this century, a "greater Chinese common market" or "Chinese economic sphere" may come into existence with Taiwan as a major partner.

All these new developments are bound to enhance the ROC's economic role in the twenty-first century. As a major trading power with rising overseas financial assets, the Republic of China on Taiwan will become a foreign aid donor, a new regional financial center, and a chief investor in mainland China. All of these developments will make Taiwan a major participant in the world economy.

NOTES

1. Per capita income in Taiwan was US$50 in 1952. By 1990, it had reached US$8,000.
2. By the end of 1991, Taiwan's foreign exchange reserves had reached US$82 billion, surpassing those of Japan and Germany.
3. Samuel C. Shieh, "The Outlook for Taipei as a Regional Financial Center in Asia," *Industry of Free China* (Taipei) 76, no. 5 (November 1991): 31-41. (Shieh is governor of the Central Bank of China).
4. For details see Chu-yuan Cheng, "The Doctrine of People's Welfare: The Taiwan Experiment and Its Implications for the Third World," in *Sun Yat-sen's Doctrine in the Modern World*, ed. Chu-yuan Cheng (Boulder, Colo.: Westview Press, 1989), 244-71.
5. *Taiwan Statistical Data Book 1991* (Taipei: Council for Economic Planning and Development, 1991), 2.
6. Ibid.
7. Ibid., 62.
8. Ibid.

9. *World Development Report 1991* (New York: World Bank, 1991), 209.
10. *Ching-chi jih-pao (Economic Daily)*(Taipei), January 7, 1992, 2.
11. Kuai-jeou Wang, "Economic and Social Impact of Export Processing Zones in the Republic of China," *Economic Review* (Taipei), no. 200 (March-April 1981): 10-11.
12. *Kuo-chi jih-pao (International Daily News)* (Los Angeles), February 18, 1992, 12.
13. In 1990, Taiwan's exports were worth US$67.2 billion., compared with US$25.7 for Indonesia, US$22.8 billion for Thailand, and US$17.8 billion for India. See *Monthly Bulletin of Statistics* (New York, United Nations), June 1991.
14. In comparison, Japan had reserves of US$71.1 billion. See *Chung-yang jih-pao (Central Daily News)* (Taipei), June 6, 1992, 1.
15. *Taiwan Statistical Data Book 1991*, 213.
16. Chuang Chia-cheng, "Balance of Payments and Economic Development in Taiwan" (in Chinese), *Industry of Free China* 76, no. 5 (November 1991): 11.
17. Chu-yuan Cheng, "United States-Taiwan Economic Relations: Trade and Investment," *Columbia Journal of World Business* 21, no. 1 (Spring 1986): 87-96.
18. Liao Ping-tsai (Liao Bingzai), "Mutual Investment between Taiwan and Developed Countries," *Kuo-chi mao-i (Intertrade Monthly)* (Peking), 1991, no. 6: 29-32.
19. Chu-yuan Cheng, "Taiwan's Economy in Transition: New Challenges and Prospects," *Asian Outlook* (Taipei) 26, no. 5 (July-August 1991): 5-11.
20. *Shih-chieh jih-pao (World Journal)* (New York), June 17, 1992, 16.
21. See note 3 above.
22. *Chung-yang jih-pao* (Overseas edition), February 3, 1992, 4.
23. *Ching-chi jih-pao*, May 7, 1992, 10.
24. *The World Journal*, June 3, 1992, 14.
25. *Chung-hua min-kuo, T'ai-wan ti-ch'u chin-ch'u-k'ou mao-i t'ung-chi yueh-pao* (Monthly Statistics of Exports and Imports, Taiwan Area, the Republic of China)(Ministry of Finance, ROC), May 20, 1991, 9-77.
26. For example, Simon Kuznets, "Growth and Structural Shifts," in *Economic Growth and Structural Change in Taiwan*, ed. Walter Galenson (Ithaca, N.Y.: Cornell University Press, 1979), 15-131.

27. Ma Hung, *Ching-chi chieh-kou yu ching-chi kuan-li* (Economic structure and economic management )(Peking: Jen-min ch'u-pan-she, 1982), 4-5.
28. He Chunlin, "Eight Years of the Open Policy," *China Reconstructs* (Peking) 36, no. 11 (November 1987): 12-15.
29. According to the PRC's State Statistics Bureau, mainland China's foreign trade in 1990 was worth 556 billion yuan (jemminpi), while its GNP was 1,768.6 billion yuan. The trade/GNP ratio was 31.4 percent. In terms of U.S. dollars, however, the ratio was 27.3 percent.
30. Gabriel Pulma, "Dependency: A Formal Theory of Underdevelopment or a Methodology for Analysis of Concrete Situations of Underdevelopment," *World Development* 6, no. 7/8 (July-August 1978): 881-924.
31. *World Development Report 1991*, 206-207.
32. Chu-yuan Cheng, "Taiwan's Economy in Transition."
33. Theodore S. S. Cheng, "Asia-Pacific Regional Cooperation Under the Backdrop of Tripolar Relationship," *Economic Review*, no. 265 (November/Deccmber 1991): 8-9.
34. *Ching-chi jih-pao*, August 24, 1991, 2.

*Reprinted by Permission of* Issues & Studies

# IV.
# Agriculture and
# the Environment

Previous page: The lush fields of Yunlin county in south central Taiwan attest to the island's natural bounty.

# Adjusting Agricultural Policy: Building Prosperous and Beautiful Farming Villages

Sun Ming-hsien

*Sun Ming-hsien is chairman of the Council of Agriculture, Executive Yuan.*

Over the past four decades, the ROC's agricultural development strategy has successfully transformed the Taiwan area, economically and socially, from a state of impoverishment and backwardness to one of prosperity and progress. In establishing this important developmental model for developing countries, Taiwan has made the transition from a conventional economy to a modern one and is advancing from a high-income to high-quality society. As a result, agriculture now accounts for an increasingly smaller percentage of the economy. In view of this trend and the rapid changes in the agricultural environment, the Republic of China has shifted its goals in policy planning from increased production to agricultural and rural village development, and concern for the farming population.

It is obvious from this structural change in the economy and the ROC's current developmental strategy of economic internationalization and liberalization of trade that the agricultural sector will be increasingly affected by world economic and trade competition. The impact on farm products is bound to grow when economic and trade opportunities open up for the ROC after it enters the General Agreement on Tariffs and Trade. Some of the ROC's farm products are already facing competition from mainland China as Taiwan-mainland relations and agricultural technology exchanges have expanded. In addition, the Republic of China must, as a member of the international

169

community, keep pace with the global trend of conserving natural resources, and attend to both economic development and ecological conservation.

Given these developments, it has become imperative for the ROC to redefine its agricultural growth. The ROC government is working on a white paper on agricultural development that focuses on industrial, farmers' and farmland policies, resource management, and scientific and technological development. This development blueprint is designed to usher in a new era in ROC agricultural development in the 21st century.

## Current Issues in the Agricultural Sector

Taiwan's agricultural sector is currently facing six major issues:

■ Small area of arable land: Over 800,000 farm households in Taiwan have an average of only 1.1 hectares of arable land, and about 75.2 percent of the total farm households have less than 1 hectare of arable land.

■ Aging of farmers: The average age of farm owners has risen to 52.4.

■ Anticipated rise in land prices: Economic development has raised the demand for land; and an anticipated increase in land prices has dampened the interest of farmland owners in farming, which in turn has hampered agricultural modernization.

■ Urgent demand for farmers' welfare: Farmers earn less than non-farmers, leading to an urgent need for improved welfare, services, and living standards.

■ Heavy pressure brought about by conservation of natural resources: Chinese have traditionally used rare animal species in medicines and winter tonics. These practices have drawn criticism from world conservation groups, have tarnished the ROC's image, and are likely to provoke trade sanctions.

■ Competition from agricultural imports: When the ROC becomes a GATT signatory in the not-too-distant future, it will have to open its domestic market to agricultural imports in accordance with GATT regulations, which will inevitably affect local agricultural products.

## Basic Orientations of the Current Agricultural Policy

Agriculture is a nation's basic industry, but modern agriculture has transcended the level of simply supplying food and raw materials. It has evolved into a commercial sector that integrates production, life style, and ecology. Consequently, the ROC has oriented its agricultural policy along four principal lines.

■ Agricultural economics: to transform farming operations into an ever-growing business enterprise.

■ Agricultural technology: to raise productivity and marketing efficiency through advanced technologies.

■ Agricultural environment: to conduct farming operations with social and public interests in mind, such as the security of national territory, ecological conservation, and rural culture.

■ International agriculture: to strengthen agricultural technological exchanges and uphold global economic and trade codes.

In order to fulfill these functions, the ROC is steering its agricultural sector towards high quality, high efficiency, and modern management in a number of ways.

■ By raising the quality of farm labor, using farmland more efficiently, adjusting the industrial infrastructure, increasing the added value of farm products, reducing the costs of agricultural production and marketing, and enhancing product competitiveness.

■ By ensuring the continued use of agricultural resources, achieving a balance between agriculture and the environment, maintaining the farming ecological environment, replenishing green resources, and meeting recreational and tourism needs.

■ By enhancing farmers' welfare and spiritual culture in rural areas, improving the rural quality of life, bridging the gap in living standards between urban and rural areas, and realizing the ideal of equitable prosperity.

## Recent Administrative Measures and Achievements

Since 1973, the ROC government has adopted a series of agricultural development measures to provide better care for its farming populace, develop agriculture, and set up farm villages. These measures include:

■ Important Measures for Accelerating the Development of Farm Villages

■ Plan for Raising Farmer Income and Accelerating the Development of Farm Villages

■ Comprehensive Plan for Promoting the Construction of Basic Facilities

■ Plan for Strengthening Basic Facilities and Raising Farmer Income

- Plan for Improving the Agricultural Infrastructure and Raising Farmer Income

- Comprehensive Agricultural Adjustment Plan

Between 1973 and 1993, the central and local governments invested a total of NT$217.7 billion in agricultural development in coordination with these measures. The money was spent mainly on improving production, farm extension, laboratory research, public investments, resource development, guaranteed prices, subsidies, development of rural communities, enhancement of farmer welfare, and agricultural financing. Some of their major accomplishments in recent years are as following.

- Second phase of the Six-Year Program for Rice Production and Rice Field Conversion: About 178,000 hectares of rice paddies have been converted to cultivation of other crops. Rice and other food grains are purchased at guaranteed prices. In the first quarter of 1993, the government purchase of food grains increased 20 percent, and in the second quarter, the purchase price was raised by 10 percent.

- Adjustment of hog-raising policy: Hog prices have been stabilized through better production and marketing management. Stronger preventive measures have been taken against pollution created by livestock. By October 1993, about 85 percent of the farmers raising more than 200 hogs had adopted appropriate waste water treatment; and in the Kaohsiung-Pingtung water conservation area, the figure is as high as 91.5 percent.

- Guidance program for pisciculture, cultivation of coastal and inshore fishing resources, and development of deep-sea fishing: A plan to establish 46 pisciculture production zones in the Taiwan area has been drawn up. Public facilities have been renovated and guidance provided in production and marketing in ten of these zones. Conservation zones for fishing resources have also been established, artificial reefs built, and coastal and inshore fishing resources developed. As many as 525 worn-out fishing boats have been purchased under a policy to reduce the number of aging fishing boats.

Pelagic fishing and international fishery cooperation have been strengthened. Currently 900 fishing boats are participating in global cooperation programs. The ROC has signed intergovernmental fishery pacts with five countries, and conducted private commercial cooperation with 23 other nations. The government has been providing guidance to fishing boats under 50 tons to engage in fishery cooperation with neighboring countries. Fishing harbors and onshore public facilities have been constructed and management of fishing boats and fishermen has been systematized.

■ Comprehensive plan for farmland use: In 1993, public facilities were improved and guidance provided in production and marketing to 91 rural townships in 12 Taiwan counties. A total of 34,428 hectares of farmland in 139 zones were covered in this program. This regional operations model is designed to overcome the shortcomings of small farm operations, slash the costs of production and marketing, and raise the efficiency of regional production and marketing operations. Data on farmland that may be converted to use for other purposes has been provided in coordination with the Economic Stimulus Package.

■ Forestry plans, and water and soil conservation: Logging is strictly restricted to a maximum of 200,000 cubic meters of logs and five hectares in each lumbering area each fiscal year. Afforestation and forest protection have been strengthened. Mountain slopes are better managed and inspected to prevent destruction of the ecological environment due to overuse of land and illegal cultivation. Water and soil conservation and flood prevention programs have been implemented in Lanyang and eastern Taiwan. Similar programs and emergency measures for major mountain disasters in western Taiwan have also been implemented. These programs and the development of forest recreational areas have been incorporated into a forestry operation system for resource conservation and tourism.

■ Environmental improvement in farming and fishing communities: Plans for 15 villages have been drafted and 106 villages have been constructed. Some 880 farm and fishing households were given guidance in obtaining home improvement loans.

■ Preliminary plan for farmers' annuity system: A farmers' annuity system has been established to improve the lives of aging farmers in their final years and to enhance farmer welfare under a social insurance and welfare policy.

■ Program for agricultural natural disaster relief: Aid is available in the form of loans and cash in the event of natural disasters encountered in the course of agricultural operations. Security is provided to farmers and fishermen by rehabilitating their operations and helping them rebuild their homes.

■ Irrigation association membership fee subsidies: As part of a concrete effort to provide better care for farmers and to alleviate their burdens, irrigation association membership fees have gradually been reduced beginning in fiscal 1990 by increasing the subsidy ratio from 70 percent to 92.22 percent. The fees will be fully subsidized by the government beginning in FY1994.

## Future Emphases in Agricultural Administration

The construction of beautiful and prosperous farming villages and the improvement of the agricultural structure are both the long-range goal as well as the fundamental means employed to implement modern management in agricultural production, modernize farmer livelihood, and maintain the natural rural ecology. The ROC has drafted a concrete strategy for agricultural development, focusing on issues arising from entry into GATT; management of production, farmers, farmland and resources (including natural conservation); and scientific and technological development.

## Strategies for Minimizing the Impact of Entry into GATT

After the ROC becomes a GATT signatory, the government will make a comprehensive study of GATT regulations, the status of the domestic industrial development, and the conclusions of the Uruguay Talks, then will request time to adjust its industrial infrastructure in order to reduce impact on the agricultural sector. The ROC government has drawn up the following concrete counterstrategies.

■ Overall negotiation strategy: The ROC will demand that agricultural imports be subject to less tariff reductions, as in developing countries, and will ask for a longer period of adjustment time and a more advantageous form of adjustment. All available bargaining chips will be employed to conduct an effective integrated campaign, and the direction of the comprehensive plan will be adjusted in accord with the nation's industrial developmental strategy and the degree of concern from countries involved.

■ Trade strategy: Seasonal tariffs and quota tariffs will be imposed and a timetable for tariff adjustment drawn up according to the nature of individual products and the overall environment surrounding the GATT talks. For regulated imports and those that require import permits, appropriate protection will be maintained or a tariff system established by raising tariffs in lieu of import restrictions, setting a timetable for tariff reduction, and increasing the import quota yearly. The ROC will, as part of its effort to win time for making industrial adjustments, consult with trading partners concerning restricted imports from certain areas, and will implement tariffs and quotas or increase import quotas yearly.

■ Production adjustment strategy: Agricultural production in the ROC will, based on market conditions, develop high-quality products, work to produce more unique domestic products, and rationalize and automate operations, to achieve higher returns. By operating in the form of a conglomerate, agricultural technological alignment will be accelerated, farm management carried out, production and marketing costs reduced, and product competitiveness raised. The ROC will promote the ecological and recreational aspects of agriculture and adjust its industrial developmental strategy in conjunction with farmland conversion to other uses and the exodus of the rural labor force for urban areas.

■ Transportation and marketing adjustment strategy: As the ROC's industrial infrastructure is transformed, a consumer-oriented marketing strategy will be advanced to meet the interests of both consumers and producers, and middleman costs will be reduced by promoting direct distribution. Brand names of domestic farm products will be established and promoted to enhance competitiveness. Distribution will be automated to modernize the transaction system.

The quarantine inspection system for agricultural products will be strengthened by setting inspection standards and regulations. Farm products affected by imports will be aided on a broader scale; compensation or direct payment will be provided depending on the nature of the industry so as to reduce the impact of imports on domestic agriculture.

## Industrial Policy

In formulating its industrial policy, the ROC must take into consideration overall domestic and international economic development, changes in agricultural resources, and the improvement of agricultural techniques. It must also focus on the supply of principal cereals as well as comparative advantages and market orientations before orienting its industries towards developing high value-added products with a low environmental cost and high market potential.

■ The ROC will maintain self-sufficiency in rice production, since food grains are staple foods and are imperative for social stability. But in keeping with overall economic and trade development and resource relocation overseas, production targets will be reduced and cultivation of quality rice will be encouraged. A rotation system for paddy fields and dry farmlands will be set up to maintain continuous farm operations.

■ The ROC will develop indigenous products capable of bringing in high returns, and will also develop capital- and technology-intensive quality agriculture. Automated production and distribution will be promoted, techniques for controlling plant diseases and pests developed, production and marketing costs lowered, product quality raised, and market competitiveness increased.

■ Hogs will be raised on a larger scale, wastes will be handled with greater efficiency, and the social costs of environmental pollution lowered. The ROC's objective is to become self-sufficient in poultry and fresh milk production. Measures will be taken to develop a sound system of production and distribution of farm products and livestock.

■ Due to water pollution and controls on the use of underground water, future pisciculture development will concentrate on establishing pisciculture zones, cultivating high-value fish species, and increasing salt-water fish production. For high-sea fishing, international cooperation will be strengthened and new fishing grounds opened up. Coastal and inshore fishing will also be developed. A fishing operation code will be established and fishing grounds developed along Taiwan's east coast.

■ The role of forests in national security, water conservation, tourism and recreation far outweighs that of production. Under a principle of natural conservation taking precedence over lumbering, the ROC has adopted a strategy of natural conservation, rational utilization of resources, and planned afforestation to maintain the ecological balance of forest resources.

## Farmer Policy

The ROC's policy on farmers is to cultivate farming and managerial talent and to keep capable people in farming through an improved rural environment and enhanced welfare. While conventional production-oriented guidance no longer meets farmers' needs, there is growing demand for systematic cultivation of farming professionals, planning of integrated rural projects, and establishment of a farmers' social security system. A farmer surplus has impeded the expansion and development of farming operations; the farming population must be gradually reduced in conjunction with transformations in the agricultural structure.

179

■ Modernized agricultural operations require core farm families with new concepts and advanced technology. The ROC's farmer policy is directed primarily at providing guidance to core farmers, including both full- and part-time farmers. This will help realize the ideal of expanding small farms into agribusinesses.

■ In order to enhance social security for farmers, plans are under way to launch an annuity system to guarantee the security of elderly, retired farmers. This system will encompass both social insurance and welfare, as well as other retirement factors or measures each year. The ultimate goal is to improve the agricultural structure. Security measures already adopted include implementation of farmers' health insurance and fishermen's safety insurance programs, the establishment of rural medical networks, and provision of relief in cases of sea and natural disasters.

## Farmland Policy

Farmland, the foundation of agricultural production, is a nonrenewable resource. With the agricultural operation structure on the verge of major reform, the important issues in farmland policy are how to coordinate with transformations in the industrial structure to rationally and effectively utilize farmland, conserve superior farmland resources, achieve a balance between individual and public interests, and protect the long-term interests of future generations.

■ An appropriate amount of farmland must be reserved for food production, natural ecological conservation, and preservation of open space and greenery. But in view of the ROC's integrated developmental needs, comprehensive plans for farmland use will include schedules and selected areas for farmland conversion while taking into consideration regional balance, efficient use of land resources, and maintenance of the ecology. The incremental value thus acquired from land conversion will be diverted back to rural development and enhancement of farmer welfare.

■ The public shares a consensus on relaxing the policy of "restricting farmland ownership to farmers and the use of farmland to farming." Currently, the pertinent laws on limiting the use of farmland to farming are not strictly enforced, and the related restrictive measures on farmland ownership must for the time being continue to be implemented. Nonetheless, the ROC will move toward easing the restrictions on farmland transactions and will strictly monitor and regulate legitimate use of farmland.

■ Taiwan's county and city governments will be asked to work out comprehensive plans for greater utilization of farmland. A system for farmland resource planning will be established and serve as the base on which a rationalized and business-like regional operations model will be formed. Farmland transfer will be encouraged to promote its effective use.

## Resource Management Policy

As a means to ensure unbroken use of water resources, resource management primarily emphasizes natural ecological conservation over the long term and environmental protection in the short term. The natural environment should have been protected by agriculture, but it was instead neglected in the ROC's overzealous pursuit of economic gains in the past. Consequently, the environment has been polluted by some farming activities, lowering agricultural productivity and incurring inestimable social costs. Agriculture must be directed at sustainable development, increasing its industrial value and quality, natural conservation and environmental protection, and ensuring harmony between man and the natural environment.

## Natural Conservation Measures to Be Adopted:

■ Conducting more in-depth surveys of biological resources and creating a data bank of natural landscapes and wildlife.

■ Protecting natural landscapes and distinctive topography, strengthening environment impact assessment work, and fortifying the management and preservation of natural resources to enable natural conservation and development to coexist in harmony.

■ Protecting rare native wildlife, promoting wildlife conservation, raising public awareness of natural conservation, joining international natural conservation organizations, strengthening international cooperation, publicizing the ROC's successes in natural conservation, investigating the transactions of endangered species parts, such as rhinoceros (for their horns) and tigers; and revising the *Wildlife Conservation Act*.

■ Strengthening afforestation, awarding and encouraging private afforestation and farmland afforestation to ensure the conservation and utilization of forest resources and maintenance of environmental ecology.

■ Strengthening the operation and management of catchment areas and the conservation of water resources.

## Environmental Protection

■ Preventing the pollution of water and land resources, establishing a monitoring system for agricultural pollution, monitoring the quality of irrigation water, guiding farmers to plant non-edible crops or to stop farming polluted farmland, and conducting chemical tests for heavy metal content in farm products from areas suspected to be polluted to ensure a safe food supply.

■ Preventing agricultural pollution, regulating the use of pesticides, promoting the use of non-pesticide techniques to prevent plant diseases and pests, developing methods for treating and using livestock wastes, accelerating the installation of pollution prevention facilities for hog farmers, and encouraging these farmers to switch to other businesses so as to reduce pollution caused by hog production.

■ Cracking down on illegal pisciculture ponds and promoting harmonious relations between pisciculture development and the environment.

## Scientific and Technological Development Policy

Scientific research and technological innovation are the driving force of agricultural productivity and quality improvement. In recent years, the Council of Agriculture has, in accordance with the Twelve-Year Long-Term National Scientific and Technological Plan, drawn up agricultural policies for scientific and technological development aimed at modernizing the agricultural sector. Efforts will be directed toward the following areas.

■ Developing advanced technology to control pollution and conserve energy in the production of value-added farm products.

■ Upgrading ROC industry by expediting market-oriented development of biotechnology and mass production techniques in coordination with the local agricultural environment.

■ Encouraging mechanized and automated production and distribution in coordination with the Plan    *183* for Automation in Agricultural, Fishery and Livestock, and Service Sectors, boosting the efficiency of farming operations, and sharpening the competitive edge of agricultural products.

- Promoting Taiwan as an international agricultural technology center in the tropics and subtropics and strengthening cooperation with technologically advanced countries with abundant resources.

## Conclusion

Industrial upgrading and transformation of the infrastructure are essential to economic development. Backed by rich experience in rapid agricultural development, the ROC regards its upcoming admission into GATT as an opportunity for agricultural reform and the dawning of a new era. The government agencies concerned with agriculture will adjust the agricultural infrastructure in coordination with the Six-Year National Development Plan and the Economic Stimulus Package. The ROC's new agricultural policy and adjustment strategy will lead to rational and effective use of agricultural resources, which in turn will ensure efficient farming operations in coordination with overall national development. Agricultural production, transportation, distribution, prices and quality will become rationalized and systematized as production is adjusted, a marketing system is established, and technological innovations achieved.

Environmental sanitation and beauty will be maintained and rural communities will be given a face-lift. Farmers will enjoy higher incomes and social status as well as a better quality of life. Private organizations will be set up to promote correct concepts of natural conservation. Only through joint conservation efforts can natural conservation, economic development, and the quality of life gain fair and equal consideration. The ROC envisions a complete transformation

of Taiwan's rural communities with business-like production, modern life styles, and natural ecology.

# Sustainable Development and Our Living Environment

Ouyang Chiao-hui

*Ouyang Chiao-hui is a professor at the Graduate Institute of Environmental Engineering of National Central University.*

A nation's living environment is vital to the life and survival of its people, and to national growth. Accordingly, the ROC government has asserted that the major goals of its environmental protection policy are "...to protect the natural environment and maintain the ecological balance to ensure the sustainable use of resources by future generations" and "...to pursue a healthy, secure and comfortable living environment for the citizenry and protect both the people and their living environment from public hazards."

The idea of "sustainable development" was first introduced in a 1987 report entitled "Our Common Future" presented to the United Nations General Assembly by the U.N. Environmental Development Commission. According to the report, sustainable development means pursuit of a global development policy that meets contemporary needs but does not impede future development or the ability of future generations to pursue developmental policies to satisfy their needs. In other words, the nations of the world have reached a consensus that environmental protection should give equal consideration to the needs of global development and prosperity.

Geographically, Taiwan is in a subtropical location characterized by steep terrain, short rivers, mountains covering two-thirds of the island's total land area, limited arable land and scarce natural resources. Fortunately, abundant rainfall, clean rivers, verdant mountains, and agreeable weather make Taiwan a pleasant place to live. In recent decades, however, Taiwan's environment has been overburdened and its resources excessively exploited as a result of rapid population growth, and the increasing concentration of population in urban areas throughout the central plains and the southern and northern parts of the island, as well as rapid growth of heavy industry, livestock raising, and the development of the transportation infrastructure. Taiwan now faces serious environmental pollution and ecological destruction, with forests being indiscriminately felled, rivers becoming fouled, and new public hazards constantly being discovered. Taiwan has lost its original beauty and in many places, local inhabitants live in a badly deteriorated environment.

Cognizant of these environmental crises, the ROC government in 1987 promulgated the *Guidelines for Environmental Protection Policy at the Present Stage.* Since then, significant progress has been achieved in certain aspects. Nevertheless, clear-cut overall environmental policies are still needed, particularly those pertaining to eliminating various environmental problems and setting the direction of future endeavors. Much more needs to be done in this regard before people can once again enjoy luxuriant mountains, clean rivers, fresh air, safe land on which to live and farm, and a balanced natural ecology, and achieve the goal of ensuring the sustainable use of resources for generations to come.

## Background and Current State of Environmental Problems

Following World War II, Taiwan was a war-exhausted society in which its six million residents lived in poverty. Nevertheless, the citizenry was generally

## Table 1.
## Evolution of Social Change, Environmental Problems and Government Policies in the Taiwan Area

### Economic, Social and Urban Development

|  | Society | Industry | Primary Technology | Dominant Energy | Transportation & Information |
|---|---|---|---|---|---|
| 1950s | social instability | industrial backwardness |  | hydroelectricity and coal | flow of goods (via roads, railroads and harbors) |
| 1960s | farming and animal husbandry on mountain slopes | (canning and sugar cane production) | food industries | petroleum | |
| 1970s | "One's living room can be a factory" | processing industries | household appliances and electronics | nuclear power | flow of people (via highways and international airports) |
| 1980s | high economic growth | (textiles, toys, computers and machines) | petrochemical and information industries | Liquid Natural Gas | |
| 1990s | industries move overseas; internationalization | | optoelectronics & robotics | conservation and diversification of energy sources | flow of information (via communication satellites and domestic airlines) |
| 2000s | emergence of a mature society | | biotechnology | new energy sources | flow of knowledge |

| | | Life | | Environment | |
|---|---|---|---|---|---|
| | Urban growth | Goals | Satisfaction | Problems | Government policies |
| 1950s 1960s | population dispersed | (being producers) | simple & industrious lifestyle | forest and mountain slope; natural environments change | |
| 1970s | population base shifts | (being consumers) defending one's life-style | minimal level of satisfaction (quantitative sufficiency) | industrial public nuisances | prevention and management of public hazards |
| 1980s | road network expanded; urban population swells | (living well) improved living standard | overall satisfaction (qualitative satisfaction) | (soil erosion) public nuisance disputes | environmental protection (environmental regulations drafted); construction of antipollution facilities (Environmental lmpact Assessments) |
| 1990s | rapid increase of motor vehicles; transportation network planned and built; for mation of suburbs around large cities | (living and creating) enjoyment of life | satisfaction based on choice (sophistication and pluralization) | (urban public nuisances) deterioration of urban environment | conservation of natural resources; national environmental protection plans |
| 2000s | public transport and shipping; multicenter metropolis and ecological cities | (cherishing happiness; symbiosis between man and his environment) enrichment of life | self-fulfillment and (simple lifestyle) | (damage to global environment) global environmental protection | life-style adjustments; education and promotion; participation in international agreements and cooperative efforts |

law-abiding and frugal. In the decades that followed, the island, in spite of numerous internal and external pressures and political setbacks, witnessed meteoric economic growth. Wise government stewardship, the hard work of the people and equal educational opportunities for all citizens combined to achieve the world-acclaimed "economic miracle." However, overemphasis on high economic growth and a higher standard of living drastically changed consumption habits and lifestyles, in the process exacerbating environmental problems. Table 1 summarizes the social changes, environmental problems and pertinent government policies in the Taiwan area since the 1950s.

Taiwan's current environmental problems are primarily the result of rapid social change, industrialization, urbanization, and development of energy, communication and information technologies; as well as changes in lifestyles and values. Among these factors, excessive exploitation and improper utilization of natural and energy resources, and changes in values are the two biggest factors contributing to the worsening of the living environment. Looking ahead to the 21st century, Taiwan must effectively resolve the environmental problems it is facing and make adjustments to cope with future needs and avoid a global environmental crisis.

Major environmental problems in the Taiwan area include serious air pollution in urban areas, severe pollution in catchment areas and rivers, a growing amount of solid waste, soil conservation problems, soil erosion, and land subsidence. The number of motor vehicles in the Taiwan area has increased four-fold in the past four years, rising from 7.7 million in 1988 to 14 million in 1992. During the same period, the number of factories has also risen by 12.4 percent, from 84,163 to 94,673. Despite strenuous efforts by environmental protection authorities, the volume of various pollutant emissions in the air have jumped from 6.39 million metric tons in 1988 to 6.51 million metric tons in 1992, an increase of 1.8 percent. The number of days when the average Air Pollution Index broke the 100 mark (signaling air quality poor enough to endanger human health) increased from 15.09 percent of the whole year in 1988 to 16.25 percent in 1992. The problem is even more serious in urban areas.

The main sources of water pollution in Taiwan are waste water discharged from factories, livestock farms, and ordinary households. Hogs in the Taiwan area numbered 9.7 million in 1992, for example, a tremendous increase from the 7.129 million of 1988. This pushed the $BOD_5$ of industrial waste water to a record 557,000 metric tons in 1992 and that of waste water from livestock farms to 287,000 metric tons. Consequently, seriously polluted sections of Taiwan's 21 major rivers increased from 13 percent of total river length in 1988 to 14.2 percent in 1992. Meanwhile, seriously polluted sections of Taiwan's 29 secondary rivers increased from 20.5 percent of total river length in 1988 to 22.7 percent in 1992. Even worse, more than a dozen catchment areas for tap water have also been polluted, thus seriously affecting the quality of drinking and irrigation water. This is a major obstacle to better quality of life for our citizenry.

Solid waste has also been increasing rapidly as a result of a swelling population and changes in lifestyles. In the Taiwan area, annual solid waste production increased from 14,475 metric tons in 1988 to 21,914 metric tons in 1992, with each person creating 0.78 kg to 1.09 kg of refuse per day. Clearly, efforts to raise environmental awareness and reduce production waste need to be intensified. Taiwan's current garbage treatment rate is 70 percent. Furthermore, in some areas, garbage dumping and treatment remains a big problem while "garbage wars" have frequently been waged in some districts. This issue must receive due attention. Ultimately, the large quantity of industrial refuse poses the greatest problem to Taiwan today. In 1992, the total volume amounted to 13.65 million tons, excluding illegally dumped waste earth from construction sites.

Plains make up 25 percent of the total land area in Taiwan, while slopelands comprise 27 percent. In the 1950s, the government encouraged farming and animal husbandry on slopelands and helped retired servicemen grow fruit, tea leaves, and vegetables on hillsides in order to ensure a sufficient food supply for the people and as a welfare measure for the former servicemen who had come to Taiwan with the government. This led to decades of environmental destruction of mountainous areas. Later on, such large-scale development projects as highway construction, urban development, and recreational facilities contributed to further deterioration. Due to a lack of careful planning, many such projects have damaged the soil, impeded the functioning of reservoirs, reduced the water retention capability of forests, caused drought, and even threatened the lives of residents in low-lying areas. Fortunately, the government later shifted its policy emphasis from slopeland farming and animal husbandry to slopeland soil conservation. According to unofficial statistics, however, there are still over 140 recreational areas—including 33 forest recreation areas and over 80 golf courses—on slopelands nationwide, and this number is still growing. They pose a great threat to the environment by causing soil erosion and impairing water quality.

Water quality is also affected by pumping underground water for aquacultural use, which has resulted in land subsidence and an inflow of sea water into lower coastal inland areas. This has not only threatened the lives and properties of local residents; it has also resulted in a loss of land and a lowering of water quality. Regrettably, no effective actions have been taken thus far to tackle this problem.

## Government Environmental Protection Efforts: An Evaluation

Environmental protection in the modern sense means that human beings should make the best use of administrative, legal, economic, scientific, and educational measures to ensure rational use of natural resources, while also cultivating a set of environmental ethics. This will prevent environmental pollution or damage, thereby achieving the global goal of sustainable development and maintaining the ecological balance. Furthermore, resource recycling and the sustainable use of resources must be promoted to safeguard the public welfare over the long term.

The world's developed nations began paying attention to environmental protection in the 1970s. To date, environmental protection has become a universal consensus and even been used as a weapon in international trade. The Republic of China got off to a later start in environmental protection, so its environmental problems are more serious than those of the developed nations. What is worse, Taiwan is a densely-populated island with rapid development in industry, business, and livestock raising, as well as a rapid increase in the number of motor vehicles, all of which make environmental problems even more difficult to resolve.

Under these circumstances, Taiwan has to pay a greater price and devote more time and effort to put its environmental management on the right track and effectively implement pollution control measures. Accordingly, the ROC government in 1987 promulgated the *Guidelines for Environmental Protection Policy at the Present Stage* as a basis for an all-out environmental protection campaign. Moreover, in August of the same year, the cabinet-level Environmental Protection Administration (EPA) was inaugurated. Later on, specialized environmental protection units and personnel were also set up in other pertinent agencies such as the Ministry of Economic Affairs, Ministry of Education, National Science Council, and Council of Agriculture. The government's efforts at environmental protection over recent years have been devoted to consolidating the legal foundation for environmental protection, strengthening the administrative system, protecting natural, social and human resources, making reasonable and effective utilization of resources, increasing government investment in public environmental protection facilities, assisting in the implementation of industrial pollution control, providing assistance to private environmental protection-related businesses, requiring environmental impact assessments, and stepping up environmental education as well as environmental research and development.

Laws and regulations pertaining to the environment are aimed at helping to solve the various environmental problems that have arisen from manufacturing and daily living activities, bringing the various social factors related to the environment under effective control, coordinating the relationship between economic development and environmental protection, and minimizing the adverse impact of human activities on the environment. Therefore, well-considered legislation serves to lay a solid foundation for sustained and consistent environmental protection efforts.

The Republic of China in recent years has made significant progress in its environmental legislation. Quite a few laws regulating air pollution, water pollution, solid waste disposal, noise levels, and the like have been revised or instituted. Many forward-looking systems have been set up, such as standards for environmental quality to be implemented in stages, a permit system for stationary pollution sources, an environmental monitoring system, and a self-declaration system. Taiwan will soon be a society where environmental protection is fully supported by a legal base. Although some laws and regulations still need to be revised or enforced, such as those regulating the disposal of toxic refuse, Taiwan has already built up a relatively complete legal framework.

A sound administrative system is imperative for successful environmental protection endeavors. The EPA in the past six years since its inauguration has gradually increased its manpower to the present size of 586 staff members. In fact, the EPA now has a total staff of 644 (173 of them are unofficial employees), excluding 438 contracted inspectors and examiners assigned to assist local environmental agencies. However, the fundamental problem remains that the ministries and commissions at the central level have not had full-fledged specialized departments to deal effectively with environmental issues. This has inevitably impeded Taiwan's overall environmental protection effort.

In contrast, the Taipei Municipal, Kaohsiung Municipal and Taiwan Provincial governments have already set up their own specialized environmental protection departments to tackle pertinent problems. These three agencies have a total of 1,508 staff members, compared with the nation's overall environmental protection manpower of 2,590 persons (excluding 26,078 sanitation workers). In the Republic of China, therefore, there is roughly one environmental protection official for every 7,500 citizens, a ratio slightly higher than that of Japan.

The environmental protection authority at the central level is responsible for policy formulation, proposing legislation, supervision, and subsidies to local governments, while the local environmental protection agencies attend to matters concerning policy implementation, since they are usually close to the various pollution sources. However, because some local government administrators have given inadequate attention to environmental protection and there exists an unbalanced distribution of environmental manpower (with central government agencies constituting one-fourth of the total environmental manpower), environmental problems in Taiwan have not been properly addressed. Corrective measures are needed in streamlining governmental administration, and more specialized personnel and units are also required by both central and local governments to handle water pollution control and sewage systems.

In an effort to protect our natural environment, the ROC government has designated 15 nature reserves, 25 state-owned forest reserves, five national parks, one wildlife conservation area, and 91 catchment areas around the country. Some of them—for instance, the five national parks—are under the management of specialized units and have special budgets, and hence have produced satisfactory results. But others such as catchment and coastal areas still fall short of effective protective measures and are suffering from pollution. This should be attributed to an unsound legal system and ineffective law enforcement. For example, although laws pertinent to the protection of slopelands have already been enacted, the problems have yet to disappear. Significant progress has been made, however, regarding the ban on hunting wildlife and trading in animal skins and horns.

Our industrial sector has already started to implement reduction, recycling, and re-use of refuse in the manufacturing process. But more needs to be done, particularly in enhancing energy efficiency and implementing more effective energy- and water-conservation, as well as waste water-recycling measures. A special environmental protection Green Mark has been designed to promote "green products" and "green consumption." However, the volume of garbage is increasing rapidly, so Taiwan has to double its efforts at garbage reduction and resource recycling while avoiding the use of plastic bags or containers.

The government has spent a large sum of money on building incinerators and acquiring garbage disposal sites to solve the garbage disposal problem. Two incinerators, in Homei and Neihu, have been completed. Four others in Hsintien, Shulin, Mucha, and Taichung are under construction. Construction of additional incinerators is currently delayed due to land acquisition problems. Overall, however, Taiwan is making good progress with a garbage treatment rate of 70 percent.

In the construction of sewer systems, however, the Republic of China lags far behind the developed nations. Specifically, only 3.5 percent of this country's towns and cities are equipped with modern sewer systems. This is in fact the main reason behind Taiwan's serious river pollution. The government is cognizant of the problem, and is constructing a comprehensive sewer system for the Tamsui River drainage system of northern Taiwan, while sewer systems in catchment and urban areas are under planning, and a "Development Plan for Sewer systems" has been drafted. To increase the country's sewer system availability rate by 2 percent, the government would have to spend NT$15 billion each year. The budget appropriated so far for this, however, is substantially less than that figure.

The government's efforts at assisting industries in pollution control over the past years have seen significant results. Progress is also being made in the control of waste water discharged by medical institutions, livestock farms and tourist hotels. Currently, about 80 percent of them have their own pollution-control facilities. To regulate other industries that are major sources of pollution, the environmental protection authorities have used a combination of suspending business operations, ordering compulsory closures, or imposing heavy fines to achieve satisfactory results. While some steps have been taken to treat industrial waste, this problem has yet to be solved; thus industrial waste continues to be a serious threat to Taiwan's environment. The use of unleaded, low-sulfur gasoline for motor vehicles is becoming popular, thus greatly alleviating air pollution problems.

One legacy of the government campaign of the 1960s to "Make your living room into a factory," which successfully encouraged housewives to work at home to help develop light industry in the ROC, was that a lot of illegal factories were built. Later on, these illegal buildings came to adversely affect the living environment of urban areas; but no effective measures have yet been undertaken to remove them.

The government has in recent years adopted a series of preferential measures to encourage more private investment in environmental protection-related businesses and help strengthen the ability and efficiency of local enterprises in controlling pollution. These measures, which include setting up special assistance units, offering low-interest loans for industries to install pollution control facilities, offering incentives to enterprises that make substantial achievements in environmental protection, and giving citations to public servants and school teachers who make contributions to environmental causes, have been relatively successful.

The practice of conducting Environmental Impact Assessments (EIAs) has been introduced by the government as the principal means for preventing any adverse impact local development projects might have on the environment. At present, as stipulated in the "Follow-up Plan for the Promotion of Environmental Impact Assessment," an EIA must be conducted by a special committee before any major development project can begin; and after the assessment procedure, there are follow-up checks and continuing supervision of the process. This system serves as an effective screening mechanism for environmental protection. Currently, the Environmental Protection Administration is drawing up a "National Environmental Development Plan" to put an end to excessive exploitation of our natural resources. This is a laudable step forward. However, the cooperation of land and resource authorities is required for its success.

Environmental protection, moreover, requires more than just governmental effort. Every member of society must be involved to assure long-term success. To promote such involvement, the fundamental task is to step up environmental education and foster environmentally ethical behavior among the general public. The government is working on this right now through, for example, efforts by the Ministry of Education to set up an environmental education center to help promote environmental education in schools at all levels. An environmental education committee has also been inaugurated to draw up "Highlights of Environmental Education" as the basis for further operation. The Environmental Protection Administration is engaged in educational and promotional campaigns for environmental causes in order to enhance the people's environmental awareness. Efforts made by the Council of Agriculture and the Ministry of Economic Affairs along this line have also produced notable results.

Currently in the ROC, more than a dozen universities and colleges have environment-related departments, which serve to supply high-caliber environmental manpower for the country. The EPA's Environmental Personnel Training Institute not only helps train specialized personnel for government agencies at all levels, but also plays an important role in upgrading the quality of Taiwan's environmental manpower. Nonetheless, in spite of all these measures, environmental education in Taiwan still requires greater effort to coordinate and integrate various agencies. Civic environmental groups can play a part in this respect. The government should therefore seek the help of environmental groups and religious groups.

More than 1,000 environmental research projects for both academic and practical purposes have been conducted over the past few years. They have contributed greatly to enhancing public understanding of environmental problems, upgrading the level of environmental technology, and streamlining government administration. In the light of the aforementioned efforts made by the government in recent years, Taiwan can boast that an all-out effort is being made by both the government and the people in environmental protection. Nevertheless, how effective these efforts prove to be remains to be seen.

Why, then, are some of Taiwan's environmental problems so difficult to solve? There are a number of answers to this question. The public has failed to make sufficient efforts to reduce waste and save energy, resulting in an ever-increasing rise in the amount of garbage and the consumption of water and electricity. The reluctance shown by citizens to utilize public transportation and delays in the construction of mass rapid transit systems in Taiwan's urban areas have contributed to a rapid increase in the number of personal motor vehicles, thus causing serious air pollution and traffic congestion in the cities. The construction of sewer systems has been delayed, allowing large volumes of raw sewage to flow into Taiwan's rivers, comprising a major source of river pollution. Although many businesses have installed pollution-control facilities, they have failed to put these facilities into full operation so far, or at times have simply chosen not to use them. As a result of inadequate attention paid to industrial waste, waste earth left by construction projects and other industrial waste materials are dumped randomly, creating not only environmental but also social problems. And finally, the failure of the government to enforce the pertinent laws for the protection of the natural environment has resulted in such problems as indiscriminate reclamation of slopelands, soil erosion, and poor water conservation. For example, excessive pumping of underground water by aquaculturalists in the coastal areas has caused serious land subsidence and damaged coastal areas. Clearly, "Prevention is better than cure." To eliminate the problems mentioned above, the government should strengthen its promotional campaigns and make forward-looking plans.

## The Evolution of Taiwan's Environmental Problems

In view of the history of environmental problems in advanced nations and the solutions employed, it is evident that a nation's efforts at environmental protection are closely connected with its living standard and degree of economic development. More specifically, in the early stage of economic development, before pollution is really serious, the government cannot afford the cost of environmental protection measures, and the people are unaware of the potential seriousness of the consequences of environmental pollution, so potential environmental problems are generally ignored. But once the economy is strong and people are materially well off enough to demand a better quality of life, environmental pollution may already be out of control. It is at this stage that environmental protection becomes a major concern.

This is true in the ROC where both the causes and solutions for environmental problems have evolved step by step over a period of time. At present, major pollution sources are the targets of pollution control measures taken by the government. Unified emission standards have been set to control pollution nationwide. However, different areas often face different pollution situations, and thus in some areas these standards might not meet local needs. In the future, therefore, different standards have to be set for different areas depending on their respective conditions, and local governments should also be allowed to set standards based on their individual requirements.

The existing environment-related laws and regulations and pollution control measures were designed mainly with industrial pollution in mind. In the future, however, pollution caused by everyday sources such as automobiles, household waste water, noise, vibration, ecological imbalance in the urban areas, and solid waste will all be targets. Since many of such pollution sources are mobile and therefore more difficult to control, the best solution would be for the general public to change from its current consumption culture and way of living to a more frugal and simple lifestyle.

Pollution control efforts by industry should be aimed at saving energy and resources. The government must be strict with local industries that have so far refused to implement pollution control in their factories, discharging raw waste into water sources, and thus polluting the environment. Since pollution control is costly, manufacturers should be compelled to improve their manufacturing processes to reduce pollution, find replacement raw materials that cause no or at least less pollution, introduce low-pollution technology and switch to the manufacture of products with high added value, adopt effective energy-saving measures, recycle usable materials to avoid resource waste, and improve personnel training, particularly for production and pollution control.

In almost every country, environmental protection starts with pollution control, then pollution prevention, and finally the creation of a comfortable living environment. Therefore, active environmental planning and management in land use, manufacturing, and the living environment are essential for creating a healthy and sound society. Furthermore, in making environmental impact assessments, the views of local residents, the businesses affected, and the pertinent government agencies must be considered.

Social demand for a better living environment increases with the economic growth and material affluence a society attains. At first the public is primarily concerned with having a safe and healthy living environment. Then, as individual and overall material attainment progresses, demand shifts toward the goals of achieving a sanitary and pollution-free place to live. This is followed by the need for quiet and peaceful surroundings. But as a society reaches the highest levels of economic and material achievement, people are no longer content with merely minimizing pollution and maximizing convenience, but instead start to seek a refined, cultured, tasteful, and comfortable environment in which to live. Government long-term environmental planning has to take into account this progression of people's demands.

In recent years, as a result of expanding urbanization and development, much of Taiwan's natural beauty has been damaged or has disappeared. Taiwan must adopt a three-pronged strategy to upgrade the quality of life in three areas: pollution control, natural conservation, and environment creation. It must constantly keep in mind that the creation of a comfortable living environment should be in harmony with the local natural conditions, historical background, cultural values, and the special features of each community. This, however, requires the initiative and concerted efforts of local people themselves.

## Future Efforts

Taiwan's social evolution over the past four decades or so suggests that its environmental problems have actually resulted from long-term changes in economic and social conditions, urban development, lifestyles and values. Naturally, then, improvement in environmental quality can by no means be attained overnight. By the 21st century, people will demand an even higher quality of life, and environmental problems will be an issue of yet greater global concern; so the Republic of China must have an international vision in its environmental protection policy.

Undeniably, this country has in the past few years made remarkable progress, particularly in pushing for environmental legislation, offering assistance to environmental organizations, and fostering technological upgrading. The general public today is much more aware of and concerned about environmental issues. This has broadened and brightened the prospects for environmental protection in Taiwan. However, in practice, what should be done to meet the people's increasing demand for higher environmental quality, and to promote a comprehensive and on-going environmental protection and natural conservation campaign for the sustainable development of the living environment? A number of concrete measures are worthy of consideration. First, Taiwan needs to establish a comprehensive national environmental planning and management system to safeguard the environmental and ecological balance and create a comfortable living environment. Under such a system, a development project can be approved only if it is determined not to have adverse impact on the natural environment and ecological balance. Historical relics belong to all the citizenry and should be properly preserved. Proper planning should be made to make the living environment not only comfortable, but also refined and cultured.

Another step would be to increase environmental manpower and strengthen the administrative system at the local level. This would involve recruiting more environmental specialists for local-level agencies, particularly those at the county and city levels or below, which have more industries under their jurisdiction, so as to help them more adequately tackle environment-related problems. It would also involve consolidation, in terms of both organization and manpower, of the units responsible for the construction of sewer systems at the local government level, particularly at the county and city level, in order to accelerate sewer system construction, for effective control of waste water.

Taiwan should also institutionalize environmental laws and regulations and revise old ones to establish the rule of the law at every level of society. The first step toward this is effectively implementing the existing laws and regulations. This can be encouraged by evaluating the efficacy of environmental protection efforts by local governments. The evaluation results can then be used as a major consideration in deciding the amount of subsidies provided them, thus encouraging local administrators to attach greater importance to environmental issues. In addition, Taiwan must put an end to excessive development of slopelands and coastal areas, unauthorized pumping of underground water for pisciculture, indiscriminate disposal of solid waste into rivers, and illegal dumping of waste earth left by construction projects.

It is not just the current thinking of local government officials that needs changing. Taiwan must also raise the environmental protection awareness and foster environmental ethics of the citizenry. This involves stepping up environmental education, enhancing popular understanding of environmental protection and natural conservation, and cultivating environmental ethics among the populace to make environmental protection an integral part of everyone's daily life. People should be encouraged to actively participate in educational activities and promotional campaigns by joining environmental groups or activities and assist in the establishment of local, regional, and national environmental groups. Providing the people with sufficient environmental information is also essential. This would involve setting up a nationwide online information system.

Beyond informing the citizenry about the need to protect the environment, Taiwan must advocate a new lifestyle that conserves energy and resources. To offer a reasonable alternative to today's wasteful transportation practices, the government must accelerate the completion of mass rapid transit systems in metropolitan areas and introduce electric buses and motor vehicles to curb air pollution. Furthermore, it should advocate reasonable water consumption practices by industry and the public, while developing water-conserving sanitary facilities. Taiwan must also encourage the design of energy-saving houses, offer loans only to buyers of houses meeting the energy-saving requirements, as well as encourage the purchase of energy-efficient household appliances. Green consumption, resource recycling, and market acceptance of the environmental protection Green Mark designed for environmental-friendly products should be promoted. Local governments should also make reasonable use of rate hikes to curb unnecessary energy and resource consumption.

Perhaps the most precious resource that is in immediate need of quantitative and qualitative protection is water. To this end, Taiwan must fortify protection of catchment areas and slopelands, and carry out reforestation projects to facilitate soil conservation. Development and construction projects inside catchment areas must be severely restricted to ensure water quality, and utilization of some of the multipurpose reservoirs for purposes other than supplying water must be curtailed. This means limiting recreational activities and restricting the influx of people in reservoir areas in order to prolong the life spans of reservoirs and ensure water quality.

In addition, a registration system should be instituted for pumping underground water under which overpumping would be strictly forbidden, to protect underground water resources and better safeguard the lives and properties of the surrounding residents. The government should purchase privately held land within government-designated catchment areas where development is restricted or compensate the owners for their losses. In addition, consumers of water coming from this area should share the expense of water conservation and maintaining water quality. Furthermore, a specialized institute should be set up to conduct research on the development and management of running water. Its budget should be subsidized by the general public under the "users pay" principle.

Setting environmental standards should start at the micro level, and then gradually expand to the macro level. Standards should be set for smoke, dust, sulfur oxide, and nitrogen oxide emissions to curb air pollution, and follow-up checks should be conducted. Standards should also be set regarding energy efficiency in daily living, manufacturing, and transportation, as well as government energy policies, so as to reduce carbon dioxide emissions. In addition, the government should formulate and carry out energy and resource development policies aimed at alleviating environmental problems, strictly enforce laws and regulations governing such environmental issues as land subsidence, soil depletion, logging, the extinction of plant and animal species, and the dumping of hazardous waste in developing nations, and foster the concept of symbiotic ecology in urban areas by preserving an ecological and environmental balance there, thus making cities a more comfortable place to live.

One of the most pressing infrastructure needs in improving the living environment of Taiwan involves the construction of a sewer system to ensure effective control of waste water in urban areas. This construction should take place step by step while taking into consideration the river ecology and environmental conditions of each area to ensure good water quality and ecological balance. The established policy of combined waste-water treatment facilities in new communities is worth continuing while the current technology is improved. Taiwan should also study the feasibility of temporarily building, in areas without modern sewer systems, treatment facilities for human waste to be located at sites reserved for future waste water treatment plants. Finally, Taiwan should recruit more manpower and introduce advanced technology in constructing sewer systems, as well as upgrade the quality of pipelines and equipment produced locally for undertaking such work.

In the future, Taiwan must adhere to the principle that "environmental protection takes precedence over economic development," by keeping foreign trade, investment and financial activities in line with the objective of sustainable development. Furthermore, the government must always bear in mind the global aim of sustainable development in formulating policies and setting up business management, energy utilization, and resource management systems. To this end, Taiwan must set up an "environmental cost system" to regularly "tally the accounts of environmental resources" by periodically assessing the quantity and quality of such environmental resources as lands, forests, rivers, lakes, and petrochemical fuels.

Ultimately, the government must encourage the industrial and agricultural sectors to fulfill their respective responsibilities for protecting the environment. This means ensuring that all investment and development projects are in accord with our society's long-term and overall interests, and that environmental impact assessment is conducted in advance of such projects. It also means making sure that all development projects proceed in compliance with laws and regulations pertaining to environmental protection so as to lessen environmental pollution.

The manufacturing process must receive similar scrutiny. Assessments should be made of the environmental impact of the manufacturing, transport, sales, and uses of a product before a product is allowed to be manufactured. The government should also conduct further research into the application of such natural energies as solar energy, solid waste heat, and wind to manufacturing production in order to reduce air pollution from the emission of sulfur oxide, nitrogen oxide, and carbon dioxide. Taiwan should also develop advanced manufacturing technologies and more efficient mechanical and electrical equipment that will not be detrimental to the environment, assist manufacturers and farmers in obtaining production equipment and creating a work environment that conforms to environmental protection standards, and help them provide their employees with proper environmental education programs.

To achieve the long-term environmental protection goals, Taiwan must look beyond its own borders by pursuing an international trade and investment policy that can ensure sustainable development through cooperation. This means emulating the administrative and technological experiences of advanced nations in the field of environmental protection, and promoting related cooperation and exchange programs to upgrade environmental protection capability. Taiwan must also make sure that its international economic cooperation and development projects are aimed at sustainable development, and can offer technological assistance, personnel training and financial support to developing nations in their environmental protection endeavors.

## Conclusion

Environmental problems often result from long-term neglect of the need for environmental protection, and therefore tend to be too complicated to solve in a short time. In the Republic of China, thanks to collaboration between the public and private sectors, significant progress has been made, particularly in the reduction of public hazards. Much remains to be done, however, in the areas of water pollution, air pollution, solid waste disposal and the protection of the natural environment. The ROC should continue to take bolder, more effective action based on the future needs of the natural environment, so as to ensure sustainable development by making environmental protection an integral part of every citizen's daily life, strengthening pollution control measures, protecting its natural environment, and creating a comfortable living environment. To be sure, as a member of the global village, the people of the Republic of China are committed to the protection of a beautiful Earth.

**Bibliography**

*Guidelines for Environmental Protection Policy at the Present Stage.* Environmental Protection Task Force, Executive Yuan, October 1987.

*The Environmental Protection Administration Administrative Over-view*. EPA, March 1993.

*Key Points of Environmental Education*, Environmental Protection Group. Ministry of Education, June 1992.

*The Concept of Environmental System*. Ministry of Education, Japan, March 1991.

*The Planning of Environmental Protection Policy*. Ouyang Chiao-hui, June 1992.

*The Problem and Solution Strategy on the Protection of Water Quality*. Ouyang Chiao-hui, June 1992.

# V.
# Mainland Affairs
# Policy

Previous page: SEF Secretary-General Chiao Jen-ho meets ARATS Deputy Secretary-General Sun Yafu during the 1993 cross-Straits talks in Taipei.

# Building a Democracy for Unification

Lee Teng-hui
*World Affairs*
Winter 1993

Editor's Note: This is a statement released by Lee Teng-hui as president of the Republic of China when he terminated in May 1991 the "Period of National Mobilization for Suppression of the Communist Rebellion," a feature that was used to justify many previous autocratic measures taken by the Taipei government. The following is reprinted from *President Lee Teng-hui's Selected Addresses and Messages* (Taipei: Government Information Office, 1992), 56-61.

*Lee Teng-hui is President of the Republic of China.*

TAIPEI, Taiwan—The Republic of China is going through a rapid political transformation that will be no less dramatic in its consequences than the current transformation of Eruope. Though this process may seem somewhat perplexing to some abroad, my countrymen and I know exactly what we are doing and where we are going.

Democratization characterizes our present endeavor, reunification with mainland China is most certainly our future aim. These two goals are not unrelated.

On May 1, the "Period of National Mobilization for Suppression of the Commuist Rebellion" was officially terminated, allowing us to deal with Mainland affairs on a more pragmatic basis.

The "Temporary Provisions Effective During the Period of Communist Rebellion," originally passed in

1948, were also abolished, thus paving the way for further democratization in my country.

As a result of constitutional changes first proposed at a meeting last July of the National Affairs Conference — a roundtable of all political forces in the Republic of China — voters will be able to directly elect a new National Assembly by the end of the year and a new Legislative Yuan (Congress) by 1993.

We have also adopted "Guidelines for National Unification" which affirm our determination to reunify China.

The "mobilization period" began in the late 1940s in response to military threats from the Chinese Communists that endangered the survival of the Republic. For more than four decades, emergency measures instituted during the mobilization period have contributed significantly to our stability and security.

We are increasingly convinced that we must not seek the reunification of our country through a military solution. We believe that freedom, democracy and prosperity have become our most valuable and powerful assets. We must earn the recognition and support of our compatriots in Mainland China by demonstrating what we can achieve in Taiwan in economic and especially political terms.

This was why I made it clear in my May 20, 1990 inauguration speech that I would soon terminate the mobilization period and would do everything in my power to ensure that the task of constitutional reform would be completed within two years.

About one month after I assumed office, the National Affairs Conference met. After the conference produced its recommendations, the ruling party established, under my instruction, a "Constitutional Reform Planning Committee" to carefully study all important constitutional issues.

The committee worked for eight months, during which time a broad range of views were solicited from numerous experts and members of the public. It then delivered an outline of constitutional modifications to those deputies of the National Assembly who are also members of the ruling party, so that these deputies could draft the clauses of the constitutional amendments for presentation to the Assembly.

After intensive deliberation and three readings, a final version of the draft was approved. In all, 10 articles were passed during the first stage of constitutional reform. They provide a legal basis for upcoming comprehensive parliamentary elections. In any other country, it might not be necessary to divide the work on constitutional reform into two stages. This is, however, not the case for us.

The Constitution of the Republic of China was democratically adopted in Nanking when our government was still located on the Mainland. Therefore, we feel it is our duty to preserve the constitution's integrity and extend it to the entire Chinese people when our country is reunified.

We take this position not with any self-interested considerations, but based on our unyielding commitment to constitutionalism. The central parliamentary bodies defined in our constitution were designed, quite understandably, for the whole of China, and it is not feasible for us to hold comprehensive parliamentary elections in the Taiwan area based on the original scale and composition envisioned in that constitution.

Therefore, we must first make some necessary adjustments through the amendments from the first stage of reform to enable the voters of my country to elect, for instance, the Second National Assembly — which will work on constitutional reform with the support of the most recent popular sentiment.

The second stage of our constitutional reforms is crucial and complicated. Many of the vital constitutional issues, such as organization of central and local governments, the election process for the presidency, organization of the government and the legislature, and so forth, must all be thoroughly examined to see if further revisions are required.

It is my belief that the foundations for further national development and eventual unification can only be laid by firmly institutionalizing democratization and broadening political participation.

Besides more smoothly facilitating the process of constitutional reform, termination of the mobilization period on May 1, 1991, also demonstrates our sincere desire to improve relations with Mainland authorities.

In October of 1990, five months after my inauguration, the "Guidelines for National Unification" were adopted to express our hope that, from this point on, both sides of the Taiwan Straits will uphold the principles of peace, reason, parity and reciprocity; that both will work to create an environment conducive to congenial interaction. In such an environment, we can all strive for reconstruction of a reunified China characterized by freedom, democracy and equitable distribution of wealth.

But we cannot do it alone. Despite all the pragmatic initiatives we have recently made, the Mainland authorities have yet to respond with any sincere and concrete measures. They have not even echoed our call to give up the use of force to achieve unification.

I am naturally not expecting any magic or instant solution. In fact, it is only prudent and responsible for us to advocate a gradual reduction of hostility between Taiwan and the Chinese Mainland, leading to a step-by-step building of mutual understanding, trust and goodwill.

I would like to see China reunified at the earliest possible opportunity, but I will not give up my insistence on guaranteeing the welfare of the entire Chinese people, nor will I ever sacrifice the security of the people in the Taiwan area.

I must reiterate that reunification cannot be separated from our commitment to democracy and from our concern for the welfare of the people on both sides of the Taiwan Straits. This is clearly stated in the "Guidelines for National Unification," which says: "The unification of China should be for the welfare of all its people and not be subject to partisan conflict."

It is imperative that the Mainland authorities appreciate that what divides the Mainland and Taiwan is really not the Taiwan Straits. It is the gap between what we can each offer to our people with our two opposing sets of economic and political institutions.

As we now open this new and historic page, my government is ready to share with people and authorities of the Mainland the lessons of our four decades of the "Taiwan experience."

It is exactly for this reason that we are currently embarking on further economic progress with the "Six-Year National Development Plan" and further democratization with constitutional reform. We are building a prosperous democracy — not just for the Taiwan area itself, but for the whole of China. We are building a democracy for unification. That is my presidential commitment.

Copyright 1991, by *New Perspective Quarterly*; distributed by Los Angeles Times Syndicate

# ROC Policy toward Mainland China: Planning and Prospects

Huang Kun-huei

The Republic of China's mainland policy has a far-reaching impact on the survival and development of the ROC, and is thus one of the ROC government's most important administrative programs. The ROC's mainland policy is designed to build a democratic, free, prosperous, and unified new China. The first step in creating the necessary conditions for China's unification is to promote relations between the two sides of the Taiwan Straits. This can be accomplished only if a consensus is reached among the Chinese people and the two sides can work together.

*Huang Kun-huei is chairman of the Mainland Affairs Council, Executive Yuan.*

## Evolution and Development of Cross-straits Relations

Cross-Straits relations are closely intertwined with developments in the international community and with conditions in Taiwan and the mainland. To fully understand the relationship between the two sides of the Taiwan Straits, one must first analyze the external environment.

Recent dramatic changes in the international community have signaled the direction of global trends that will shape the future of mankind. The greatest changes in the international community have been the dissolution of the Soviet Union, which ended 40-odd years of Cold War between the two superpowers, and the collapse of the communist regimes in Eastern Europe, which contributed to an unprecedented surge in the tides of freedom and democracy.

International focus has shifted from political and ideological issues to areas such as economics, environmental protection, and human rights. The armed confrontation of the Cold War era has given way to dialogue and cooperation on both a global and regional scale.

The Republic of China is a member of the international community, and changes in that community have naturally had a profound effect on the ROC's development. The ROC's zeal and steady progress in promoting democracy and constitutional reform in recent years have been in line with global trends and have earned worldwide acclaim. President Lee Teng-hui's proposal to construct a collective security system in the Asia-Pacific region is regarded highly by many countries and has spurred discussion throughout the region. Furthermore, the ROC's timely Six-Year National Development Plan has helped boost the world economy, and many countries have expressed willingness to participate in the plan. The ROC's efforts in environmental protection, conservation, and copyright protection are also in line with international trends and have achieved noteworthy results.

The Chinese communist regime is one of the few remnants of the communist world. The Chinese communists can no longer close the door on democracy for the mainland and control an awakened Chinese people. They have no choice but to introduce a capitalist market economy, though they try to hide it behind slogans of "upholding Marxism-Leninism and Mao Tse-tung thought," "socialism with Chinese characteristics" and "politically left, economically right." These phrases are intended to gloss over ideological contradictions and palliate uneasy minds; and "preventing peaceful evolution" and "adhering to communist leadership" clearly show that the Chinese communist authorities have heard the death knell of communism.

Relations between the two sides of the Taiwan Straits have developed apace over the last six years. By the end of 1993, the ROC government on Taiwan had adopted more than 60 different measures to stimulate cross-Straits interaction—and with stunning results. Residents of the Taiwan area have made over 5.79 million trips to the Chinese mainland. Indirect trade between the two sides has totaled more than US$30.6 billion. And over 74 million letters and 92 million telephone calls and telegrams have been exchanged. Private exchanges between the two sides are clearly growing, and they are receiving international attention.

News of the ROC government's move in November 1987 to allow Taiwan residents to visit their relatives in the Chinese mainland made other Asian countries stand up and take notice. In March 1991, the ROC government passed the *Guidelines for National Unification* to gradually build a democratic, free, prosperous, and unified China under the principles of reason, peace, parity and reciprocity. The Guidelines promptly received recognition and support from the international community.

In April 1993, the talks between Koo Chen-fu and Wang Tao-han, heads of the two private intermediary agencies (the ROC's Straits Exchange Foundation and the Chinese mainland's Association for Relations Across the Taiwan Straits) were widely noted, and intensively covered by international media. According to the ROC's Government Information Office, Ministry of Foreign Affairs, and Mainland Affairs Council, foreign media released over 1,000 news reports on the event in the weeks before and after the talks. Most of the commentaries viewed the talks as a constructive force in the development of cross-Straits relations. The political statement issued at the last G-7 summit also indirectly affirmed the positive effect of the talks on security in the Asia-Pacific region.

Cross-Straits relations can be characterized by the following statements.

• The political standoff between the two sides has not yet been completely eliminated, and the Chinese communists remain hostile.

• Private exchanges have become more common since the two sides lifted restrictions on such exchanges. Nevertheless, a few of the exchange activities show signs of spinning out of control.

• It is difficult for the people on the Chinese mainland to learn about Taiwan because of the communists' tight control over the dissemination of information. For the same reason, Taiwan residents lack a true understanding of the Chinese mainland because Taiwan's media are unable to obtain true and meaningful information about the mainland.

• The Koo-Wang talks have institutionalized the communication channels between the two private intermediaries, an important step in the advancement of cross-Straits relations. Whether or not such progress can be maintained depends on negotiations following the Koo-Wang talks.

• The international community asks that the ROC on Taiwan take responsibility and fulfill its international obligations, but fails to pay due respect to the ROC. This imbalance obscures the fact that the two sides of the Taiwan Straits are politically equal but separately governed entities. Asking the international community to recognize this reality and treat the ROC fairly, and getting the Chinese communists to face up to this reality, are major tasks in the development of cross-Straits relations.

224    Since international developments and conditions in the relationship of the two sides of the Taiwan

Straits are consistent with the principles of reason, peace, parity and reciprocity outlined in the *Guidelines for National Unification*, we are confident that the goals set forth in our mainland policy and our strategies for attaining them represent the only real chance for the unification of China. Due to the efforts of the ROC government, cross-Straits relations have changed radically over the past six years. Taiwan-mainland relations can continue to seek out new horizons once the Chinese communists abandon their dated ideas and methodology and boldly accept our tiered plan for national unification.

## Basic Position and Principles of the ROC's Mainland Policy

Drawing upon the collective wisdom and will of the people, and after exhaustive research, the National Unification Council under the Office of the President drafted the *Guidelines for National Unification* in February 1991. After receiving approval by the Executive Yuan Council, the Guidelines have become the highest principles of the ROC's mainland policy. The spirit of the Guidelines evinces the ROC's dedication to reunifying China under the Three Principles of the People. The Guidelines are timely, and are based upon the principles of reason, peace, parity and reciprocity. The Guidelines state that national unification should be for the welfare of the people; that in the process of reunification, Chinese culture should be promoted, human dignity safeguarded, basic human rights protected, and democracy put into practice; and that reunification should be divided into short-term, mid-term and long-term phases to gradually eliminate hostility between the two sides and build a democratic, free, prosperous and unified China. The *Guidelines for National Unification* is thus a major document that bases its goals and ideals in pragmatism and feasibility.

The Guidelines have helped the Chinese people to understand the goals, guiding principles, and various steps of the present mainland policy, and they have played a leading role in the development of cross-Straits relations.

The Chinese communist authorities remain hostile to the ROC. They are reluctant to renounce the use of force against Taiwan and face the fact that the ROC is an equivalent political entity. They have also worked hard to exclude the ROC from the international community. Therefore, in accordance with the Guidelines, the ROC government has limited the cross-Straits relations to private exchanges so as to distinguish the Chinese people from the Chinese communist regime in order to build mutual understanding between the people of the two sides. Limiting exchanges to the private sectors also ensures that the Chinese communists will have no chance of endangering the safety and well-being of the people of Taiwan.

Drawing upon the German idea of a Gemeinschaft or a closely knit community, President Lee Teng-hui recently encouraged the people of Taiwan to identify themselves with the Republic of China, build a consensus, take a firm position, develop the nation, and work for unification. Consensus-building, therefore, is a high priority in implementing mainland policy.

Premier Lien Chan also proclaimed in his March 2, 1993 administrative report to the Legislative Yuan:

"We will never give up the ideal of national reunification, nor will we ever seek a unification in form only while glossing over real differences. We truly wish to enter as soon as possible into the medium-term phase of mutual trust and cooperation as mapped out in the *Guidelines for National Unification* and to work for the collective interests of the Chinese people."

226

Premier Lien's remarks not only indicate that fundamental policies of the mainland program must be compatible with the scheme set forth in the *Guidelines for National Unification*, but also specifically express the sincerity and confidence the people of the Republic of China have in achieving the goals therein.

## Concrete Results of Efforts

The ROC government's mainland program has progressed steadily. Whereas the two sides of the Taiwan Straits were completely separated in the past, Taiwan residents now make 1.5 million visits to the Chinese mainland every year. Indirect trade between the two sides has grown from nothing to more than US$9 billion by 1993, and cross-Straits news and cultural exchanges have progressed from no contact at all to frequent exchanges. Cross-Straits interactions are obviously growing in frequency, in line with the goals of the ROC government's mainland policy.

It would be difficult to describe in detail each and every specific result of the government's mainland program over the past six years. Listed below are some of the more important accomplishments.

First, a number of agencies have been set up to carry out the mainland program. In October 1990, the Office of the President set up the National Unification Council (NUC) to advise the president on matters concerning national unification. In January 1991, the Executive Yuan set up the Mainland Affairs Council (MAC) as a special body to handle mainland affairs. In February 1991 the Straits Exchange Foundation (SEF) was founded, with government authorization, as a private intermediary agency to deal with mainland affairs. The establishment of these governmental and private organizations has laid the groundwork for implementing the ROC's national unification policy.

Second, the ROC government has decided upon the guiding principles of its mainland policy. As mentioned above, the NUC drafted the *Guidelines for National Unification* in February 1991. The Guidelines were then submitted to the Executive Yuan Council, which approved and passed them the following month. The goals and principles set forth in the Guidelines represent the government's consistent position on national unification. The process and pace outlined in the Guidelines take the security and well-being of the Taiwan area fully into account. The Guidelines are thus a more specific and more pragmatic extension of the government's established national unification policy.

Third, the handling of cross-Straits affairs has become more institutionalized. The ROC has insisted upon maintaining its juridical sovereignty in all interactions between the two sides of the Taiwan Straits while upholding the principles of reason, peace, parity and reciprocity. As a result, the ROC has been able to react speedily and appropriately to any sudden disputes or conflicts (e.g., the Ying Wang Hao incident, the Min Shih Yü incident, the Hsia Kung Chi No. 2 incident, and the dispute over the Chinese communists' demand that Taiwan residents must submit photocopies of their household registration when applying for mainland travel passes). An institutionalized procedure for handling cross-Straits incidents has thus evolved.

Fourth, the legal framework in which cross-Straits exchanges can take place has been mapped out. Regulating private exchanges between the two sides of the Taiwan Straits is one of the ROC's major policy objectives. The first legal document specifically covering such exchanges was the *Statute Governing the Relations Between People of the Taiwan Area and the Mainland Area*. The statute provides an adequate legal framework for interaction and private exchanges between the two sides. In accordance with the Statutes, the MAC has worked with various other government offices to draft and promulgate 18 sets of permit regulations designed to bring order to cross-Straits exchanges.

Fifth, negotiations on practical matters represent a new page in the history of cross-Straits interactions. The first meeting between the two heads of private intermediary agencies from the two sides was held in Singapore in April 1993. During the Koo-Wang talks, the ROC government stuck to its established positions and policies and did its best to avoid political traps set by the Chinese communists. The Koo-Wang talks went smoothly and concluded with the signing of four technical agreements. Nevertheless, the signing of the agreements represents merely the establishment of consensus. Only full implementation of the agreements can really denote progress in cross-Straits relations.

Following technical negotiations in Peking and Amoy in August and November of 1993, the ROC proposed holding a round of talks in Taipei to demonstrate the ROC's sincerity in fulfilling the agreements. This proposal was made in the spirit of the Agreement on the Establishment of Systematic Liaison and Communication Channels Between the SEF and ARATS. The ROC will continue to implement the four agreements signed at the end of the Koo-Wang talks in order to establish an order for private exchanges, to resolve the disputes growing out of the cross-Straits exchanges, and to ultimately eliminate hostility and build mutual trust between the two sides of the Taiwan Straits.

Lastly, the ROC has implemented a program for dealing with changes in the status of Hong Kong and

Macao. The Department of Hong Kong and Macao Affairs was set up under the Mainland Affairs Council when the latter was founded in January 1991, replacing the Hong Kong and Macao Affairs Task Force under the Executive Yuan. Hong Kong and Macao are due to be turned over to the Chinese mainland in 1997 and 1999. In response to the coming change, the MAC, working extensively with other government agencies, has drafted a Current Agenda for Hong Kong and Macao. The plan, approved by the Executive Yuan, is now being implemented.

Cross-Straits relations have progressed rapidly and dramatically, making it difficult to recount each of the government's initiatives vis-à-vis the Chinese mainland. Generally speaking, cross-Straits relations are moving in the direction set forth in the *Guidelines for National Unification* and the concrete results of the government's mainland policy are increasingly apparent.

## Current Problems and Orientation of Future Efforts

Despite initial progress, however, cross-Straits relations are still plagued by several tenacious problems. First, as yet no absolute public consensus on mainland policy exists in the ROC on Taiwan. Second, news and information do not yet flow freely between the two sides of the Taiwan Straits. Third, the Chinese communists have yet to respond positively to ROC initiatives, and, fourth, the gap between the ROC's mainland policy and actual implementation remains to be closed.

The ROC government, of course, follows the *Guidelines for National Unification* when dealing with mainland affairs. However, a public consensus has yet to be formed on national unification. A few partisan voices still advocate Taiwan independence and do not accept government policies, hampering the implementation of the mainland policy. Dissenters boycotted the Koo-Wang talks and caused problems for the MAC and the SEF. Thanks to the clear instructions of Premier Lien Chan and the trust and support of the majority of the people, many obstacles have been overcome. Nonetheless, the lack of public consensus on mainland policy weakens the ROC government's efforts to fight the ideological war waged by the Chinese communists.

Matters are further complicated by the lack of information and news exchanges between the two sides. The Taiwan area and the Chinese mainland have been separated for over 40 years. Enhancing mutual understanding is the first step towards unification. Full and free exchange of information is essential. The ROC government has allowed Taiwan-based media to cover events in the Chinese mainland area, but the Chinese communists have imposed many restrictions on Taiwan-based journalists traveling in the Chinese mainland. This form of indirect censorship has made it virtually impossible for the Taiwan public to have timely access to information about the mainland. In addition, the Chinese communists have controlled mainland media visits to Taiwan and censored reports on developments here.

Such practices are typical of the Chinese communists' negative response to our show of goodwill. The ROC has done its best to obtain a positive response from the Chinese communists. For example, the ROC terminated the Period of National Mobilization for Suppression of the Communist Rebellion, and publicly recognized the Chinese communists as a political entity governing the mainland area. However, the Chinese communists have not as yet renounced the use of force against Taiwan. They also deny the ROC's status as an equal political entity, thwart its efforts to join the international community, and indirectly obstruct many of its activities. Moreover, they have continued to tout their "one China, two systems" policy and demand that the ROC allow direct postal, transportation and commercial links with them. On August 31, 1993, they even released a hostile white paper titled *The Taiwan Question and the Reunification of China*. Such acts have hindered cross-Straits exchanges and the unification of China.

In view of this situation, the ROC must strengthen the implementation of its mainland policies. The government's mainland policies have been devised and implemented in accordance with the *Guidelines for National Unification*. The drafting of mainland policies, however, is subject to limitations imposed by considerations of national security and the people's welfare. Some people have responded very emotionally to how cross-Straits affairs are being handled. They make a big stir over the gap between their expectations and the government's implementation of mainland policies, making the government the butt of unnecessary criticism and further hampering government operations.

Implementation of the mainland policy over the past year has made it possible for cross-Straits relations to develop in a stable and orderly environment. While no major breakthroughs were achieved in the face of Chinese communist obstruction, the ROC's mainland policies have played a dominant role in cross-Straits interaction and have kept relations moving along the path mapped out in the *Guidelines for National Unification*. To build upon this foundation, the government will solidify its positions, enhance private exchanges, strengthen strategic planning, and promote public consensus.

The government has repeatedly asserted the public that national unification must be predicated on the safety and welfare of the people of Taiwan. The *Guidelines for National Unification* take these preconditions into account. Developing cross-Straits relations in accordance with the phased approach set forth in the Guidelines is the best guarantee for our safety and welfare, and immunizes the ROC against the united front tactics of the Chinese communists. The people and government of the ROC ought to work hand in hand in developing the economy, pushing for constitutional reform, and seeking domestic stability and prosperity.

Certainly there is no need to bend to the whims of the Chinese communists by revising the positions and principles set forth in the *Guidelines for National Unification*. On the contrary, the ROC should solidify its position and assume a leading role in the development of cross-Straits relations.

Under the *Guidelines for National Unification*, progress in cross-Straits relations in the present phase should focus on enhancing private exchanges and reciprocity. The ROC's open policy toward the mainland over the past six years has contributed greatly to the growth of private cross-Straits exchanges. In the future, more planning efforts should be made to make private exchanges an active catalyst in promoting mutual understanding and to insure that all such exchanges are carried out in an orderly and mutually beneficial fashion.

Many imponderables remain in the volatile cross-Straits relationship. The only way for the ROC to maintain its initiative and strategic advantage is to set its sights on the future and come up with forward-looking policies. Thus the ROC will continue to focus its efforts on setting up a flexible policy framework, systematically using a large pool of information, identifying emerging trends, and strengthening policy research and planning work.

Mainland policy is inseparable from national identity. The public's identification with the Republic of China is the most important source of support for the government's mainland policy. The issue of national identity belongs to a level higher than that of mainland policy. To win public support, each specific mainland policy must be patiently and thoroughly promoted, and channels for public input must also be widened.

## Cross-straits Relations: Prospects

Development of cross-Straits relations depends on constructive interaction between the two sides. The ROC has proposed its *Guidelines for National Unification* and has pushed for exchanges and reciprocal measures based on them, in hopes of enhancing mutual understanding and dissolving hostility. The ROC has also taken the initiative by announcing the termination of the Period of National Mobilization for Suppression of the Communist Rebellion and advocating a reasonable and peaceful way to unify the nation. The fact remains, however, that the ROC government cannot unilaterally improve relations.

The Chinese communist authorities must respond pragmatically and stop putting up roadblocks in the path of China's eventual reunification. The Chinese communist authorities should carefully weigh the need for interactive relations. They should face the fact that China is divided and ruled by two distinct political entities; immediately renounce the use of force as means to unification; recognize the necessity of respecting each other's status in the international community; and undertake political, economic, and social reforms.

234

China's division is temporary. Separate jurisdictions are a historical misfortune but a political reality. If the Chinese communist authorities overlook this fact, they will obstruct China's eventual reunification. While separated by the Taiwan Straits, Chinese on both sides share the conviction that national unification should be accomplished peacefully and democratically. Threatening to use force against compatriots is anachronistic and certain to elicit aversion. With memories of the Tienanmen massacre still fresh in people's minds, the Chinese communists must renounce the use of force, or they risk disgracing Chinese the world over, and further impeding China's unification.

The Republic of China government on Taiwan is a member of the international community. This fact connot be overlooked or changed by any country or person. Efforts to exclude the ROC from the international community and to pressure us into accepting the "one China, two systems" arrangement are misguided. Both sides of the Taiwan Straits would benefit from mutual trust and cooperation in a non-zero-sum competition.

The Chinese mainland has achieved certain success in its fourteen years of economic reform. However, its failure to institute political, media, social, and educational reforms are creating a boottleneck in the mainland's economic development, and threatens to send it spining out of control. The *Guidelines for National Unification* remind the Chinese communists to lift their restrictions on public opinion and democratization. By reflecting on Taiwan's success story, the Chinese communists can prevent their society from slipping into chaos, and promote the welfare of the 1.2 billion Chinese under their jurisdiction.

# Conclusion

The rapid development of cross-Straits relations over the past six years has served the interests of both sides. The relationship is multidimensional and focuses on social, cultural, and trade exchanges. This phenomenon is in full accord with the *Guidelines for National Unification*. Under the Guidelines, national unification is divided into phases but there is no timetable. Judging by the development of cross-Straits relations to date, the ROC should stick to the Guidelines without either hesitation or haste.

The present mainland policy centers on private exchanges. The results of frequent and orderly private exchanges over the past six years are increasingly apparent. Continued success hinges upon the involvement and constructive input of all ROC citizens. The Mainland Affairs Council willl continue to abide by the government stance, adhere to the *Guidelines for National Unification*, and promote cross-Straits relations for a democratic, free, prosperous and unified new China.

**Appendix**

## The Guidelines for National Unification

Adopted by the National Unification Council at its third meeting of February 23, 1991, and by the Executive Yuan Council (Cabinet) at its 2223rd meeting on March 14, 1991.

### I. Foreword

The unification of China is meant to bring about a strong and prosperous nation with a long-lasting, bright future for its people; it is the common wish of Chinese people at home and abroad. After an appropriate period of forthright exchange, cooperation and consultation conducted under the principles of reason, peace, parity, and reciprocity, the two sides of the Taiwan Straits should foster a consensus of democracy, freedom and equal prosperity, and together build anew a unified China. Based on this understanding, these Guidelines have been specially formulated with the express hope that all Chinese throughout the world will work with one mind toward their fulfillmentt.

## II. Goal

To establish a democratic, free and equitably prosperous China.

## III. Principles

1. Both the mainland and Taiwan areas are parts of Chinese territory. Helping to bring about national unification should be the common responsibility of all Chinese people.

2. The unification of China should be for the welfare of all its people and not be subject to partisan conflict.

3. China's unification should aim at promoting Chinese culture, safeguarding human dignity, guaranteeing fundamental human rights, and practicing democracy and the rule of law.

4. The timing and manner of China's unicication should first respect the rights and interests of people in the Taiwan area, and protect their security and welfare. It should be achieved in gradual phases under the principles of reason, peace, parity, and reciprocity.

## IV. Process
1. Short term—A phase of exchanges and reciprocity.

(1) To enhance understanding through exchanges between the two sides of the Straits and eliminate hostility through reciprocity; and to establish a mutually benign relationship by not endangering

each other's security and stability while in the midst of exchanges and not denying the other's existence as a political entity while in the midst of effecting reciprocity.

(2) To set up an order for exchanges across the Straits, to draw up regulations for such exchanges, and to extablish intermediary organizations so as to protect people's right and interests on both sides of the Straits; to gradually ease various restrications and expand people-to-people contacts so as to promote the social prosperity of both sides.

(3) In order to improve the people's welfare on both sides of the Straits with the ultimate objective of unifying the nation, in the mainland area economic reform should be carried out forthrightly, the expression of public opinion there should gradually be allowed, and both democracy and the rule of law should be implemented; while in the Taiwan area efforts should be made to accelerate constitutional reform and promote national development to establish a society of equitable prosperity.

(4) The two sides of the Straits should end the state of hostility and, under the principles of one China, solve all disputes through peaceful means, and furthermore respect—not reject—each other in the international community, so as to move toward a phase of mutual trust and cooperation.

## 2. Medium term—A phase of mutual trust and cooperation.

(1) Both sides of the Straits should establish official communication channels on equal footing.

(2) Direct postal, transport and commercial links should be allowed, and both sides should jointly develop the southeastern coastal area of the Chinese

mainland and then gradually extend this development to other areas of the mainland in order to narrow the gap in living standards between the two sides.

(3) Both sides of the Straits should work together and assist each other in taking part in international organizations and activities.

(4) Mutual visits by high-ranking officials on both sides should be promoted to create favorable conditions for consultation and unification.

## 3. Long term—A phase of consultation and unification.

A consultative organization for unification should be established through which both sides, in accordance with the will of the people in both the mainland and Taiwan areas, and while adhering to the goals of democracy, economic freedom, social justice and nationalization of the armed forces, jointly discuss the grand task of unification and map out a constitutional system to establish a democratic, free, and equitably prosperous China.

## The Meaning of "One China"

Adopted at the eighth meeting of the
National Unification Council
on August 1, 1992

1. There are marked differences of opinion between the two sides of the Taiwan Straits over the meaning of "one China." To Peking, "one China" means the "People's Republic of China (PRC)," and after unification of the two sides Taiwan would become a "Special Administrative Region" under PRC's rule. Our side, on the other hand, considers "one China" to mean the Republic of China (ROC) that has existed since 1912, with *de jure* sovereignty over all of China. However, the ROC's current jurisdiction covers only Taiwan,

Penghu, Kinmen and Matsu. Taiwan is part of China, and the Chinese mainland is a part of China as well.

2. China has been temporarily divided ever since 1949. This has resulted in each side of the Taiwan Straits being administered separately by two political entities. Such is a simple reality that any proposition for China's unification should not fail to consider.

3. For the progress and the welfare of the people, and the prosperity of the nation, the government of the Republic of China adopted the *Guidelines of National Unification* in February 1991, seeking to establish consensus and to start the process of unification. The ROC government earnestly hopes that the mainland authorities will adopt a progmatic attitude, set aside their prejudices, and the two sides will cooperate in contributing wisdom and efforts to the building of a free, democratic and prosperous China.

# The Koo-Wang Talks and Cross-Straits Relations

Chang Liang-jen

The meeting between Koo Chen-fu and Wang Tao-han in Singapore in late April 1993 was the first contact between the heads of two private, but government-authorized, intermediary organizations[1] since 1949 when China was divided. The Koo-Wang talks became the focus of media attention and were closely followed by Chinese people around the world. The process that led up to the talks and the issues that were discussed were fully and publicly disclosed; however, the high degree of public concern and the rampant political speculation produced by the talks sowed seeds of doubt in the minds of some people. It is thus necessary to provide a comprehensive explanation to the public.

*Chang Liang-jen is director of the Department of Cultural Affairs at the Mainland Affairs Council, Executive Yuan.*

## The Origin of the Koo-Wang Talks

The primary concern of the Koo-Wang talks was to resolve problems that had arisen from the people-to-people exchanges between the two sides of the Taiwan Straits within the limits of the short-term phase outlined in the *Guidelines for National Unification*.

Residents of the Taiwan area have made 5.79 million visits to relatives in the Chinese mainland since November 2, 1987 when the Republic of China government lifted a ban on such visits. Over the past five and a half years, indirect trade between the two sides has reached US$30.6 billion, and nearly 10,000 factories from Taiwan have invested more than US$6.4

billion in the Chinese mainland. During the same period, more than 64 million letters have been exchanged between the two sides.

As the number of exchanges has grown, so has the number of ensuing problems, hence the urgent need to institutionalize the channel for resolving problems that arise between the two sides. Problems that must be given priority attention include verification of marriage certificates, inheritance papers, and academic records; checking, tracing, and compensating for lost mail; providing guarantees and benefits for Taiwan investors on the mainland; protecting travelers; jointly cracking down on rampant maritime smuggling and illegal immigration; and, resolving increasingly frequent fishing disputes.

The two sides have had to set up a system for holding periodic talks and to establish organizations specifically empowered to handle these issues.

The Straits Exchange Foundation (SEF) was established in February 1991 and was authorized by the Republic of China government to handle cross-Straits problems. After a ten-month wait-and-see period, the Chinese mainland founded the Association for Relations Across the Taiwan Straits (ARATS) as a counterpart to the SEF. The two agencies have since met in Peking and Hong Kong to exchange views on problems stemming from people-to-people exchanges. However, the results have not been ideal because the mainland has mixed political issues with practical problems, and also because the two sides have lacked a systematic channel of communication and negotiation. It became apparent that a meeting between the heads of the two organizations was necessary.

As chairman of the SEF Koo Chen-fu and his vice chairman Cheyne J.Y. Chiu attended the talks, the expectations of the majority of people in Taiwan were very high. During the talks, the chairman and vice chairman spoke appropriately and contended the necessary points in order to protect the welfare of the 21 million people in the Taiwan area. In the end, Chairman Koo and Vice Chairman Chiu were able to achieve the anticipated results.

## The Nature of the Koo-Wang Talks

The subjects discussed in the Koo-Wang talks were set forth by the ROC government in accordance with the goals of the short-term phase as defined in the *Guidelines for National Unification*. This phase stresses promotion of mutual understanding through private exchanges and the elimination of hostility through reciprocity, in hopes that the order and rules for such exchanges can be established between the two sides. This was the highest authorized guiding principle for the SEF in the talks with its mainland counterpart.

When SEF and ARATS held preparatory meetings for the Koo-Wang talks that were held in Peking during early April of 1993, the two sides agreed that the talks would be non-governmental, practical, economic, and functional. In the preparatory meetings, delegates from both sides scrupulously abided by their commitment to not touch on any political subjects, thus enabling the smooth completion of the preparatory meeting and laying a favorable foundation for the formal talks held later on in Singapore.

During the formal talks, the SEF delegates carefully stayed within the parameters set by the Mainland Affairs Council, and limited the discussion to subjects agreed upon in the preparatory meetings, thus avoiding all political topics. While the communists did bring up the political issue of "direct transport, mail and trade," the SEF delegates ignored this and stuck closely to the authorized range of issues previously agreed upon. As is apparent from the nature of the four agreements signed in the talks[2], as well as from the SEF-ARATS decisions to give high priority to a dozen other issues emerging from increased exchanges across the Taiwan Straits, the Koo-Wang talks were obviously in no way political.

While Mr. Koo Chen-fu is a member of the Kuomintang Central Standing Committee, he took part in the talks in his capacity as the SEF chairman rather than as a KMT representative. In view of the ROC's gradually maturing multiparty system of democracy, the ROC government has either opposed or ignored the repeated demands made by the Chinese communists in recent years for party-to-party negotiations. The ROC government's stance on this issue will not change.

According to the *Guidelines for National Unification*, mutual visits by high-ranking officials can only take place in the medium-term phase, and discussions on unification are not to be held until the long-term phase. Since cross-Straits relations at this point are still in the short-term phase of private-sector exchanges, the ROC government will not hold any political negotiations with the Chinese communists.

## The Goals and Results of the Koo-Wang Talks

The three principal objectives of the Koo-Wang talks were to institutionalize a channel for consultations between the SEF and ARATS, to remove obstacles to non-governmental exchanges while safeguarding the people's welfare and security, and to lay down the principles of reason, peace, parity and reciprocity for cross-Straits interactions.

The SEF has found that correspondence, telecommunication exchanges, and occasional meetings have not been able to provide timely and effective solutions to cross-Straits problems. The SEF felt it was essential to establish a system of regular meetings between SEF and ARATS staff so problems could be solved as they arose.

The subjects discussed during the Koo-Wang talks corresponded with the government's current mainland policy and the needs of the public. The talks were designed to solve problems that had infringed upon people's rights and interests during the course of bilateral exchanges. The overall objective was to set up orderly and safe cross-Straits exchanges by solving problems that involved both sides such as counterfeiting, illegal activities at sea, smuggling, and illegal immigration.

During the Koo-Wang talks, SEF delegates steadfastly upheld the principle of parity when discussing the various subjects on the agenda as well as such technical matters as meeting procedures, conference sites, and seating. This made it impossible for the Chinese communists to overlook the fact that the Republic of China is a political entity and their equal.

Solving problems, reducing hostilities, promoting understanding, and establishing mutual trust are essential steps towards developing positive interactions between Taiwan and the Chinese mainland. Only with sincerity and goodwill on both sides will the interactions be conducive to peace and stability in the Taiwan Straits, and contribute to the stability and prosperity of the Asian-Pacific region. Owing to the deliberate indifference of the Chinese communists, the two sides were unable to substantively explore and reach agreements on issues pertaining to the people's rights and interests, such as the protection of property and guarantees of the rights and interests of Taiwan businessmen. Nevertheless, the four agreements signed during the talks do reflect substantial progress and merit closer inspection.

## The Four Agreements Produced in the Koo-Wang Talks

*The Agreement on Document Authentication Between the Taiwan Area and the Mainland Area.*

The increasing number of private-sector exchanges between the Taiwan area and the Chinese mainland has made it necessary to present, for use on the other side of the Taiwan Straits, documents concerning the claims of rights or the receipt of payments, or for resettlement or residential purposes. However, given the different legal systems on the two sides of the Taiwan Straits, and in particular, the extensive area of the Chinese mainland and its numerous agencies, it is difficult to determine whether a document is authentic. Liberal authentication could adversely affect the interests of a party with genuine rights, whereas strict authentication might create inconvenience for the public. It is, therefore, essential that documents be authenticated through a simple verification process common to both Taiwan and the mainland.

Formerly, neither side had been able to provide a method of document authentication for the other side. When handling cases of document verification, the SEF had to make written requests for verification by the issuing agency on the mainland. Not only was the exchange of correspondence time-consuming, but the communist Chinese Taiwan Affairs Office ordered that no mainland agency should respond to SEF inquiries. This resulted in inefficient document authentication, a big backlog of verification cases, and a great deal of trouble.

In the *Agreement on Document Authentication Between the Taiwan Area and the Mainland Area*, both sides agreed to send copies of documents concerning inheritance, adoption, marriage, birth, death, consignment, academic degree, residence, dependency, and property ownership for verification purposes to the other side. Documents will be authenticated by comparison with copies sent by the other side, and verification may be requested in writing in case of any doubt. This method should provide better and more effective service for the people. The SEF and ARATS also agreed to consult and provide mutual assistance in individual cases concerning non-notarized documents.

*The Agreement on the Tracing of and Compensation for Lost Registered Mail Between the Taiwan Area and the Mainland Area.*

Ordinary mail is sent across the Taiwan Straits via a third area, but registered mail service has not been provided. The difficulty in the conveyance of important correspondence has mainly been due to a lack of arrangements by either side over the scope of the registered mail service between the two sides to be offered and the tracing of and compensation for lost registered mail.

In the *Agreement on the Tracing of and Compensation for Lost Registered Mail Between the Taiwan Area and the Mainland Area*, both sides agreed that the registered mail service would cover letters, post cards, aerograms, printed matter, newspapers, magazines, and Braille letters. Registered mail will continue to be sent indirectly. Both sides agreed to provide mutual assistance to track down lost registered mail, and to respond within three months of receiving a written inquiry. Should it be found that a registered letter of parcel has been lost, stolen or destroyed, the sender shall be compensated by the area from which it was mailed in order to simplify matters.

*The Agreement on the Establishment of Systematic Liaison and Communication Channels Between the SEF and ARATS.*

The SEF and the ARATS have, since their inception, met several times to discuss such issues as a joint crackdown on illegal activities at sea, document authentication, and the tracing of and compensation for lost registered mail. Communication on all other matters was made through fax or mail. This has solved a few individual cases, but overall operations have not proven entirely satisfactory. There is a need to establish a system of liaison and consultation that will allow the two agencies to better fulfill their functional purposes, and to effectively solve the problems arising from private exchanges between the two sides of the Taiwan Straits.

The *Agreement on the Establishment of Systematic Liaison and Communication Channels Between the SEF and the ARATS* is aimed primarily at building up a systematic form of communication and dialogue between the two agencies. In principle, the agreement calls for regular or irregular meetings between SEF and ARATS chairmen, vice chairmen, and secretaries-general. Department directors or office heads shall meet once every three months to discuss more timely issues in their area of responsibility. The deputy secretary-general or personnel of equivalent status in the two agencies will be the contact person in emergency cases. In addition, the SEF and the ARATS shall mutually facilitate the entry and exit of SEF and ARATS personnel.

### The Koo-Wang Talks Joint Accord

SEF Chairman Koo and ARATS Chairman Wang met in Singapore on behalf of their respective agencies to proceed with non-governmental talks on economic, practical, and functional matters. The *Koo-Wang Talks Joint Accord* set up a priority list for topics of mutual concern which both sides agree require further discussion. Topics to be discussed this year include repatriation of illegal immigrants, efforts to crack down on illegal activities at sea, the resolution of fishing disputes, the protection of intellectual property rights, and mutual assistance on judicial issues. As for economic exchanges, the development and exchange of energy resources, and cultural, educational, and scientific and technological exchanges, the SEF and the ARATS will continue to hold talks to resolve matters of concern to people on both sides of the Taiwan Straits and to facilitate more orderly private exchanges between Taiwan and the Chinese mainland.

## The Follow-up Consultations

The *Agreement on Document Authentication*, the *Agreement on Tracing of and Compensation for Lost Registered Mail*, the *Agreement on the Establishment of Systematic Liaison and Communication Channels Between the SEF and the ARATS*, and the *Koo-Wang Talks Joint Accord* that were signed by the SEF and ARATS at the Koo-Wang talks went into effect on May 29, 1993. Full compliance with these agreements is sure to benefit exchanges between the two sides.

The various issues arising from private exchanges between the two sides of the Taiwan Straits are extremely complex. Nonetheless, they were discussed in full during the Koo-Wang talks and were given priority in the order of their magnitude and urgency. According to this priority list, the following topics were to be discussed by the end of 1993: "repatriation of people entering the area of the other party in violation of pertinent regulations, and related issues," "joint efforts to combat smuggling, hijacking and other crimes," "consultation on the handling of fishing disputes at sea," "handling of marine fishing disputes between the two sides," "protection of intellectual property rights of the two sides," and "mutual assistance between judicial organs of the two sides." Both parties agreed to select a different time and place to continue discussions on economic issues, on which the two sides have widely divergent views, and to further discuss cultural and scientific exchanges. The priority issues to be discussed in future talks were thus clearly delineated.

In order to fulfill the agreements, SEF's delegation[3] made a trip to Peking on August 28, 1993, hoping to discuss the five subjects specified above. Due to time limitations, the SEF proposed that "mutual assistance between the judicial organs of the two sides" and "repatriation of people entering the area of the other party in violation of pertinent regulations and related issues" be discussed first. The SEF was also willing to discuss the other three priority issues agreed upon in the *Koo-Wang Talks Joint Accord*. ARATS, however, proposed that either the agenda stipulated in the joint accord be "rearranged" or priority issues for 1993 should be "specifically arranged." ARATS also proposed a timetable that would have had both sides discussing 13 issues in the last four months of 1993. Among the 13 subjects raised by ARATS were issues which fell outside the scope of the *Koo-Wang Talks Joint Accord*, such as the opening of Taiwan's labor market to mainland workers.

During the August talks in Peking, SEF delegates fully respected the opinion of the ARATS and stated that if specific conclusions were reached by the end of this year, ARATS' new proposals could be discussed. The ARATS delegates, however, insisted that a timetable for holding talks on economic issues had to be set, and they were willing to listen but refused to speak about the two previously agreed upon priority issues of "repatriation of illegal entrants" and "judicial assistance."

The non-interactive nature of the discussions stripped the talks of any meaning. Both sides should have, as is common practice, simply abided by the agreements already reached. Making random changes, advancing unreasonable interpretations, and changing the order of the talks as one pleases are all inappropriate behavior. The ARATS' attempt to rearrange the agenda under the pretext of carrying out agreements reached during the Koo-Wang talks was in stark violation of the *Koo-Wang Talks Joint Accord*. In addition, discussing generalities was of no help at all in solving the practical problems at hand.

Faced with less than ideal circumstances, the SEF delegation chose to return to Taipei on September 3, earlier than originally scheduled. Though the talks in Peking had failed to reach any conclusion, the SEF is still willing to continue consultations in line with the *Koo-Wang Talks Joint Accord*.

## Cross-Straits Relations after the Koo-Wang Talks

Just as relations across the Taiwan Straits were becoming less tense, and the ROC government was actively promoting friendly relations with the Chinese mainland, the Chinese communists released a white paper titled *The Taiwan Question and the Reunification of China* on August 31, 1993. This move sufficiently demonstrated the Chinese mainland's rigid stance toward the ROC on Taiwan. It is necessary, then, to clarify the ROC government's policy vis-à-vis the Chinese mainland and the ROC's views on relations between the two sides.

First, the Republic of China will stick to the unification process set down in the *Guidelines for National Unification* and slowly but surely promote its Chinese mainland policies. Second, the ROC is a member of the international community; the Chinese

251

communists are unable to represent the 21 million people in the Taiwan area. Third, the Chinese communists' "one country, two systems" position is the main obstacle to China's unification. Fourth, the two sides of the Taiwan Straits should resolve the question of unification peacefully. And fifth, the "China question" can be thoroughly resolved only under a democratic, free, and equitably prosperous system.

By observing the talks between the SEF and the ARATS, we have learned more about the Chinese communists' strategy regarding Taiwan, and we appreciate more than ever before the three-stage, no-timetable design of the Guidelines. It sets clear conditions for progress towards unification, and allows no room for rash advances. The problems that have accumulated between the two sides of the Taiwan Straits cannot be solved overnight. We will give priority consideration to the wishes of the people in Taiwan and Chinese people living abroad, and we will safeguard the safety and welfare of the people in the Taiwan area. While the SEF-ARATS talks have institutionalized channels of communications to solve problems arising from the exchanges between the two sides of the Taiwan Straits, the effectiveness of this communication channel is still unproven. The Koo-Wang talks did not diminish Chinese communist hostility towards Taiwan. Their release of *The Taiwan Question and the Reunification of China* proves this fact. The Chinese communists' unreasonable attitude harms relations between the two sides. It would be premature to move, at this point, into the medium-term phase of relations with the Chinese mainland as outlined in the *Guidelines for National Unification*.

Taiwan is undeniably a part of Chinese territory. Though the government and the people of the ROC have lived under constant threat of military attack from the Chinese communists for more than forty years, the ROC on Taiwan has maintained official or substantive relations with most countries in the world and has actively participated in international activities. In view of the fact that the ROC government effectively and independently exercises jurisdiction over the area comprising Taiwan, Penghu, Kinmen, and Matsu, and in order to protect the basic human rights of the 21 million people in this area, the ROC must strive for the right to participate on an equal basis in the international community. The Chinese communists have never extended their governing power to the Taiwan area, so they are not entitled to represent Taiwan in the international community. Indeed, the Chinese communists have never spoken up for the rights of the people in the Taiwan area or fulfilled their international obligations. The Chinese communists' continued suppression of and exclusion of the ROC internationally can only imply their ignorance of political realities, and impede any improvement in relations between the two sides of the Taiwan Straits.

The Chinese communists' united front tactics against Taiwan have, in recent years, been based upon the "one country, two systems" scheme. According to the Chinese communists, the "one country, two systems" scheme would require the Taiwan area to immediately hand over its diplomatic and military rights, accept rule by the Chinese communists, and become a "special administrative region" under their jurisdiction. The ROC on Taiwan would, in effect, disappear forthwith. Under this formula, the 21 million people in the Taiwan area would be allowed, for some years, to enjoy a "high degree of autonomy" under Chinese communist rule, but the lifestyle and basic human rights enjoyed by the people in the Taiwan area would not compare to what they already have. The Chinese communists stress the superiority and dominance of socialism. The "one country, two systems" formula would thus be a transitional arrangement. In the long run, the Taiwan area would have to abandon its democratic and free system and completely accept the Chinese Communist Party's socialist system. It is clear that the "one country, two systems" premise is nothing but a demand for the Taiwan area to surrender to the Chinese communists. Thus the "one country, two systems" scheme is unfeasible and unacceptable to the people in the ROC.

The ROC government has always maintained that China should not be divided indefinitely. In 1991, the ROC government proposed the *Guidelines for National Unification* to serve as the lodestar for promoting China's unification. The ROC government pursues China's unification not only to unify the territories of China through peaceful and reasonable means. Its loftier goal is to allow the 1.2 billion people on the Chinese mainland to enjoy the same democratic, free, and equitably prosperous lifestyle and basic human rights and freedom that the people in the Taiwan area do. The significance and value of the kind of national unification that the ROC envisions far surpasses the "one country, two systems" model proposed by the Chinese communists.

In *The Taiwan Question and the Reunification of China*, the Chinese communists state that the "Taiwan question has long been a destabilizing factor in the Asia-Pacific region." In fact, the Chinese communists themselves have exported revolution since their very establishment. Yet, because the Chinese communists have strictly enforced the Leninist principle of communist dictatorship, they have not held themselves accountable to the public for any of their actions, or taken international condemnation into account. Therefore, we believe that the threat posed by the Chinese communists to the stability and prosperity of Asia and to the world at large will continue so long as they refuse to implement democracy and the rule of law, and to renounce the use of force in solving problems.

The ROC government has consistently emphasized the importance of stability in the Asia-Pacific
region. ROC President Lee Teng-hui recently suggested setting up a collective security system in the
Asia-Pacific region. In recent years, investments by
Taiwan businessmen have also spurred economic
growth and trade expansion in some Southeast Asian
nations, increasing employment and raising incomes
among Southeast Asians. Taiwan is not only the foun-
tainhead of hope for the mainland people in their
pursuit of democracy, freedom, and equitable prosperity; Taiwan will also be a major contributor to the creation of an Asia-Pacific era in the 21st century. We sincerely hope that the Chinese communists will renounce the use of force in the Taiwan Straits and build
a foundation of mutual respect, peace, and prosperity
in order to create objective conditions beneficial to
national unification.

The communist regimes in the former Soviet
Union and Eastern Europe have all collapsed, leaving
the Chinese communist regime as one of the few
remaining communist influences in the world. In the
six years since 1987, when the ROC government began
adopting a variety of more open measures vis-à-vis
the Chinese mainland, the people on the two sides of
the Taiwan Straits have exchanged over 5.79 million
visits and almost 74 million letters. Over 92 million
messages have been made via telephone, telegram, and
fax services. Indirect investment by Taiwan businessmen in the Chinese mainland has helped to improve
the economic lives of the people there and to increase
their understanding of how a free economy works. In
addition, cultural exchanges between the two sides
of the Straits have breathed new life into the waning
traditional Chinese culture on the Chinese mainland
and brought in much information on freedom and
democracy. The people on the two sides of the Taiwan
Straits are related by blood. The numerous exchanges

255

and face-to-face contacts between the people on the two sides of the Taiwan Straits have effectively broken through the information blockade erected by the Chinese communists. These exchanges have also enabled the Taiwan experience (forty-some years of development, democratization, increased educational opportunity, and liberalization) to reach the mainland. The ROC experience shows that the "China question" can be resolved only if a democratic, free, and equitably prosperous system comes into being on the Chinese mainland.

NOTES

1. Koo Chen-fu is the chairman of the Republic of China's Straits Exchange Foundation, and Wang Tao-han is the chairman of the Chinese mainland's Association for Relations Across the Taiwan Straits.
2. The *Agreement on Document Authentication*, the *Agreement on the Tracing of and Compensation for Lost Registered Mail*, the *Agreement on the Establishment of Systematic Liaison and Communication Channels Between the SEF and the ARATS*, and the *Koo-Wang Talks Joint Accord*.
3. The SEF delegation that traveled to Peking in 1993 comprised ten SEF staff members.

# The Significance of the Taiwan Experience in Mainland China's Modernization and Cross-Straits Economic Integration

Shih Chi-ping

The "Taiwan experience" has often been cited by social scientists as a model of success for post-war developing economies. Thus far, academic analyses of the "Taiwan experience" have been made mainly from the perspective of economic development. On the other side of the Taiwan Straits, industrial and trade development in the Chinese mainland has become increasingly liberalized since the economic reforms launched in 1979, and has made considerable progress. Naturally, the feasibility of transplanting the Taiwan experience to the mainland to hasten its modernization and catalyze positive cross-Straits integration is a matter of great interest.

*Shih Chi-ping is a deputy secretary-general of the Straits Exchange Foundation.*

Both propositions require careful study. We must first determine if the Taiwan experience can be regarded as a model of success. Our concept of "development" should not be restricted solely to the economy. Extended to the domains of society, politics, and culture, the degree of developmental success Taiwan has achieved is open to debate. An examinination of the various difficulties that Taiwan has encountered in recent years reveals that these reservations are justified. Second, even if such a model is examined in terms of economic modernization, it is still necessary to separate historical from policy factors.[1] Policy factors are often the central concern in developmental and comparative economics. The contribution of policy factors, however, is often exaggerated in studies of the Taiwan experience. Third, the Taiwan experience is a political, economic, social and even cultural phenomenon, and it is therefore theoretically difficult to isolate a certain part of it (e.g. the economy) and transplant it into another environment. This does not mean that different developmental models cannot borrow useful portions from each other. The question is how to recognize the fine line between what can and what cannot be transplanted. I believe that for the Chinese mainland (or other less developed areas) ascertaining what can and should be transplanted from the Taiwan experience is at least as important and meaningful as ascertaining what cannot or should not be transplanted.

The Chinese mainland launched its current economic reform program in 1979, and took comprehensive measures to promote the responsibility system of joint production and contract production in the agricultural sector. Impressive achievements have been made, even in the beginning years from 1979 to 1984. In the industrial sector, the Chinese communists have set up "test points." They first established four "special economic zones" at Shenzhen, Zhuhai, Shantou and Xiamen, and employed an "outside-to-outside strategy"[2] in the localized and export-oriented economic development of these areas. Hainan was subsequently added to the list. Recently, the Pudong area has also been included as a special economic zone. This model of development has made laudable achievements in the introduction of capital and technology, the creation of job opportunities, and in boosting income and foreign exchange reserves. From a perspective of comparative development, it is interesting to contrast the differences and similarities between the development of Taiwan and the mainland. This comparison will be significant in the future development and economic integration of the two areas. This essay is an exploratory analysis of this subject.

# Historical and Political Factors in the Taiwan Experience

## A. Historical Factors

Taiwan's modernization is generally considered to have begun in the 1950s, but the starting point should in fact be set at the end of World War II in 1945. Historical development, however, is an ongoing process. We should not overlook the role of pre-1945 Japanese development of Taiwan in the evolution of the Taiwan experience. Theoretically, the economic development of a country depends on both supply and demand. On the supply side, land, labor, capital, technology, infrastructural construction, efficiency of the administrative branch, and system software, statutes, and social discipline all are fundamental to the growth of an economy. Fifty-one years of Japanese developmental efforts in colonial Taiwan[3] made contributions in at least three major areas: (1) infrastructural construction, including harbors, railway and highway networks, water conservation and electric power facilities; (2) a complete land and household registration system; and (3) sound social discipline. Compared with Hainan, Taiwan began its development in better initial condition.

Thanks to the pre-war construction of railways, highways and harbors by the Japanese, Taiwan did not suffer from bottlenecks[4] caused by insufficient infrastructure in its economic and social development for at least two decades, until the mid-1960s. This was undeniably a major contributing factor in the Taiwan experience.

The capital, labor, technology and administrative capabilities introduced into Taiwan following the government's relocation from the mainland were the other major initial elements of the Taiwan experience. More than a million Chinese came to Taiwan. Although their arrival aggravated inflation in Taiwan's

259

war-ravaged economy, they provided massive and efficient manpower to the development of labor-intensive industries and major communication and transportation projects, such as the East-West Highway.

In addition, large numbers of technocrats and elite accompanied the government to Taiwan. They contributed greatly to raising efficiency in the public sector and to progress in the private sector.

In addition, Taiwan's strategy of spearheading industrial and economic development with the development of export-oriented manufacturing in the 1960s was basically successful. Beyond government policy, post-war international economic prosperity and trade expansion also helped Taiwan in a big way. Taiwan was on the bandwagon to prosperity.

In short, the Taiwan experience must be considered in its specific historical context. These factors should not be overlooked in examining the Taiwan experience as a potential "model" to be transplanted to other economies.

## B. Policy Factors

Most studies tend to stress policy factors. The policy adopted by Taiwan was a system characterized by respect for basic market functions, and government intervention when necessary. The degree of government intervention in economic activities, or from the opposite viewpoint, the degree of liberalization, has evolved over time. The following three points regarding the origin, formation and evolution of this system are noteworthy:

(1) The success or failure of a government's role in the functioning of a market economy is closely related to the efficiency of the public sector. This was especially important[5] in the 1950s when import-sub-

stitution industries were being developed with heavy government intervention. As mentioned above, Taiwan had a relatively efficient bureaucracy.

(2) It is interesting to note that in the 1950s after the government moved from the Chinese mainland to Taiwan and began to develop the economy in a new environment, the authorities boldly did away with the concept of economic control and replaced it with a market economy. One convincing explanation for this decision is that it was due to American influence. After the outbreak of the Korean War, the United States resumed military and economic aid to Taiwan and nudged Taiwan's strategy of economic development toward liberalization. This was undeniably crucial in Taiwan's success. When Taiwan launched its second set of liberalization reforms in the 1980s, we again saw massive influence from the United States. Such outside influence (mainly from the U.S.) was very important and significant in the development of the Taiwan experience[6] and to the pursuit of modernization in other areas.[7]

The government played a dominant role in industrial and trade development, be it through agricultural reform, development of import-substitute industries in the 1950s, export expansion in the 1960s, or the second-push development of import-substitute industries in the 1970s. It is noteworthy that the government strategy in each case was linked to the relative advantages of Taiwan's industry and trade, demonstrating the high standards achieved by the public sector.

## An Evaluation of Taiwan's Modernization and the Keys to Its Success
### A. The Current State of the Taiwan Experience
Basically, the Taiwan experience is a neutral concept. An evaluation of its current state shows both

good points and bad. The good points are mainly rapid growth, increase in incomes, stable price levels and equitable distribution of wealth[8] sustained over a considerable period of time. Most studies of the Taiwan economy, including this analysis, stay within this scope. More and more data have, however, revealed the downside of the Taiwan experience, which should also be addressed and studied.

Taiwan has undeniably faced many unprecedented difficulties in recent years. These include tense labor-management relations, clashes over environmental protection, skyrocketing land prices, underground investment, rampant stock and other monetary games, protests by people unable to buy a home and other disadvantaged groups, erosion of the work ethic, the labor shortage and deluge of foreign labor, growing material greed, speculation, and lack of public order.

Excepting labor-management relations and environmental protection, no theory or empirical experience can support the assertions that these problems are the natural result of economic development. These negative phenomena are to a large degree related to the following two facts: (1) a sustained trade surplus since the 1980s and intentional suppression of the appreciation of the NT Dollar, and (2) a long-term failure to build sound, modern institutions, including a modern civil service system. Trade surpluses and deferred appreciation of the NT Dollar have resulted in a sharp increase in foreign exchange reserves, an influx of hot money, excessive expansion of the money supply, a deluge of mobile capital, and soaring land prices caused by massive demand, which have led to further monetary games, speculation, erosion of the work ethic, introduction of foreign labor and deteriorating public order. The long-term trade surplus is related to relatively high productivity and insufficient liberalization; but basically it is a result of an overemphasis on export and economic growth by the government and business, and a neglect of the social costs incurred by producer and consumer activities. The government and the private sector have avoided facing up to these problems in order to strengthen Taiwan's export competitiveness. Incessant clashes over environmental protection, tension in labor-management relations, and the imbalance between economic and social development are clearly related to the massive long-term trade imbalance.

The economic and social aftereffects that have surfaced in recent years amply reflect the error in a policy that put too much emphasis on economic growth. This will hurt the future development of Taiwan's economy and society to a certain extent. An analysis and evaluation of the history and chain of interaction of socio-economic modernization must be based on data collected over a considerable length of time. In this context, the study of the Taiwan experience is an apt example.

One fact that has emerged from the Taiwan experience is that once an economy has developed to a certain level, the accompanying diffusion of knowledge will have an impact in the political and social domains. According to the theory of progressive demand, once one's basic livelihood is assured, he will be increasingly conscious of his rights, and his desire to participate in politics will also increase. The accumulation of wealth, emergence of a middle class, rise in the educational level, wider availability of information, and closer human relations provide the conditions for social and political progress.

B. Prospects of the Taiwan Experience
Whether Taiwan can overcome its present difficulties and return to its previous path will hinge on two conditions.

First, in the face of an irrevocable trend toward liberalization, contradictions and conflicts of interests in the course of the redistribution of resources will be inevitable. To reconcile these contradictions and defuse conflicts, pluralistic interests in society must be respected, and the existence and operation of organizations representing different interests in society must be protected by law. For example, the establishment and operation of political parties, trade unions, farmer associations, industrial guilds, environmental protection bodies, consumer groups and other civic groups in society must be institutionalized. This is social pluralism.

Once a society becomes pluralistic, how the interest bodies express and reconcile their interests through rational political operations will be a vital precondition for the smooth redistribution of resources. That is, social pluralism must be followed by political reform. In other words, a successful follow-up to the Taiwan experience depends on a close coordination of political reform with the progress of economic liberalization.

Second, the Taiwan experience must ultimately be extended from the narrow sphere of economic development to the social and cultural spheres. While economic breakthroughs may create momentary prosperity, they cannot last if they are not buttressed by parallel social and cultural developments.

Two crucial preconditions will be required. First, the public must reconsider and adjust their concept of development. This will be a long social and cultural process, and it is also a social responsibility of entrepreneurs. The second precondition on which the government can bring its policies to bear is a strategic adjustment involving the allocation of a greater proportion of total resources for the social and cultural sectors. Certainly, the effects of such efforts will take time to be felt. Unfortunately, Taiwan has yet to begin.

## The Significance of the Taiwan Experience for Modernization in the Mainland

What is the significance of the Taiwan experience in the economic integration between the two sides of the Taiwan Straits and the modernization of the Chinese mainland?

First, the economic reforms initiated on the mainland in 1979 were basically a move toward the establishment of market mechanisms within a socialist system. It is expected that as long as the reforms and liberalization measures continue, the economic vitality and social prosperity Taiwan experienced in the 1950s will emerge in areas in the mainland where reforms and liberalization are promoted. It is noteworthy that market mechanisms must be built on private ownership. The Chinese mainland has made impressive progress in its move toward a market economy, but privatization of property is still strongly resisted. In the short term, a market-oriented economy in a setting of public ownership may bring prosperity, but a concomitant low efficiency in production and other woes will be unavoidable. This will hamper further liberalization and modernization of the mainland economy.

We must concede, however, that the social sciences have been unable to provide a feasible and effective method of ownership reform for state enterprises. Judging from the Taiwan experience, privatization of state enterprises is a very slow process. As a result of decades of rapid growth in the private sector, the percentage of state enterprises' contribution to the GNP has consistently declined. The same process of "dilution" has appeared on the mainland as a result of the rapid growth of local enterprises, private enterprises and production by individual households since the economic reforms and liberalization measures were initiated. This trend should be affirmed.

Second, the Taiwan experience has demonstrated that in the operation of market mechanisms, failure to address external costs is often a major cause of labor and environmentalist disputes. The mainland has not yet come as far as Taiwan in advancing a market-oriented economy, and there is no reason to believe that the administrative branch on the mainland can force enterprises to absorb these external costs. Actually, the situation of environmental protection on the mainland has steadily worsened owing to the economic growth of the past decade. There is evidence that many industries that once caused much pollution in Taiwan, such as ship scrapping, petrochemicals, pisciculture, and metal recycling, have relocated to the mainland. This transfer of environmentally unfriendly industries to the Chinese mainland will have a negative effect on the modernization of the mainland and the development of cross-Straits relations.

Third, there are two other noteworthy points in Taiwan's economic liberalization. Taiwan's economic liberalization has been retarded by two forces: deeply ingrained traditional ideas and resistance from vested interests. The former involves the people's overall level of education and the ideology of national and social development. The latter stems from the inevitable redistribution of resources accompanying liberalization, something that is resisted by vested interests.

In Taiwan, liberalization has been able to move ahead despite the hindrance of tradition and vested interests, mainly due to a number of external and internal factors.

As already mentioned, even in the 1950s when Taiwan's economy was just beginning to develop, the government adopted policies favorable to the development of a market-oriented economy and private enterprise. Some believe this had a great deal to do with the "policy advisors" who followed U.S. aid to Taiwan. The quickened pace of liberalization starting in the mid-1980s, which included such steps as reducing trade barriers, opening up the market and liberalizing the foreign exchange rate mechanism, was also closely tied to U.S. pressure.

Since liberalization leads to the redistribution of resources, it unavoidably causes friction and clashes among interest groups. If the friction and clashes are not resolved, liberalization is certain to be affected. To effectively resolve such problems, multiple interests must be reconciled.

Incorporating a resolution mechanism into political and social development has become a serious task. In this respect, Taiwan's recent developmental experience can perhaps offer some valuable lessons.

## The Path to Cross-Straits Economic Integration

The two sides of the Taiwan Straits meet many of the criteria for unification. Economic integration and a reduction in ideological and socio-economic differences are unquestionably the most feasible path to unification. The Chinese mainland began to reform its economy in 1979 in the direction of a market economy and liberalization, and now it is beginning to reap the fruits of modernization. But, according to the Taiwan experience, there are theoretically unavoidable pitfalls and barriers on the road to modernization. Some pitfalls could be avoided if policies and their application could be adjusted and improved based on the Taiwan experience. What is difficult to deal with are mutually antagonistic forces within the establishment, which often cause paralysis to reform efforts inside the structure.[9] This will be the major barrier the Chinese mainland will face in its modernization drive. This paralysis is sure to hurt an otherwise smooth integration of the two sides of the Taiwan Straits.

In order to give the mainland opportunity to overcome this obstacle, a well-designed experiment in economic, political and social reforms might be worth trying. The policy of setting up special economic zones has helped to free up economic resources and establish value-added industries, but it cannot become a complete experiment in reform due to its overemphasis on production.

Future economic experiments should be carried out in an area which is large enough, where there are few political and social restrictions, and where the scope of reform could be expanded as much as possible. The experiment would require land, regional and urban planning, and a dynamic plan for infrastructural and other development required by a modern society. The experiment would also encompass education, the civil service system, statutes and institutions, and the system of legal administration. The reform might perhaps take a leaf or two out of the Taiwan manual, but should also draw upon the experiences of Singapore, Japan, and even Europe. This experiment could provide an arena to the two sides of the Taiwan Straits for further cooperation, and also experience and a basis for future economic integration.

This project could be called an experimental "Special Modernization Zone." If successful, it would be highly significant for both sides of the Taiwan Straits. For the mainland, the success would offer a clear direction for the economic modernization of all of China. The experiment could also diminish ideological differences and the socio-economic operational gap between the two sides of the Taiwan Straits, and have a highly positive effect on the economic integration and positive political interaction between Taiwan and the mainland.

## NOTES

1. The historical factors included pre-war construction by Japan, the influx of capital and talent at the time of the ROC government's relocation to Taiwan. The policy factors refer to the political, economic and social measures taken by the ROC government after the war.
2. The "outside-to-outside strategy" means to import capital and raw materials from the outside and then to export the finished products to the outside.
3. Colonial development refers to Japanese development of Taiwan into an agricultural basis. This strategy made Taiwan to remain an agricultural economy in the early years of its return to the Chinese rule. It led to Taiwan's development of import-substitute industries, a major part of the Taiwan experience.
4. After the mid-1960s, because of rapid expansion of production triggered by increased export, Taiwan began to face bottle-necks in communications, transportation and power supply, seriously hampering economic progress.
5. In many areas of the world (like Latin America), the development of import-substitute industries are often hind-ered by public sector inefficiency, resulting in the stall of political and economic progress.
6. Theoretically, any liberalization will involve the redistribution of established resources and, therefore, will encounter strong resistance from the circles of vested interests. Outside pressure was decisive to the success of liberalization.
7. There are indications that in recent years the Chinese mainland has faced similar U.S. pressure during trade negotiations.
8. From 1961 to 1990, Taiwan's annual economic growth aver-aged 9.1 percent, ranking first among Asia's four little dragons. During the same period, the averages were 5.7 percent for industrialized nations and 25.9 percent for developing nations. In income distribution, the ratio between the top one-fifth and the bottom one-fifth of Taiwan's population declined from 5.23 in the 1960s to the lowest level of 4.17 in 1980, comparable to Japan's record.
9. Two of the major examples would be the restraining forces of ideology and the restraining forces of vested interests.

# VI.
# Foreign Relations

Previous page: President Fidel Ramos of the Philippines hosts a dinner for President Lee Teng-hui and his entourage during their trip through Southeast Asia in February 1994.

# Let the Cry for Justice Spread Far and Wide![1]

## Lien Chan

I am deeply honored to have been invited to this
cocktail reception celebrating the 30th anniversary of
the National Press Council. Founded thirty years ago
by senior members of the press corps, the National
Press Council has had a far-reaching impact on our
society. It has imparted to our society a high regard
for press freedom and a deep sense of social responsibility. Therefore, on behalf of the government of the
Republic of China, I would like to express my respect
and gratitude for the contributions made over many
years by the National Press Council and the senior
members of the press. I firmly believe that under your
excellent guidance, the National Press Council has
preserved press freedom, safeguarded individual
rights, advocated self discipline for the media, and
brought about justice in the media. I also believe that
the National Press Council will score even greater successes in the future and will most certainly make a
direct and active contribution to the development of
the Republic of China's mass communication industry.

The senior members of the press corps seated
here today are among the most knowledgeable and
informed media professionals in the ROC. This is a
rare opportunity for me to consult with you. I, therefore, would like to explain the government's position
on the issue of the ROC's participation in the United
Nations, and I hope that all of you will be generous
with your comments and suggestions.

*Lien Chan is Premier of
the Republic of China.*

## The Response, Both at Home and Abroad

Few people realize that over two years ago President Lee Teng-hui ordered the relevant government ministries to look into the issue of the ROC's participation in the United Nation, and had indicated that the ROC should begin to solicit understanding and support in the international community. Over the last two years, not only have political parties reached a measure of consensus over the issue, but extensive international coverage of the issue has also created quite a stir both in Taiwan and abroad.

I can report to you that many voices favoring the ROC's participation in the United Nations have made themselves heard in the international media. For instance, newspapers in Boston, San Francisco, and other areas have recently carried letters to the editor submitted by the ROC government's information offices stationed abroad, calling to the attention of the American public the rights and the interests of the ROC to participate in the United Nations. On July 3, 1993, the British Broadcasting Corporation broadcast a special program about the ROC's position and perspective on this issue. Likewise on August 4, 1993, *The West Australian* published an article written by David Goodman, the head of the Asia Research Centre at Murdock University. In the article, Dr. Goodman, a scholar specializing in Chinese affairs, emphasized that if the United Nations excludes the ROC from participating, "the refusal of admittance . . . may limit the U.N.'s room for maneuver." The media in other countries, including Germany, Holland, France, and Belgium, have all conducted similar coverage that has directed international attention to the ROC's aspiration to expand the scope of its international activities and to participate in international organizations. Even more heartening, on August 6, 1993, seven Central American countries jointly forwarded a letter to U.N. Secretary-General Boutros Boutros-Ghali asking the United Nations to seriously consider the importance of parallel representation in the U.N. for the divided China and requesting the United Nations to begin drafting a feasible package for the resolution of this issue.

Each time when I met with foreign dignitaries, I have explained with utmost clarity and sincerity why the ROC has adequate and sufficient cause to participate in the United Nations.

## The ROC Should Never Be Overlooked

Since its withdrawal from the United Nations, the ROC has not disappeared from the world map. Instead, it has, thanks to the combined efforts of its people, won worldwide recognition for its extraordinary successes. Today, everyone knows that the ROC is the fourteenth largest trading nation in the world, holding foreign exchange reserves that rank either first or second in the world. The ROC has the world's 25th highest per capita income. Demographically, the Republic of China on Taiwan has a larger population than two-thirds of the 184 member countries of the United Nations. By any criterion, the ROC is a strong and resourceful country, entitled to a seat in the U.N.

Some people who were supporting the Chinese communists' entry into the United Nations emphasized that the world must not overlook the strength of the Chinese communists, and that to isolate the Chinese communists would be disadvantageous to global interests. I think the same can now be said of the Republic of China. On November 10, 1990, the *New York Times* published an editorial, "Taiwan: Too Big to Ignore," which appealed to the United States and other nations to consider the existence and development of the Republic of China on Taiwan. This undoubtedly demonstrates that it would be unwise and inappropriate of the United Nations to continue to ignore the

275

ROC. Many specialists in international affairs might have noticed that up to now the United Nations and its peripheral organizations rarely publish statistical information on the Republic of China on Taiwan. This omission has not only detracted from the thoroughness and usefulness of these organizations' publications, but has also encroached on the rights and interests of the users. This situation must be rectified quickly.

In addition, for the last few decades, Western democracies have unceasingly advocated the importance of freedom and democracy. Today, the Republic of China on Taiwan has attained outstanding results in democratic reform. Several surveys further reveal that participation in the U.N. is the freely expressed desire and will of the majority of the people in the ROC. Therefore, there is no reason for any country that truly treasures freedom and respects democracy to pretend to not notice our aspirations.

## Willing and Able to Make Contributions

It is particularly worth pointing out that the international community would certainly benefit practically from the ROC's participation in the United Nations. The ROC has both the will and the wherewithal to actively contribute to maintaining international order, to promoting economic and trade cooperation, and to providing international humanitarian relief. Everyone knows that the ROC became a donor nation about ten years ago. We began parceling out money from the International Disaster Relief Aid Fund in 1980. We established the International Economic Cooperation and Development Fund in 1988, and we have sent 43 technical cooperation teams to assist in the development of 31 countries. These actions demonstrate that the ROC has taken concrete steps to pay back the international community for its help in the past and is now serving as a contributor, partner, and participant to countries and regions in all stages of development.

The ROC is, regrettably, not a member of the United Nations. This means that the ROC is often unable to carry out its charitable missions to pay back to the international community. For instance, during the Gulf War two years ago, the ROC was eager to provide economic aid to some of the countries ravaged by the war. Who could have guessed that these countries had reservations about accepting the aid just because the ROC is not a member of the United Nations. As a result, many delays and complications undermined the effectiveness of the aid. Another example is the recent global effort to ameliorate the worsening greenhouse effect. The United Nations launched a massive effort to protect the ozone layer and rallied various countries to sign the *Montreal Protocol.* Although the ROC wished to participate, it was excluded from the treaty strictly because the ROC is not a member country of the United Nations. This is not only unfair to a country that has the desire to participate in international cooperative efforts, but it also undermines the effective solution of environmental problems. Furthermore, it sets a bad precedent for political interference in environmental protection and inevitably "limit[s] the U.N.'s room for maneuver." Surely the United Nations must understand that without active global cooperation, the ability of mankind to resolve its common problems will be undermined. It is not unreasonable to expect the United Nations, as the highest international governing organ in the world, to abide by the "principle of universality" of membership.

## Righting Wrongs and Restoring Justice

The ROC has yet another reason to assert its right to participate in the United Nations: The ROC wants to fight for the basic rights and dignity of the

21 million Chinese people in the Taiwan area. From the viewpoint of international law, the United Nation's *Universal Declaration of Human Rights* in 1948, *The International Covenant on Civil and Political Rights* in 1966, and *The International Covenant on Economic, Social and Cultural Rights* passed in the same year all emphasize that every person is entitled to participate in political, cultural, and economic activities. These rights are part of the fundamental rights and basic dignity of every person in the world, and these rights differ from the general rights that every government should guarantee. The people of the Republic of China, without any assistance from other nations, already enjoy the full spectrum of human rights. However, in the 22 years since we were excluded from the United Nations, the 21 million citizens in the Taiwan area have been seriously discriminated against and their dignity and basic rights to participate in political, economic, and cultural activities in the international community have been violated. This is a very immoral, unfair, and unreasonable situation. The issue of "China representation" has not been resolved at all, because the Chinese communists have neither the capability nor the right to represent the Chinese people in the Taiwan area. The United Nations must not continue to just sit by and watch. The United Nations should prove its esteem for human rights by promptly taking action to correct the situation and by compensating the 21 million people in Taiwan whose rights have been violated. I firmly believe that the time has come for the international community, and in particular the United Nations, to right its wrong and to restore justice.

Members of the United Nations must realize that while the U.N. Assembly may have, in its 1971 resolution, accepted the Chinese communist authorities and barred us from its organizations, the U.N., nevertheless, ignored the fact that the Chinese communists cannot and are not entitled to represent the 21 million people in the Republic of China on Taiwan. We are not represented in the United Nations today. Nor do we have anyone who can stand up for our rights or promise to take on our responsibilities. Is it normal for such an important international intergovernmental organization to ignore the existence of our 21 million people? Is it normal for our children, women, aged, and handicapped to be excluded from U.N. activities and deprived of their rights and the benefits which their counterparts in other countries around the world enjoy? Is it normal for our police to be deprived of full international cooperation in their mission to crack down on international crimes and drugs?

## Joining the U.N. Helps National Unification

Of course, we all realize that the greatest resistance to our participation in the U.N. comes from obstacles placed in our path by the Chinese communists. I strongly disapprove of the various actions taken by the Chinese communists in the last few days to suppress us in the international community and to oppose our participation in the United Nations. The Chinese communists should face reality. If the Chinese communists cannot rationally and practically think through this issue and examine this very serious question, they will betray their solemn obligation to the Chinese people.

The ROC is entitled to enjoy its rightful national status, even prior to unification. The ROC's decision to participate in the U.N. was never intended to create a permanent split between the two sides of the Taiwan Straits. On the contrary, the ROC believes that participation in the U.N. would increase our confidence in the unification of China and trigger more active measures to pursue the eventual unification of China according to the *Guidelines for National*

*Unification*. The Chinese communists would be enlightened if they would only look at the classic case of East and West Germany, which were simultaneous members of the United Nations and yet unified without any obstacles. North and South Korea is another example of simultaneous participation by a divided nation in the United Nations and the best evidence that the two political entities can simultaneously belong to an international organization. Whether in terms of theory or in terms of practice, the ROC's advocacy of participation in the United Nations is reasonable and feasible. The ROC's position on this issue is totally clear. The ROC's efforts to participate in the United Nations must be carried out in line with the principle of a unified China, and will certainly have positive effects on the eventual unification of China. We hope that the Chinese communist authorities will calmly evaluate the situation and not impede the unification of China.

The Chinese communists must realize that the United Nations was formed in the aftermath of the Second World War when mankind had set its will on pursuing peace after having experienced bloodshed and catastrophe. The highest ideal of the United Nations is to turn swords into plowshares, or as the Chinese would say, turn hostility into friendship. A renowned Western scholar of international relations, David Mitrany, once placed emphasis on "peace by pieces." The Republic of China has always been a peace-loving nation and its intention to rejoin the United Nations is based on its sincere desire to promote peace in the world and in China. The Chinese communists should not oppose the numerous opportunities for bi-coastal contact and interaction provided by international forums. Is it possible that the Chinese communists are opposed to fostering bi-coastal understanding and mutual trust through such contacts and interaction? Can they be opposed to working for "peace by pieces" that would pave the way for the peaceful unification of the Chinese people?

## Time to Work for U.N. Membership

Of course, it should be emphasized that we know we are entitled to participate in the United Nations, that we are strengthened by this knowledge, and that we realize that we must do our best. We shall not weaken in the face of opposition from either the Chinese communists or anyone else. We are confident that our future status in the international community will be commensurate with the expansion of our national strength. The scope for our international activities can only continue to expand, regardless of any plans to obstruct us. If we are only willing to work hard, we will surely gain strength, and if we are strong, we will surely have a future — a future that will not depend on the Chinese communists or on any outsider. The ROC will determine its own future.

Ladies and gentlemen, President Lee once reminded us that "to be alive is to have hope." Today, the ROC is not merely alive, it has taken a strong first step in its bid to participate in the United Nations. We know, however, that a long sinuous and treacherous road lies before us. Nevertheless, participation in the United Nations is not some unattainable dream. If we only bolster our confidence, redouble our efforts, unite all the people, consolidate national resources, and if our political parties are of one mind, then the ROC can make an even greater impact on the international community. In this way, I believe the ROC can gain international support and attain its goal to participate in the United Nations.

## Let the Cry for Justice Spread
## Far and Wide

I sincerely hope that the National Press Council will expand its pervasive influence on the mass media, and through various media and communication channels, spread our calls and our expectations to every corner of the globe. Let the cry of justice spread far and wide. Let us create more opportunities to participate in the activities of the United Nations, so that we can finally participate in that organization at an early date.

NOTES

1. A speech delivered by Lien Chan, Premier of the Republic of China, at the 30th Anniversary of the National Press Council on September 2, 1993.

# A View from Taipei

Fredrick F. Chien
*Foreign Affairs*
Winter 1991/92

Fredrick F. Chien is minister of foreign affairs of the Republic of China.

Developments in East Asia may appear sluggish compared to the momentous changes in Europe and the Soviet Union. The Cold War lines that divide both China and Korea remain firmly in place, although rendered more permeable by flexible policies. East Asia's three communist countries—mainland China, North Korea and Vietnam—are still ruled by first-generation revolutionary leaders. In stark contrast to the peaceful unification of Germany, Vietnam was unified by a vast communist army. And mainland China (the People's Republic of China) is soon to extend its domination to Hong Kong—the citadel of capitalism in the East. Moreover the string of arms control measures achieved in the West has not found a counterpart in East Asia. Soviet President Mikhail Gorbachev's policy of accommodation, sweeping as it is, has only begun to thaw the chilly relations between the Soviet Union and Japan. For different reasons the major powers in this area appear unwilling or unable to change the current situation.

Yet beneath the surface important currents of change are discernible. First, East Asia ranks as the fastest growing area of the world in terms of economic output. Japan's gross national product, 50 years after Pearl Harbor, is double that of Germany. Japan is now the world's largest creditor, while its victorious World War II adversary, the United States, has slipped into being the world's largest debtor. Other East Asian economies are also doing well, with average growth rates that far outstrip those of the European Community.

Second, the process of democratization is moving apace in the Republic of China (R.O.C.) on Taiwan, the Republic of Korea and the Philippines. The light of democracy that flickered to life in 1989 on the Chinese mainland has only been dimmed, not extinguished. In fact the collapse of communism in the Soviet Union and eastern Europe may portend similar developments in mainland China after the passing of its first-generation leaders.

Finally, a spirit of reconciliation seems to be prevailing in East Asia as well. The normalization of relations between mainland China and the Soviet Union and also Vietnam, as well as the establishment of diplomatic ties between Moscow and Seoul and expanding people-to-people interchanges between the two sides of the Taiwan Straits are but a few examples. In short, while the Cold War structure remains largely intact in East Asia, global trends toward democratization, development and détente have deeply penetrated the area, and there are grounds for optimism about the future.

Since its withdrawal from the United Nations in 1971, the R.O.C. has aimed to maintain and expand its substantive relations with other countries. It has also sought to upgrade its economic structure and make itself more democratic. Today it is the fifteenth largest trading nation in the world, with a GNP more than one-third that of mainland China. The R.O.C. is widely recognized as having emerged from an era of isolation and irrelevance to become a potentially valuable contributor to the emerging new world order. By furthering trends toward democratization, development, international integration and détente, Taiwan may play an important role in promoting stability and prosperity in East Asia. In fact Taiwan's experience may someday be especially relevant to the future of a unified and democratic China.

## II

The 1911 revolution led by Dr. Sun Yat-sen brought the Ching dynasty to an end, but failed to create a suitable environment for economic and political development. The following four decades were marked by fierce fighting among rival warlords, a communist insurgency and a Japanese invasion that eventually helped lead to the communist conquest of the mainland.

Since 1949 Taiwan has made slow progress toward democratization, the timing and direction of which was narrowly controlled by the government, taking into account the threat from mainland China and Taiwan's own socioeconomic development. By the mid-1980s Taiwan and Singapore had become the only non-oil exporting countries in the world with per capita incomes of at least $5,000 a year that did not have fully competitive democratic systems. But today Taiwan has finally developed the proper economic and social base for successful democracy.

An important step toward Taiwan's political reform came in 1986, when opposition forces formed the Democratic Progressive Party (DPP), defying a government ban on new political parties. The ruling Kuomintang (KMT, or Nationalist Party) not only refrained from taking action against the opposition but made a series of moves in the following years that decidedly liberalized and democratized the nature of Taiwan's political system. The liberalization measures adopted by the KMT included replacing martial law with a new national security law, lifting press restrictions, revamping the judiciary and promulgating laws on assembly, demonstration and civil organization. The democratization measures legalized opposition parties, redefined the rules for political participation—such as the electoral law—and include the ongoing reform of the legislature (the Legislative Yuan), the electoral college (the National Assembly) and the R.O.C. Constitution.

This process of democratization, begun by President Chiang Ching-kuo before his death in January 1988, was given further impetus by his successor, Dr. Lee Teng-hui. At his inauguration in May 1990, President Lee set a two-year timetable to complete the country's democratic transformation, including major structural and procedural reforms. A National Affairs Conference was convened in June 1990 with delegates drawn from all major political and social forces. After much public debate the NAC decided to end Taiwan's "mobilization period," begun in 1949, which had allowed the government extraordinary national security powers.

A declaration to this effect, made by President Lee in May 1991, also included recognition that a "political entity" in Peking controls the mainland area. On the recommendation of the NAC the "temporary provisions," appended in May 1949 to the 1947 constitution, giving the government sweeping powers to deal with external and internal threats, were abrogated in early 1991. By the end of the year all the senior members of the Legislative Yuan and National Assembly elected on the mainland prior to 1949, and who have never been subject to reelection, will have retired. A new National Assembly composed exclusively of representatives elected in Taiwan will then undertake the final phase of democratic reform: revision of the R.O.C. Constitution. Upon its completion in mid-1992, and after Legislative Yuan elections scheduled for the end of that same year, the R.O.C. will have become by any standard a full-fledged democracy.

The R.O.C.'s democratization process is unique. It has not been initiated or monitored by external forces, as it was in Japan and West Germany. Nor was it undertaken after political or social upheavals, as in Greece or Argentina and lately in the Soviet Union. Rather it has evolved peacefully within the country and is mainly the result of prosperity. Tensions and divergent views exist, to be sure. For example, although both sides of the Taiwan Straits maintain that Taiwan has been, legally and historically, an integral part of China, the Democratic Progressive Party insists that Taiwan is a sovereign, independent entity. The DPP's position is contrary to the R.O.C. government's claim to represent all of China. Furthermore, the DPP's foreign-policy platform holds that Taiwan should develop its own international relations, including membership in the United Nations and all other international organizations, on the basis of independent sovereignty and under the name "Taiwan." The R.O.C. government, however, maintains that "Taiwan," as a geographical area, is merely an island province of the R.O.C.

These kinds of differences are inevitable in an open society. But the point is that the government of the R.O.C. itself has largely set the timing for its own democratization; the clock cannot and will not be turned back. It is worth noting that the R.O.C. is the first Chinese-dominated society to practice pluralistic party politics. In that sense what we have been witnessing is truly revolutionary. It realizes the dreams of many of our founding fathers—a dream for which many have sacrificed their lives. And yet R.O.C. prosperity and democratization have been achieved without bloodshed and without overturning the existing socioeconomic order.

These changes, however, do not come without a price. They have unleashed societal forces that present new challenges to the government, which still needs to coordinate reforms in other areas, such as economic policy, mainland policy and foreign affairs. As various societal interest groups stake their claims on public policymaking, the quality of government will increasingly have to rise to meet the needs of its various constituents.

## III

Despite Taiwan's economic miracle, rapid social change and political liberalization, the R.O.C. has an artificially low international status and remains an outsider to the emerging international order. Between the urgent necessity for greater integration into the international community and an underlying desire not to forsake the future reunification of China, the R.O.C. has adopted a flexible approach to foreign relations, commonly called "pragmatic diplomacy."

Pragmatic diplomacy did not emerge overnight. The R.O.C.'s diplomatic fortunes suffered their first major setback in 1971, when its seat in the U.N. General Assembly and Security Council were taken by mainland China. Its diplomacy reached its lowest point in 1979, when the United States switched diplomatic recognition to Peking. At that time the R.O.C. maintained formal diplomatic relations with only 21 countries and had only 60 offices abroad, and it feared that other nations would follow Washington's lead. Taiwan suffered yet another blow in 1982 with the "August 17 Communiqué," signed by Washington and Peking, which committed the United States to reducing the quantity and quality of arms sold to Taiwan.

But Taipei learned much from these reversals. A spirit of pragmatism emerged among its foreign-policy makers as well as the nation's public. Amid increasingly strident popular calls for change, the government chose on several occasions to adopt a more flexible

approach. For instance, the R.O.C. agreed to participate in the 1984 Los Angeles Olympics under the title
"Chinese Taipei," not "Republic of China," as in previous games. It protested Peking's entry in 1986 into the
Asian Development Bank (ADB), but refrained from
withdrawing itself.

Under President Lee the R.O.C.'s search for international visibility and participation became more
vigorous. In April 1988 an official delegation was sent
to Manila to attend the annual ADB meeting under the
name "Taipei, China." This was the first time that the
R.O.C. and mainland China had both attended a meeting of an international governmental organization. In
his opening address to the KMT's Thirteenth Party
Congress in July 1988, President Lee urged the party to
"strive with greater determination, pragmatism, flexibility and vision in order to develop a foreign policy
based primarily on substantive relations," a passage
incorporated into the party's new platform.

In March 1989 President Lee led an official delegation on a highly successful visit to Singapore, where
he was referred to in the local press as "the President
from Taiwan." That May the R.O.C. made an even
more dramatic decision to dispatch its finance minister, Dr. Shirley Kuo, to the annual ADB meeting, this
time in Peking. President Lee explained the decision in
a June 3, 1989 speech to the Second Plenum of the
KMT's Thirteenth Central Committee: "The ultimate
goal of the foreign policy of the R.O.C. is to safeguard
the integrity of the nation's sovereignty. We should
have the courage to face the reality that we are unable
for the time being to exercise effective jurisdiction on
the mainland. Only in that way will we not inflate ourselves and entrap ourselves, and be able to come up
with pragmatic plans appropriate to the changing
times and environment."

In 1988 Taipei established an International Economic Cooperation and Development Fund and appropriated $1.2 billion for economic aid to Third World countries. This new foreign aid program, plus the 43 teams of technical experts already working in 31 countries, places the R.O.C. firmly in the ranks of significant aid-providing nations. Moreover 1989 saw the establishment of the Chiang Ching-kuo Foundation for International Scholarly Exchange with an endowment of over $100 million. A fund for International Disaster Relief also provided tens of millions of dollars to the Philippines, the Kurdish refugees and others who suffered during the Gulf War.

These and other efforts resulted in a sharp increase in the R.O.C.'s international ties. As of 1991 the R.O.C. has formal diplomatic relations with 29 countries and maintains 79 representative offices in 51 countries with which it has no diplomatic relations. These offices, some of which bear the Republic of China's official name, facilitate bilateral cooperation in areas such as trade, culture, technology and environmental protection. The R.O.C. is also a formal participant in the newly formed ministerial-level organization, the Asia-Pacific Economic Cooperation, and has been active in regional groupings such as the Pacific Basin Economic Cooperation and the Pacific Economic Cooperation Council. It also stands ready to join the General Agreement on Tariffs and Trade as the representative government of the "customs territory of Taiwan, Penghu, Kinmen and Matsu," not the whole of China.

While pragmatic diplomacy enjoys wide support at home—so much so that the country's foreign relations were not an issue during the hotly contested 1989 election campaign—it has invited relentless criticism from mainland China. Characterizing it as a plot to create "one China, one Taiwan," or "two Chinas,"

Peking has taken a number of steps to forestall the R.O.C.'s international integration. Those countries that have shown interest in establishing air links with Taipei, receiving or sending official delegations, setting up offices in Taiwan or simply striking major business deals are warned of "deleterious consequences." In 1991 alone twenty countries, including Poland, Hungary, the Philippines, Malaysia and the Soviet Union, have been forced to reaffirm that "the P.R.C. is the sole legitimate government of China, and Taiwan is part of China."

This has not deterred the R.O.C. from its charted course. Pragmatic diplomacy is part and parcel of the R.O.C.'s democratic transformation, reflecting the nation's collective yearning for change. Just as the domestic political process is being democratized and its economy opened to the world, so its foreign relations must become more flexible as well.

## IV

Taiwan is directly susceptible to winds of change from the Chinese mainland. In recent years the relationship between the two sides of the Taiwan Straits has undergone a sea-change. From 1949 to 1979 Taiwan was constantly threatened by direct military invasion. The shelling of Kinmen and Matsu in 1958, which almost brought the two superpowers into confrontation, was a dangerous example.

But beginning in 1979, when Deng Xiaoping led the Peking leadership to embark on its "four modernizations" program, mainland China's need to maintain a peaceful image eased its hard-line policy. The new goal was not to coerce but to cajole Taipei back into the fold with a variety of devices, such as the "one country, two systems" formula advanced by Deng in 1984. According to this formula, Taiwan would be downgraded to a "highly autonomous region," thus conceding the right to conduct its own foreign relations and national defense. The R.O.C. resisted by adopting its "three nos" stance toward mainland China: no contact, no compromise, no negotiations.

This deadlock was broken in November 1987 when President Chiang Ching-kuo decided to allow people on Taiwan to visit family members on the mainland. Subsequently, longstanding bans on indirect trade and investment, academic, sports and cultural exchanges, tourist visits and direct mail and telephone links were lifted in rapid succession. This opened the floodgates to people-to-people exchanges between the two sides of the straits, unprecedented at any period of Chinese history. In the early part of this year alone, an estimated two million people from Taiwan visited the mainland, more than 28 million letters were sent in both directions—an average of 40,000 per day—and telephone, fax and telex exchanges numbered five million. Moreover, by conservative estimates, indirect trade reached $4.04 billion in 1990 and investment topped $2 billion.

In November 1990 a cabinet-level Mainland Affairs Council was established. At the same time the R.O.C. created the Straits Exchange Foundation, an organization funded primarily by private money. The SEF serves as an intermediary between the people of Taiwan and the mainland on an entire range of functional issues. If necessary the SEF may engage mainland representatives in non-political negotiations. Thus far SEF personnel have visited the mainland on three occasions and received one Red Cross delegation from mainland China—events all highly publicized by the R.O.C. press. The two sides have agreed on procedures for the repatriation of criminals and have indicated an interest in the joint prevention of crimes committed on the high seas. It is hoped, at least by the R.O.C., that through these exchanges "peace by pieces" may be achieved.

A National Unification Council was set up in October 1990 with President Lee as its chairman. To further clarify the R.O.C.'s stance on mainland-Taiwan relations, new Guidelines for National Unification were proposed by this council and accepted by the Executive Yuan (Cabinet) in March 1991. The guidelines state: "After an appropriate period of forthright exchange, cooperation and consultation conducted under the principles of reason, peace, equity and reciprocity, the two sides of the Taiwan Straits should foster a consensus on democracy, freedom and equal prosperity, and together build anew a single unified China."

The guidelines envision unification after three consecutive phases. For the immediate future is a phase of exchanges and reciprocity, during which the two sides are to carry out political and economic reforms at home and "set up an order for exchanges across the straits . . . [to] solve all disputes through peaceful means and furthermore respect, not reject, the other in the international community," and "not deny the other's existence as a politicl entity."

In the medium term a phase of mutual trust and cooperation is envisioned, in which "official communications channels should be established on an equal footing," direct trade and other links should be allowed, and "both sides should jointly develop the southeast coastal areas of the mainland." Both sides should also "assist each other in taking part in international organizations and activities" and promote an exchange of visits by high-ranking officials to create favorable conditions for consultation.

In the final phase both sides may jointly discuss the grand task of unification and map out a constitutional system built on the principles of democracy, economic freedom, social justice and nationalization

293

of the armed forces. In today's Taiwan context "nation-alization" means enhancement of the nonpartisanship of the armed forces.

Public opinion polls show a hard core of "unification" supporters in Taiwan, amounting to about 10 percent of the population. There is also a group of "independence" advocates whose strength ranges between 5 and 12 percent of the population. In between is a silent majority whose views tend toward the R.O.C. government's long-standing position of "one China, but not now" and its emphasis on phased advances toward the goal of unification. However, as in other democracies, the minority may be vocal and aggressive, and their voices are often amplified through the democratic process, thus complicating the formulation of mainland policy. While the push and pull involved in formulating the R.O.C.'s mainland policy may seem natural to those familiar with Taiwan's increasingly democratic political system, it at times appears inscrutable to the aged leaders in Peking.

Given the widening gap—politically, socially and psychologically—between the two sides of the straits, the danger for the R.O.C. appears to stem not so much from Peking's capricious and expansionist tendencies as from its unwillingness or inability to comprehend the changes in the R.O.C. The mainland's aged leaders seem all too ready to take extreme positions by drawing parallels between the R.O.C.'s democratization and what is derisively called "Taiwanization," and between "pragmatic diplomacy" and "two Chinas." At the heart of these misperceptions is Peking's stereotype of Taiwan as a small island province located on the Chinese periphery and ruled by mainland China's defeated civil war enemies. From this vantage point there is no way Peking can treat Taipei as an equal. The same attitude seems to have led the Peking leadership to deny, or at least suppress, the fact that the R.O.C. has come far in the last four decades in overcoming age-old feudalism, poverty and the last vestiges of imperialism. One hopes that in time the Peking leadership will realize that the R.O.C., as a dynamic polity and vibrant economy with ideals, hopes and fears of its own, likewise cannot agree to hold political negotiations with Peking from an unequal position and while mainland China continues to rattle its saber.

V

For too long too many foreign observers have cast the R.O.C. in a unidimensional mold. For those who hailed the R.O.C. as a bulwark of anti-communism, it was to be supported at any price. For those who favored better relations with mainland China, Taiwan was viewed as a "problem" or an "obstacle" to China's unification. When many in the United States were obsessed with the deteriorating bilateral trade situation, Taiwan even became a "threat" to be curbed by protectionist legislation.

Yet the Republic of China is rapidly coming of age. It is evolving into something that fits none of the old stereotypes. Along with the old stereotypes, we must throw out the old prism through which events on the island were once perceived. No analysis of issues relating to China is complete if it fails to take into account the views, ideals, aspirations and fears of the people of Taiwan.

Just as Taiwan is a part of China, so is the mainland. Neither should seek to lord it over the other or to claim superiority by dint of size, population or past performance. Both should instead recognize the fact that two different systems exist in these separate parts of China. While unification is the ultimate goal of Chinese on both sides of the Taiwan Straits, it should not be pursued simply for its own sake. As the breakup of the Soviet Union has shown, a forced union will ultimately end in divorce. The primary task for both governments in the next few years is therefore not to accelerate artificially the wheels of history, but to carry out reforms at home in order to narrow the political and economic gaps between the two sides. Most important, the unification process should be peaceful and voluntary, so that it will neither constitute an imposition by one side on the other nor cause undue concern among China's neighbors.

As the world celebrates the end of the Cold War, the people of the Republic of China are looking forward to making greater contributions to a new world order. Taiwan's experience shows that the Chinese people, like any other people, are fully capable of practicing democracy, promoting rapid economic growth with equitable income distribution and living peacefully with their neighbors. For this the R.O.C. welcomes the arrival of the global tides of democratization, development, international integration and détente in East Asia.

Reprinted by permission of *Foreign Affairs*, (Season & Year) Copyright 1991 by the Council on Foreign Relations, Inc.

# Pragmatic Diplomacy in the Republic of China: History and Prospects

Bernard T. K. Joei

*Bernard T.K. Joei is a professor at the Graduate Institute of European Studies of Tamkang University.*

Before discussing the development of the Republic of China's pragmatic diplomacy in the 1980s, we must first clarify a prerequisite and reach a common understanding, to wit, that both sides of the Taiwan Straits, speaking either in mid-term or in long-term objectives, basically have in mind "One China," and that this "China" should be a free, democratic, and prosperous "China" before it can be acceptable to both parties. However, as for the actual situation, clearly two Chinas, or perhaps more fittingly "two realities," do exist in the international community. It is evident that in the Republic of China on Taiwan's pursuit of reunification of China, it has one China as its ultimate goal. The Chinese communists in Peking have also made reunifying China as their policy. How to reach this common goal pursued by both parties is basically a question of when and how. Little can be done about the factors of timing that are beyond our control, but the question of method is an aspect which is relatively possible to deal with through political wisdom and finesse, along with the addition of positive ingredients.

However, we must perceive the factual existence of the "two realities" mentioned above clearly lest we stray into some specious constructs as "one China, two systems," or "one China, one Taiwan." Instead, the formula of "one China, but not now" or "one China, two realities"[1] advocated by contemporary scholars, which remains true to the objective while demonstrat-

297

ing flexible adaptability, will allow a positive response to the situation. Therefore, the pursuit of our national rights and our promotion of good relations in the international arena can, in keeping with this formula, be termed flexible or pragmatic diplomacy.

## The Origins of Pragmatic Diplomacy

Pragmatic diplomacy in its basic sense consists of expedient measures and methods adopted to deal with external relations and matters when normal diplomacy or official diplomacy are not operable, the practice of which is called "pragmatic diplomacy" or "subtle diplomacy."

*Webster's Third New International Dictionary* defines diplomacy as "...the art and practice of conducting negotiations between nations for the attainment of mutually satisfactory terms." Judging from the results obtained through the practice of pragmatic diplomacy by the ROC government, its pragmatic way of conducting nation-to-nation or government-to-government negotiations fully meets *Webster's* definition.

In addition, according to *Webster's* definition, diplomacy is an art, not a science. Since it is not a science, there are no fixed rules to follow. Basically, diplomacy inherently contains flexible factors. It can take a hard line or a soft one, a combination of both, first a hard line followed by a soft one, or the other way around. On occasion, "one must turn the other cheek," i.e., give a little in order to gain a lot. In the practice of diplomacy one can advance and one can retreat, or even advance through retreat. The process is at times direct, and at times circuitous. Infinite variations in technique and skill are possible as long as the objective is reached.

Diplomacy is like a battlefield involving a fight for a nation's rights, except that it is with negotiation rather than the use of lethal weapons. As Sun Tzu said, "The supreme skill is to subdue the enemy without firing a shot." Indeed, the current diplomatic methods of ROC diplomatic authorities have fully demonstrated the art of diplomacy.[2]

Pragmatic diplomacy dates from a time when normal diplomacy suffered setbacks. The ROC's first setback in diplomacy occurred when the ROC was ousted from the United Nations General Assembly and the Security Council in October 1971. The second setback happened when the United States switched diplomatic recognition to Peking in January 1979. The statement in the Joint Communiqué heralding the establishment of diplomatic relations between the U.S. and PRC states that "the Government of the United States acknowledges the Chinese position that there is but one China and Taiwan is part of China." This statement was a bodily blow to the Republic of China.

The government and people of the ROC learned a lesson from these setbacks. A spirit of pragmatism emerged among its foreign policy makers as well as the nation's public. Amid increasingly strident calls for change, the government chose on several occasions to adopt a more flexible approach."[3]

In fact, the late president Chiang Ching-kuo once declared that, "The practice of diplomacy consists of adhering to national policy, facing reality, creating favorable opportunities, weighing the pros and cons, and negotiating at the appropriate time for the sake of safeguarding the supreme interests of the nation." He also remarked that "in certain cases one may act, in others one should not act." These simple statements contain a profound philosophical implication: the supreme guiding principle of flexibility. This grand principle is not only applicable to diplomacy but also other political spheres, and ultimately, to everything.

In his opening address to the KMT Thirteenth Party Congress in July 1988, President Lee Teng-hui also urged the Party to "exercise greater confidence in adopting more pragmatic, flexible and forward-looking actions to raise the quality of and score breakthroughs in a foreign policy based primarily on substantive relations."[4]

On June 3, 1989, President Lee Teng-hui addressed the Second Plenum of the KMT's Thirteenth Central Committee, saying, "The ultimate goal of the ROC's foreign policy is to safeguard the integrity of our national sovereignty. However, we should have the courage to face the reality that we are unable for the time being to exercise effective jurisdiction over the mainland. Only by so doing will we be able to avoid inflating our self-importance or tie ourselves down with details, and only by so doing will we be able to come up with pragmatic plans appropriate to the time and situation that open up new possibilities and scenarios." It could be said that what is now understood under the term "pragmatic diplomacy" was actually launched by President Lee Teng-hui.

President Lee spoke to the Sun Yat-sen Institute on Policy Research on this topic on another occasion in his capacity as KMT chairman. In his speech, entitled "From uncertainty to pragmatism," he quoted Harvard Professor Kenneth Galbraith's book *The Age of Pragmatism* to expound the concept of pragmatic diplomacy, including the basis and orientation of the ROC's practice.

## What Is Pragmatic Diplomacy, and What Is Its Goal?

As for the nature of the ROC's pragmatic diplomacy, ROC Foreign Minister Fredrick Chien has explained that, "Pragmatic diplomacy consists of conscientiously and responsibly maintaining the ROC's existing diplomatic relations as well as its substantive relations, initiating new external relations, and going after opportunities to participate in international activities and international organizations." He has also stated: "Pragmatic diplomacy is assertive, and possesses a selectivity and intensity of competitive spirit." Foreign Minister Chien expresses these beliefs in the motto "Why not the best?"

Minister Chien succinctly explained the goal and orientation of pragmatic diplomacy: "to bolster ournational strength and broadly establish good relations...to force the Chinese communists, through conditions both within and beyond their control, to compete peacefully with us in the process of national reunification." "[By] attaching importance to gathering information...[and] rejoining international organizations...diplomatic policy must be based equally on our best interests and what is right,"[5] he said.

Speaking on the concept of pragmatic diplomacy, Minister Chien stated, "In response to changes in the international situation and to trends in our national development, our all-out effort to develop new relationships with a pragmatic and flexible attitude and positive, assertive approaches while adhering to the One China principle has already produced concrete results. What is meant by "flexible and pragmatic," as well as "positive and assertive" is that we will not retreat even when we encounter a worse situation but will face reality and seek a solution. While seeking to establish, maintain or improve our external relations, we shall strive for the 'very best' goal first, and if that is unattainable, then we shall strive for 'second best,' as long as circumstances both within and beyond our control permit, and neither national policy nor the welfare of our people is compromised."[6]

Fredrick Chien briefly explained the goal of pragmatic diplomacy in his report entitled "Taking the pulse of international developments, creating new diplomatic opportunities," delivered at the Sun Yat-sen Monthly Commemorative Meeting held at the Presidential Office on March 18, 1991. He said: "Our long-range national goal is a reunified China, but in the near-term our national goal is to seek survival first, then development. Diplomacy itself is a means and not an end. The basic method should be do all possible to reach our national goals. However, in the process of so doing, we must be able to stick to our principles while adapting to change, and, based on the precept of pragmatism, make appropriate adjustments to the role the ROC plays in the international community and bring it to fruition according to the national resources we presently have."

To summarize the process, pragmatic diplomacy stems from the inability of classic diplomacy to function. And we cannot exercise classic diplomacy because of an all-out effort by the Chinese communists to isolate the ROC in the international political arena and squeeze our vital space on the world scene.

Therefore, pragmatic diplomacy consists of breaking through all conventional entanglements in classic diplomacy and adopting a strategy exactly like the "Multidimensional Diplomacy" referred to by Foreign Minister Chien, in which we exercise our considerable economic and trading clout to actively participate in international organizations and compete for the friendship of Third world nations, and, based on the principle of mutual benefit and reciprocity, earn international recognition and approval, to "...create pressure that forces Peking to change peacefully, thereby leading to China's peaceful reunification, and the establishment of a democratic, free and equitably prosperous new China."[7] In this way, we can attain the supreme goal of One China or a reunified China sought by pragmatic diplomacy.

## The Theoretical Foundation for Pragmatic Diplomacy

Theoretical bases for pragmatic diplomacy, in the words of one scholar, "...can be found everywhere."[8] However, due to limitations of space, we shall only mention the fundamental ones here. They respectively define pragmatic diplomacy as: (1) an international act performed by a political entity, (2) as equivalent to the exercise of a nation's sovereign rights, (3) as having its origins in the ROC Constitution, and (4) as a proper and logical means of expressing a nation's struggle for its "international right of survival."

### An International Act Performed by a Political Entity

The practice of pragmatic diplomacy is basically an international act of sovereign right by an independent and sovereign state. The subject of an international act is either a state or a political entity that qualifies as an international person. This is the most fundamental theoretical basis of pragmatic diplomacy.

The Republic of China on Taiwan is a political entity, and is indeed a state in the full sense of the term according to international law. It also qualifies as an international person.[9]

As a "political entity" is something of factual existence, it requires no further recognition; whether or not it is recognized does not affect the *de facto* existence of this very "political entity." Therefore, even if Peking does not recognize the Republic of China as a "political entity," this is surely insufficient to obscure the fact that this political entity does exist.

Article 1 of the Montevideo Convention of 1933 on the Rights and Duties of States asserts that:

A nation with the status of an international person possesses the following characteristics: (a) a permanent population; (b) a defined territory; (c) a government; and (d) a capacity to enter into relations with other States.

The Republic of China on Taiwan, established in 1912 and having continuously existed as a State since then, definitely possesses the four characteristics defined by the Montevideo Convention mentioned above. The fact that the ROC is not recognized diplomatically by all states internationally does not affect its being a political entity with the status of an international person that enjoys state sovereignty in terms of international law. This should be beyond any doubt.

It follows that, being a sovereign state that qualifies as an international person in terms of international law, the Republic of China on Taiwan *ipso facto* is a member of the international community, and as a *bona fide* member it has made contributions to the international community and world peace in trade, economics, technology, and finance. Therefore, the ROC is fully entitled to exercise its international rights and duties.

In addition, even though the ROC moved to Taiwan from the Chinese mainland in 1949 and lost a major portion of its territory, according to the "principle of state continuance" in international law, the status of a state as an international person is not affected by the gain or loss of population or territory.[10]

In addition, it should be further clarified that the territory cited above as a necessary condition for a state, may not be lightly construed as what the PRC claims, namely that Taiwan is part of China represented by the Chinese communists. We should emphasize, rather, that Taiwan is part of the Republic of

China, as discussed and affirmed in the author's article entitled "The International Status of the Republic of China and its 'Quasi'-Diplomacy."[11] This legal point is crucial, and if we were to fail to clarify it, the international community might be misled into believing that Taiwan is part of the People's Republic of China. Thus, should the Chinese communists invade Taiwan or intervene in Taiwan affairs, it would be construed as an "internal PRC problem about which the international community (including the United States) could do little."[12]

**An equivalent to the exercise of a nation's sovereign rights**

The practice of pragmatic diplomacy, like the exercise of sovereign rights, is subject to no foreign interference.

According to a French international lawyer, Hubert Thierry, the sovereignty of a state is the supreme right exercised by a state in total independence, which is not subject to intervention by another state.[13]

Although the tendency toward regional realignment is likely to restrict nations' sovereignty or call for self-restriction, no concession should be made on the fundamental national sovereignty relating to territory, or territorial air and waters. On the contrary, the notion of sovereignty in certain domains needs to be interpreted according to new theories in a broader sense.

For instance, the Republic of China is entitled to exercise its basic sovereign rights relating to its own domestic affairs, which, among others, should include the right to uphold its national appellation or designation, to raise its national flag and to perform its national anthem. Hence, in conformity with the principle of "non-interference with national sovereign rights," issues of national designation, national flag and national anthem being part of national sovereign rights in this broadened interpretation are equally subject to non-interference.

In the 1960s, former colonies emerged as new independent states forming the Third World or the bloc of developing nations. They sought economic independence as well as political sovereignty. As a result, the International Law of Development took shape, making economic sovereignty an inalienable part of the inviolable national sovereignty.

A resolution of the United Nations General Assembly adopted in 1970 on the principle of non-interference illustrates this state of mind very aptly. It read, in part, as follows:

"No State or group of States has the right to intervene, directly or indirectly, for whatever reason, in the internal or external affairs of another State. Consequently not only armed intervention but also every other form of interference and all threats directed against the personality of a State or against its political, economic, and cultural organs are contrary to international law...No State may apply or encourage the use of economic or political measures or those of any other nature to compel another State to subordinate the exercise of its sovereign rights or to obtain from it advantages of whatever nature." (Res. 2625 (XXV) of October 24, 1970)

In view of the above doctrine of international law and U.N. resolutions, the Republic of China, in practicing its pragmatic diplomacy, either in the category of "we should act" or in the category of "we should not act," will not tolerate international interference.

## Having Its Origins in the ROC Constitution

The legitimacy of the Republic of China since its establishment more than 80 years ago has never been interrupted. The government, which has been installed according to the Constitution, enjoys autonomy and independence, is free from foreign interference, and exercises effectively its sovereign rights. It is a *de facto* as well as *de jure* government. It is at the same time a political and legal entity. The fact that it moved to Taiwan in 1949 does not affect the legal existence of the ROC government.

Ever since its establishment after the 1911 revolution which overthrew the Manchu dynasty, the Republic of China has involved itself in international affairs: the Paris Peace Conference, the League of Nations and the United Nations. The ROC has shown its capacity to found international organizations and participate in them; its capacity to enter into relations with other states and establish diplomatic relations with them; its capacity to dispatch diplomatic envoys; its capacity to negotiate, sign, ratify, and adhere to treaties; its capacity to fulfill international obligations, to contract loans and debts, to grant political asylum, to extradite foreign criminals, to protect its own citizens as well as aliens and overseas Chinese... All have proven that the ROC is indeed an independent and sovereign state in the full sense of its definition under international law.[14]

Today, mainland China, taking advantage of its improved position in the international community, hampers and boycotts every effort the ROC is undertaking in the field of diplomacy, making the latter's work for expanding its external relations and enlarging its international activity space much more difficult, even to the extent of menacing the country's survival.

To counteract Peking's tricks in the international arena, the ROC has been obliged to implement pragmatic diplomacy. To do so, it has recourse to the Constitution of the Republic of China, which happens to be also the *raison d'être* of the Republic of China on Taiwan.

Not only does the Constitution make the survival of the Republic of China and its government in Taiwan possible; it even, over the long term, serves as a valuable instrument for realizing the great work of China's unification.

This is because the Constitution of the Republic of China is the very fundamental law that was solemnly promulgated at the National Assembly convened in Nanking on December 25, 1946, thirty-five years after the establishment of the Republic. The Constitution emerged from meticulous discussions by all parties (including the Communist Party) and interested groups based on the Draft Constitution of May 5, 1936, in Constitutional National Assemblies and the Political Consultative Conference during the war against Japan.

The Constitution even had the support of Mao Tse-tung who, at the Communist Party's Sixth Plenum in October 1938, advocated a "republic of the Three Principles of the People" based on Dr. Sun Yat-sen's doctrines. Later, Mao Tse-tung, in a meeting with American journalist Edgar Snow, regretted that the designation of Republic of China was altered. This proves to a certain extent that Mao Tse-tung had some respect for the Constitution.

The government of the Republic of China was set up based on the Constitution of the Republic of China. Despite its move to Taiwan, its legitimacy has never been interrupted. Based on the Constitution, the government is able to exercise its sovereign rights, including that to practice pragmatic diplomacy. Therefore, only by adhering to the Constitution can the ROC Government enjoy its legitimacy and claim to represent part of China.

Article 1 of the Constitution reads: "The Republic of China, founded on the Three Principles of the People, shall be a democratic republic of the people, to be governed by the people and for the people."

This is the first ever Constitution in China's history that was instituted by delegates elected under a democratic system and in a democratic atmosphere according to the principles of justice, equity and openness. Therefore, it belongs to the whole Chinese nation. As an embodiment of China's cultural heritage, it should be shared by the entire Chinese people on both sides of the Taiwan Straits, and cherished forever.

The collapse of the Soviet Union and communism in Eastern Europe together with Mainland China's economic evolution provide a good opportunity for integration between the two sides of the Taiwan Straits, hastening the realization of a "unified China." It would not be extravagant to again call on mainland China "to return to the Constitution of the Three Principles of the People"[15] The existing Constitution serves as the best basis for promoting pragmatic diplomacy.

## A Proper and Logical Means for Expressing a Nation's "Right to Survival"

With the end of the Cold War following the tumultuous collapse of communism in Eastern Europe in 1989 and the disintegration of the Soviet Union two years later, at a time when the PRC was officially recognized as a "political entity" by the ROC Government coupled with increased trade between the two sides of the Straits, time ought to be propitious for the ROC to expand its scope of foreign relations through pragmatic diplomacy. But this is only wishful thinking.

The Chinese communists have not loosened their grips on the ROC's international life. On the contrary, they have chosen to further boycott or obstruct the latter's external activities—such as its application for GATT membership. This communist maneuvering has aroused criticisms that the concept of Peking's national sovereignty is outdated, that it runs against the trend of history and that it ought not hamper the ROC's international life and its endeavors to participate in some international organizations.[16]

The ROC, as a member of the international community, should normally be granted equal treatment based on the principle of equality, which is inseparable from the principle of sovereignty. What the PRC has been doing against the ROC is contrary to international law and practice.

Since World War II, new independent states emerging from former colonies constituted a majority of two thirds among nations called the "Third World," thus underlining the importance of the right of equality. As Guy Feuer and Herve Cassan have emphasized, "From the principle of equality in the classical sense, developing countries in particular deduce the idea that all states should participate in an equal way in international economic life. The international law of development takes up the struggle against situations where states are deprived of certain advantages."[17]

The Third World, for the sake of safeguarding its rights, provoked the emergence of a new doctrine of international law, called the "right to development."

The concept of the "right to development" was adopted by the Human Rights Commission in 1977 and was recommended in 1978 in a report of the Secretary General to become a Resolution of the U.N. General Assembly, which asserted that "the right to development is a human right." (Res. 34/46, November 23, 1979)

Two years later, Resolution 36/133 of December 14, 1981 adds that this right is "inalienable" and the Assembly registered its desire to see the promotion of a "New International Humanitarian Order" (Res. 36/136 of December 14, 1981, and Res. 37/201 of December 18, 1982).[18]

From the concept of the right to development it is easy to deduce that theoretically this right to development should function in both directions: for the developing countries to claim the right to development, and for the developed countries to help these developing countries in their development.

Consequently, the ROC, being a *bona fide* member of the international community and, according to the principles of natural law derived from national sovereign rights, is entitled to exercise its international rights and duties. The ROC set up an International Economic Cooperation and Development Fund and a Fund for International Disaster Relief to strengthen its foreign and humanitarian aid operations and to support President Lee Teng-hui's appeal for "sharing the Taiwan experience" and Foreign Minister Chien's call for putting into practice the "traditional virtue of helping those in need and relieving those in distress as contained in his crusade of 'Universal Brotherhood'."[19]

These and other efforts illustrate eloquently the purpose of the international law of development and serve, at the same time, the needs of pragmatic diplomacy.

Given the remarkable performance of its economy and rapid progress in the scientific and technical domains, the Republic of China could claim to be a developed country while at the same time a developing country. Because of this dual role it is called on to play in the international arena, the ROC will need more room for its activities for survival than other countries.

Thus, the ROC's need for survival space has emerged from both subjective and objective circumstances. It has been driven naturally by the interactive momentum of the international community. This right could be called the "right to survival." Following the foregoing logic, one could derive from the concept of the right to development the concept of the right to survival in the international community. And one could also realize that like a human right, the right to survival is an inalienable right corresponding to the "New International Humanitarian Order" called for in the United Nations resolutions.

Therefore, Taipei's recent flexible and temporary measures to expand her international reach and responsibilities are only natural and spontaneous reactions and, to some extent, reflect the right of légitime défense deriving from its right to survival.

All the malicious doings or unilateral claims by Peking for the purpose of depriving *mala fide* the ROC of its right to survival within the international community are immoral and contrary to international law and international ethics.

## The Fruits of Pragmatic Diplomacy

In the early 1980s, diplomatic authorities hit upon the idea of pragmatism, yet they were still bound by the traditional all-or-nothing concept of a zero-sum game. Policymakers were a bit shy and conservative. Without bearing the tag of "pragmatic diplomacy," the

ROC's foreign policy has gradually absorbed the essence of pragmatism under the name of "total diplomacy" or "substantive diplomacy."

Only in recent years did people first start talking about "flexible diplomacy" and "pragmatic diplomacy," and the terminology began to appear in newspapers, magazines, written documents, and administrative reports to the Foreign Affairs Committee of the Legislative Yuan.

At present, people have been psychologically influenced by academics and the media. New interpretations of international law, open-mindedness of the government and the public, as well as personal practices of the ROC president have combined to create a "culture of pragmatic diplomacy," which has succeeded in bringing the Republic of China into an age of pragmatic diplomacy. By agreeable coincidence, the brunt of pragmatic diplomacy lies upon the shoulders of Foreign Minister Fredrick Chien, who was an avant-garde soldier on the front line of the battlefield as ROC envoy to the United States, and who had been dubbed in Washington the "master of pragmatic politics."[20] Chien indeed is the right person for the implementation of pragmatic diplomacy.

It goes without saying that many people still put national strength first. Should there be no support from a solid national might, it would be difficult to score any great successes in diplomacy.

Fortunately, the ROC's economy has grown strong enough to serve this purpose. It ranks second in foreign exchange reserve holdings, the 14th largest global trading partner, its per capita income exceeds US$10,000, making it the 25th highest in the world, and the ROC has replaced Japan as the biggest U.S. creditor in terms of bonds. Given these economic indicators, plus the Six-Year National Development Program, a more receptive international environment has been created for Taipei, on which the world's eye is focusing. As a *Newsweek* report put it, "over the years Taiwan's increasing wealth and its pragmatic emphasis on building bilateral trade relationships have put it back on the world stage."[21]

Taipei's pragmatic diplomacy actually draws its strength from an array of sources including economic cooperation, trade, finance and banking, high technology, medical aid, cultural exchange and agricultural assistance. The results of ROC pragmatic diplomacy are that we have consolidated and reinforced our relations with friendly countries, established substantive relations or upgraded diplomatic relations with countries formerly lacking diplomatic relations with Taipei, and gained active participation in international organizations and related activities.

The ROC at present maintains diplomatic relations with 29 countries. For fear that Peking might hamper its existing diplomatic relations, the ROC government has never ceased to consolidate and reinforce its cooperation with the states that maintain diplomatic ties with it.

In September 1992, the first Conference of the Mixed Committee of the Foreign Ministers of the Central American Countries and the Republic of China was held in Taipei. During the conference, ROC Foreign Minister Fredrick Chien and his counterparts from Costa Rica, El Salvador, Guatemala, Panama, Nicaragua and Belize discussed issues ranging from politics and cooperation projects to trade and investments. In the conference, the ROC's application for participating in GATT and the Montreux Protocol obtained the unanimous support of these countries.

The exchange visits by government leaders have also contributed to enhancing mutual friendship. Visitors to the ROC included President Rafael Leonardo Callejas of Honduras, President Frederik W. de Klerk of South Africa, King Taufa'ahu Tupou IV of Tonga, President General Andre Kolingba of the Central African Republic, President Violeta Barrios de Chamorro of Nicaragua, Vice President Ossio Sanjines and Speaker Gaston Encinas Valverde of Bolivia, Vice President Espina Salguero of Guatemala and President Guillermo Endara Galimany of Panama.

ROC Vice President Li Yuan-zu visited three Central American countries in August 1991—Costa Rica, Honduras and Nicaragua—on behalf of President Lee Teng-hui. Li's visit left a lasting impression of friendship on the governments and peoples of the these nations.

Foreign Minister Fredrick Chien, at the invitation of relevant authorities, participated in the Twelfth Summit Conference of Central American Countries held in Nicaragua in June 1992. It was a particularly significant event for the ROC, because Chien was the only non-Latin American guest to be invited to attend this Summit Conference. After the conference Chien visited Guatemala, El Salvador and Panama. Thanks to these visits, ties between the ROC and countries in Central America were further strengthened and consolidated, helping to promote the ROC's role in this part of the world.

Among the twenty-nine countries with which the ROC currently has diplomatic relations, the Bahamas, Grenada, Liberia, Belize, Lesotho, Guinea-Bissau, Nicaragua, the Central African Republic and Niger are countries with which the ROC has newly established or re-established diplomatic ties in the last three years. Some of the ties were established when Premier Lien

Chan served as foreign minister. The fact that the ROC was able to establish relations with countries such as Grenada that formerly had relations with Peking illustrates the success of pragmatic diplomacy.

Thanks to adequate exercise of economic strength and pragmatic diplomacy, the ROC has made quick advances in the field of substantive relations. In 1992 alone, consulates-general, representative offices and trade missions have been set up in several countries with which the ROC has no diplomatic relations, including Australia, Uruguay, Latvia, Canada, Angola, Poland, Jamaica and Vietnam. The number of missions and offices in the areas where the ROC does not maintain diplomatic relations has increased to 89 in 58 countries. Seventeen of these offices use the official designation of "Republic of China."

In the meantime, some ROC missions in Japan, Europe and ASEAN countries have changed their names into the Taipei Economic and Cultural Office. The official tone of the new name reflects a better relationship with these countries. On the other hand, a new model of relations and communication channels have been also established with the Commonwealth of Independent States as well as with the three Baltic countries. The signing with Russia of the Agreement on the Taipei-Moscow Economic and Cultural Coordination Committee is a case in point.

Also noteworthy is that the ROC signed with the Republic of Vanuatu a Joint Communiqué in June 1992 which, starting from September 24, 1992, mandates the two countries to grant mutual recognition based upon principles of international law, thus creating a new model of pragmatic diplomacy.[22]

In the era of the new world order since the end of the Cold War, the instrumental role of international cooperation and international organizations have become all the more evident. Important international matters are solved through international organizations by negotiations in the spirit of international cooperation. President Lee Teng-hui, in his New Year's Day Message of 1993, rightfully declared that "We have to knock on the doors of international organizations one by one until they open, shoulder a greater international responsibility, and contribute to the building of a new world order."[23]

President Lee's message fully reflects the ROC's ambition of fully participating in the international arena. Consequently, the ROC Foreign Ministry has made active involvement in international activities and participation in international organizations, including the U.N., its major task.

In fact, provisions relating to active participation in international matters are prescribed in the ROC Constitution. Article 141 of the Constitution states: "The foreign policy of the Republic of China shall, in a spirit of independence and initiative and on the basis of the principles of equality and reciprocity, cultivate good-neighborliness with other nations, and respect treaties and the Charter of the United Nations, in order to protect the rights and interests of Chinese citizens residing abroad, promote international cooperation, advance international justice and ensure world peace." Evidently, the Foreign Ministry's mottoes of "being actively involved in international matters and planning to rejoin the United Nations" are based on the constitutional provisions to "promote international cooperation, advance international justice and ensure world peace."

Due to the Foreign Ministry's unflagging efforts, voices appealing for justice and for the U.N. not to ignore the ROC's existence have been heard in international forums. Nicaraguan President Violeta Barrios de Chamorro, in her speech delivered at the 47th Session of the United Nations General Assembly, told nations that the time had come for recognizing the Republic of China's achievements in many fields.[24]

This was the first time since the ROC's retreat from the U.N. that a head of state from a friendly country took an official stand on behalf of U.N. membership for the ROC.

Following the Nicaraguan Head of State, President Alfredo Christiani of El Salvador, President Guillermo Endara Galimany of Panama, President Anatolijs Gorbunovs of Latvia, and foreign ministers and permanent representatives of Costa Rica, Guatemala, Belize, Honduras and Guinea-Bissau all stood up to echo Nicaragua's appeal and demanded that the ROC be re-admitted into the world body.

Of course these moves could be construed as "pin-prick diplomacy" (*diplomatie à coups d'épingle*) or be compared to a drop in a bucket of water, but this trickle could someday swell into a powerful tide. One may recall that it took Peking more than twenty years to oust the ROC from the U.N. after India first submitted in 1950 a draft resolution calling for its expulsion. Now the originator is to be paid back in his own coin. The ROC would need much less time to attain its goal, given its current national strength and the more favorable environment in which the ROC finds itself.

Furthermore, the ROC is close to success in its effort to join the General Agreement on Tariffs and Trade (GATT) under the name of "the Separate Customs Territory of Taiwan, Penghu, Kinmen and Matsu." It acquired the status of observer in the November 1991 Board Meeting, marking a great step forward toward formal participation in this international gathering.

Presently, the people of Taiwan have successively defended their participation in a number of multilateral groups, including the Pacific Basin Economic Council (PBEC) and the Pacific Economic Cooperation Conference (PECC). In November 1991 the ROC was invited to attend the ministerial Conference of the Asia Pacific Economic Cooperation forum (APEC). In July 1992 the South Pacific Forum agreed to accept the Republic of China on Taiwan as a "Post-Forum Dialogue-partner" among the Forum countries. The ROC has to date participated in 777 governmental or nongovernmental international organizations.

Also, many world nations are interested in participating in projects under the Six-Year National Development Program. Even European countries that in the past kept a low profile towards the ROC, like France, Germany, the United Kingdom, Ireland and Italy, started sending high level officials to visit Taiwan. The years 1991 and 1992 saw visits by 48 ministerial officials. The United States also bent its rules to send its first cabinet rank Trade Representative Hills for a visit to Taiwan in December 1992.

These facts attest to the success of the ROC's pragmatic diplomacy. However, because of Peking's diplomatic offensive, Taipei suffered successive losses in the severance of diplomatic relations with Saudi Arabia and South Korea. This made Simon Long of *The Guardian* state that in the larger picture, Taipei is losing the diplomatic battle; and he suspected South Africa would be likely to follow suit.[25] But in any case, as to the success of the ROC's pragmatic diplomacy so far, one may well cite Simon Long's remark that "in a world unwilling to give diplomatic cake, Taipei eats it anyway."[26]

## Pragmatic Diplomacy Needs Ammunition for Support

To paraphrase Karl von Clausewitz, foreign policy is an extension of domestic policy. This means that foreign policy needs domestic backing in the form of political, economic and financial support. There is also an old Chinese saying that "a housewife, however clever, cannot prepare a meal without rice." The rice in the case of pragmatic diplomacy is a strong domestic policy, which includes a prosperous economy, an enlightened and orderly political administration, a solid defense, good education, and abundant wealth.

As a matter of fact, pragmatic diplomacy and domestic policy are causally interrelated. Given the present situation of the ROC at home and abroad, and assuming the government continues to give mainland policy the highest national priority as it is doing now, pragmatic diplomacy would be merely a strategic exercise of external relations of its mainland policy.

Since mainland policy is a part of domestic policy, pragmatic diplomacy could be said to be a logical extension of domestic diplomacy. Let us consider what the impact on domestic policy would be if the ROC joined GATT or even the U.N. It is thus clear that pragmatic diplomacy and domestic policy are closely interlinked.

Under the above perception, Taipei successively established an International Economic Cooperation and Development Fund, appropriating US$1.2 billion for economic aid to Third World countries; a Humanitarian Fund for International Disaster Relief, providing aid and assistance to refugees and those who suffered during the Gulf War; and the Chiang Ching-kuo Foundation for International Scholarly Exchange, promoting cultural exchange and research. All are intended to back up pragmatic diplomacy.

This foreign aid policy fully corresponds with the needs of the Third World countries, while living up to the spirit and principle of the international law of development. It also constitutes a kind of international duty and obligation of advanced nations vis-à-vis developing countries.

At a time when the ROC is seeking to join the ranks of the developed countries and is managing to use unconventional formulae to expand its diplomatic space, "foreign aid and assistance" will no doubt play an important role in pragmatic diplomacy.

The U.S. foreign aid program amounted to US$10 billion in 1991, about the same as Japan's program. Even a country like the Netherlands, whose economic and trade volume are comparable to that of the ROC, has a foreign aid program amounting to US$1 billion. Hence the Asia Development Bank suggests that the ROC should earmark 0.025% of its GDP for foreign aid. The United Nations sets a standard aid budget of 0.07% of the GDP for the developed countries. The ROC's foreign aid in 1990 amounted to a mere 0.02% of its GDP, far less than these countries. The foreign affairs authorities are hoping that in the not too distant future the foreign aid program budget can reach 0.07% of the GDP.[27]

The problem is, the ROC does not possess a consistent set of standards for foreign aid, nor does it have experience in its operations. Nor even does its public opinion possess any modern perception or conception of international moral obligations and economic assistance, which explains the absence of an adequate legal framework for the foreign aid program. It is time for the ROC to pass appropriate legislation on foreign aid, according to its budget capacity, in order to manage the much-demanded international aid and assistance that the already insufficient Foreign Ministry budget is unable to cover. People need to be educated to revise their incorrect conceptions of foreign aid as "money diplomacy" or "fool's diplomacy."

We must be cognizant of the existence of principles, practices, and international responsibilities to the global community, such as interconnectedness, mutual assistance, the right to development advocated by the new-style international law of development, North-South and South-South cooperation—none of which allows a country to stay outside the global community. It is all the more true that pragmatic diplomacy needs ammunition, i.e. domestic policy support, to continue to fulfill its mission, thereby creating a full interaction and harmonious exercise of foreign and domestic policies.

## Pragmatic Diplomacy and the All-Or-Nothing Policy Strive for the Same Goal

The notion of a zero-sum game which we consistently maintained toward the Chinese communists for several decades was the ROC equivalent of the Hallstein Doctrine embraced by the former Federal Republic of Germany. It summarized the ROC's policy on matters involving the PRC until at least the 1970s. At a time when the ROC was still able to maintain the upper hand on the diplomatic front throughout the 1960s, this "zero-sum" approach had its positive function in helping bar the PRC from the United Nations and in forestalling or obstructing the PRC's bid for diplomatic relations with other countries.

However, as international currents shifted against the ROC diplomatically, the question was no longer one of coexistence of both the "good guy" and the "bad guy". It has become a question of the "bad guy" being accepted and the "good guy" expelled. It was a question of how to keep the ROC in the U.N. when it was no longer possible to keep the PRC out. By then the challenge for the ROC was how to handle the sensitive issues of flag raising and national designation, among others, in its rivalry with the PRC in the diplomatic arena. Such concepts as "choosing the lesser of two evils" and "staying alive to fight for another day" gradually gained acceptance. Thus "flexible" or "pragmatic" diplomacy became the basis for the ROC diplomatic offensive waged at the time.

Now that times have changed, it may seem anachronistic to again drum up the "good guy-bad guy" theme. However, for purposes of analysis, there is still a need for clarifying what it means. The term "good guy", of course refers to the Republic of China, a democratic republic of, by, and for the people, established in accordance with Dr. Sun Yat-sen's Three Principles of the People, and therefore the true lineal descendent of the Chinese cultural legacy. The term "bad guy", on the other hand, implies betrayal of that legacy, since Communist China professed to believe in Marxism-Leninism under Mao Tse-tung's dictatorship.

By the nature of its juxtaposed elements, the motto implies the orthodox legitimacy over the heretic illegitimacy. Yet it makes no sense if the ultimate goal is to reunify China. In this context, all Chinese should give their allegiance to a free, democratic and prosperous China. The inherent assumption is that the legitimate shall triumph over the heretic, hence, the "good guy" over the "bad guy", and the loyalist over the traitor. Seen in this light, both the "good guy-bad guy" rationale and pragmatic diplomacy share a common implied goal, that is, one China. They differ only in tone and means. In tone, the former doctrine is flinching, negative, rigid, and demonstrates defensiveness, reluctance to change and passivity. The latter policy, on the other hand, by being relatively active, assertive and flexible, demonstrates aggressiveness, willingness to take on challenge and adaptability.

The "good guy-bad guy" rationale is basically one of "the less done, the better" that argues for more or less maintaining the passive attitude of a weaker nation without diplomatic relations. It preaches hiding behind the shield of principled disdain to avoid squarely facing the reality of the existence of the two entities. The doctrine of pragmatic diplomacy, on the other hand, disparages inaction as a mistake. The imperative of active diplomacy is meant precisely to compensate for the relatively weaker position one is in. The way out of the present jam, according to this view, is to distinguish the end from the means. While the end may be one China, the means is the reality that there are presently two Chinas. Acknowledging the reality is not an end in itself, but a means to an end. It is diplomacy at its best, if one's end is an ultimately reunified China.[28]

Thus, in terms of their logic and ultimate objectives, both the notion of noncoexitence between the "good guy" and "bad guy" or between the loyalist and the traitor, and the philosophy of pragmatic diplomacy, anchor on nothing other than national reunification. In an interview with the *Asian Wall Street Journal* in September 1990, President Lee Teng-hui stated, "In reality, it is undeniable that China has two political entities at the moment, but China will ultimately be reunified. Our hope is that China will reunify under the principles of a free-market economy, democracy, and free elections." This stance clearly has one China as its long-term goal.

Foreign Minister Fredrick Chien has likewise stated that "the basis of our current pragmatic diplomacy is predicated on the premise of one China with two separate entities for a period of time that co-exist in equality and peace, wherein we would first use our political and economic might with a pragmatic attitude and flexible methods in the pursuit of existence and then development."[29] When translated into the "good guy-bad guy" terminology, our objective in stages would be to ensure the "good guy's" existence while temporarily tolerating the existence of the "bad guy", followed ultimately by the stepping down of the "bad guy". Thus, the two scenarios envision reaching the same destination, though via different routes.

## Conclusion

The symbiotic relationship between the above-mentioned concepts of foreign policy as an extension of domestic policy and domestic policy as an extension of foreign policy, when transposed to the ROC's mainland policy, are even more evidently connected and mutually enabling.

If our mainland policy can be termed a fundamental policy of our nation at the moment, then pragmatic diplomacy is the strategic exercise of external relations under our mainland policy, and diplomacy is an extension of domestic policy. Conversely, if the exercise of pragmatic diplomacy results in some diplomatic breakthroughs or gains (such as joining GATT or some other international institutions) that are sufficient to break down the obstacles and shackles imposed upon us internationally by Peking, or even to go so far as to provoke some fundamental changes within the PRC toward freedom, democracy and the respect for human rights, then domestic policy is an extension of foreign policy. With the flexible exercise of the two, the ultimate goal of "One China"—an ideal and wonderful China—will be reached more easily.

However, given the international situation and the current cross-Straits context, we must not expect to attain the "One China" goal on the first try. Whether in terms of theory or practice, there is a long way to go. We are bound to experience a series of successive phases of exploration, feeling each other out, buffer-

325

ing, confrontation, competing, dialoging, and negotiating, while passing through a *de facto* temporary and transitory coexistence.

The concept of "One country, two systems," proffered by Deng Xiaoping, consisting of one predominant communist system and one subordinate capitalist system, is evidently unacceptable to the ROC. Some believe "Peking's 'One China, two systems' could be interpreted as two different political systems coexisting under one China—one of the Three Principles of the People and one communist regime, there should be no dispute over central or local government. In terms of diplomacy, there are no reservations, either: official diplomacy represents China, pragmatic diplomacy represents also China, treating countries with or without diplomatic ties on an equal footing. And this kind of diplomacy could be called 'diplomacy of equal deeds.'"[30]

Some foreign academics argue that the "one China, two systems" concept could be accepted under certain conditions, as stated by James Liley, former U.S. ambassador to Peking: "One country, yes, but a free and democratic one," "Two systems, yes, but equal and based on full reciprocity."[31]

Another academic, Shen Chiun-shan, at an earlier stage countered Peking's "One China, two systems" by advocating "One China, two administrations."[32] Shen Chiun-shan's conception matches in a way the direction pragmatic diplomacy is pursuing.

Professor Lee Wen-lang of Ohio State University innovated a reverse process, in order to avoid falling into Peking's trap of "One China" by advocating the conception of "Two administrations, one China." By reversing the process and putting emphasis on "Two administrations" Lee deems it better reflects the current objective existence of "two realities." Lee thinks also that it would be more logical to attain the "one China" goal by trading space for time (time being to the ROC's advantage), while each of the two administers its affairs in its own way without interference in the other's. This China, in the future, according to Lee, will value moral principles, democracy and the people's welfare.[33]

All the above-mentioned concepts or theories concerning the "reunification of China" or "one China" reflect generally the background and implementation of the ROC's current pragmatic diplomacy, as well as its ultimate goal. But the probability of its success relies on the word "change." Diplomacy is, by nature, a changing force since it constantly adapts to changing situations. As to how to adapt the change, even to provoke the change and make the change turn into benefit for the ROC, and for the latter to take the lead, it is a tremendous challenge that Taipei diplomatic authorities must take.

The evolution of the international situation is favorable to the Republic of China. While recognizing that the collapse of the Soviet Union has made Peking—this remnant of Marxism and Leninism—more isolated, chances are that in the foreseeable future, mainland China will catch up by adjusting itself to the world's new changing mood. And its adaptability should not be underestimated. At a time when Peking has been so active in isolating the ROC and intimidating the latter's friends, Taipei should double its vigilance in moving every step on the way.

Fortunately, in terms of domestic policy, elections of members of the Second National Assembly and Legislature have been successively held, and the Six-Year National Development Program will soon be pushed forward. Democratization and economic reconstruction are bound to reach new heights and will serve as a pole of attraction for the 1.1 billion people of mainland China. Together with the efforts of pragmatic diplomacy, the international situation will turn out to be more favorable to the island republic. The political space that has been widened thanks to skillful interaction of foreign and domestic policies will surely allow the ROC to play a more important international role on the world stage.

## NOTES

1. Dr. Jason Hu, "President Lee's pragmatic diplomacy and China's reunification," *The Daily Telegraph*, May 21, 1990.
2. Bernard T. K. Joei, "Basic Theories of Pragmatic Diplomacy," *Theory and Policy Quarterly*, No. 1, Vol. 6, Taipei, October 31, 1991.
3. Fredrick Chien, "A View from Taipei," *Foreign Affairs* quarterly, 1991/92 Winter issue, p. 22.
4. Lee Teng-hui, opening address to th KMT's Thirteenth Party Congress, July 1988.
5. Fredrick Chien, Speech on "New Developments on Pragmatic Diplomacy" at a Symposium on "Current National Policy's Great Concepts and Orientations," jointly organized by the *China Times* and the *21st Century Foundation,* April 13, 1990.
6. Fredrick Chien, in his administrative report to the legislature on "Recent developments in the intenational situation and diplomacy," March 18, 1992, Foreign Affairs Committee, 89th Session of the Legislative Yuan.
7. Fredrick Chien, "New trends of the ROC's diplomatic policy in the 1990s," *Issues and Studies*, 10th issue, October 1991.
8. I-shing Chen, "Theories and practice of the ROC's pragmatic diplomacy," *Theory and Policy Quarterly*, Vol. 4, No. 4: 27-38.
9. *Taiwan, Hearings before the Senate Committee on Foreign Relations*, 96th Congress, 1st session, on Bill S. 245, February 5, 6, 7, 8, 21, and 22, 1979, Washington, D.C.: U.S. Government Printing Office, 1979, p. 148
10. Bernard T.K. Joei, "The concept of recognition in Latin American countries," *Issues and Studies*, 30: 8, Taipei (June 10, 1991).
11. Bernard T.K. Joei, "The International Status of the Republic of China and its 'Quasi'-Diplomacy," *Area Studies*, published by

the Center of Area Studies, Tamkang University, Taipei, IX, 2:4-6.
12. Hongdah Chiu, "Questions in Taiwan-American relations," *China Times Cultural Press*, Taipei, 1979, p. 138.
13. Hubert Thierry, Jean Combaccau, Serge Sur and Charles Vallé, *Droit international public*, Paris Editions Montchrestien, 1984, pp. 4-7.
14. See Note 10.
15. Bernard T.K. Joei, "PRC urged to 'return to the Constitution' under the ferver of mainland exodus," *Central Daily News* (international edition), April 1, 1988.
16. See Wang Ching-hong's report on "The U.S. favors pragmatic diplomacy," *Central Daily News* (international edition) July 24, 1991, p. 1; Fu Chien-chung, "U.S.'s China policy: reality and illusion," *Central Daily News* (international edition), August 5, 1991, p. 1.
17. Guy Feuer and Hervé Cassan, *Droit international du développement*, (Paris: Dalloz, 1985), p. 33.
18. Bernard T.K. Joei, "ROC and the International Law of Development," *Area Studies*, Special Issue: "ROK & ROC in Transition — Political and Economic Developments," Tamkang University Press 1989, Vol. X, No. 1, pp. 94-6.
19. See Fredrick Chien, Note 5.
20. Mark London, quoting *Asiaweek* in his article on "Fred Chien and the Tobacco War." Rigardie's, August 1987, collected in Fredrick F. Chien *Faith and Reliance: The Republic of China on Taiwan Forges Ahead*, Kwang Hwa Publishing (USA) Inc., 1988, pp. 330-7.
21. Steven Strasser, "Taiwan Reaches Out," *Newsweek*, October 5, 1992, p. 28.
22. Fredrick Chien, Report to Foreign Affairs Committee, Legislative Yuan, 90th Session on "Latest International Situation and Diplomatic Administration," October 28, 1992; Ouyang Jui-hsiung, Director of Information and Cultural Affairs, "Current Diplomatic Situation," November 1992.
23. *United Daily News*, Taipei, January 1, 1993, p. 1.
24. Chien, Report, October 28, 1992, p. 18.
25. Simon Long, "In a world unwilling to give diplomatic cake, Taipei eats it anyway," *The Guardian*, June 22, 1992.
26. Ibid.
27. Chien, "New Trends."
28. Bernard T.K. Joei, "To Act or Not to Act and Flexible Diplo-

macy," Column, *China Times*, Taipei, January 10, 1988. p. 2.

29. Chien, "New Trends."

30. Teng Li-hao (former senior parliamentarian) in his written interpellation "Five suggestions on national policies," *Official documents relating to resolutions*, Legislative Yuan, 84th Session, September 29, 1989, 5th Plenary Meeting, Document No. 038, p. 7.

31. James Liley, "A Formula for China-Taiwan Relations," *Asia Wall Street Journal*, September 6-7, 1991.

32. Shen Chiun-shan, "'One China, two administrations' vs. 'One China, two systems'," *China Times*, Taipei, September 1, 1987, p. 2.

33. Lee Wen-lang, "Getting out of the dilemma of Unification and Independence by the way of 'Two administrations, one China'," *United Daily News*, Taipei, January 3, 1993, p. 6.

# ROC's Foreign Aid Policy

Lee Wei-chin
*Asian Affairs*
Spring 1993

Taiwan's diplomatic stand in the global community has faced challenges since 1971, when it lost its UN seat to the PRC (People's Republic of China). More and more countries shifted their official recognition from Taipei to Beijing, and fewer and fewer international organizations accepted Taiwan's membership. By 1988, countries having diplomatic ties with Taiwan numbered only twenty-two, the majority of them insignificant players in the international arena. Moreover, not all of them had full-fledged diplomatic missions in Taiwan. Although Taiwan's total world trade volume went from $3.9 billion in 1971 to $39.5 billion in 1980, fifty countries severed diplomatic relations with Taiwan during the same period. In 1989, only 5 percent of Taiwan's trade was with countries that officially recognized Taiwan.[1] Its official membership in international organizations in 1988 had declined to only eight international bodies.[2] These developments cast doubt on Taiwan's continuing viability as an independent political entity. In order to break out of its diplomatic isolation, Taiwan has employed its economic strength to gain friendship, not only deepening interactions with friendly countries but also enlarging its web of connections. One way it has beefed up this effort has been through the use of foreign aid.

This article focuses on Taiwan's foreign aid policy since the late 1980s by examining the extent of its success and failure and investigating its scope, durability, and implications. How and where is this foreign

*Lee Wei-chin is an associate professor of political science at Wake Forest University, North Carolina.*

aid delivered? What is the limitation of this "dollar diplomacy," as some Taiwanese politicians call it? Is it designed to allay suffering and promote development in needy nations, or is it intended instead to serve the interests of the donor? The findings will shed light not only on the utility of foreign aid in Taiwan's diplomacy but also on Taiwan's future status in the international community.

Information on Taiwan's foreign aid has not been systematically documented and placed in the public domain. The government considers these statistical data and documentary sources to be sensitive and confidential and only discloses information selectively. This makes exhaustive evaluation impossible, but an examination of the available materials offers enough hints for us to draw sensible conclusions about its foreign aid policy.

## Foreign Aid: Design and Implementation

There is no consensus regarding the definition of foreign aid. Some view it as including any flow of materials and financial resources, including grants, loan packages for which the interest is below the market rate, non-compensatory technical assistance, officially guaranteed credits, and reparation pay. Others regard foreign aid as only the transfer of resources on terms easier than those that could be obtained in the capial market.[3] Notwithstanding these various definitions, it is usually considered to be a transfer from the haves to the have-nots for the purpose of economic development, military security, and disaster relief and rehabilitation.

At one time or another, most industrialized countries have been donors of aid. The implementation of the Marshall Plan and the wooing of third world countries by foreign aid since the 1950s occurred within the context of the East-West confrontation.

Likewise, in the 1950s and 1960s, the competition between mainland China and Taiwan for international recognition also led each of them to offer extensive foreign aid to the third world. For China, the purpose of foreign aid was not only to isolate and diminish Taiwan's international standing but also to pose as a third choice for developing countries by claiming a noble purpose of offering genuine help, unlike the exploitative intention of both the American capitalist imperialist and the Soviet socialist revisionist.[4] For Taiwan, the purpose of foreign aid was not to bid for a leadership role but to focus on survival by winning friendship and support for its legitimacy as an acceptable actor in world politics, particularly to ensure its UN seat.[5] By the 1970s, however, Taiwan was engaged in a losing battle with Beijing for diplomatic recognition as the legitimate government of the whole China.[6]

Most of the financing of Taiwan's foreign aid programs before the late 1960s came from American surplus agricultural products sold in Taiwan. Even though the idea of aiding other developing countries was partially initiated by Taiwan, the money then was mostly from the United States.[7] The objective was to demonstrate Taiwan's experience and was aimed at self-sufficiency, but the emphasis was on simple, low-cost, labor-intensive programs by disseminating know-how in the field. By 1980, over two thousand technicians from Taiwan had served in some fifty different countries, mostly African and Latin American countries having diplomatic ties with Taiwan. In contrast, because of its great financial resources and economic clout, Taiwan's foreign aid program since the late 1980s has been more extensive than this early grass-roots approach. Technical and agricultural assistance projects are still part of aid projects, but financial loans, grants, and contributions to multilateral organizations have been added to the list of provisions. Although Taiwan's foreign affairs have been less influenced than before by the United States after the latter withdrew its recognition in 1979, its foreign aid policy indicates the trend of its increasing autonomy. Taiwan · no longer needs to rely on U.S. financing to launch its aid efforts.

Taiwan's foreign aid program rests in the decision-making process of the Ministry of Foreign Affairs (MOFA) and the Ministry of Economic Affairs (MOEA). Two implementing arms are the Committee of International Technical Cooperation (CITC) and the International Economic Cooperation and Development Fund (IECDF). The CITC was initially known as Operation Vanguard, established in 1961 to provide agricultural technical assistance to African and Latin American countries. The IECDF was created in 1988 with a five-year goal of allocating $1.2 billion in aid to friendly developing countries. Although the IECDF was set up by the MOEA and the official who is in charge of daily administration is the political vice-minister of the MOEA, the IECDF is ultimately steered by a seven-member cabinet-level council with representatives from various agencies.[8] Additional agencies and departments are called in whenever help is needed. For example, when the project involves agricultural assistance, the Taiwan provincial government's Department of Agriculture and Forestry is consulted. When the aid is concerned with extending credit to foreign governments and the financing of outward investment, the Export-Import Bank (Eximbank), a specialized government bank established in 1979, is brought into the implementation process.[9]

Although the assumption is that both the MOFA and the MOEA hold joint jurisdiction over decision making, each ministry sees aid from a somewhat different angle. The MOEA sees it more from an economic viewpoint, examining aid proposals carefully in order to ensure efficient and effective use of money. Without denying the necessity of wise planning of aid for the commercial interest and development needs of recipients, the MOFA is more concerned with aid as a diplomatic lever. Aid programs are sometimes employed as expedient political means to win diplomatic favors. The MOEA prefers a detailed and careful screening process, which might take more than a year; the MOFA tends to favor a shorter period of deliberation for approval in order to take advantage of changing international circumstances or to sustain relationships with countries deemed "politically correct" and important to Taiwan. Most recipients of the MOFA's aid are friendly countries, meaning that they either have recognized Taiwan or that they are willing to construct substantial relations without fear of Beijing's reprisals.

In the 1991 fiscal year, the allocation for the IECDF was $48 million, and the CITC received $32 million. The MOFA budgeted $188 million for international activities, partly to be used for external assistance and humanitarian disaster relief. If we assume that the MOFA's budget was completely dedicated to external aid and that this funding was used in its entirety, the total of the IECDF, CITC, and MOFA portions — $268 million in all — would account for 0.16 percent of Taiwan's gross national product (GNP).[10] Although it cannot be determined if the scheduled budget has been spent completely due to the political sensitivity of some aid programs, and although it is clear that not every penny of the MOFA's international budget was spent on external aid, a conservative estimate of Taiwan's 1991 foreign aid spending would be about 0.1 percent of the GNP, less than that of the United States (0.15 percent) in 1989. Even so, in total dollars, Taiwan's aid compares favorably with some OECD (Organization for Economic Cooperation and Development) members such as Ireland and New Zealand, and it is higher than that of most of the OPEC (Organization of Petroleum Exporting Countries)

countries.[11] In the 1992 fiscal year, the budget allocation for the IECDF alone has been increased to $120 million.[12]

## Who Gets What

Taiwan's foreign aid covers six geographic areas (Table 1). In Latin America, Taiwan promised $10 million aid to Grenada and $50 million aid to Belize for housing and hydraulic power plant projects in 1989.[13] The amount of aid for Costa Rica and Panama totaled $16.8 million dollars in 1989-90.[14] In August 1991, Vice President Li Yuan-zu made a highly publicized official visit to Costa Rica, Honduras, and Nicaragua, despite charges from the Taiwanese opposition party of buying friendship with aid pledges of millions of dollars to these countries.[15]

The arm of aid has also reached Africa, a target of Taiwan's aid program since the 1960s, when Taiwan was competing with the PRC for UN membership and recognition. In the 1980s, Taiwan focused on regaining recognition from some previously friendly countries. Liberia received fifteen thousand tons of rice in 1988-89 to relieve its food shortage crises and then $212 million to cover road construction and educational improvement after its decision to normalize relations with Taiwan in 1989. Lesotho received $30 million in aid from Taiwan in 1989-90. In 1991, Nigeria was offered a $38 million aid package.[16] South Africa also received a $60 million low-interest loan in 1991 to provide black people in South Africa with technical and agricultural assistance.[17]

In 1989, Papua New Guinea, a country in the Southern Pacific without official ties with Taiwan, agreed to exchange trade missions with Taiwan. This accord was reached after Taiwan's pledge of $17.65 million in aid and occurred amid Beijing's protests.[18] The year 1991 witnessed additional aid to Papua New

Guinea as well as $710,000 to the Solomon Islands, which recognize Taiwan as a nation.

Delegations from Southeast Asia are likewise beating a path to Taipei for aid. Southeast Asia has been the top priority of Taiwan's foreign aid programs because of its geographical closeness and recent economic vitality. In 1991, for example, Indonesia and Thailand each received $1.7 million in aid to further so-called "substantive" relations.[19] The government has also begun to evaluate the possibility of a $15 million loan to Vietnam (with 3.5 percent interest rate) in addition to technical assistance to a proposed highway construction project in Vietnam.[20]

The latest aid effort in Taiwan's "flexible diplomacy" is in the Baltic states and other republics of the defunct Soviet Union. The IECDF has included these countries in its list of states eligible for assistance.[21] Though the Baltic states have established relations with the PRC to win China's crucial vote regarding their UN membership applications, they appear to have a strong sense of affinity toward the thriving capitalist economy of Taiwan. It has become a pattern for newly independent countries to establish diplomatic relations with China first to gain UN seats and then to develop relations with Taiwan later. The possibility of economic assistance, something more tangible than an economic model, led to exchanges of legations or consulates between Taiwan and Latvia, Estonia, and Lithuania. Ukraine also allowed the establishment of Taiwan's trade representative office in Kiev with Taiwan's promise of food assistance in return. Taiwan also focuses on technical assistance. For example, it has established a variety of training programs for managers from East European countries. All these developments have given Taiwan an "official presence" in these countries, accompanied by limited diplomatic privileges and immunities.[22]

# Table 1. Selected List of Taiwan's Foreign Aid

| Recipient | Year(s) | Amount/Content | Remarks |
|---|---|---|---|
| **Europe** | | | |
| Belarus | 1992 | $1 million/financial and medical aid | |
| Estonia | 1991 | Aid consideration | Exchanged legations |
| Hungary | 1991 | Technical training for managers of light industry | |
| Latvia | 1991 | Aid consideration | Exchanged legations |
| Lithuania | 1991 | Aid consideration | Exchanged legations |
| Russia | 1992 | 10,000 tons/rice | Unofficial coordination councils, trade offices established |
| Ukraine | 1992 | $15 million/medical aid | Trade agreements and offices established |
| **Asia** | | | |
| Indonesia | 1989-91 | $1.7 million/unknown | |
| Philippines | 1990 | $200,000/aid for earthquake; $300,000/vocational training; $1.5 million/fish research (jointly with Indonesia) | High-level official visits |
| Thailand | 1989-91 | $1.7 million/unknown | |
| Mongolia | 1992 | 2,000 tons/rice | |
| **Latin America** | | | |
| Bahamas[a] | 1989 | $2.5 million/unknown | Diplomacy established in 1989 |
| Belize[a] | 1989 | $50 million/road and power plant projects | Diplomacy established in 1989 |
| Costa Rica[a] | 1988-90 | $9 million/export processing zones; $55 million/low-interest loan | |
| Grenada[a] | 1989 | $10 million/unknown | Diplomacy established in 1989 |
| Honduras[a] | 1991 | $20 million/low-interest loan | |
| Nicaragua[a] | 1990 | $100 million/3-year low-interest loan | Diplomacy established in 1990; ROC vice-president visit in 1991 |
| Panama[a] | 1989-90 | $7.8 million/export processing zones | |
| Paraguay[a] | 1989-91 | $3.2 million/relief aid and project funding | |
| **Africa** | | | |
| Cen. African Republic[a] | 1992 | $200,000/Sudanese refugees and technical assistance | Diplomacy established in 1991 |
| Lesotho[a] | 1989-92 | $30 million/unknown; | |

# Table 1. Continued

| Recipient | Year(s) | Amount/Content | Remarks |
|---|---|---|---|
| Liberia[a] | 1989 | $1 million/food aid for drought | |
| | | $212 million/loans for highway projects and education | Diplomacy established in 1989 |
| Malawi[a] | 1992 | $3 million/aid for drought damage | |
| Niger[a] | 1992 | $50 million loan/economic assistance | Diplomacy established in 1992 |
| South Africa[a] | 1991 | $60 million/low-interest loan | |
| Swaziland[a] | 1992 | $1 million/food aid for drought | |
| Southern Pacific | | | |
| Papua New Guinea | 1989 | $17.65 million/building project | |
| Solomon Islands[a] | 1989-91 | $710,000/unknown | |
| Middle East | | | |
| Jordan | 1991 | $20 million/relief aid for the Gulf War | Representative office name is changed to the "Commercial office of the ROC (Taiwan)" |
| Kurdish refugees | 1991 | $10 million/relief aid for the Gulf War | |
| Turkey | 1991 | $2 million/relief aid for the Gulf War | Rejected a further $3 million |
| Multilateral Aid | | | |
| Asian Development Bank | 1992 | $15 million/Asian Development Fund | ROC has paid back a total of $100.4 million in loans acquired from the ADB |
| Central American Bank for Economic Development | 1991 | $150 million/"Fund for the Economic and Social Development of Central America" | Membership of the bank |
| European Bank for Reconstruction and Development | 1991 | $10 million/"Taipei China-European Bank Cooperation Fund" for Eastern Europe | Observer status on the bank's board |
| South Pacific Forum | 1992 | Possible economic assistance to individual members | Post-Forum Dialogue Partner status |

Note:Sources are taken from various issues of *Free China Journal, Far Eastern Economic Review, Asiaweek*, and newspapers in Chinese and English. This list is intended for readers to have a general view of Taiwan's aid programs. Aid figures may vary in different sources. As aid may be pledged and carried out for several years, figures here do not necessarily mean the total amount of aid delivered to the recipient in the years indicated in this table.

[a]Has official diplomatic relations with Taiwan.

In cases where direct assistance has been politically inappropriate, Taiwan has employed a multilateral approach to aid. In Southeast Asia, for example, the IECDF appropriated $15 million in 1992 to the Asian Development Equity Fund, which is supported by the Asian Development Bank.[23] In addition, a $150 million donation was pledged in 1991 to the Central American Bank for Economic Integration to help needy countries in that region in the early 1990s. As a result, the bank revised its charter to allow Taiwan to join in as a non-regional member in 1992.[24] Moreover, the South Pacific Forum, a regional organization of 15 member states in the South Pacific, admitted Taiwan to be the eighth Dialogue Partner in 1992 for its annual Post-Forum Dialogue in order to request economic assistance from Taipei. It is noteworthy that only four member states of the Forum recognize Taiwan (the other seven partners include the United States, Canada, Japan, France, Britain, the PRC, and the European Community).[25]

In dealing with cash-strained Eastern Europe, Taiwan has channeled aid through the European Bank for Reconstruction and Development by promising a $10 million contribution to a special fund to help develop market-oriented economies. A huge portion of the $10 million subscription will be loans to help republics of former Soviet Union and East European countries; 20 percent of it will be used to advise Taiwan's investors in Europe and help make related purchases from Taiwan. As of June 1992, 90 percent of the fund had been used.[26] This gives Taiwan a link with an international financial organization, even though it is not qualified to join the bank because it is a non-European country and a non-IMF (International Monetary Fund) affiliate. In fiscal year 1992, Taiwan's contribution to the three regional banks — the European Bank for Reconstruction and Development, the Asian Development Bank, and the Central American Bank — totaled $32.5 million, accounting for 0.07 percent of the government's budget.[27]

Taiwan is also willing and ready to offer help whenever needed in the international community. Amid the intensive pledge efforts to offset the costs of military operations in the Persian Gulf, Taiwan's initial offer was about $100 million. Although it was not comparable to the amounts offered by Japan and Germany, Taiwan's offer was larger than that of most other nations. For example, South Korea, which is larger in territorial size and population, responded with an offer of $50 million in cash and $70 million in goods and services over a two-year period. Even after the United States turned down Taiwan's offer because of its concern with the PRC's critical vote in the UN Security Council, Taiwan still pleged $30 million to the Middle Eastern countries hurt by the crisis.[28] All of this aid is on top of other humanitarian programs, for example, $20 million to Jordan to offset losses during the gulf crisis and $10 million to Kurdish refugees in Iraq.[29]

Several observations about Taiwan's new aid efforts can be made. First, in all cases, Taiwan apparently did not set up the strict precondition that new "friends" first break ties with China. Instead, Taiwan was willing to accept their dual recognition of both Chinas. Even if countries are not enthusiastic about the idea of diplomatic recognition, Taiwan is still willing to use aid to promote official contacts between countries. Accepting that some developing countries, particularly those in Southeast Asia, more or less realize China's role and weight in their national security and regional stability, Taiwan's expectation is not the acquisition of full-scale diplomatic ties but (at least) the establishment of official trade or representative offices under the name of "Taipei" or "Republic of China." The mere existence of such an office helps Taiwan's trade and investors in the host country.

Moreover, official interaction signifies a breakthrough in diplomatic isolation, a beach-head for further development, and a change of international image.

Another example is Europe. Perhaps because of Taiwan's recent aid programs, in combination with its trade and investment, European countries and the European Community have started to take Taiwan seriously, allowing their cabinet-level officials to visit Taiwan since 1991. Europe also accounts for 18 percent of Taiwan's two-way trade in the early 1990s.[30] Reinharde Drifte once pointed out that in the early 1980s, Taiwan was considered only an object of trade and tourism, without any political leverage in East Asia or the international community. There seemed no way for Taiwan to circumvent its diplomatic isolation.[31] In the early 1990s, however, Taiwan's image has undergone a significant change in Europe.

Second, aid and investment are apparently complementary to each other. In 1990, Sam Shieh, the president of Central Bank, estimated that Taiwan's total outward investment might reach twelve to fifteen billion dollars.[32] Aid furthers the expansion of Taiwan's outward investment, as clearly seen in its interaction with Southeast Asia. Given its geographical closeness and cultural affinity, Southeast Asia catches Taiwan's eyes. In 1989, Taiwan directly invested $1.96 billion, 11 percent more than in 1988, in Thailand, Malaysia, Indonesia, and the Philippines. The total investment in these four Southeast Asian countries together during the 1986-1989 period was $4.1 billion, along with $15.9 billion in trade.[33] By 1991, Taiwan had become the largest foreign investor in Vietnam, injecting more than $400 million into the Vietnamese economy. Vietnam also agreed to allow Taiwan to set up a trade representative office to protect the interests and rights of Taiwanese investors there.[34]

Aid and investment walk side by side in Latin America, too. In 1988, the MOFA issued a special policy to encourage investment in this region. The program offers eligible projects a lower loan rate, a percentage of financing up to 80 percent of total investment, and an excellent deal in investment insurance.[35] Nevertheless, Latin America has remained a less attractive investment venue, from Taiwanese investors' perspective, than Southeast Asia because of the latter's cultural affinity and better work ethics.

Even so, experts from Taiwan provided managerial guidance for the establishment of export processing zones in Guatemala, Panama, and Costa Rica. For example, Taiwan paid most of the start-up costs for Taiwanese firms locating in Costa Rica, buying land for sites and offering tax incentives. It is clear that this foreign aid was based as much on export need as on diplomacy: Taiwan was able to use these countries as duty-free launching pads to enter the U.S. market by taking the advantage of the U.S. Caribbean Basin Initiative, which began in 1983 to assist export earnings of twenty-eight Caribbean and Latin American countries by offering trade benefits in the U.S. market.[36] As U.S. resistance to East Asian exports has grown, the idea of lending a hand to the establishment of export processing zones certainly has benefited Taiwan's trade.

Third, though Taiwan's aid has concentrated on Africa, Latin America, and Southeast Asia, South Asia and the Middle East have been relatively neglected, partly because of the lack of regular dialogue and substantial trade relations between Taiwan and some countries in these regions, partly because of the volatile political situation in the Middle East. Another reason may be that certain oil-producing countries have accumulated more than sufficient petrodollars. Upon a recipient's request, however, Taiwan still provides some oil-producing countries with an insignificant amount of technical and agricultural assistance.

Fourth, Taiwan is willing to adopt either the bilateral or multilateral approach to aid, as the situation requires. It seems to be to Taiwan's advantage to engage in bilateral aid relations, which allow the recipient country to identify the donor more easily than in the case of multilateral aid packages. Such relations give Taiwan more discretionary power in negotiation as a donor and allow it to control the initiative. Even though no political strings are attached, indirect persuasion is at work. As long as give-and-take is established, Taiwan's goal of "substantial diplomacy" has been partially fulfilled.

At times, the multilateral aid approach is employed, however, to reduce the political sensitivity incurred from bilateral aid. Moreover, when the organization in charge of the multilateral aid decides to accept Taiwan's contribution, Taiwan sometimes acquires membership in order to participate in the management and governance of aid allocation. Even without such membership, the multilateral route establishes communication between Taiwan and other major donors. This facilitates Taiwan's "networking and bonding" capability, improves its chances of eventual membership in international organizations, and strengthens its claims as a de facto entity separate from the PRC.

## The Objectives of Taiwanese Aid

The political transition of 1986-1988 to a democratic regime, with the establishment of opposition parties and the lifting of martial law, freed Taiwan from its decades-long ideological stance of non-coexistence with the PRC. Though the principle of non-coexistence satisfied the self-justified sense of morality in rhetoric, it in effect entrapped Taiwan in a self-limiting situation without sufficient freedom to maneuver for creative diplomacy. The gradual thaw in domestic politics has been reflected in external relations. Pragmatism seems to be taking the lead in Taiwan's foreign policy, and foreign aid seems to be an indispensable and effective tool to achieve one of its top foreign policy objectives: to win more international support, preferably official recognition, for Taiwan's existence as an independent political entity and Taiwan's participation in international organizations, thus warding off diplomatic isolation and deterring the PRC from taking drastic measures against Taiwan. This explains why Taiwan's aid sometimes goes to some mini-states with which Taiwan has no extensive trade or investment relationship at all.

This objective certainly cannot be easily achieved. The PRC has consistently argued that Taiwan's foreign aid policy is "silver-bullet diplomacy" to cloak its intention of establishing a "two Chinas" or "one China and one Taiwan" policy, resulting in the "creeping officiality" of Taiwan's international status.[37] The PRC still has influence in blocking Taiwan's aid offensive. For instance, Taiwan was excluded from a two-day conference in Tokyo in May 1992 that aimed at providing economic aid to Mongolia, at which seventeen countries and five international organizations participated.[38] After receiving $2 million in aid from Taiwan during the gulf crisis, Turkey turned down a further $3 million because of Beijing's protest. Egypt also rejected a $5 million aid offer from Taiwan.[39] Partly because of the changing Middle East situation, and partly because of the reliance on the PRC for missile supplies and satellite launching, Saudi Arabia finally agreed to establish ties with the PRC.[40] When a recipient country is greatly concerned with security, Taiwan's money-oriented aid packages still have difficulty in competing with the PRC's offer of arms. In order to head off further diplomatic setbacks such as those created by Saudi Arabia, Indonesia, and Singapore when they recognized the PRC in 1991 and South Korea in 1992, Taiwan has pushed for more aid offensives in the developing countries.

Aid supporters, however, claim that aid is not strictly for political purpose. The need to maintain vigorous external economic relations for Taiwan's sustained growth becomes another top priority. Aid paves the way for increasing Taiwan's outward investment and acts as leverage to enable its investors to enjoy better treatment in recipient countries. "Aid constituency" in Taiwan apparently includes business groups who see foreign aid as one way to increase trade sales and investment opportunities. The commercial nature of Taiwan's aid stimulates trade between donor and recipient and indirectly leads to more earnings because of viable trade cash flows.

Aid also creates relocation options so that Taiwan's manufacturers can consider locations in Southeast Asia rather than just in mainland China. Taiwan's total investments in China reached well over $5 billion in 1991,[41] but the government has long warned that the PRC intends to entrap Taiwanese enterprises and investment in China's market and production in order to create irremediable dependency for future political black-mail. Dependence on the mainland has also pulled Taiwan into disputes that are not its own making. The United States has constantly threatened economic retaliation against the PRC for its unfair trade practices, lack of human rights protection, and violations of intellectual and property rights. Through its investments in mainland China, Taiwan is indirectly entangled in these disputes. A variety of aid packages in Southeast Asia gives Taiwanese business and industry the option of switching from the mainland to enjoy similar benefits of low labor costs and extensive investment advantages elsewhere.

Moreover, overseas investment eases pressures from the appreciation of Taiwan's currency, labor shortages and wage increases, the growing demand for environmental protection, excessive foreign exchange reserves, and trade imbalances with other countries. Outward investment also facilitates exports by setting up offshore production to bypass quota restriction in the fenced markets of major trading partners such as the United States.[42] Aid serves the role of lubricant to smooth relations between host countries and investors and makes it easier for Taiwan's companies to put down roots without stirring up any existing racial resentment against ethnic Chinese and outside Chinese investors in local economies, especially in Southeast Asia. Taiwan's investment is therefore seen to be of little threat to the local government and societies. Thus, an "underlying rationality" concerning Taiwan's trade and investment opportunities pushes forward the foreign aid programs.

In addition to the two top priorities of a solid international standing and trade and investment promotion, other objectives have been discussed, but they have received relatively lower priority and less attention. One is to address the need to help the less developed countries (LCD), an idea that gained momentum in domestic political dialogues in the 1980s. The government claimed that Taiwan's aid is considered not only an answer to the call for "burden sharing" in international development issues but also an indication of the economic power shift to the Pacific. U.S. aid to Taiwan from 1949 to 1965 partially contributed to Taiwan's political stability and economic prosperity. Now it can be said that it is time for Taiwan to pay back its due. Moreover, using the words of foreign minister Fredrick F. Chien, Taiwan becomes "a potentially valuable contributor to the emerging new world order" by helping others.[43] Although countries still resist the idea of recognizing Taiwan, aid provides Taiwan with some room for diplomatic give-and-take in the international community. "Being there" in the international aid regime at least cultivates a positive image of Taiwan as a burden sharer, not a free rider. Therefore, the U.S. Brady Plan intending to reduce the LDC debt problem in 1989 initially received a positive, enthusiastic response from Taiwan. No doubt the government's enthusiasm for the Brady Plan is more or less related to image maintenance for the sake of downplaying Taiwan's trade surplus in recent years. No one can deny, however, that Taiwan's aid, at least in part, arises from humanitarian considerations of inequality between states. This concern serves as one legitimate reason for policy initiation and reinforces the justification for Taiwan's continuing aid efforts.[44]

Another objective of aid is to enhance national pride. Taiwan's rush toward advanced economic status has dazzled outsiders. The bestowing of foreign aid fosters a sense of pride because it indicates that Taiwan is capable of assisting others. The hidden implication behind such aid is that the government policies guided by the Nationalist party must have been correct all along in the past because they achieved such remarkable economic prosperity, which in turn has allowed Taiwan to offer help to others. The impact of foreign aid affects domestic politics in that it reinforces regime legitimacy and stability.

## The Effectiveness of Aid: Criticism at Home

Taiwan's foreign aid program has not been implemented without controversy. At a time when people in Taiwan have been increasingly demanding extensive social and public services and an upgraded economic infrastructure for further economic development, they have been questioning the government's priorities regarding domestic needs and external aid. The demand to look homeward has drawn the government back to the domestic needs and has somewhat restrained Taiwan's external aid offensive to avoid internal criticism. For opponents of foreign aid, the first beneficiary of any "free lunch" should be the people of Taiwan.

Critics are particularly rankled by the Brady Plan. Several advanced industrialized states, the World Bank, and the International Monetary Fund are all involved in the multifaceted projects of the Brady Plan to relieve the third world debt. Although Taiwan received a tacit invitation to participate in this project, critics of foreign aid maintain that Taiwan has no obligation to join because it is no longer a member of these international organizations and has no diplomatic relations with participating industrialized countries. They add that the United States would use Taiwan's contribution to promote its own philanthropic image and that Taiwan would remain anonymous. Pointing to the lukewarm response of the United States to Taiwan's application for the GATT (General Agreement on Tariffs and Trade) in 1989, these critics argue that it seems pointless to participate in the Brady Plan.[45] It is like sending a huge donation to a charity dinner without even receiving a ticket to attend the event.

Moreover, critics argue, most aid recipients are developing countries, hardly serious players in the world arena. Spending millions of dollars in aid in exchange for symbolic recognition does not seem to be a smart bargain. After all, Taiwan has been isolated for so long that to add a few more countries to the list of diplomatic recognition hardly improves the situation.

The pro-Taiwan independence groups, particularly those inside the opposition party (the Democratic Progressive Party), consider this "dollar diplomacy" a waste of Taiwan's hard-earned foreign currency reserves and a tool to stall the natural course of Taiwan independence. In their view, the governing party, the

KMT (Nationalist party), tries to use foreign aid to sustain its claim of the "Republic of China." They argue that the basic strategy for a diplomatic breakthrough is to claim Taiwan's independent identity first. Only then can foreign aid be truly free from bondage, enabling Taiwan to offer genuine help, instead of using aid as a bargaining chip to purchase or to cling to a national title that has lost appeal to the international community.[46]

Opponents also raise the issue of the effectiveness of foreign aid. Although it is considered to be an excellent chance to participate in the international community, it has raised doubts about the worth of putting money into the deep, dark hole of third world countries. If advanced countries such as the United States and Japan have not been able to solve those thorny problems of debt and economic underdevelopment in the third world, how can one expect tiny Taiwan to achieve it? There is evidence that foreign aid has done little to promote economic development in recipient countries. A typical case is Liberia, where two decades of foreign aid seem to have made little contribution to its economic development and agricultural production.[47]

Liberia is also an example of the two-China diplomatic tango: Liberia accepted help from Taiwan and mainland China, switching sides in 1977 and again in 1989. Another example is the Central African Republic, which established diplomatic relations with Taiwan twice in 1962 and 1968 but switched recognition from Taipei to Beijing in 1964 and 1976.[48] The establishment of diplomatic ties is built upon monetary assistance, but there is no guarantee that countries will not switch sides easily once the well of the aid package dries up. There is ample reason to question the use of foreign aid as a way to win international popularity.

In order to placate opponents' criticism, much of Taiwan's aid has been given on a request and application basis, which allows careful screening of the appropriateness of aid projects. This screening probably explains why so far the government has been slow to approve grants from the recently established IECDF. Until the end of 1991, the government had budgeted $400 million for the fund, but only $114 million (28.5 percent) had been delivered to twelve countries. Only seventeen out of eighty-three formal applications for IECDF assistance had been approved by 1991, although twenty were still under evaluation.[49] Most applications have been from countries in Southeast Asia and Central America for the development of industrial parks or export processing zones in which Taiwan's industrial investors can benefit.[50]

## The Effectiveness of Aid:
## Donor Interest vs. Recipient Need

In order to assess the utility and limitation of Taiwan's aid, it is necessary to examine whether Taiwan's foreign aid policy follows the recipient need approach or the donor interest approach.[51] The former allocates aid in proportion to the recipient's needs, whereas the latter employs aid programs to promote the interests of the donor. The bargaining position of the donor is strengthened during the aid relationship because the donor is able to terminate aid at its option.

Because access to government information is limited, no systematic relationship between aid and development can be established to substantiate the recipient need approach. Nevertheless, a variety of Taiwan's aid programs do allow recipients to improve agricultural production, meet immediate socio-economic needs, and supplement the capital accumulation process.[52] On the other hand, it is undeniable that there is a hidden agenda behind Taiwan's decisions. As the deputy foreign minister once commented, "We

*351*

think it's the right thing to help countries in need, and what's wrong with getting some political benefit?"[53] In fact, it seems naive to assume that most foreign aid efforts stem from purely humanitarian motives. Political expediency rides along with the aid programs.

Moreover, aid creates a reciprocal situation of commitment and reliance between Taiwan and aid recipients. Taiwan relies on the recipients, at least to facilitate investment, trade, and travel for the Taiwanese people, and at most to support its bid for membership in international organizations such as GATT and to help it gain diplomatic recognition. Aid from Taiwan is used as a carrot to reward countries pursuing policies favorable to Taiwan.

Aid efforts, nevertheless, are no guarantee of recognition or diplomatic ties. Taiwan's bargaining advantage is unlikely to increase tremendously after the aid program begins, in part because the recipients see the PRC, a competing donor with Taiwan, waiting outside the door to strike a deal. A recent case is Niger: in 1992, Niger intended to resume official ties with Taiwan because of Taipei's promise of loans but faced diplomatic pressures as well as a significant aid counter-offer from Beijing.[54] This means that Taiwan may not be able to exact whatever it wishes from the recipient. The existence of the PRC lessens the likelihood of a recipient's dependency on Taiwan as a donor.[55] Therefore, the argument that the donor's bargaining position will be reinforced during the aid relationship is limited in Taiwan's case.

This should not lead one to conclude that Taiwan suffers severely from the "reversed dependence" incurred by the aid relationship. Although Taiwan seems desperate to welcome any kind of official linkage, it is unreasonable to believe that Taiwan would fulfill every recipient's demand. The proliferation of states and the demise of ideological confrontation in the post-cold war era have given Taiwan more access to various channels to improve its international status. One country's decision to switch sides will not cause great damage. Taiwan has become used to external denials of its status in the international community. The threat of a recipient's switching sides is unlikely to force Taiwan to yield to a recipient's wishes. Because money talks louder than politics to cash-hunting developing countries, aid donors still have some leverage. Though "reversed dependence" indeed exists, it is hard to imagine that Taiwan would reduce its autonomous position to a significant extent to fulfill any recipient's demand.

Many recipients in fact view Taiwan's foreign aid as less threatening than aid from other industrialized countries, which usually generates charges of a sellout to imperialism or foreign intervention. Unlike other countries, Taiwan has never explicitly mentioned human rights improvement in the recipient's society as a contingency for aid. Other than its requests for diplomatic support, trade convenience, and investment benefits, Taiwan offers aid that allows a large degree of freedom for deliberation. In particular, Taiwan's status as a newly industrialized economy, a country only recently advanced from a developing condition, more or less relieves a recipient's concern with foreign exploitation. That is, Taiwan's aid is perceived less as a malignant intention to set the parameters of development choices and processes in the recipient societies, as world system approach or dependency approach scholars would proclaim, than as a coherent burst of pragmatism in Taiwan's diplomatic approach. Aid therefore occurs when both donors and recipients see the convergence of national interests and willingness to accommodate each other. The modification of Taiwan's stand on coexistence with the PRC in international affairs and the material incentives Taiwan offers give recipient countries a reasonable possibility of accepting the deal. The objectives of recipients and donors can be quite diverse yet complementary.

The twin crises of foreign debt combined with the lack of real substantial economic growth in the third world have apparently made Taiwan's offers very tempting. So far, several countries have taken advantage of Taiwan's economic aid and established official ties with Taiwan. Even though these nations are just "little friends," the numbers game remains significant to Taiwan. In comparison with the more than 140 countries that have official ties with the PRC, thirty countries in total recognized Taiwan in 1992, an increase from twenty-two countries in 1988. China's initial response has usually been a suspension of relations with these countries, a step short of severing relations completely.[56]

## Conclusions

In comparison with other industrialized countries, the total dollar amount of Taiwan's aid looks small, yet it provides Taiwan with an image of "non-free-rider," a nation willing to participate in international affairs and ready to offer help whenever needed. Through this image-building process, Taiwan may be able to participate in international organizations such as GATT, IMF, World Bank, or even the United Nations. Taiwan is learning from the experience of Japan and Germany: both emerged from isolation at the end of World War II into full participation in international politics.

Taiwan's diplomacy, long steeped in straight anti-communist policy, has grown more flexible. Today it has been seen less in terms of a Manichaean struggle between the forces of right and the forces of wrong. Foreign aid is a good example of this new tendency. Taiwan's diplomacy is not strongly affected by a recipient country's ideological leanings.

Taiwan's foreign aid can be deemed successful because many developing countries have accepted this aid and improved their relations with Taiwan. Even if countries are reluctant to endorse Taiwan's official identity separate from the PRC, the sheer existence of aid programs still serves the function of diplomatic linkage. And even if a recipient country establishes official ties with Beijing, Taiwan's aid has continued if desired by the recipient, as is shown in the example of Senegal.[57]

Taiwan's foreign aid helps convince industrialized countries, moreover, of its contribution to the international community and willingness to cooperate with the others in international affairs. Undoubtedly, decisions of developed countries to accept Taiwan back into the community in full scale also depend on the PRC's tolerance of Taiwan's effort to project itself as an independent political entity and whether the rest of the world is responding to the PRC's pressure.

With the emergence of "donation fatigue" in most industrialized countries and the subsidence of ideological competition in the post-cold war era, Taiwan's entrance into the club of donors is welcomed. The major challenge to the future of Taiwan's foreign aid policy comes not so much from recipients but from criticisms of powerful opposition groups and suspicious constituencies within Taiwan. In order to diffuse criticism for its "black box" (secret) operations and the ambiguous delimitation of authority between governmental departments in the decision-making process, the Ministry of Foreign Affairs has started to draft a law to restructure all aid deliberation as well as implementation under an umbrella body. It would also make aid subject to parliamentary approval.[58] This would avoid the mixture of policy voices and make aid more accountable to the legislative discretion. Nevertheless, the question of whether Taiwan's international status will be greatly improved due to this restructuring of its aid policy still remains to be answered in the coming decade.

NOTES

1. *Wall Street Journal*, 16 August, 1989, A8.
2. *Republic of China Yearbook, 1989*, 229; Hung-mao Tien, *The Great Transition: Political and Social Change in the Republic of China*, Standford: Hoover Institution Press, 1989, 216, 222-23.
3. Karl Holbik and Henry Allen Myers, *West German Foreign Aid*, 1956-1966, Boston: Boston University Press, 1968, 27; Chiao Chiao Hsieh, *The Strategy of Foreign Aid*, London: Sherwood Press, 1985, 1-2; Robert E. Wood, *From Marshall Plan to Debt Crisis: Foreign Aid and Development Choices in the World Economy*, Berkeley: University of California Press, 1986, 10-15.
4. John F. Copper, *China's Foreign Aid*, Lexington, Mass.: D. C. Heath, 1976, xii, 127-30. China outlined "Eight Principles on Economic and Technical Assistance" in the 1950s and 1960s. See *The Foreign Relations of the People's Republic of China*, Winberg Chai, editor, New York: Capricorn Books, 1972, 214, 225-26.
5. Chiao Chiao Hsieh (note 3), 4.
6. Deon Geldenhuys, *Isolated States: A Comparative Analysis*, Cambridge: Cambridge University Press, 1990, 421-22. One region where both Beijing and Taipei competed for influence by employing foreign aid was Africa. See Liang-tsai Wei, *Peking Versus Taipei in Africa*, 1960-1978, Taipei: The Asia and World Institute, 1982.
7. *Far Eastern Economic Review*, 73 (28) (10 July 1971), 30-32. Also see K. T. Li, "Republic of China's Aid to Developing Nations," *Pacific Community*, 10 (4) (1970), 666. For an examination of the impact of U.S. aid to Taiwan, see Wen Xinying, *Jing Ji Oi Ji De Bei Hou: Tai Wan Mei Yuan Jing Yan De Zheng Jing Fen Xi* (1951-1965) [Behind the Economic Miracle: Political and Economic Analyses of the U.S. Aid Experience in Taiwan(1951-1965)], Taipei: Zi Li Wan Bao [Independent Evening News], 1990.
8. The MOFA also established the Economic and Trade Department in 1992. One of its major tasks is to monitor operation of the IECDF. See *Free China Journal*, 17 April 1992, 1.

9. "How Much? Do You Know About Foreign Aid?" *Sinorama*, 17(1) (January 1992), 92-93; Trenholme J. Griffin, *Taiwan, Republic of China: Opening Up to the World*, London Euromoney Books, 1989, 75-76; Liang-tsai Wei (note 6), 303-6.

10. "How Much? Do You Know About Foreign Aid?" (note 9). Their respective NT$ amounts are separately 1.2 billion (IECDF), 800 million (CITC), and 4.7 billion (MOFA). Here the currency exchange rate is roughly US$1 = NT$25 as it stood in late January 1992. However, Taiwan's foreign minister stated that the annual amount of foreign aid was more than 0.02 percent of the GNP. The discrepancy may be attributed to what should be included in the category of foreign aid. See JPRS-CAR-91-058 23 October 1991, 83; FBIS-CHI-91-166, 27 August 1991, 72.

11. Aid outflows of Ireland and New Zealand in 1989 were, respectively, $49 million and $87 million. Readers certainly can question the appropriateness of the comparison between Taiwan's 1991 foreign aid figure and other countries' 1989 figure. However, the comparison is to give readers a general view of Taiwan's foreign aid portfolio. The 1989 figure is the latest information published by the World Bank. See World Bank, *World Development 1991*, New York: Oxford University Press, 1991, 240.

12. *Central Daily News*, 17 April 1992, 1.

13. The $50 million aid was neither confirmed nor denied by the spokesman of Belize's Foreign Ministry. *China Times Weekly*, no. 243, 21-27 October 1989, 7.

14. Information provided by the Coordination Council for North American Affairs, Washington Office. The *L.A. Times* reported that about $9 million apiece had been approved by 1990 for Costa Rica and Panama. See *L. A. Times*, 8 January 1990, D8.

15. *Far Eastern Economic Review*, 14 November 1991, 35. For example, Nicaragua acquired $30 million low-interest loans from Taipei. See *Free China Journal*, 14 February 1992, 1.

16. *China Times Weekly*, no. 242, 14-20 October 1989, 17-19. *Far Eastern Economic Review*, 14 November 1991, 34.

17. *China Times Weekly*, no. 311, 9-15 February 1991, 12.

18. Taking advantage of the diplomatic competition between Taipei and Beijing, Fiji in 1989 also received a $2.62 million interest-free loan agreement and a $5.8 million grant for rural electrification from the PRC. *Far Eastern Economic Review*, 25 May 1989, 35-36.

19. *Shi Jie Ri Bao* [*World Journal*] 7 August 1992, 6; *Far Eastern Economic Review*, 19 October 1989, 11; *Far Eastern Economic Review*, 14 November 1991, 34.

20. See *Central Daily* (overseas edition), 8 July 1992, 1; FBIS-CHI-91-191, 2 October 1991, 56; *Shi Jie Ri Bao*, 14 October 1992, 6.

21. *Hai Wai Xue Ren* (Taipei), no. 231 (November 1991), 25-26.

22. *Christian Science Monitor*, 27 December 1991, 6; *Free China Journal*, 17 December 1991, 1. Taiwan also sent food aid to Russia in 1992. As for Taiwan's official presence in other countries, please see Hungdah Chiu, *The International Legal Status of the Republic of China*, Baltimore, Md.: School of Law, University of Maryland, 1990, 13-16.

23. *Shi Jie Ri Bao.* 25 September 1992, 16.

24. *Free China Journal*, 22 October 1991, 2; 10 December 1991, 1. *Shi Jie Ri Bao*, 5 June 1992, 7.

25. *World Journal*, 11 July 1992, 1. For information about the South Pacific Forum and the Post-Forum Dialogue, see *The South Pacific Forum: 21 Years of Regional Cooperation*, Information Bulletin No. 38, Ministry of External Relations and Trade, New Zealand, December 1991, 3-4, 17.

26. *Free China Journal*, 22 October 1991, 2; 19 June 1992, 2; FBIS-CHI-91-182, 19 September 1991, 60.

27. *Central Daily News*, 24 December 1991, 7.

28. *Los Angeles Times*, 29 September 1990, A8.

29. *Far Eastern Economic Review*, 14 November 1991, 34.

30. *Far Eastern Economic Review*, 14 November 1991, 31. Some European countries also allow the name change of Taiwan's representative offices. For example, the Free China Center in London was recently changed to the Taipei Representative Office in the U.K.

31. Reinhard Drifte, "European and Soviet Perspectives on Future Responses in Taiwan to International and Regional Developments," *Asian Survey*, 25 (11) (1985), 1115-22.

32. Trenholme J. Griffin, *Taiwan, Republic of China: Opening Up to the World*, London: Nestor House, 1989, 123; *Asia and Pacific Review 1991/92*, Edison, N.J.; Hunter, 1991, 216.

33. *Far Eastern Economic Review*, 19 April 1990, 84-88. For recent information, see *Free China Journal*, 28 April 1992, 8. For Taiwan's investment in Southeast Asia before 1986, see Sheng-yi Lee, *Trade and Investment Relations Between Taiwan, R.O.C. and ASEAN Countries*, Taipei; Chung-Hua Institution for Economic Research, 1986.

34. *Washington Post,* 5 July 1990, D4: *Free China Journal,* 18 October 1991, 3; *Free China Journal,* 20 December 1991, 8.
35. Shug-ren Mao, *Taiwan's Outward Direct Investment,* University of Wisconsin Law School, Madison, Wisconsin, LL.M. thesis, 1990, 78-79.
36. *Christian Science Monitor,* 7 December 1989, 9.
37. *New York Times,* 3 December 1989, 615; October 1989, 10; *Far Eastern Economic Review,* 19 October 1989, 11.
38. FBIS-CHI-92-107, 3 June 1992, 53-54.
39. *Far Eastern Economic Review,* 14 November 1991, 34.
40. *China Times Weekly,* no. 283, 28 July-3 August 1990, 10-11.
41. *The Economist,* 4 January 1992, 31; FBIS-CHI-92-073, 15 April 1992, 69.
42. Chi Schive, *The Foreign Factor: The Multilateral Corporation's Contribution to the Economic Modernization of the Republic of China,* Standford: Hoover Institution Press, 1990, 86-87.
43. Fredrick F. Chien, "A View from Taipei," *Foreign Affairs,* 70 (5) (1991), 94.
44. For theoretical discussion, see Roger C. Riddell, *Foreign Aid Reconsidered,* Baltimore: Johns Hopkins University Press, 1987, 68.
45. *China Times Weekly,* no. 222, 27 May-2 June 1989, 47; no. 240, 30 September-6 October 1989, 14-15; no. 274, 26 May-1 June 1990, 50-51.
46. *Shi Jie Ri Bao,* 23 August 1992, 6.
47. *China Times Weekly,* no. 242, 14-20 October 1989, 17-19. For a concise debate concerning the contribution of aid, see World Bank, World Development Report, 1991, Oxford: Oxford University Press, 1991, 48.
48. FBIS-CHI-91-131, 9 July 1991, 73-74.
49. *Far Eastern Economic Review,*14 November 1991, 34-35.
50. It would certainly be interesting to know what portion of aid builds infrastructure for Taiwanese investments. Unfortunately, no reliable source is available.
51. A good discussion of these two models can be seen in R.D. McKinley and R. Little, "The U.S. Aid Relationship: A Test of the Recipient Need and the Donor Interest Models," *Political Studies,* 27 (2) (1979), 236-50.
52. Foreign aid can, of course, help the recipient state's power relative to that of civil society. See Keith Griffin, "Foreign Aid After the Cold War," *Development and Change,* 22 (1991), 669-70.
53. *New York Times,* 19 January 1989, A13.

54. *Free China Journal*, 30 June 1992, 1.
55. Certainly, the increase of aid availability in the world for developing countries from donors since late 1970s also contributes to the decline of donor dependency. See Robert E. Wood (note 3), 86-91.
56. Of course, there are exceptions. For example, Niger established diplomatic ties with Taiwan in 1992. Taiwan has promised to provide loans ($50 million) to Niger to help establish its credit to borrow money from the IMF and the World Bank. The PRC promptly protested and lowered its flag. See *Free China Journal*, 28 July 1992, 1; *Shi Jie Ri Bao*, 1 August 1992,6.
57. K. T. Li (note 7), 664-71.
58. *Far Eastern Economic Review*, 14 November 1991, 35; JPRS-CAR-91-049, 30 August, 1991, 58.

Reprinted by Permission of *Asian Affairs*

# VII.
# Culture

Previous page: Chinese Opera continues its long
tradition of artistic excellence in
the Republic of China on Taiwan.

# My Perception of President Lee Teng-hui's Cultural Development Program for the Nation

Huang Shih-cheng

Chairman of the Chinese Cultural Renaissance Promotion Commission, President Lee Teng-hui, upon being sworn in to the eighth presidential term of the Republic of China, said in his inaugural speech that cultural development was to be one of five key tasks in his administration. "The government of the Republic of China has worked for many years toward the rejuvenation of Chinese culture. It is our sincere hope that in this generation of Chinese we can establish a model of democratic government under the rule of law." This clearly tells us that President Lee bases the development and rejuvenation of Chinese culture on the establishment of a model of democratic government under the rule of law. This has long been the direction and style of his leadership.

*Huang Shih-cheng is secretary-general of the Chinese Cultural Renaissance Promotion Commission.*

## Spiritual Rejuvenation through Cultural Development

Despite his extremely busy schedule, President Lee gladly accepted the concurrent position of chairman of the Chinese Cultural Renaissance Promotion Commission upon its reorganization on March 28, 1991. This is a concrete expression of his commitment to cultural development. He often attends Commission meetings and personally guides Commission business. He also once quoted the following Chinese poem, written by the Sung dynasty Confucian scholar Chu Hsi, of which a rough translation follows:

363

*Reflected on a half-acre square pond,*
*Sunlight and cloud shadows dance to and fro.*
*Why is this pool so crystal clear?*
*Living water is its source.*

President Lee chose the term "living water" mentioned in this poem for the name of the Commission's newsletter, and wrote it in his own hand with a Chinese brush pen for the publication. In the message he wrote for the inaugural issue, President Lee earnestly encouraged the people of the ROC thus: "When a society enjoys the wealth brought about by a high rate of economic growth, we must look back, and drink the living water of our culture; let music and the arts enrich our lives; let ethics and morals fill our being. If we are far from the living water of culture, our society will be blinded by wealth and seduced by desire for profit and material goods. Our horizons will shrink, and we will become narrow-minded. At this point, life in this world loses its truth, goodness, and beauty, and becomes trivial and barren."

It is his hope that the living water of culture can, through the efforts of the Chinese Cultural Renaissance Promotion Commission and various sectors of society, reach the people, and become a clear flowing spring that fills people's spiritual lives and guides them out of the growing spiritual darkness and confusion of our society to a reassessment of their spiritual lives and to enlightenment. President Lee's ardent hopes coincide with the founding objectives of the Chinese Cultural Renaissance Promotion Commission, and the guiding principles for the implementation of each of the Commission's programs.

## A "Cultural" President

Over the past three years, President Lee has energetically advanced constitutional democracy in the ROC, ushering in a new era for our nation following the lifting of the *Emergency Decree*. He has also made significant and continued efforts in the area of cultural development. As chairman of the Chinese Cultural Renaissance Promotion Commission, he has participated in numerous cultural activities, including grassroots cultural events, Taiwanese culture activities, and folk art activities, as well as high culture activities and arts, representative of both mainland Chinese and local Taiwan culture—all are important in his eyes, and he is fond of them all. He is an internationally noted scholar in agricultural economics, but is at the same time an appreciator of the humanities, the arts, and culture. Due to his frequent appearances in galleries, concert halls, and folk museums, the news media have dubbed him the "cultural president." And it is an appropriate moniker.

President Lee cultivates a serious interest not only in the fine arts and music, but also has a deep understanding and appreciation of Taiwan aboriginal culture and arts. In 1992, at an exhibition of Paiwan Wood Carvings held by the Chinese Cultural Renaissance Promotion Commission, President Lee could describe each exhibit as though it were an object displayed in his own home, deeply impressing the artists and Paiwan tribespeople who accompanied him.

During the Chinese New Year holiday in 1992, President Lee, in his capacity as chairman of the Commission, hosted a New Year's Reception for Artists, which brought together writers, painters and others involved in the arts from the entire country. President Lee greeted each one individually, and in his address to the reception, he encouraged those engaged in artistic activity to work hard for the nation's cultural development. He believes that cultural development cannot rely solely on the efforts of the Council for Cultural Planning and Development or the Chinese Cultural Renaissance Promotion Commission, but requires the contributions of everybody in society. This New Year's Reception for Artists is the first major arts event in ROC history in which the nation's president received artists from all over the country. This is a clear indication that President Lee's commitment to the arts is a comprehensive one. The Chinese Cultural Renaissance Promotion Commission has since made the New Year's Reception for Artists a regular annual event.

## Concern over the Degeneration of Wedding and Funeral Customs

President Lee often attends local community arts activities during his visits to the Taiwan countryside. He feels that popular culture can be set on the right track by folk culture activities, and that grassroots level and community cultural activities must receive special attention in cultural development and renaissance programs. "Only by raising people's awareness on the community level will it be easier for us to raise the level of folk culture," he has said. "By proceeding step by step from this foundation we can move to the next level of promoting a more refined kind of culture." He has expressed a deep concern for ritual vehicles with pornographic displays sometimes used for weddings and funerals, and other decadent cultural practices. He has, on the one hand, directed the Commission to launch specific programs to counter such trends by holding lectures and demonstrations; on the other hand, he has brought together local government officials, responsible people of local Commission chapters and subchapters to follow up on progress made in correcting these practices. The Commission's secretariat has also commissioned experts to plan and produce television commercials encouraging the people to celebrate weddings and funerals in a dignified, befitting manner. These commercials have been broadcast on local television stations, and the powerful and direct appeal of their content has elicited strong viewer response, demonstrating their effectiveness in getting the people to rethink current practices. The Commission is now in the process of drafting a second set of measures to deal with this issue.

## Focus on Television Culture

In the Commission's fourth meeting of members and consultants, a number of participants expressed their serious concern over the pornography and low-class culture frequently seen in television programs in the ROC. They also noted an urgent need to cultivate cultural workers on the local level. At the conclusion of the meeting, Chairman Lee directed the Commission to set up a Television Research Committee of outstanding members of society as quickly as possible, and to work together with the relevant agencies to draft a concrete program on how to cultivate and appoint cultural workers on the local level. This was a decisive and timely move, and it received broad and immediate response and support from all sectors of society. The Commission subsequently invited scholars and experts in related fields to establish a Television Cultural Research Committee. This committee has been in operation now for over a year. Its various achievements have received the full support of the people, and have been quite effective in helping clean up the content of TV programs and raising program quality. The number of people serving as "culture volunteers" has also been steadily increasing. These volunteers consist mainly of enthusiastic intellectuals from local communities with an interest in cultural work and an appreciation for President Lee's concepts of cultural development. These people are making their presence felt throughout the country by making cultural contributions. The Commission is currently working in close cooperation with the Council for Cultural Planning and Development under the Executive Yuan to further enhance the effectiveness of the volunteers.

## Reestablishing Moral Ethics

President Lee has voiced concern over the deteriorating moral atmosphere of society and the growing disdain shown toward ethical standards. To address this problem, he has, in addition to visiting local communities and urging local government officials to pay special attention to cultural development, often gathered local cultural and educational representatives and personally given them encouragement and presented awards for outstanding achievements in these areas. By conveying the idea that the nation's president places high importance on models of culture and education work worthy of emulation, he hopes to mobilize others to follow his example. He does not, of course, think that he is the only one who can do work in the area of social culture, ethics and morals; his greatest hope is that all the people become involved and realize the importance of cultural development. It is for this reason that the Commission established a task force for reestablishing moral standards, and asked Judicial Yuan President Lin Yang-kang to serve as convener. At present, this task force, under the direction of President Lee and Judicial Yuan President Lin and through the efforts of the committee members, is launching a series of programs. They have adopted the approach of revamping morals by promoting their work on the grassroots level, i.e. through rural and community activities, with the aim of reaching each sector of society.

## Promoting the Concept of an "Interdependent Community"

Recently, President Lee has in his capacity as Chairman of the Kuomintang (KMT) of China reiterated his concept of cultural development. He has said that the "Taiwan experience" that we have accumulated over the past forty years has involved mainly the establishment of an economic system and political innovation; but we should now concentrate our efforts on how to use the essence of traditional Chinese culture to create a new culture never before seen in our history. He particularly emphasized that we must use our Taiwan experience to create a new culture and create a new life with a national and collective consciousness. This does not mean a break in our relationship with mainland China; he offers instead a model on how to guide the mainland along a path similar to the one we have taken here in Taiwan. We must take the lead in writing our own history; in other words, we must use the essence of traditional Chinese culture as a basis for creating a whole new culture unknown in our history.

I have two thoughts on these comments of President Lee. First, the Taiwan experience is a new culture built upon traditional Chinese culture with the dignity of the 21 million people of Taiwan as its premise; it is a culture that is enjoyed by and that benefits all of these people. It is a renaissance and re-creation of traditional Chinese culture, which requires a collective realization of what President Lee has constantly reminded us of: that we are all part of one interdependent whole. This interdependent whole requires solidarity, harmony, humanity, and morality. Stated in different terms, it is an "awakening" to the basic values most important to our society.

Second, creating a new culture does not mean that we cut ourselves off from traditional culture; it means rather filtering out the best and discarding the rest, based on current and future needs and trends. We of course cannot forget our past. Nobody who has walked the path of our past will forget the suffering, the poverty, the hard times. For this reason, we must know and appreciate what we have now, and not be ready to give up just anything for immediate gain or profit without a view to our long-range ideals. We must be careful not to act like nouveaux riches who carelessly fritter away hard-won wealth, so that the values that Taiwan has treasured most, namely industriousness, endurance, filial and fraternal piety, loyalty and trust, do not fall by the wayside. If this were to happen, our culture would lose its roots, morals would deteriorate, and we would return to being known as an "island of greed." For this reason, every person who lives on this piece of land should actively encourage each other, show concern for others, and identify with this piece of land, this society, and this nation so we can create a new culture based on our Taiwan experience.

## Reaching the People

Cultural work includes just about anything and everything under the sun, and success of this enterprise requires long-term, basic efforts for which immediate results cannot be expected. Since the establishment of the Chinese Cultural Renaissance Promotion Commission, I have had the good fortune to serve as its secretary-general, and work together with the committee chairman. This experience has given me the opportunity to observe the chairman's selfless dedication to our task, and to realize how much this is contributing to cultural development in the ROC, and to the people of our country as well. I became particularly aware of this after recently meeting with some people who had just returned from a trip to the Chinese mainland and who reported that senior cultural workers there thought very highly of President Lee's directive to place greater stress on Taiwan-mainland cultural work, and that they had very high expectations of it. This illustrates how Chinese everywhere have become familiar with President Lee's cultural program.

## Returning to Chinese Culture

In closing, I would like to quote a passage from the message President Lee gave at the New Year's Reception for Artists: "We should realize that by 'modern Chinese culture,' we do not mean either just Taiwan culture or just mainland Chinese culture, but rather a confluence of these two cultural forces," and this is what should be used to elucidate the goals of the Chinese cultural renaissance movement, and the basic direction of the work of the Chinese Cultural Renaissance Promotion Commission. I am confident that under the leadership of our chairman, the Chinese Cultural Renaissance Promotion Commission will be able to unite the forces of all sectors of society to work for cultural development in the ROC, to infuse Chinese culture with the vitality of living water, complementing government achievements in other areas. Let us rejuvenate Chinese culture, bringing out its uniqueness and color, so as to transform our society into a cultural entity in which courtesy, integrity, and human caring are our central values, thus achieving the objectives of our President and Chairman's vision of "cultural development."

# The Taiwan Experience in Chinese Culture

## Fang Peng-cheng

*Fang Peng-cheng is deputy-director of the Department of Cultural Services at the Straits Exchange Foundation.*

Chinese culture boasts a long history and far-reaching influence. For the past several millennia, Chinese culture has guided the integration and development of the Chinese people. And because of this, Chinese culture has absorbed the essence of other cultures, a process that has greatly enriched Chinese culture.

Since the Republican era, men of good will worked for the modernization of China and sought new development for Chinese culture in the hope of guiding their country into the ranks of the developed and modern nations. The May Fourth Movement set the stage for China's modernization by proposing a new culture characterized by democracy and scientific growth. Yet civil war and external threats came one after the other. Then communism made inroads into China by taking advantage of the ensuing chaos. Soon the ravaging tides of communism swept China, rocking the nation to its very foundations, leading to the fall of China, and turning it into a laboratory for Marxism and Leninism.

By a twist of fate, the Chinese race was spared from total destruction. Taiwan, known in ancient times as the "Island of the Immortals," fortuitously became the bastion of national recovery. For the past forty-some years, the Republic of China on Taiwan has been actively propagating Chinese culture based on the existing foundation of traditional culture. By a gradual process, Western cultural components of science and democracy have been absorbed into Chinese culture. In this silent process of transformation, Taiwan has witnessed the most democratic, free and prosperous era in the history of the Chinese people.

## The Attributes of Chinese Culture

Culture is a set of ways created by man to change, harmonize and adjust to his environment or to pursue development. Culture is an all-encompassing term that includes philosophical thought, systems, scholarship, technology, crafts, education, art, customs, habits, and lifestyles.

Traditional Chinese culture is typified by an emphasis on ethics and the "golden mean," veneration of Heaven, benevolence to our fellow man, emphasis on wisdom, and integration.

Emphasis on ethics led to the "Five Relationships" (*wu lun*) governing relations among ruler, officials, parents, offspring and spouses, which helped establish a social hierarchy, and assure order within it.

The "golden mean" calls for moderation in all matters and avoidance of extremes.

Veneration of Heaven stimulated the development of natural law based on a "unity of Heaven and man." It calls for acting in accordance with Heaven's will.

Benevolence toward one's fellow man mandated a reign of benevolence whose ultimate political objectives lie in safeguarding people, encouraging universal prosperity, national stability and peace, as well as effective administration of the nation.

Emphasis on wisdom means respect for knowledge and the learned. This led to progress in scholarly knowledge and the appointment of learned people to official positions, which paved the way for the formation of the traditional elite political culture.

Finally, integration is the moving force behind cohesion and progress in Chinese culture. Since time immemorial, the concept of unification has been a recurring theme in the meldings and solidarity of the Chinese people over their 5,000-year history.

Taiwan has received a Chinese cultural baptism since ancient times. When generations of Taiwan's ancestors crossed the Taiwan Straits to the shores of Taiwan, they brought with them a process of cultural integration as they took refuge from dynastic chaos and in their search for paradise on earth.

During the Ming and Ching dynasties, wave after wave of immigrants from the provinces of Fukien and Kwangtung came to Taiwan in great numbers. Whether pioneer farmers, traders or war refugees, these immigrants brought with them seeds of culture which they soon disseminated in every place they settled. Starting with the Ming and Ching dynasties, schools and academies were established in many places in Taiwan, where they spread Chinese cultural ideas with dedication. Poetic societies were common, and these contributed to a literary flowering. Artists and craftsmen introduced traditional techniques and art to Taiwan.

In spite of Taiwan's geographical location, our ancestors' thoughts, systems, customs, habits, scholarly interests, arts and crafts, technology, and lifestyles were all intertwined inextricably with Chinese culture.

Backwardness and corruption in the closing years of the Ching dynasty led to the Sino-Japanese War in 1894-95, after which Taiwan was ceded to the Japanese. Yet in spite of painstaking efforts to uproot Chinese culture during the Japanese occupation, it remained deeply ingrained in the local populace.

After the eight years of the War of Resistance against Japan, Taiwan was returned to China. What followed was a resumption of the development of Chinese culture under government leadership. The relocation of the central government to Taiwan at the end of 1949 accelerated the process of Chinese cultural integration.

On July 28, 1967, the ROC Government established the Promotion Committee for the Chinese Cultural Renaissance Campaign in an effort to promote cultural renaissance by encouraging reform and transformation in traditional Chinese culture. Among its objectives was the development of a Chinese culture based on the Taiwan experience.

## The Taiwan Experience in Chinese Culture

After Taiwan's retrocession, Chinese culture again came out into the open after years of being hidden among the grassroots population. The many aspects of Chinese culture thus began a process of rapid growth and development.

The rise and fall of cultures is closely connected with the vicissitudes of time and the environment. The government's cultural policies, economic development and support from mass media all have contributed to the integration and growth of Chinese culture in the Taiwan area.

Academia is the main source of cultural progress. All systems and norms, technology and social activities can be traced to academia. Since the Spring and Autumn and the Warring States periods, Confucian ideas became the major cultural force that shaped China's political psyche, with the Legalist philosophy given a lesser, supplementary role. Even in times of chaotic divisions and wars, Confucian moral ideals remained the single major force that helped maintain stability in society.

Confucianism emphasizes humanism and moral values. It proposes that rulers must take popular will into consideration, understand the people's yearnings and administer with responsibility and concern for the people. One who is to administer the country must first rectify himself and his intentions, cultivate virtue, and govern his family well.

The Legalists stress the rule of law in administering a country; but they tend toward severity. Chuang Tzu's philosophy propounds administration with passivity and reverting to what is natural. Both of these philosophical trends also exerted significant influences on Chinese culture.

A look at the historical development of Taiwan reveals that since the Ming and Ching dynasties, Confucian ideals have always found their way into the thinking of the local populace. Temples dedicated to Confucius and academies devoted to the teaching of Confucianism were built throughout Taiwan. All these contributed to an emphasis on ethics at the family and societal levels. In the past forty-some years, the traditional extended family has gradually evolved into a nuclear family structure; moral ideals, however, have remained deeply rooted, a phenomenon that is perhaps the greatest stabilizing force in Taiwan's society.

Politics, economics, society, education and other systems are also component parts of culture. The imperial system inherent in traditional Chinese culture disappeared following turbulent transformations. It has been replaced by a democratic system characterized by free and fair elections.

Although Western democracy dates back to ancient Greece, its development was interrupted during the Dark Ages. It resumed its development after the Revolution in England in 1688. After more than three centuries of trial, democracy evolved into its two main versions: the British Parliamentary System and the U.S. Presidential System.

Democracy became the Republic of China's key objective soon after its founding. Despite successive disturbances from warlord secession, foreign invasion and civil war, democratic constitutional rule was established in 1947.

Constitutional rule developed apace after the central government moved to Taiwan. In July 1987, the late President Chiang Ching-kuo lifted martial law, allowing the formation of new political parties, the publication of new newspapers, family visits to the mainland, and the launching a series of political reforms. President Lee Teng-hui took over as president on January 13, 1988 after the death of President Chiang, then in May 1991 was subsequently inaugurated as the eighth president of the Republic of China. He continued constitutional reform, announced the termination of the Period of Mobilization for Suppression of the Communist Rebellion, completed the two-stage constitutional amendment process, restructured the National Assembly and actively promoted party politics.

Democratic constitutional rule has progressed peacefully over the past forty-some years, a phenomenon later acclaimed worldwide as Taiwan's "political miracle." This achievement of democracy made a valuable contribution to Chinese culture.

Taiwan's economic development represents another glorious chapter in Chinese cultural history.

Before Taiwan's recovery, Japanese exploitation and the ravages of war had left Taiwan's economy in a sad state. After Taiwan's retrocession in 1945, the task of economic rebuilding had to begin on the ruins of war.

In 1951, the "37.5% Rent Deduction Program" was initiated, followed by the "Land to the Tiller Program" in 1953. These two important land reform measures laid a firm foundation for stability and progress in rural areas. While farmers gained ownership of the land they were tilling, landlords used funds they obtained to invest in basic necessity industries. Mutual assistance between the agricultural and industrial sectors expanded the manpower and economic strength of rural areas, which soon became the heartland of industry. With planned government guidance, Taiwan gradually became active in international trade, which increased Taiwan's potential for economic development. This contributed to the creation of the Taiwan "economic miracle."

In the past four decades, Taiwan was at various times the largest producer of more than 10 products. In fact, Taiwan's economic strength was ranked among the top 20 in the world.

External trade was an important factor behind Taiwan's economic development and prosperity. In 1952, Taiwan's international trade totaled a mere

US$300 million, with US$110 million in exports and US$190 million in imports. By 1992, the figure rocketed to US$153.45 billion, with exports totaling US$81.47 billion, ranking Taiwan the 12th largest exporter in the world. Imports totaled US$70.98 billion, 14th highest in the world.

In 1965, the ROC's per capita income was US$211. By 1992, the figure had shot to US$9,332.

For the past four decades, Taiwan has been enjoying the fruits of peaceful economic and political reforms. In fact, other areas such as society, education, technology, lifestyles, and the arts are also undergoing reform and transformation in an environment of stability.

Taiwan's social development received a boost with the arrival of the central government and millions of soldiers and civilians in 1949, who brought with them needed funds, talent, knowledge and social integration. This triggered robust growth in the Taiwan area.

During the past forty years, integration and fusion were brought about in Taiwan through marriage, the practice of professions and other means. Such integration has contributed much to the essence of Chinese culture in the Taiwan area.

The fusion of different social groups is beneficial to the reaching of consensus on the concept of building an "interdependent community that functions as an organic whole." It also has brought about a gradual homogenization of customs, habits and lifestyles.

Traditional rural society has gradually experienced change in Taiwan. The extended family system has given way to smaller family units. Urban develop-

379

ment has started a process of population outflow from rural villages. However, aging parents remain an important reason why village emigrants return to their places of origin during the Lunar New Year. This attests to the fact that social and ethical values inherent to Chinese culture remain strong.

Ancestral genealogical inscriptions which identify the ancestral origins of each clan, commonly found on the facades of homes in rural Taiwan, have recently started to disappear as old houses give way to new buildings. Most ancestral inscriptions in Taiwan point to Central Chinese origins. Studies suggest that the Southern Min dialect common among local residents traces its origins to ancient central Chinese dialects. This is proven by the fact that Tang Dynasty poems, when recited in the local dialect, take on the proper rhythm and tempo. From this, it can thus be said that ancient central Chinese culture remains richly preserved in Taiwan.

Education is one of the pathways for the transmission and dissemination of culture. Chinese culture has always stressed knowledge and education. This tradition remains in practice in Taiwan. In the past four decades, education has benefited a countless number of people, a process that continues to contribute to the propagation of Chinese culture in Taiwan.

During the Japanese occupation, Chinese culture was transmitted clandestinely among the local populace, thus making possible the uninterrupted continuity of cultural traditions. After Taiwan's retrocession, education provided a ray of hope for improving difficult living conditions. No matter how difficult the situation was, each family tried hard to give their children a chance to receive higher education, or even to send them abroad to be educated. The accumulation of knowledge and the training of talent laid a strong foundation for national and social progress, while providing an impetus for Chinese cultural propagation and creation.

Education in Taiwan over the past forty years has emphasized cultural training. The majority of citizens who have received at least a secondary school education have become the pillars of social progress and contributed to the development of various professions.

Another important aspect in the Taiwan experience is technological development. In the past four decades, achievements in developing applied science and high technology were made through study overseas, technological cooperation with other countries, education in technology and research, and experimental programs.

Chinese technology was surpassed by that of the West after the Ming and Ching dynasties. In the early years of the Republican era, emphasis was placed on science and democracy. However, a turbulent situation prevented any significant achievements in these areas. At present, however, technological progress has taken root in an atmosphere of freedom in the Taiwan area. The absorption of technological concepts from Europe and North America has added new dynamism to Chinese culture. It is expected that in the future, Taiwan will catch up with Western technological achievements.

Other areas of Chinese culture, namely literature, painting, film-making, opera, sculpture, dance and music have likewise witnessed robust growth in Taiwan over the last four decades.

Chinese folk arts have long been preserved through activities held by civic groups, communities and temples. A rich variety of literary and art activities sponsored by communities and temples presents traditional culture to the people. Opera, which reflects Chinese historical, cultural and philosophical elements, exerts a particularly significant influence on the local population.

Traditional Chinese culture is well preserved in Taiwan, particularly in the form of literature, opera, painting, music and dance. In fact, the essence of Chinese culture can be seen in the collections of the National Palace Museum in Taipei. Through research work and propagation of traditional scholarship, Taiwan has become the center of world sinological studies.

Customs and traditions in Taiwan have undergone significant changes over the last forty years. The same can be said of popular lifestyles. Undesirable customs and habits prevalent earlier in the Chinese cultural tradition, such as putting baby girls up for adoption, polygamy, foot-binding, pre-arranged marriages and village wars have largely been eradicated through education and law enforcement. The traditional mentality that favors attachment to one's native place has long been changed. Improvement in economic conditions has led to increased opportunity for foreign travel and overseas investments.

A most significant change is the modernization of lifestyles. In the years that followed the recovery of Taiwan, people lived difficult lives. Coarse rice with bits of sweet potato formed the main staple of people's diets. With economic progress, the people's livelihood gradually improved. Rice, meat, poultry and seafood, refrigerators, television sets, telephones, stereos, automobiles have now become daily necessities. The residents of Taiwan now enjoy the most prosperous, stable, free, and democratic life in China's 5,000-year history. Indeed, Chinese culture has flourished in the Taiwan area.

In recent years, however, growth in spiritual culture has failed to keep pace with rapid developments in material culture. People now show a tendency toward utilitarianism. Cultural progress lags behind material growth. Noting these negative social trends, schools, social groups and families have voiced a need for spiritual and cultural development. A case in point is religious groups, which have cast off their previous detachment from secular matters and have started to show concern for the general welfare of society. They are now promoting participation in secular events aimed at providing guidance to those in need. Joining forces with social and family groups, the religious sector is leading the charity movements, offering medical services and organizing cultural activities, with the aim of contributing to the attainment of a peaceful, harmonious and contented, cultured society,

## The Taiwan Experience:
## A Dominant Force in China's Unification

Four decades of progress in the Republic of China on Taiwan have yielded the Taiwan experience, which has enriched the essence of Chinese culture as well as injected new vitality into it.

The Taiwan experience in Chinese culture can be summarized as political democracy, economic freedom and social prosperity. These have been the ideals of traditional Chinese culture over the last 5,000 years.

The extensive absorption of Western cultural values has inevitably affected Chinese culture. Individualism, although transitional, has widened the distance between people and has affected consensus on moral issues. Distorted utilitarian ideas have led to opportunistic behavior and confusion on the meaning of freedom and democracy, and has resulted in the disruption of social order. An affluent lifestyle deprived of literary and artistic components has debased life to a vulgar, extravagant and brutish level. Economic prosperity, which contributes to national power, must be utilized in combination with traditional Chinese benevolence and nationalism in helping developing countries attain prosperity and promote world peace.

It was in this light that President Lee Teng-hui delivered an address at the First National Conference on Culture on November 8, 1990. He encouraged the people of the Republic of China to upgrade their quality of life by immersing themselves in the literary and artistic traditions inherent in Chinese culture. He cited the role of Chinese moral teachings in re-establishing social order, and the need to return to Chinese nationalism for the unification of China. President Lee also cited the high value placed on peace in traditional Chinese culture, and the potential contribution it could make to the promotion of global harmony.

Traditional Chinese culture has always placed great stress on benevolent government. The Taiwan experience, with its roots in traditional Chinese culture, can be summarized as political stability, economic freedom and social prosperity. This is precisely the benevolent government pursued by generations of Chinese intellectuals and common people. This benevolent government contrasts strongly with the communist dictatorship of the past four decades in mainland China.

Family visits to mainland China have been allowed since November 2, 1987. During the past six years, we have witnessed ever-growing people-to-people interaction between the two sides of the Taiwan Straits. The Taiwan experience in Chinese culture has been transformed into tens of thousands of seeds scattered to every corner of mainland China. These seeds will germinate, flower and bear fruit when the time is ripe.

Mencius once said: "...For a kingdom to be successful, it need not be powerful. King Tang of the Shang dynasty ruled a territory measuring 70 square *li* in area. King Wen of the Chou dynasty territory was no larger than 100 square *li*." We are all aware that since ancient times, "the benevolent make no enemies." Shao Kang, Prince of Hsia, regained his land with only one brigade. Similarly, the National Revolutionary Army unified the whole of China by launching the Northern Expedition from Kwangtung province. History will attest to the dominant role to be played by the Taiwan experience in the eventual unification of China. When that time comes, we will be able to write a new glorious page for the Chinese people which will usher in a bright new era.

# The Development and Organization of Foundations in Taiwan: An Expression of Cultural Vigor in a Newly Born Society

Hsiao Hsin-huang

*Hsiao Hsin-huang is a researcher at the Institute of Ethnology of Academia Sinica.*

Research into the development of endowed foundations in Taiwan has not yielded very impressive results, indicating that the development of such foundations has not received due attention. No attempt has ever been made to systematically record even their most basic data.

While government authorities which oversee foundations (namely the Ministry of Education, the Council for Cultural Planning and Development, the Ministry of the Interior, the Department of Health, the Environmental Protection Administration, and the Ministry of Economic Affairs) do keep lists of the names of Taiwan's foundations, the information therein is incomplete. Apart from the names and addresses of foundations and their directors, the lists provide virtually no other background information which would facilitate further analysis. Supposedly more thorough information is included in the *Introduction to the Cultural and Educational Foundations of the Republic of China* published by the Council for Cultural Planning and Development in June, 1989, but references available are limited only to the dates foundations were established, the size of their endowments, their founding principles, organization, and main undertakings. The work, therefore, can hardly form a basis for further research.

The only academic study dealing with foundations in Taiwan is *Foundations in the Changing Taiwan*

*Area*[1]. Commissioned by the Asia Foundation, this report gathered and analyzed data on 96 of Taiwan's foundations. Subjects explored include each of the 96 organizations' founding principles, classification, organizational type, major activities, financial status, directors' attitudes towards social welfare, and the policy and legal environment. It is pointed out in the introduction to *Foundations in the Changing Taiwan Area* that "To date, scholars have made no attempt to study issues such as the organizational alignment of Taiwan's foundations, the projects they have undertaken, their financial status, or the government's policies for foundations." This statement is as true now as it was then.

Nevertheless, public attention has, in recent years, increasingly focused on foundations. The main reason for this rise in interest is that several large foundations have been established (namely the 21st Century Foundation, the Institute of National Policy Research, the Chiang Ching-kuo Foundation for International Scholarly Exchange, and the Democracy Foundation). Other foundations focusing on academic and educational issues, cross-Straits relations, and the study of mainland affairs, for example, have also been set up. For the most part the public is concerned with three questions.

First, foundations for studying government policies have been emerging in Taiwan in recent years. These foundations are similar to Western think tanks. What are the political and social implications of these Chinese counterparts to think tanks?

Second, how can a foundation set up by a political personage maintain its image as an independent organization and allay fears that it is tainted by political influence?

Third, foundations supported by one or more corporations have become quite common. Is the for-profit nature of corporations compatible with the non-profit nature of foundations? How can the borderline be maintained between corporations and corporate foundations?

These questions have become focuses of public interest and favorite subjects of columnists and editorialists for some time. While these questions might not be suitable as serious objects of inquiry in social sciences, they have at least caught the public's attention and given rise to many discussions. Even the government is becoming more serious about the management and guidance of foundations.

In recent years, more attention has also been directed toward the American counterparts of Taiwan's foundations. Several newly-established foundations specializing in public policy have often cited their U.S. counterparts as models for emulation. Newspapers too have discussed the functions of a few U.S. foundations, but their opinions and the information yielded are usually half-baked or taken out of context. Academia and administrative authorities in Taiwan therefore lack a general understanding of U.S. foundations.

This article seeks an initial understanding of the 309 foundations in Taiwan for which data have been collected, sorted, and recorded, by first describing current conditions and then their purposes, financing, organization, and operations in the light of historical changes.

The data pool for this study is based on the facts and opinions obtained from the 309 foundations by means of a specially-designed questionnaire on their organization and operations. Research was carried out in three stages. In the first stage, the data to be studied were selected and verified. First, the names and addresses of 677 foundations were culled from lists provided by government offices such as the Council for Cultural Planning and Development, the Ministry of Education, the Ministry of the Interior, the National Health Administration, the Environmental Protection Administration and the Ministry of Economic Affairs.

While compiling this master list of foundations, the author also was designing a questionnaire on the organization of foundations. A draft of the questionnaire was tried out so that flaws in its content and phraseology could be eliminated. The executives of the ROC Consumers' Foundation, the Sampo Foundation, the Homemakers' Union and Foundation, and the Hsin-yi Foundation were invited to attend a seminar where they could comment on the first draft of the questionnaire.

The final version of the questionnaire was then mailed to the 677 foundations on the master list. Foundations that did not return a questionnaire by the deadline were contacted by phone. This constituted the second stage of research. Altogether 314 completed questionnaires were eventually returned. The answers to be used for the third stage of the research were recorded and in-depth interviews were carried out to ensure a better understanding of the development of foundations. In terms of location, categorization (based on the source of their funds, the targets of their services, and the nature of their activities), and image, 16 of the 300-odd foundations were chosen as subjects for more thorough interviews. The results were used as information for another supplementary analysis, undertaken in the second stage of the research.

## The Development of Foundations and Taiwan's Changing Society— the Transformation of Foundations

While one can trace the development of foundations in Taiwan back to the mid-1960s, foundations remained few in number until after the 1970s, and it was not until the 1980s that foundations became a salient social feature. Most of the samples noted in the study on Taiwan's foundations carried out by Tsai Cheng-wen et al. in 1982 already existed in the 1970s. Three fourths of the samples in the present study, carried out ten years after Tsai's, comprise foundations established in the 1980s. Although the studies were carried out a decade apart, they indicate that the respective decades on which they focus were periods of rapid growth for foundations. Furthermore, the studies draw attention to two long-term implications of the development of the foundations.

First, these two periods show a connection between Taiwan's economic development and the growth of foundations in Taiwan. Taiwan entered a period of economic growth during the 1970s, promising a more solid basis for further stability and prosperity than in the previous two decades. As the economic environment was conducive to the establishment of foundations, the 1970s can be described as the "formative era" for foundations. In the 1980s, Taiwan entered another phase in which economic prosperity lent a new surge of strength to the local community. Such a congenial environment gave a strong boost to the establishment of foundations, making the 1980s the "developmental era" of foundations.

Second, social and political development in Taiwan during the 1980s was unique. One dominant event during this period was the lifting in 1987 of the Emergency Decree, which had been in effect for more than forty years. This move unleashed the potential of Taiwan's private sector. Since foundations are one form used by the private sector to build community ties, foundations were naturally stimulated by the move. More foundations were established in the 1980s than in all other years combined. The growth of foundations in the post-Emergency Decree era has a special political significance. For one thing, there was a rapid decline in the number of government-established foundations. Balancing this decline was the staggering growth of foundations established by corporations and private individuals within a few years after the lifting of Emergency Decree.

Apart from the two historically significant facts mentioned above, there were yet a few more trends heralding further changes in a transforming society. The first trend was the emergence of activist foundations and a corresponding rise in the pressure of the appeals for social reform. The second trend was the establishment of "think tanks" that sought to influence government public policies. Third, there was a change in the orientation of foundations set up by corporations. Whereas such foundations had traditionally dedicated themselves to charitable undertakings, they now based their new aims and appeals on a broader concern for the development of community and culture.[2]

These trends not only reflect the three different directions in which foundations have evolved, they also serve as clues in predicting, observing, and understanding the development of Taiwan's foundations in the decade ahead. Generally speaking, the more economic prosperity and political freedom a country enjoys, the more pronounced the development of its foundations becomes. Such a principle applies also to Taiwan. Foundations in Taiwan were established in one of four periods, which this study defines as (1) 1971 and before, (2) from 1972 to 1981, (3) from 1982 to 1988, and (4) after 1989. The year 1989 was chosen as the break between the third and fourth period in order to better understand how the lifting of the Emergency Decree influenced the growth of foundations.

Table 1 shows the first period to be the one in which the fewest foundations existing today, only 6.8 percent of the total, were established. Approximately 19 percent of all foundations were set up in the second period. This spurt of growth was linked to Taiwan's rapid economic growth at the time. The third period witnessed yet greater growth in the number of foundations, accounting for 45.6 percent of all present foundations, while 27.8 percent of all foundations were founded in the fourth period. Such a high growth rate in the third and fourth periods demonstrates that the 1980s marked the zenith of growth for Taiwan's foundations. Special attention is drawn to the fact that 86 new foundations, over a quarter of all the samples, were established in the two years just after the termination of the Emergency Decree. It can thus be concluded that political liberalization and the gradual demise of authoritarian rule were definitely conducive to the rise and renewal of various forces in the private community. Nevertheless, while the growth of foundations in the 1980s was no doubt a reflection of the tremendous political and economic changes that took place in Taiwan during this period, it still remains to be seen whether or not these foundations can exert a positive influence in the 1990s and whether or not they presage a healthier relationship between private and governmental forces.

## Table 1.
## Establishment of Foundations by Period

| | | |
|---|---|---|
| 1971 and before | 21 | 6.8% |
| 1972-1981 | 59 | 19.1% |
| 1982-1988 | 141 | 45.6% |
| 1989 to August 1990 | 86 | 27.8% |
| Not Available | 2 | 0.7% |
| Total | 309 | 100.0% |

This table shows that three quarters of currently existing foundations were founded during the 1980s and have less than a ten-year history. Another 20 percent of the foundations are between ten and 20 years old. Those with a history of over 20 years account for a mere 7 percent of all the samples.

When registering with the government authorities, a foundation must provide clear statement of its overall mission. After studying the statements of the 309 foundations, we classified each foundation under one of seven categories: philanthropy, social activism, education, research, culture and art, scholarships, and international cultural exchange. This classification is presented in Table 2.

**Table 2.**
**Foundations: Classified by Primary Focus**

| | | |
|---|---|---|
| Philanthropy | 77 | 24.9% |
| Research | 65 | 21.0% |
| Education | 57 | 18.4% |
| Culture and Art | 43 | 13.9% |
| Scholarships | 35 | 11.3% |
| International Cultural Exchange | 12 | 3.9% |
| Social Activism | 11 | 3.6% |
| Not Available | 9 | 2.9% |
| Total | 309 | 100.0% |

The majority of foundations in this study, nearly one fourth of the total, are philanthropic. The second most common type concentrates on research. These foundations are followed, in descending order, by those that focus on education, culture and art, scholarships, international cultural exchanges, and social activism. If we consider foundations concerned with philanthropy and scholarships to be the traditional type of foundation interested in charity and the promotion of learning, then almost 38.8 percent of Taiwan's foundations belong to this more traditional type. If foundations set up for research can be regarded to include the recently formed think tank-type of corporate juristic persons, then they are the second most common type of foundation.

The promotion of education for the general public has always been an objective of foundations, both inside and outside of Taiwan. Foundations established for this purpose are third on the list. Fourth on the list are the foundations for the promotion of culture and art. This new type of foundation focuses particularly on the promotion of Taiwan's indigenous culture and art. The existence of foundations of this nature reflects community concern for cultural affairs. In terms of absolute numbers, foundations that focus on international cultural interchange and social activism appear at the end the list. However, their concerns in promoting cultural interactions with other countries and in promoting social movements in Taiwan are manifestations of Taiwan's underlying social and cultural vigor.

Taiwan's foundations are diversifying beyond the traditional models that once focused on charity and scholarships. Any new topics and new directions that cater to social and cultural needs may in time generate the establishment of new kinds of foundations.

By tracking the development of foundations in Taiwan, we can see that social and economic changes in Taiwan have redefined the objectives of Taiwan's foundations in a meaningful way. The philanthropic aims that dominated foundations in earlier stages are gradually giving way to a diversity of aims. To a large extent, this basic developmental pattern reflects the fact that foundations are usually established in response to the needs of a changing society (See Table 3).

In the first period (until the 1970s), all foundations were primarily concerned with social welfare and education. In contrast, no foundations at all promoted social activism or culture and art, and only one foundation each promoted scholarships and international interchange.

It was not until the 1970s that foundations began to diversify. Foundations that promoted culture and art or a particular social movement began to appear. The number of foundations that provided scholarships rose the most sharply. Although the number of foundations concerned with social welfare or education also increased, they accounted for a steadily decreasing percentage of the total, indicating that such foundations have been gradually eclipsed by new types of cultural foundations.

Table 3.
Founding Years of Foundations and Trends of Change in Foundation Purposes

| Founding year/ Purpose | Up to 1972 | 1972- 1981 | 1982- 1988 | After 1989 | * Subtotal |
|---|---|---|---|---|---|
| Philan- thropy | 9 | 16 | 35 | 16 | 77 |
|  | 42.9 | 27.1 | 24.8 | 18.6 | |
|  | 11.7 | 20.8 | 45.8 | 20.8 | |
| Social Movement | 0 | 4 | 4 | 3 | 11 |
|  | 0 | 6.8 | 2.8 | 3.5 | |
|  | 0 | 36.4 | 36.4 | 27.3 | |
| Education | 5 | 8 | 24 | 20 | 57 |
|  | 23.8 | 13.6 | 17.0 | 23.3 | |
|  | 8.8 | 14.0 | 42.1 | 35.1 | |
| Research | 3 | 6 | 31 | 25 | 65 |
|  | 14.3 | 10.2 | 22.0 | 29.1 | |
|  | 4.6 | 9.2 | 47.7 | 38.5 | |
| Culture and Art | 0 | 10 | 18 | 15 | 43 |
|  | 0 | 16.9 | 12.8 | 17.4 | |
|  | 0 | 23.3 | 41.9 | 34.9 | |
| Scholar- ships | 1 | 10 | 20 | 3 | 35 |
|  | 4.8 | 16.9 | 14.2 | 3.5 | |
|  | 2.9 | 28.6 | 57.1 | 8.6 | |

| Inter- | 1 | 3 | 4 | 4 | 12 |
| national | 4.8 | 5.1 | 2.8 | 4.7 | |
| Cultural | 8.3 | 25.0 | 33.3 | 33.3 | |
| Exchange | | | | | |
| **Subtotal | 21 | 59 | 141 | 86 | 309 |

*Deviation: 9.
**Deviation:2.

Numerous kinds of foundations grew noticeably during the third period (1982-1988). Foundations focusing on research grew the most rapidly, while philanthropic and scholarship foundations, in the meantime, dropped in comparison with the others. The percentage of foundations focusing on education picked up once more, but their concerns became more comprehensive, and thus they were more in keeping with the aims of social and cultural education in a modern society.

In the two years after the lifting of the Emergency Decree, more academic-oriented foundations were established than other types. Those focusing on scholarships grew the least and suffered the greatest percentage drop. For the first time, philanthropic foundations were also outdone by the research foundations and education foundations.

It is clear from the preceding that various foundations appeared during different periods of time and that the 1980s saw the greatest increase in the variety of foundations. It should be noted that foundations associated with particular social movements were basically products of the 1980s. Foundations focusing on research or the promotion of culture and art also mushroomed during this decade. This again shows that, through the formation of foundations during the 1980s, the private sector was able to demonstrate its strength in three regards—in a vigorous fight for social rights and reforms, in active participation in the formulation of government policies, and in concern for the interests of the community at large.

Generally speaking, foundations can be further sub-divided into four categories according to their primary funding sources: (1) corporate foundations, which receive funds from a single corporation; (2) official foundations, which are government-supported; (3) mixed foundations, which are funded by both corporations and the government; and (4) private foundations, which are sponsored by non-governmental and non-corporate sources. The expectations imposed on foundations may differ in accordance with their funding sources. Some patrons may even subject the foundations they support to certain specific obligations. Table 4 classifies foundations by funding source.

Nearly three-fifths of the foundations studied lack long-term corporate or government sponsors. These private foundations raise funds or accept donations from a wide variety of sources, such as the general public or individuals. This does not mean that such foundations never obtain any funding from corporations, but rather that they do not rely on any single corporation or set of corporations for steady patronage. Corporations that do finance such private foundations do not make long-term commitments.

Foundations supported by specific corporations are often established with independent funds. This type of patronage may exercise a stabilizing effect on the foundation. Altogether 74 corporate foundations account for a quarter of all the samples in this study. Corporate foundations are thus the second most common type of foundation, and they are also an important type. Their relationship with their specific corporate sponsors merits closer scrutiny. Generally speaking, the more prosperous a society is and the better-developed its private enterprises are, the more corporate foundations there will be, and the more active they will be. In this study, corporate foundations account for a much higher proportion of all foundations than was found in Tsai Cheng-wen's 1982 study. Such an increase reveals the changed status of private corporations and the direction in which their role has been adjusted in the decade following Tsai's survey. Foundations co-sponsored by the government and corporations, and foundations completely sponsored by the government, account for only 5 percent and 3 percent of the foundations in the present study respectively, taking third and fourth position on the list. Thus, Taiwan's foundations are mainly non-governmental in nature.

### Table 4.
### Foundations: Classified by Funding Source

| | | |
|---|---|---|
| **Private foundations**, supported by neither the government nor specific corporations | 194 | (68.8%) |
| **Corporate foundations**, supported by specific corporations | 74 | (23.9%) |
| **Mixed foundations**, co-sponsored by corporations and the government | 15 | ( 4.9%) |
| **Official foundations**, supported by the government | 10 | ( 3.2%) |
| Information not available | 16 | ( 5.2%) |
| Total | 309 | 100% |

Table 5 reveals that while the relative ranking of funding sources does not change over the four time periods in this study, the percentage of funding provided by different sources has fluctuated over time.

The second period (1972-1981) saw a tremendous growth in the number of corporate foundations. Whereas corporate foundations accounted for 23.8 percent of all foundations in the first period (up to

1971), by the third period (1982-1988) they accounted for 35.6 percent. Mixed foundations also began to appear in the second period. While the absolute number of private foundations rose rapidly during the second period, their numbers remained relatively constant as a percentage of all foundations. Such a phenomenon underscores the great interest that enterprises took in organizing non-profit foundations. During the second period, 39 percent of all foundations received at least partial financial support from corporations, reflecting the tremendous growth of Taiwan's private sector during this time.

During the third and fourth periods (1982-1990), the ratio of private foundations grew from 50 to over 65 percent of the total, while the absolute number of private foundations increased three-fold. This is further evidence of the increased vigor of the private community.

Corporate foundations continued to grow during the third and fourth periods. A total of 26 corporate foundations were established between 1982 and 1988, prior to the termination of the Emergency Decree. In contrast, 21 corporate foundations were established in the first two years following the lifting of the Emergency Decree, equal to the number of corporate foundations set up in the entire second period. One can anticipate that corporate foundations will continue to gain in importance.

The ratio of official foundations to all others declined remarkably after the Emergency Decree was lifted. This was seemingly a result of growing strength of the private community versus the government strength.

Yet another look at the developmental pattern of each type of foundation during the four periods reveals the following. First, official foundations were the products of the period during which the Emergency Decree was in force. Second, corporate foundations have grown steadily since the beginning of the second period. Third, mixed foundations did not become apparent until after the second period. Fourth, private foundations were an important social and cultural phenomenon spawned by changing Taiwan society during the 1980s.

**Table 5.**
**Founding Years and Funding Sources**

| Funding Sources/ Founding year | Corporate Foundations | Official Foundations | Mixed Foundations | Private Foundations | **Subtotal |
|---|---|---|---|---|---|
| Period 1 | 5 | 1 | 0 | 11 | 21 |
| (up to 1972) | 23.8 | 4.8 | 0 | 52.4 | |
| | 6.8 | 10.0 | 0 | 5.7 | |
| Period 2 | 21 | 2 | 2 | 31 | 59 |
| (1972-1981) | 35.6 | 3.4 | 3.4 | 52.5 | |
| | 28.4 | 20.0 | 13.3 | 16 | |
| Period 3 | 26 | 6 | 8 | 94 | 141 |
| (1982-1988) | 18.4 | 4.3 | 5.7 | 66.4 | |
| | 35.1 | 60.0 | 53.3 | 48.5 | |
| Period 4 | 21 | 1 | 5 | 57 | 86 |
| (1989-Aug. | 24.4 | 1.2 | 5.8 | 66.3 | |
| 1991) | 28.4 | 10.2 | 33.3 | 29.4 | |
| * Subtotal | 74 | 10 | 15 | 194 | 309 |

* Deviation: 16
** Deviation: 2

Generally speaking, the endowments of most foundations in Taiwan fall within one of two ranges: from NT$1 million to NT$1.99 million, or over NT$6 million. Others fall within the ranges of NT$2 million to NT$2.99 million and NT$3 million to NT$3.99

million. Table 6 shows the correlation between the time of a foundation's establishment and the size of its endowment.

Most foundations established in the first or second period have endowments of at least NT$6 million. Starting in the third period, however, endowment sizes began to vary. Numerous small foundations with endowments of between NT$1 million and NT$1.99 million were set up. Such a trend probably reflects the fact that before the third period, few individuals, enterprises, or groups could afford to organize foundations. During the third and fourth periods, a multitude of small and medium-sized foundations appeared. Anyone who had the economic wherewithal was allowed to set up a foundation. Gone were the early days when the scene was dominated by only a few foundations.

The foundations established during the third and fourth periods whose endowments were between NT$2 million-NT$5.99 million have grown the fastest. In other words, the development of medium-scale foundations was another feature in the history of the development of foundations during the time.

The number of medium-sized foundations established since the lifting of the Emergency Decree has almost equaled the number of large foundations. Foundations with endowments of less than NT$1 million, foundations with endowment of between NT$2 million and NT$5.99 million, and foundations with endowments of over NT$6 million account for one-third of the total number of foundations respectively.

While it is ture that the earlier a foundation was established, the larger its endowment was, the size of more recently established foundations has varied from small to large.

# Table 6.
# Founding Years and Current Endowment Size

| Founding Year /Endowment Size Unit:NT$1 million | Before 1971 | 1972- 1981 | 1982- 1988 | After 1989 | *Subtotal |
|---|---|---|---|---|---|
| Below 0.45 | 1 | 2 | 3 | 0 | 6 |
|  | 4.8 | 3.4 | 2.1 | 0 | |
|  | 16.7 | 33.3 | 50.0 | 0 | |
| 0.50—0.99 | 0 | 2 | 2 | 1 | 5 |
|  | 0 | 8.5 | 1.4 | 1.2 | |
|  | 0 | 40.0 | 40.0 | 20.0 | |
| 1.00—1.99 | 0 | 5 | 47 | 25 | 78 |
|  | 0 | 6.8 | 33.3 | 29.1 | |
|  | 0 | 6.4 | 60.3 | 32.1 | |
| 2.00—2.99 | 0 | 4 | 15 | 4 | 23 |
|  | 0 | 5.1 | 10.6 | 4.7 | |
|  | 0 | 17.4 | 65.2 | 17.4 | |
| 3.00—3.99 | 1 | 3 | 6 | 12 | 22 |
|  | 4.8 | 6.8 | 4.3 | 14.0 | |
|  | 4.5 | 13.6 | 42.9 | 54.5 | |
| 4.00—4.99 | 0 | 4 | 6 | 4 | 14 |
|  | 0 | 0 | 4.3 | 4.7 | |
|  | 0 | 28.6 | 42.9 | 28.6 | |
| 5.00—5.99 | 1 | 0 | 6 | 5 | 12 |
|  | 4.8 | 59.3 | 4.3 | 5.8 | |
|  | 8.3 | 0 | 50.5 | 41.7 | |
| 6.00 and above | 17 | 35 | 50 | 27 | 129 |
|  | 81.0 | 59 | 35.5 | 31.4 | |
|  | 13.2 | 27.1 | 38.3 | 20.9 | |
| Subtotal | 21 | 59 | 141 | 86 | 309 |

The overall missions of foundations have changed over time. This change can be traced by comparing the founding years of foundations with the primary emphases of their work at the present time.

# Table 7.
# Founding Years and Primary Focus
# (Multiple Choices Allowed)

| Founding years /Foci | Before 1971 | 1972-1981 | 1982-1988 | After 1989 | Subtotal |
|---|---|---|---|---|---|
| | 12 | 23 | 43 | 19 | 97 |
| Philanthropy | 57.1 | 30.9 | 30.5 | 22.1 | |
| | 12.4 | 27.3 | 44.3 | 19.6 | |
| | 14 | 35 | 64 | 46 | 160 |
| Scholarships | 66.7 | 59.3 | 55.4 | 53.5 | |
| | 8.8 | 21.9 | 40.0 | 28.8 | |
| | 8 | 26 | 69 | 57 | 160 |
| Research | 38.1 | 44.1 | 48.9 | 66.3 | |
| | 5.0 | 16.8 | 43.1 | 35.6 | |
| | 2 | 6 | 13 | 11 | 32 |
| Social Activism | 9.5 | 10.2 | 9.2 | 12.8 | |
| | 6.3 | 18.8 | 40.6 | 34.4 | |
| International | 6 | 26 | 35 | 37 | 104 |
| Exchange | 28.6 | 44.1 | 24.8 | 43.0 | |
| | 5.8 | 25 | 33.7 | 35.6 | |
| | 6 | 28 | 68 | 41 | 143 |
| Publishing | 28.6 | 47.5 | 48.2 | 47.7 | |
| | 4.2 | 19.6 | 47.6 | 28.7 | |
| Cultural | 8 | 27 | 59 | 38 | 132 |
| Activities | 38.1 | 45.8 | 41.8 | 44.2 | |
| | 6.1 | 20.5 | 44.7 | 28.2 | |
| | 10 | 30 | 72 | 46 | 158 |
| Education | 47.6 | 50.8 | 51.1 | 53.5 | |
| | 6.3 | 19.0 | 41.6 | 29.1 | |
| *Subtotal | 21 | 59 | 141 | 86 | 309 |

*Deviation:2.

A large number of the foundations established in the first period focused on charitable causes and providing scholarships. In the second period, the percentage of foundations which focused on research, international exchanges, publishing, and cultural activities rose while the number of foundations focusing on philanthropy began to fall. This trend continued throughout the third and fourth periods, with the number of foundations dealing primarily with philanthropic projects decreasing. In the meantime, the number of foundations focusing on academic research rose.

Research, social activism, cultural activities, and education have emerged as the chief new concerns of foundations since the third period. The newer the foundation, the greater its tendency to adopt the above-mentioned concerns as a focus for its undertakings. Such a finding can also be regarded as evidence that the purposes of foundations may change over time and that foundations have been drawing upon the cohesive power of the private sector since the early 1970s.

The targets of foundation-sponsored programs have changed very little. Despite differences in their founding dates, most foundations target their services either for students or the general public. Furthermore, foundations tend to choose their target groups activity by activity. (See Table 8)

# Table 8.

| Founding dates/ Targets of Service | Period One | Period Two | Period Three | Period Four | Total |
|---|---|---|---|---|---|
| | 8 | 15 | 41 | 23 | 87 |
| Children | 38.1 | 25.4 | 29.1 | 26.7 | |
| | 9.2 | 17.2 | 47.1 | 26.4 | |
| | 3 | 19 | 36 | 27 | 85 |
| Adolescents | 14.3 | 32.2 | 25.5 | 31.4 | |
| | 3.5 | 22.4 | 42.4 | 31.8 | |
| | 7 | 11 | 23 | 17 | 59 |
| Senior Citizens | 33.3 | 18.6 | 16.3 | 19.8 | |
| | 11.9 | 18.6 | 39.0 | 28.8 | |
| | 6 | 8 | 30 | 22 | 66 |
| Women | 28.6 | 13.6 | 21.3 | 56.6 | |
| | 9.1 | 12.1 | 45.5 | 33.3 | |
| | 11 | 28 | 66 | 46 | 152 |
| Students | 52.4 | 47.5 | 48.6 | 53.5 | |
| | 7.2 | 18.4 | 43.4 | 30.3 | |
| | 8 | 12 | 20 | 19 | 60 |
| The Poor | 38.1 | 20.3 | 14.2 | 22.1 | |
| | 13.3 | 20.0 | 33.3 | 31.9 | |
| Disabled People | 6 | 12 | 25 | 16 | 59 |
| | 28.6 | 20.3 | 17.7 | 18.6 | |
| | 10.2 | 20.3 | 42.4 | 27.1 | |
| The public at large | 11 | 26 | 80 | 52 | 169 |
| | 52.4 | 44.1 | 56.7 | 60.5 | |
| | 6.5 | 15.4 | 47.3 | 30.8 | |
| Depends on service provided | 7 | 18 | 50 | 33 | 109 |
| | 33.3 | 30.5 | 35.5 | 38.4 | |
| | 6.4 | 16.5 | 45.9 | 30.3 | |
| *Total | 21 | 59 | 141 | 109 | 309 |

*Deviation:2.

405

Three quarters of the 309 foundations have existed for less than ten years, and of these three quarters, more than a quarter have been in existence for less than three years. The newness of foundations provides an excellent perspective from which to understand them, for their unique characteristics reflect their newness.

The overlapping of new foundations upon old accentuates differences in foundation type. Older foundations were set up to deal with the more traditional undertakings at the grass-roots level, namely, social welfare, philanthropy, and education. Diversification of purpose has come to characterize the new generation of foundations. No longer limited to the above-mentioned concerns of the traditional foundations, the younger generation foundations are involved in research, reviewing public policies, promoting culture and art, and campaigning for social reform.

Limiting factors in the early years—political sensitivity, lack of social consensus, and insufficient financial resources—made it almost impossible for foundations to be organized without the assistance of corporations, individuals, or groups who were in positions of power and willing to take the initiative. As a result, most foundations established in the early years were richly endowed. However, starting in the third period, as people began to enjoy more freedom and affluence and became increasingly concerned about community issues, foundations of various sizes began to appear. This change ushered in a new age in which foundations became "popularized" and were no longer the special privilege or the guarded enterprise of powerful minorities.

The diversification of target groups and the popularization of foundations once again point to the expansion of foundation affairs, the diversification of the means they employ, and the universalization of their service targets.

A close scrutiny of this study's database also reveals several unique features of foundations in Taiwan. First, almost all Taiwan's foundations are "self-run," which means that the foundations achieve their goals through their own efforts rather than through commissioned agencies. Second, most foundations are not self-sufficient in terms of financial or human resources. They must constantly rely on social resources from outside, such as occasional donations from individuals or enterprises. Fund-raising activities are thus crucial, and foundations often call in experts or volunteer workers to make up for a lack of fixed human resources. Third, foundations interact with one another or with other social groups. They co-sponsor activities, exchange publications, and provide mutual assistance. (It must be noted, however, the body of data on the interactions and exchange of resources between the foundations is not yet sufficient to warrant systematic study.) Cooperation between foundations has been spontaneous at best. Fourth, most of Taiwan's foundations have been organized along very simple lines. There is usually a lack of personnel, especially experts who can deal with the practical side of business. Consequently, obstacles are often encountered in tapping community resources and in seeking new directions for the development of the foundation.

## How Foundations Are Organized

An overall study and evaluation of the foundations in Taiwan has yielded some insights into the factors that have contributed to the establishment of Taiwan's foundations. Objectively speaking, apart from a few favorable conditions brought about by changes in society at large and by the rise of power in the private community, several other intrinsic factors are essential to the emergence of foundations. These include a

407

group of people dedicated to a common goal, powerful supporters, and opportune timing.

Usually the idea of forming a foundation is initiated and carried out by a group of people sharing the same ideals and motivated by the same purpose. From the outset, a strong conviction and a clear sense of orientation will guide this cohesive group, precluding the potential for disorientation and confusion that often besets foundations in the initial stages of their development. Foundations established through consensus seldom deteriorate into mere names registered for ulterior purposes.

Foundations must also win financial backing from individuals or groups in positions of power and influence. The commitment of long-term support to a foundation by the powerful can, to a great extent, ensure smooth sailing in the future. Furthermore, if the financial support can be efficiently utilized to manage whatever undertakings the foundation is concerned with, the foundation will stand a better chance of reaching its goals and building a name for itself.

Opportunity presents itself to foundations when a situation requiring immediate solution arises in the community or when a long-standing problem has remained unsolved. Once this situation becomes a matter of public concern, foundations that are set up to deal with the situation will gain the recognition and support of society and win patronage.

In contrast, foundations that lack consensus, powerful patrons, and good timing tend to be nothing more than registered name. Lackluster performance can also result from a lack of clearly-defined aims or mangement expertise. In some cases, a foundation may have the strong backing of powerful patrons but lack a clearly-defined aim. In other cases, foundations are established only to build individual or corporate prestige rather than to achieve the loftier aim of serving the public. Such a foundation may contract with public relations firms to plan or run its program rather than taking charge on its own. Numerous as these kinds of delegating foundations might be, they can hardly expect to make a name for themselves. Doubtless, the two indispensable ingredients for the success of a foundation are the strong support of its patrons and the dedication of its members. Foundations that lack one or both of these ingredients can never develop to their full potential.

The intrinsic features of a foundation, to some extent, determine that foundation's future development and performance. Conversely, the foundation's ability to utilize extrinsic factors to its best advantage is also indicative of future success.

The board of directors should be the top executive body in a foundation. The director represents the foundation officially, and the secretary general or the chief executive officer is the central figure in the execution of business. In some foundations, there is an executive secretary to assist the secretary general or the CEO in the management of internal administration and the general affairs of the foundation. The position of executive secretary may be a part-time position held concurrently by a staff member within the foundation or occupied full time by somebody invited from outside. There are a few foundations which do not have the position of executive secretary, and whose day-to-day affairs are handled directly by the secretary general or CEO. The position of secretary general is a full-time job or one taken up by a staff member who has been with the foundation long enough to be capable of assuming complete responsibility. The number of staff needed and the delegation of jobs depend on the financial status and the needs of the individual foundation.

Apart from the staff members within the system, some foundations also set up complementary voluntary organizations or committees as dictated by practical needs.

An analysis of documented data and the results of interviews has yielded the following information about how foundations work.

### The Board of Directors

The board may be composed of the founding members or people invited from the outside. Some of the board seats may be reserved for fund donors depending on the source of the funds. Whether the board members are qualified to meet the professional demands of a foundation depends on how that foundation was set up, the source of its funding, its human resource requirements, and the image the foundation seeks to establish. Generally speaking, a foundation established by people dedicated to achieving the same goals has better professionally-trained board members.

### The Director, the Secretary General or CEO, and the Executive Secretary

The interactions among these three key figures will have a profound impact on the foundation's internal management and operations, its image, its activities, and its development. Judging from the interviews, it can be concluded that if a foundation is to be run successfully, interactions among these three people must be guided by trust, understanding, cooperation, and a willingness to delegate responsibility. Otherwise, internal conflicts are bound to arise, and these in turn can send conflicting messages to outside observers. Furthermore, the person acting as secretary general or CEO must have considerable expertise, and he must have the trust of the director, to be able to carry out his ideals.

## The Staff

Extensive interviewing has revealed that, except for very few foundations which have numerous full-time staff members assigned to departments according to their specializations, most foundations are manged by a simple staff that usually consists of a secretary general and two to three others. Generally, most staff members work on an ad hoc basis. Very few staff members have the professional qualifications to take full charge of the planning and promotion of the foundation's projects. Lack of expertise is thus a problem that plagues most foundations. Aggravating the problem is the way in which staff are trained. Usually foundations train their own staff by engaging them in actual work. Such a training process is slow, inefficient, and unprofessional. It may result in high staff turnover and create gaps between the different levels of administration, adversely affecting the general development of business.

## Volunteers and Committees

To make up for the lack of professional expertise, foundations often resort to recruiting volunteers and establishing committees. Data obtained from the questionnaire used in this study shows that 33 percent of the foundations recruit volunteers, and 25 percent set up committees. Recruitment of volunteers may be cheap and easy, but volunteers may not be particularly well suited to the job at hand. Still, some foundations are able to utilize voluntary resources to good advantage, and cultivate volunteers as "the seeds for social and cultural work" by organizing and training them to be front-line workers. Some volunteers may be included in the general planning, so that they can one day become the "backbone" of the foundation.

Committees are usually set up as a way of recruiting professionals and enhancing the status of a foundation. As most committee members are experts

411

in some way, they provide multiple services. Data garnered from the questionnaire used in this study show
that committee members often play several roles. Some
59 percent of committee members served as consultants, 64.1 percent worked as planners, and 60.3 percent handled administrative duties. It may therefore be
concluded that the lack of human resources, especially
the shortage of professional experts, plagues foundations. In interviews, some foundations also suggested
that the government should help train professional
personnel who are genuinely devoted to the business
of foundations. The training would enable them to
have a full understanding of the judicial nature of
foundations, their rules of operation, and the various
ins and outs of the taxation system. They could learn
about social trends and how to develop and utilize
community resources. These well-informed professionals would in time become a valuable resource for
various foundations. Government authorities ought to
seriously consider adopting this approach.

Basically foundations are the products of a
changing society, and they have become a highly visible expression of vigor in the private community.
Since foundations aim to promote the social good and
since the projects they undertake are the only indicator
of how they define the social good, evaluating a foundation's planning capabilities is thus useful.

When a foundation is developing its projects, it
will typically first consider whether the propsed projects correspond with its overall mission. After ascertaining that the content and direction of a project is in
line with the foundation's mission, the foundation will
consider how to get across its "message" through a
series of events. Most foundations set goals for different phases of their work. The most commonly listed
goals include (1) promoting new concepts related to
the overall mission of the foundation, (2) paving the

way so that the public will gradually recogize and identify with the spirit and goals of the foundation, (3) experimenting with new solutions to problems in the
community, (4) establishing new criteria for guiding
Taiwan's social and cultural development, and (5)
advocating innovations in government policies and
suggesting ways to effect these innovations. For some
foundations, these are definite goals to be pursued at
certain stages in time, but for other foundations, goals
may be changed depending on how the foundation's
projects are progerssing.

The questionnaire and interviews employed in
this study reveal that foundations must overcome
many difficulties as they go about their work. For instance, foundations must figure out how to combine
"expertise" with "power" to create more opportunities
for growth. Some foundations, hobbled by a lack of
manpower or money, easily fall into developmental
ruts. They must learn from more successful foundations how to draw on the knowledge of experts and the
financial resources of powerful patrons. Foundations
must also be able to cultivate their own professional
staff and modify their organizational frameworks. And,
perhaps most importantly, foundations must:

1. Combine expertise with real political power to
create new opportunities for development. Intrinsic
limitations such as a lack of financial backing or qualified personnel create developmental bottlenecks for
some foundations; however, the experinence of successfully and aggressively managed foundations shows
principles must be tempered by pragmatism. The technical know-how of the experts and the financial backing of powerful patrons are essential. Foundations
ought to see the growing power of the private sector as
a potential resource which can be tapped by tailoring
projects to the needs occasioned by new social developments. In this regard, foundations need to win rec-

ognition from the community and to hone the business skills of their staff.

2. Upgrade staff professionalism and adjust organizational frameworks to maximize their role in the community. The lack of professionals has greatly handicapped the development of Taiwan's foundations. Such a deficiency has of course something to do with the financial background of the foundations, but there is no absolute causal relationship between the two. Interviews with foundations show that quite a few foundations with only limited financial resources and skeleton staffs have been run with extraordinary success. The keys to success are (1) capitalizing on all available human resources and (2) knowing how to delegate responsibility. Most important, staff must be backed up by experts who are given free rein in organizing and planning. For the time being, it seems that just experts can make the difference between mediocrity and success. However, it would be foolhardy to rely solely on a few experts over the long term; new recruits must be trained in case key staff members resign.

A foundation can compensate for inadequate financial and human resources in two ways. First, it can provide its full-time staff with on-the-job training, so that they will become well-versed in the nuts and bolts of the foundation's affairs. Secondly, it can solicit the know-how of interested committee members (experts and scholars) as well as volunteers and build a flexible system for integrating their expertise into the plans for promoting the affairs of the foundation.

Of course, the director and the board members of the foundation should be good policy-makers capable of exercising their powers to the fullest. Similarly, since the secretary general is the person in charge of overseeing the day-to-day operations of the foundation, one cannot be too careful in selecting candidates for this position. In addition, a foundation should be allowed to develop at a pace in keeping with its actual abilities and needs, and should never expand too fast. Nonetheless, most foundations, at one time or another, are faced with the need to modify their organizational frameworks rapidly.

3. Keep track of the latest social trends in Taiwan's rapidly developing and changing society and brace themselves for new challenges. The need for adjustments may not appear as urgent to new foundations as to old ones, but all foundations, old and new, should always be prepared to tack with the prevailing social wind. In the 1980s, some long-established foundations shifted their focuses toward social and cultural concerns and tailored their promotional drives to the new needs of the community. Similarly, some relatively new foundations have been flexible enough to make necessary changes, and for this reason they have been very active and highly productive. The key to the flexibility of the newer foundations has been a desire to seek out new issues and a willingness to adjust public relations strategies.

The 1990s saw remarkable advances in Taiwan's social and political development. The foundations established prior to the lifting of the *Emergency Decree* in the late 1980s—themselves products of a long series of social changes—have not been lax in meeting the emerging challenges. At this juncture, foundations in Taiwan should seriously consider how they can play an even more active role in setting the trends for Taiwan's social and cultural development by drawing upon the potential of the private community.

## Sound Foundations: Tapping the Cultural Vigor in a Newly Born Society

A few foundations expressed in their interviews that when they were registering with the government, if their statement of mission clashed with "established policy" or if the government feared they might threaten its "authority," it would deliberately furstrate their efforts by not approving the name of the prospective foundation or by being ambiguous about which government department would be in charge of the foundation-to-be.

Frankly speaking, the government is limited intrinsically and extrinsically in its ability to take full responsibility for all social issues. As foundations draw upon the power of the private community, they are in a position to compensate for any "inadequacy" on the part of the government. Before the lifting of the *Emergency Decree*, and the revision of the *Law on Civic Organizations*, the government often regarded foundations as a threat to its authority, fearing that if they were given free rein, they would get out of hand. Now with the lifting of the *Emergency Decree*, our society has become more open. Mass media are easily accessible and no longer monopolized by the government. And the government should be more open to differing opinions as it goes about fostering a democratic and pluralistic society. Government authorities should first forego their defensive attitude toward the establishment of foundations and replace this negative sentiment with a genuine and positive attempt to understand foundations in terms of the facts (i.e. their major concerns and activities, their fund-raising status, their organizational frameworks, and the roles they play in the community). In time, foundations may become a positive force that complements and promotes the government's policies and cultural initiatives.

Any government department can approve applications to establish foundations. However, each regulatory authority has its own rules and standards for approving such applications and sets its own quota for the number of new foundations. Since government staff may not have a real understanding of foundation operations. Foundations, in their eagerness for a license, may tailor their founding purposes or objectives to cater to the supervising authorities. One feasible remedy for the situation is to assign a single department to handle the examination and approval of applications and to invite people who are fair and just or who have expertise and experience in the operations of foundations to form an inter-ministerial committee for reviewing applications. This supervisory body could set the standards for the establishment of foundations, regulate the size of primary endowments, and unify the methods for examining and approving applications. When the examination is over, the committee could assign a supervising department. The foundation would register with this supervising department, which would then be responsible for guiding the foundation after its establishment.

Although a foundation is only an organization whose nature is to serve the public, it has the same juristic personality as any registered corporation. All of its operations, fund-raising activities, use of tax incentives, planning and implementation of projects are undertakings within the specialized realm of foundation work. People who are engaged in foundation work should mainly be those who are dedicated to serving the community. In view of the general lack of qualified staff for foundations, and the inablility to fill that gap, there seems to be a need for government authorities to help educate professionals about foundation work through lectures on the legal rights of juristic persons, the application process, criteria for tax exemption, social studies, basic administrative skills, basic accounting concepts, and business strategies. A certificate could be awarded to successful trainees, who would then be recommended to foundations where involvement in practical jobs would make them full-fledged professionals devoted to the ideals of the foundation they serve.

Foundations are professional undertakings. The government should respect their autonomy, and should not intervene too much in their administration. Government "guidance" should be directed mainly towards the provision of financial aid, the facilitation of administrative proceedings, and the provision of tax reductions or exemptions. Assistance along these lines would help foundations fulfill their potential.

Taiwan already has over 1,000 foundations[3]— large and small, official and non-official—engaged in a highly-diversified range of activities. Even though some foundations may have the same theme or structure, their emphases and work styles may differ. For example, "women's issues" may be approached from different directions, such as raising women's social status, rescuing child prostitutes, assisting women in planning their career, counseling women on marriage, and reinforcing alliances between women. Foundations developing along different lines could do better if they shared communications networks, human resources, information, and even expenses. Foundations pursuing the same objectives would gain much by such collaboration. The government should gather as much information as it can about foundations so as to facilitate communications among them. Apart from enabling the government to have a better understanding of foundations, this would also benefit the work of foundations themselves. In addition, there is a dire shortage of information about foundations abroad. The government should bridge the gap by asking consulates or liaison offices abroad to collect information about foundations in other countries. The information would be very useful to domestic foundations and could lead to future exchanges between them and their foreign counterparts.

The general provisions of the ROC's *Code of Civil Procedure* state that all competent government agencies may have their own respective regulations concerning a juristic person. Furthermore, the Executive Yuan has also set up "criteria for determining tax exemption for educational, cultural, social welfare, charitable organizations and groups." All foundations, regardless of whether or not they are really organized for one of these four purposes, will attempt to meet the requirements laid down for such foundations in order to qualify for tax-exempt status. The lack of a unified set of parent regulations has greatly impeded the governing of foundations. It is therefore essential that a specialized "Foundation Control Law" be passed, and adhered to by all foundations in Taiwan.

We can justifiably believe that if the government and the private sector take a serious look at the above-mentioned facts about foundations in Taiwan, and encourage foundations to expand their roles, Taiwan's foundations will be able to shoulder a considerable share of responsibility in social reform and cultural development. Only when foundations prove that they can make a noticeable difference in these two aspects will they be regarded as a positive social and cultural force in the 1990s.

NOTES
1. (Tsai Cheng-wen, et al., 1982)
2. (Hsiao, 1911: 113-126)
3. (Himalayan Foundation, 1991)

REFERENCES
Baron, Barnett F., ed. 1991. *Philanthropy and the Dynamics of Change in East and Southeast Asia.* New York: Columbia University, East Asian Institute.
*Catalogue of Foundations in Taiwan.* 1991. Taipei: Himalayan Research Foundation.
"Consolidating Foundations and Promoting Social Well-Being," editorial, *China Times,* Aug. 12, 1990, Taipei edition.
Hsiao, Hsin-huang M. "The New Reformism: Private Philanthropy in Taiwan in the 1980s," in Baron, op. cit., pp. 113-126.

*An Introduction of Foundations in Taiwan.* 1989. Taipei: Council for Cultural Planning and Development.

*Knowing Foundations.* 1990. Taipei: Department of Mass Communications, Ming Chuan College.

Tsai Cheng-wen et al. 1982. "Foundations in the Changing Taiwan Area," unpublished research paper commissioned by the Asia Foundation, Taipei.

# VIII.
# Miscellany

Previous page: The ROC's education system has provided the nation with a large pool of highly skilled, well-versed individuals.

# Towards a Modernized National Defense

Sung Wen

National defense is the key to national security. A country might go a hundred years without fighting a war but could not last a single day without a national defense, for with no defense, a country has nothing. By consolidating its defenses after moving to Taiwan, the Republic of China has been able to hold its ground and foil two bitter attacks on Kinmen by the Chinese communists. This has allowed the country to carry out various political and economic development projects in a secure environment and to achieve democracy, prosperity, and stability in the Taiwan area.

*Sung Wen is a counselor at the Ministry of National Defense.*

With the recent collapse of the former Soviet Union and the East European communist bloc, the conflict between the Soviet and US camps has ended. In the post-Cold War era, numerous regions and nations around the world face the challenge of shaping a new world order that, at this point, is still filled with a host of variables. Domestically, the government's major constitutional reforms have ushered in a new historical era of political and economic development. In order to establish a defensive force that is truly capable of guaranteeing security and prosperity in this new environment, the task of the ROC military will be to follow government directives and strive for structural and functional reforms in the pursuit of modernization.

While national security is the top priority of the nation's defense, absolute security is unattainable, for

423

one nation's security is achieved at the expense of another's. Security is relative. In the interactions of relative security, identifying the existence of threat is the first step toward safeguarding national security.

The most direct and serious threat to the security of the Republic of China on Taiwan is a possible armed invasion by the Chinese communists. We will for now leave aside a discussion of earlier interactions, and begin by looking at how the Chinese communists have failed to respond positively to two recent developments. The first was our announcement that we were terminating the *Period of National Mobilization for Suppression of the Communist Rebellion* and that we were committed to gradually solving problems related to the unification of China by applying the principles of peace, reason, parity, and reciprocity. The second development is the increase in economic, cultural, academic, and sports exchanges between the two sides of the Taiwan Straits that have been in progress since the ROC government lifted a ban on Taiwan residents visiting relatives in the Chinese mainland. In response, the Chinese communists have released a white paper entitled *The Taiwan Question and Reunification of China* in which they merely repeat their old slogans of "one country, two systems," "high degree of autonomy," and "peaceful negotiations" and in which they flatly refuse to renounce the use of force against Taiwan.

The military capabilities of the Chinese communists force us to acknowledge the severity of the threat they pose to the security of the ROC. Over the past decade or so, the Chinese communists have been building up their military arsenal and modernizing their armed forces for political purposes. The end of the Cold War has not been matched by a cessation of military activities on the part of the Chinese communists, who have instead revealed their ambitions by rapidly filling the vacuum left behind by the gradual withdrawal of American and Soviet power from the Asia-Pacific region. The military budget of the Chinese communists has experienced double-digit growth over the past few years; indeed, their military expenditures more than doubled between 1988 and 1993. The Chinese communists are now taking advantage of Russia's shortage of hard cash to procure large quantities of advanced naval and air weapons. These purchases of Russian armaments have allowed the Chinese communists to project their military capabilities from coastal to inland areas.

In addition to steadily reducing troop strength along the Sino-Indian and Sino-NIS borders, the Chinese communists outlined a new set of "contemporary strategic directions" in 1993 that clearly identifies the mainland's southeastern coast as the focus of future strategic development. A series of large-scale military maneuvers conducted from May to August of 1993 involving the air, land, and naval components of the Chinese communists' armed forces also confirmed this new focus and served to warn of possible future implications for our own security.

The second and most effective way to safeguard national security is to set up military forces possessing adequate self-defense capability without outside assistance. It is an unchanging truth that with strength comes security. But what kind of military force can guarantee the ability to defend oneself with outside help? It is difficult to set a standard. The arms race between the US and the Soviet Union and the concomitant notions of mutual deterrence created economic burdens that indirectly led to the collapse of the Soviet system as well as an erosion of the international power and prestige of the United States.

We are vastly different from the Chinese communists; and we have altered our strategic thinking because of changes in our political environment and the way in which we are seeking to unify China. Deterring an attack on the area comprising Taiwan, Penghu, Kinmen, and Matsu is now the main focus of our military buildup. In other words, our "defense-cum-offense" strategy has been reduced to the element of "defense." In line with this dictate, our military buildup is being conducted in accordance with the following line of thinking: "objectives—weaponry—organization—training." We have considered strategic conditions around us, evaluated the threat posed by the Chinese communist military, and included in our equation the disposition of our national resources. Over the long term, our overall objective is to strengthen naval and air defenses. We are planning to build a small, high-caliber, effective, and modern fighting force. We hope that this force will be sufficient to deter attack and make the Chinese communists think twice about invading, so that peace and stability will prevail in the Taiwan Straits, and the two sides can continue to engage in friendly competition, build prosperity, and move towards a brighter future for the Chinese people.

Chinese military thought stresses that it is the quality of the troops and not the quantity that is important. The Elite Troops Policy is a major part of the ROC's military modernization program. It comprises both a program to streamline the ranks and one to raise the quality of the troops.

Most advanced nations do not maintain armed forces in excess of two percent of their national population. The ROC's figure is slightly higher, at 2.3 percent. The ROC military has thus mapped out a ten-year plan from 1994 to 2003 for keeping troop levels under 400,000 (only 1.7 percent of the population in the Taiwan area, which is estimated to reach 22 million in the year 2003).

This far-reaching plan will not be carried out too quickly, so as to avoid jeopardizing national security. The ten-year period in which the program to streamline the armed forces will be conducted has been divided into three phases. An assessment of current conditions and future potentialities will be made as we slowly but surely implement the program, so that objectives can be met at each stage, following prudent consultation.

The first phase, lasting approximately three years, will eliminate inconsistencies in the organization of the army, navy, and air force and bring units up to full force, so as to facilitate training and the execution of normal duties. The second phase, lasting approximately four years, will adjust the organization of general staff and cut or combine redundant units so that the general headquarters of the three services can function in concert and command operations can be sped up. The third phase, lasting approximately three years, will cut or combine units in the General Staff Headquarters and in the general headquarters of the three services. In this phase, the armed forces will shed units that do not serve a military purpose, and the military academies and schools will be cut or combined, so as to create a solid military structure.

The amount of military power assigned to each of the three services will be decided by the current priority of either naval or air supremacy in defensive operations and by the needs of coastal patrols.

Troop quality is an intangible factor that affects combat strength. The Persian Gulf War demonstrated that troop quality will occupy an increasingly important position in future high-tech wars. Therefore, the ROC military is placing special emphasis on the quality of its troops as it goes about streamlining its ranks. The effort to improve troop quality begins with military education. We are working to incorporate the military academies and colleges into the national education system, which will give the military's educational institutions greater access to educational resources. We also have programs with civilian universities and research institutes to exchange professors and researchers. These programs are enriching the content of our curricula, enabling us to confer more high degrees, and raising the overall level of military education. Another step we are taking to improve the quality of troops is to begin allowing people from a wider variety of backgrounds to become non-commissioned officers. We are working to improve working conditions and create more incentives for young people to test for placement in military academies. We are also considering instituting an American-style "Reserve Officers' Training Corps" so we can allow students who are enrolled in colleges and universities to voluntarily join the military while still in school, thus giving military personnel more avenues for developing their creativity. In addition, we are increasing the number of non-combat positions available to women in administration, logistics, education, and training. This expands the available pool of human resources and facilitates raising the overall quality of the troops.

The famous futurist, Alvin Toffler, believes that war will become an increasingly high-tech enterprise. High-tech weapons systems are a major indicator of a modernized defense. The ROC military has worked for many years to develop high-tech weapons systems. The emphasis has been on developing our own weapons because of limitations in the international environment for the ROC and because we feel it is important to develop a self-defense capability without relying on outside assistance. In a little more than two decades, the following weapons systems have been or are currently being developed: the IDF fighter, the

Tien-chien I and II AAMs, the Tien-kung SAMs, the Hsiung-feng I and II anti-ship missiles, the Cheng-kung class missile frigate, and the M-48M tank. Thanks to recent progress in ROC diplomatic efforts, we have had some degree of success in procuring weapons systems from abroad and have been able to purchase high-performance fighters and naval craft.

To ensure air supremacy, we are using both self-produced and imported high-performance fighters, including the F-16, the Mirage-2000, and the IDF fighter to replace the aging F-104s and F-5Es. We are also increasing our purchases of the E-2T, an early-warning plane, and various types of mounted armaments. These weapons are being matched with ground-based anti-aircraft missile systems under operation "ch'iang-wang" to fully automate battlefield control and integrate air defenses. We are also preparing to buy C-130H transport planes to shore up our air transport capabilities.

To ensure naval supremacy, we are building PFG2 frigates, PFEG cruisers, and coastal patrol craft. In addition, we are renting Knox-class frigates and buying more submarines and more missile systems for installation in coastal batteries or on ships. We are also automating our command and control operations and deepening our anti-submarine defenses in order to boost our ability to break a naval blockade.

In preparation for repelling an amphibious landing, we are revamping the armaments of our ground forces and our electronic intelligence and command systems for use during combat. We have completed production of the M-48M tank and are now preparing to purchase AH-1W ground attack helicopters and OH-58D combat and search helicopters. These additions will help us achieve the objectives of adding more armor, filling out our defenses, using more electronics, automating, and integrating our ground and air forces.

Logistics is the key to prolonged fighting capability. Without logistical support, combat operations could not be continued. The more modernized a military is, the more important logistics becomes. Successful logistical preparation was one of the factors of success in the American victory in the Persian Gulf War. The logistics system set up by the ROC military under the old strategic doctrine of "offense and defense" assumed the establishment of logistics centers in areas outside the ROC's present defensive perimeter. This assumption called for massive expenditures of personnel and money. Now that the ROC military has adopted a "purely defensive" strategic doctrine and begun to implement the Elite Troops Policy, we have had to adjust our logistics structure. We have, for instance, regionalized logistics operations. In the past, when combat units at all levels followed the imperatives of the "offense-cum-defense" policy, they had to set up their own logistics units in order to meet the requirements of mobility. Now, the emphasis is on defense and logistical efficiency. From now on, not only will combat units have their own logistical support staffs, each combat zone will also be considered a single logistical support area. Gradually, the functions of each logistical unit in a given logistical support area will be integrated under the unified command of the particular combat zone. This should reduce the amount of time needed for supplying combat units and increase logistical efficiency.

Logistical support can be divided into two types of services, supply and maintenance. Logistical units in the ROC Army, regardless of the type of unit they were attached to, used to be responsible for both supply and maintenance, so they were generally large, redundant, and slow. To raise efficiency, logistics units will now specialize in either supply or maintenance. In other words, all supply needs will be handled by a supply system, and all maintenance needs will be handled by a separate maintenance system.

All military armaments used to come from either military aid or military procurement. Logistical support planning was limited to allowing units to apply for parts by submitting a request based on computer calculations. There was no overall plan for providing support. During the research and development of new weapons systems, the emphasis was on technical breakthroughs, while studying how to use the integration of information and planning for integrated logistical support were overlooked. The painful lack of logistical support was not felt until after a new weapons system was deployed. To prevent such painful shortcomings after the deployment of a second generation of weapons systems, we now include logistical support planning in the R&D and deployment process of new weapons systems. The goal is to have a complete support system in place for any new weapon on the day of its deployment.

The adjustments in the logistics process outlined above are being gradually introduced in two phases. The first phase was completed in June 1993. New units have been set up to evaluate the efficiency of the adjustments. After some revision based on careful consideration and discussion, the second phase of adjustments will be put into effect throughout the entire ROC military. We expect this second phase to be completed within two and a half years.

A military career differs from most professions. Military personnel must be willing to accept limits on their personal freedom, to accept personal risk, and to tackle the most demanding of tasks. The Western military theorist Richard Hartman has noted that any country which does not provide its military personnel with the same salary and benefits enjoyed by civilians at similar levels is certain not to be a strong, flourishing country. Raising morale in the ranks is thus a major but relatively intangible component of our modernization program. Raising morale entails providing better care for our soldiers.

We have increased the financial rewards for certain kinds of specializations or regional assignments. In the military, certain specializations entail high-risk challenges. And military personnel are often stationed in alpine regions or on remote islands. Appropriate financial compensation should be awarded to those who undertake the strain of such special service. While we have worked very hard in this direction for many years now, we still have not met the standards for comparable jobs in the civilian sector, such as police officers or firemen. We will continue our efforts to remedy this situation by allocating funds for gradual pay increases.

We will also be improving barracks and recreational facilities in order to reduce stress on troops during work and training. The military has done its best to clean and refurbish bath and latrine facilities, mess halls, and barracks on existing bases up to civilian standards. We have also set up recreation centers offering the best in audio-visual equipment, and are now planning to establish large recreation centers in the north, central, and southern regions of Taiwan, and in Penghu and Kenting, so that officers and enlisted men can have access to quality R&R facilities.

We have revised the retirement provisions for military personnel to bring them closer in line with the government's newly mandated retirement system for military personnel, civil servants, and educational personnel. The revisions are aimed at setting reasonable guidelines for disbursements, gradually raising pensions, and mapping out a fundraising plan for pensions. Once the new system is in effect, military personnel will be eligible for a more reasonable retirement package. We are now promoting early retirement for mid-ranking officers so that they can continue to contribute to society. To help these officers in their transition to civilian life, we offer pre-retirement training, and we are working with national labor and commercial groups to provide training and job opportunities matched to the retiring officer's previous specialization and job goals.

The armed forces are part of the nation, and military personnel are one segment of society. Military personnel come from society and one day must return to it. The armed forces thus have close relations with the civilian community, especially since modern defense is premised on the participation of all citizens. Wars are now total wars. A strong national defense requires the support of all the people. War will require total mobilization. To gain public support for the military, we must first promote military-civilian relations.

The first step is to safeguard the rights and interests of the public. The prices of usable land in Taiwan have skyrocketed in recent years as Taiwan's economy has prospered. Since relevant laws are not always clear, disputes over land use have arisen between the military and civilians. The military is working actively to resolve these problems to protect civilian rights and interests. We have solved many cases in which the military was using private, government, or school land, as well as cases in which military land was being used by others. We are doing our best to resolve problems involving monetary and legal issues as quickly as possible. Restricted military areas and prohibitions against certain kinds of development in such areas, which are necessary measures for defensive combat operations, will be frequently reviewed and relaxed as much as possible to avoid obstructing national development. The basic consideration will be to maintain the minimum of military security while contributing to the welfare of the people. In recent years, we have lifted numerous restrictions on land use.

The second step to good military-civilian relations is to provide services to the civilian community. The military is on the lookout at all times for opportunities to serve the people, as long as such service does not interfere with combat training and preparation. For instance, military personnel helped farmers harvest rice crops 328,000 times over a total 32,000 square hectares last year. We also provided free medical services 5,000 times last year, serving over 110,000 people. In addition, the military uses its equipment to provide relief in land, sea, or air disasters. We build temporary bridges, repair dikes, and straighten river courses. On national holidays, we open the doors to our bases and camps and display weapons, equipment, and the achievements of our training. This helps people to better understand national defense and to build a consensus between the armed forces and civilians.

Building a modernized defense force requires large investments of manpower and capital. Such investments naturally will have an affect on the overall economic development of the community; but the choice between "defense or economic development" has been a major issue for mankind since ancient times. At different times in history, people have chosen to emphasize one or the other to different degrees, so it is difficult to make sweeping statements or to choose one over the other. Usually the standard used for striking a balance between defense and growth is the degree of outside threat, for one cannot have security, much less prosperity, without strength. Japan, for example, has strongly emphasized economic development. Yet, even though Japan is protected by the *Security Treaty Between Japan and the United States*, Japan has continued, due to factors in the current international environment, to raise its defense budget, which now totals nearly US$40 billion, the second highest in the world. The extent to which Japan emphasizes security is noteworthy. The Republic of China has greatly reduced its defense budget in recent years in response to the needs of economic development. For the first time ever, the ROC's defense budget experienced growth this year, -5 percent, which is attributable to the greater stress placed on the military's modernization program. Numerous projects already under way were unable to proceed on schedule.

Prior to any reduction of the threat posed by the Chinese communists, we must re-examine the relationship between national security and economic growth and seek balanced development. The results of the ROC's efforts to develop national defense are gradually becoming more visible after many years of planning and promotion, and after overcoming many hardships. Nevertheless, national defense work is exceedingly intricate and complex. Many of our successes are not readily apparent. Much time and continuous effort must be spent before our goals can be achieved. Many advanced countries have had similar reform experiences. Throughout this long and ever-changing development process, we must build a consensus regarding security among all ROC citizens, and win their affirmation of the military's contributions. Only with the full support of the people for the development of national defense, can we march down the great path to a modernized national defense.

# Education in the ROC: Development and Trends

Yang Kuo-tzu

*Yang Kuo-tzu is director of the Department of Higher Education at the Ministry of Education.*

## Introduction

Education is a long-term task, and has a profound impact on national development. Political reform, economic growth, social prosperity, and cultural rejuvenation all depend on it to lead the way. We have recently been confronted with rapid social change, economic growth, structural change in the manufacturing sector, and the impact of diverse values. Accordingly, the ROC government is energetically taking the initiative to create a new educational system, reconfigure its structure, codify its rules and regulations, revise and improve school curricula and teaching materials, and introduce new teaching and guidance methods to meet the demands of our nation's current and future social development. This should cultivate manpower befitting a modern country and improve the quality of our lives.

In fact, the development of education in the ROC takes the Three Principles of the People (Nationalism, Democracy, and Social Well-being) as its supreme guiding principle; ethics, democracy, and science as its basic content; and world peace its ultimate goal. Therefore, a key mission of our educational development is to cultivate modern citizens who are lively, healthy, and productive, and who have a high degree of national and ethnic pride as well as a strong sense of responsibility, so as to join the ranks of modernized and developed countries.

# The Goal of National Development

The problems of education are extremely complex. The task of reforming and updating education will only be effective if we address subjective needs, comply with objective circumstances, and plan accordingly. Our educational development must therefore be aimed at seeking improvement, and we must use effective policies and planning to steer the task of education toward a brighter future. From this it is evident that educational development must be in accordance with the educational objectives of the nation; tally with our traditional culture, yet accommodate the reality of social progress; be in line with trends of educational thinking worldwide; acknowledge the current national exigencies; and take into consideration objective circumstances to draft concrete and feasible measures in hopes of realizing progress in the task of education.

There are four channels for us to devote our efforts to attaining the goals of our national development:

■ Assure political stability and democratic freedom. In order to build a free, equal, and democratic society, we must give democracy a prominent place in our educational work, strengthen education in democracy and the rule of law, cultivate a democratic attitude and spirit, and inculcate habits of obeying the law and taking responsibility before we can establish a foundation for democratic politics.

■ Foster economic prosperity, social well-being and wealth. We should strive to create a prosperous society in which people have access to equal opportunities. If we want our economy to prosper, education must be increasingly particular about planning; if we want science to thrive, education must increasingly stress science.

■ Making education universal and raising the level of culture. We have to develop a wealthy and courteous society. In education, we must meld Western culture with our own while giving expression to what is unique about Chinese culture and education. In particular, we must re-establish the humanistic spirit by extending artistic and cultural activities, and increase respect for human nature through the expression of its glory. Consequently, we should press forward with balanced development of the humanities and science to cultivate well-rounded students for the building of a wealthy and courteous society.

■ A society of progress, peace, and contentment. If we want to create a peaceful and orderly society, we must strenuously seek to make education universal and improve the quality of education to bring about the progressive realization of the ideal of equitable wealth in society.

Thus, education is extremely influential in the process of our national modernization. We are also convinced that only through effective development of education can we promote nationalism, spread democracy, and develop social well-being, thereby realizing at an early date the goal of modernizing our nation.

## The Important Missions of Educational Development

We know that educational development is the most important aspect of our nation's comprehensive modernization and is a principal force propelling such modernization. Therefore, educational development often plays a significant role in the process of modernization, not only in terms of cultivating the best talent to engage in national development or leading the development of science and technology, as well as academic research. It also must shoulder responsibility for steering social practices in new directions, establishing positive social norms, and promoting social and psychological development. Educational development must especially be able to spur political democracy and steady development, facilitate economic growth, foster social mobility, as well as guide cultural renovation and progress.

In the process of modernization, education must transmit and ensure the continuity of the national culture, while also allowing it to accommodate itself to the trends of social pluralism. Education must furthermore nurture the requisite quality of manpower for a modernized country, as well as quality of life for its citizenry. Therefore, there are two missions for educational development. The first is to make use of "encouraging invention" and "cultivating individual modern quality" to accelerate modernization. The second is to help solve problems arising in the process of modernization, such as cultural maladjustment, increasingly superficial relationships, and the bewildering myriad of choices. The task of national modernization, however, is integral, inclusive, and continuously cyclical. Thus, if we want to give full play to educational development and continue to accelerate the modernization of national development, we must take on three new and important missions:

■ to facilitate political socialization in order to form an appropriate political culture that will be conducive to the implementation of democracy;

■ to facilitate the realization of the ethical objectives of economic development, in the hope that the standard of material living is consistent with that of spiritual life;

■ to help uphold the ideal of a national culture to root out social disorder, and bring forth the result of harmonious social change.

439

In the case of the first of these new missions, while the theory and practice of political socialization have a long history, advanced research into this matter has only been undertaken in recent years. Civics education is deemed especially important by governments in various countries because of their bitter experience with political instability and the impact of moral decline. In fact, the success or failure of civics education can have a considerable impact on fostering an appropriate political culture and the practice of democracy. It also influences social order and renewal, the inculcation of ethical norms and the frequency of misbehavior. As a result, in a democratic society civics education must be geared to political socialization. Scholars today pay quite a great deal of attention to how specific political identification is generated among the citizenry, how certain political values are sustained, and how particular kinds of political stances are adopted.

If a nation wants to realize its political ideals, it must rely principally on the power of education. Stated concretely, the exercise of this kind of educational function is the operation and implementation of one kind of civics education. Therefore, one of the most important tasks of ROC education today is to actively bolster the education of our youthful citizens. In particular, we must stress and encourage the concepts among adolescents of love for their nation, race, and family by correcting their character, cultivating personal quality, and actively nourishing a democratic consciousness so that they will beneficially use the political rights they are legally entitled to, and increase their participation in the political process. In the course of political socialization, we must make them comprehend the operation of governmental policies, and bolster a strong identification with national politics to attain our nation's ideal of developing free and democratic constitutional government.

In short, we must start with school education if

we are to be able to design good educational measures for political socialization. Curricula, teaching materials, methodology, and each teacher's personalities must all be geared to the norms and thought of a democratic society. Through intellectual instruction, emotional guidance, and formation of good habits, we wish to mold individuals of high moral character, who cultivate themselves and care about others, and who think and act for the group, so as to promote social prosperity and progress, and build a modernized democratic country.

As for the second mission to facilitate achieving the ethical goals of economic development, the lightening pace of economic growth in recent years has led to the phenomenon of economic progress coupled with moral decline in the pursuit of fast economic growth and the creation of social prosperity. This has become the focus of social concern. In fact, every stage of economic development entails its particular social problems. Among these, not a few cases of temporary maladjustment have involved the realignment of ethical values and the restructuring of value systems. Consequently, the rebuilding of ethics must go hand in hand with economic development and other aspects of national development before social security, peace, happiness, and benefit can be assured, and the fruits of prosperity and progress enjoyed.

In a modern democratic society, education can allow people to be conscious of the increasingly important role they themselves play in economic development and the sense that they as individuals are continuing to develop in their professional niche and cultural space, resulting in the satisfaction of their psychological needs. Nevertheless, for our society to be self-satisfied but not profligate, wealthy but not spendthrift, free but not anarchic, we must start with setting ethical goals for economic development through the educational process, cultivating ethic value among students as citizens, enriching their sense of public spiritedness, and influencing them to lead frugal, simple, and vigorous lives. This depends on stepping up the moral and ethical education of our citizens in our development of education through which we can correct and improve the conduct of our people, as well as cultivate a people of modern quality to hasten societal modernization.

Finally, the third mission of helping students stay in touch with the ideals of our ethnic culture is important at the moment for education in ethnic spirit. Education in ethnic spirit must start with a comprehensive process instead of only changing certain courses. In other words, education in ethnic spirit should be implemented simultaneously with societal education and school education. Societal education entails using mass-media tools such as newspapers, magazines, motion pictures, television, and radio to exalt our traditional virtues, thereby making the traditional virtues part of their lives and conduct.

School education should, in the instruction of each subject and extracurricular activities, allow students to understand and practice traditional morals in their daily lives, and cultivate patriotic enthusiasm. This should instill an ethnic consciousness and raise their ethnic confidence. Of course, what is most important is the need for outstanding teachers that through their ardent spirit and activities personally set an example that moves students, since only then can education in ethnic spirit achieve maximal results with the least effort. In short, to uphold the ideals of ethnic culture and exalt the import of Nationalism, Democracy, and Social Well-being and to make them the guidelines for individual behavior and social development are an extremely important task in the present modernization of the nation.

# The Aims of Current Educational Development

Coping with rapid social change and the demands of future social development requires forward-looking planning and appropriate adjustments in the overall development of education to allow education in the future both to transmit our national culture and appropriately adapt to the needs of pluralistic social development. We want to proceed with educational renovation step-by-step, and then move on to pursue progress, so as to cultivate quality manpower for a modern country. Let us now examine the important aims and measures of educational development before us at five levels: primary, secondary, technical, higher, and social education.

## Primary Education

Primary education is the very foundation of the educational system, thus the quality of education at this level has a strong impact on both the individual and society. Accordingly, in order to nurture healthy citizens with balanced growth in moral, intellectual, physical, group, and beauty educational areas, the emphasis in public primary education policy is placed on regularizing teaching as well as balancing urban and rural educational development to achieve the ideal of equal educational opportunity. Another priority is the need to fortify education in life, morality, democracy and the rule of law, as well as to promote comprehensive counseling for young adults to foster healthy future generations for our country. The major tasks for primary education presently and in the future include:

■ Comprehensively revising curriculum standards at every level and rewriting textbooks to make the curriculum more appropriate and reasonable; simplifying teaching materials and drawing examples from daily life so that they may be more easily understood, to match the abilities of the majority of students and assure that the five areas of education are truly realized.

443

■ Reconfiguring the structure of central and local educational expenditures, substantially raising the level of central government subsidies of local educational expenditures, upgrading teaching equipment, improving the teaching environment, raising qualification standards for teachers to balance and unify elementary educational standards, to achieve balanced urban and rural educational development, and to realize the ideal of equal educational opportunity.

■ Upgrading the ethical mentality on school campuses and actively promoting education in ethnic spirit, life and ethics, democracy and the rule of law, as well as recreation and environmental protection in response to the rapidly changing social environment, so as to raise the caliber of the citizenry for a modernized country.

■ Promoting adolescent counseling to lower the rate of juvenile delinquency, in keeping with the policy of long-term cure of the "disease" and short-term treatment of the symptoms. At the same time, we should strengthen counseling organizations across the board, cultivate counseling professionals, combine the counseling resources of both schools and society, and establish a solid counseling network to effectively prevent juvenile delinquency.

## Secondary Education

Due to the enormous impact on educational development of social change, secondary education has undergone notable changes in its goals, function, curriculum, and teaching materials in an effort to cope with the rapid social transformation it has confronted in recent years. The major tasks at present include raising the quality of secondary education, balancing urban and rural educational development, tailoring secondary school rules and regulations to secondary education development, experimenting with the system of

444

academic-year credits to provide students with more latitude in their studies, encouraging faculty to engage in research and additional training to raise the caliber of secondary school teachers, stepping up education of gifted students, opening up varied paths to educational advancement, and trying out focal curricula in a few selected high schools to establish their uniqueness.

From the foregoing we know that secondary education must not only continue laying the educational foundation established by primary education in order to raise healthy citizens, it also must address the interests and capabilities of students when implementing a proper education, so as to adapt to the needs of young people and complete their preparation for research at a high academic level, and for acquiring professional knowledge and skills. Most important of all, it should target the practical needs of the current age to cultivate middle-level basic talent for our country and society.

## Technical Education

Technical education is the most effective way to fulfill the ideals of national development and improve the national economy and people's livelihood. In order to complete the goals of national development, we must seek the best ways in technical education to develop the appropriate talent.

In view of the upgrading and capital-intensivness of industry, increasing manpower requirements in the service sector, and the incessant structural change in the job market, the following should be emphasized in the policy on technical and vocational education: planning adjustments of the technical education system, opening up channels for students in the technical system to obtain further training, establishing more technical schools and colleges to complement the development of local communities, planning the cultivation of versatile instructors and programs for their further training, developing curriculum uniqueness for technical education, improving ways and subject matters for technical school entrance examinations, and establishing a system of gearing technical education to vocational certification. The aforementioned developmental orientations for technical education are geared toward the rapid transformation of the social structure and fast growth of the national economy that require the government to continuously improve the quality of technical education.

We must use every kind of educational and training method to cultivate superior technical talent to meet with the needs of national economic development and society for talented industrial technicians.

**Higher Education**
Higher education is currently under enormous impact from the rapid social changes in recent years and developments in many areas. Universities and colleges demand independence, while all sectors of society have greater expectations of higher education than ever before. Consequently, educational authorities must fine-tune the mechanism of their operational relationships with universities and colleges, and make timely and important adjustments to meet the demands of rapid social change and development. The question now is how to create an even more forward-looking and ideal environment for the development of higher education that will lead our country toward the twenty-first century by enabling universities and colleges to facilitate social progress.

Accordingly, in planning the development of higher education we must equally concern ourselves with the issues of quantity and quality. It is a worldwide trend for every nation to liberalize higher education as part of educational reform. We still need to establish more universities and colleges in the future to provide our citizens with more opportunities to receive higher education and to cultivate the professional talent needed for national development. At the same time, we must maintain or raise the caliber of higher education so as to avoid wasting our educational investment due to underemployment. These constitute the two principal goals for higher education development at present. In the future, we must:

■ Comprehensively plan the development of higher education. The plan should consider both the quality and ensure a balanced development of the humanities and sciences. It must also ensure a regional balance and an even-handed distribution of educational resources between public and private higher institutions.

■ Help the development of private universities and colleges. These institutions occupy an important place in the whole domestic educational mechanism. At present nearly 55 percent of all university students study at private universities, and as much as 80 percent of all college students are enrolled in private colleges. Although a distinction is made between public and private universities and colleges, such a distinction is meaningless when it comes to training the requisite talent for national development. The greatest difficulties for the development of private institutions are a lack of funding and stereotyped impressions of them by some people.

Therefore, how educational authorities can make the financial structure of privately established institutions of higher learning sound and help such institutions win the trust of society hinges upon dealing with both the symptoms and the cause of the problem. We must start by improving their image through making their finances public. Their financial resources should

447

be broadened, a flexible tuition and fee system adopted, and their scholarship funding should be made more flexible.

■ Improve the quality of instruction and academic standards. To meet the gradual growth of higher education in the future, we are maintaining definite teaching standards and quality, revising the grading and testing system to rigorously eliminate students of poor caliber, and adopting a liberal admission but strict graduation system to assure the quality of university education. Furthermore, in order to effectively raise our academic research standards, we are targeting the development of selected graduate studies with equal emphasis on the sciences and humanities. At the same time, we are continuing to work on the National Academic Computer Information Service and University Computer Network Project, utilizing this system of academic support service to raise university and college academic research standards.

■ Encourage universities to deepen their interactive relationship with society. Following the liberalization of higher education, universities should establish a positive mutual relationship with society. This is in part because society provides the resources and assistance that universities need for future development, and in part because it will allow universities to better mesh with the needs of social development.

■ Establish a pluralistic higher educational order. We must map out a flexible academic system that will spur universities toward pluralistic development. In addition to promoting better use of educational resources, this can also allow universities and colleges more space to develop, in response to the pluralistic demands of society.

448  In short, looking to the future, we believe that breaking through the developmental bottlenecks of

higher education at the present stage is a phenomenon we must face. Guided by lofty ideals and forward-looking goals, we have already begun to sketch out an ideal scenario for the future development of higher education.

## Social Education

The goal of implementing social education lies in mass as well as individual life-long education. Therefore, the important areas of development for social education at present involve comprehensively mapping out a life-long educational system in line with the Six-Year National Development Plan, equalizing urban and rural social education, and making plans to promote educational measures that meet public demand. This should build a society that is self-satisfied but not profligate, wealthy but not spendthrift, and free but not anarchic. The important tasks at hand include:

■ Comprehensively mapping out a system of life-long personal education and expanding educational opportunities. This involves actively promoting education through mainstream and non-mainstream educational institutions such as cram-school instruction, broadcast media instruction, and universities and colleges. It also involves running all kinds of adult educational activities through social agencies at every level, the mass media, and private institutions and groups.

■ Building additional social education institutions on a wide scale and bolstering their social education functions. In order to effectively make social education a reality, we must continue to plan the establishment of institutions of social education and actively map out setting up a social education network and guidance system. This will allow the task of social education to reach down to the lowest levels and perform its socializing function.

■ Stepping up family education and promoting artistic and literary activities as well as leisure education. Indeed, the primary issues in the current process of educational development within our rapidly changing social environment involve increasing parental understanding of child and adolescent physical and psychological development, stepping up promotion of parenting education, and placing family education on a firm foundation from the start so as to prevent juvenile delinquency and learning problems. In addition, we must comprehensively promote a large variety of artistic and literary educational activities to enrich the lives and raise the living quality of our citizens. At the same time, in line with the trends of social development, we should improve leisure activity facilities for young people, cultivate healthy leisure and entertainment habits among our citizenry, and develop positive social practices.

## Conclusion

Society in the ROC is presently in the midst of swift development. Because of the extreme rapidity of such change, some chaos in the political, economic, social, cultural, and daily living spheres is unavoidable. The task of educational development, therefore, must be carried out in a comprehensive, continuous, and balanced way. Although we rarely witness educational results immediately, their influence is long-term and far-reaching.

National modernization is an inevitable trend for the development of countries. Raising the quality of life for the citizenry and cultivating a modern citizenry are two important tasks that will spur national modernization. We must promote the task of educational development in the ROC with unparalleled faith and devotion, and through continually devising measures to revamp education, combine the energy of society, family, and schools to move forward together and complement each other's strengths in order to raise physically and emotionally healthy citizens for our society and nation. We must also stay on top of academic trends worldwide and attune ourselves to the pulse of national development, planning with foresight how to nurture the talent needed for the ROC to enter the ranks of modernized nations. On the fertile ground tilled by educational development, we wish to cultivate an affluent but courteous society and attain the ideal of national modernization.

# The Development of Social Welfare in Taiwan

## Chan Huo-sheng and Yang Ying

*Chan Huo-sheng and Yang Ying are professors of sociology at National Taiwan University.*

While structures set up in advanced welfare states in Europe and North America have served as a blueprint for the development of social welfare in Taiwan, conceptions of social welfare or social security in Chinese society were not products of Western influence. The ideal of a utopian society is firmly rooted in traditional Chinese culture, as evidenced in the oft-quoted axiom, "Extend filial piety for your parents to other parents, and extend your love for your children to other children. Let the old be taken care of. Let the strong put their talents to use. Give the young the opportunity to learn, and let the widowed, lonely, handicapped, and sick be taken care of." Political systems in China through the ages have also focused on eradicating poverty among the people.

Since its establishment, the Republic of China government has gradually taken on much of the responsibility for social welfare, due to the influence of imported welfare concepts and to the advocacy of domestic government agencies and private organizations. In 1912, the ROC government organization responsible for the implementation of social welfare was the Ministry of the Interior. Its duties then were fivefold: to provide relief in times of need, to extend aid, to sponsor charitable events, to convert wrongdoers, and to provide health care. In actuality, however, operations did not begin until October 11, 1940, when the government promulgated the *Organic Law for the Ministry of Social Affairs*. In November, the

Ministry of Social Affairs was formally established. Its duties can be categorized as follows: social aid, social welfare, the organization and regulation of private social welfare associations, social movements, social service, labor administration, and the administration of cooperative ventures.

The social welfare policies of the Republic of China before the implementation of the ROC Constitution can be found mainly in the platforms adopted during the national assembly sessions through the years. Social welfare policies were included in the *Kuomintang Platform* adopted during the First National Assembly Session held in 1924, the *Recent Platform of the Kuomintang* adopted in 1926, the *Kuomintang Government Platform During the Period of Political Tutelage* adopted in the Third Plenary Session of the Kuomintang Central Committee, and the *National Development Directives During the War of Resistance* adopted in an ad hoc session of the National Assembly in 1938. Of the various welfare programs under way in the ROC before the implementation of the ROC Constitution, the *Outline of the Four Major Social Policies* adopted in 1945 was the most complete. Nevertheless, the social welfare policies of the ROC at that time were directed towards passively solving the problem of poverty and providing social relief. Few policies contained an active approach to social welfare by instituting concrete measures.

After the ROC Government moved to Taiwan in 1949, the administrative authorities responsible for social welfare were reorganized. The Ministry of Social Affairs was dismantled and its operations were divided between the Department of Social Affairs and the Department of Labor Affairs, both of which were under the Ministry of the Interior. At the provincial government level, a Department of Social Affairs was also set up. Bureaus of Social Welfare were established in

Taipei City and Kaohsiung City after the two cities were placed under the direct jurisdiction of the central government. Later, the Department of Labor Affairs under the Ministry of the Interior was merged into a new Council of Labor Affairs (COLA) that was set up under the Executive Yuan in 1987. Departments and bureaus for labor affairs were also set up at the provincial and municipal levels to deal with labor affairs.

The ROC's welfare policies before the 1970s were based essentially on the *Social Policies for the People's Livelihood at the Present Stage* adopted in 1965. This administrative program covered social insurance, vocational training, social aid, housing, welfare services, social education, and community development. From the present social welfare viewpoint, this policy was considerably "beneficiary" in tone. In light of the circumstances at that time, however, the policy was rather visionary. Unfortunately, it is now more than thirty years old and unable to meet present needs. The *Guidelines for Developing Social Welfare at the Present Stage* adopted in 1969 provided a preliminary outline for a social welfare system, but was still limited in scope. The government has continued to draft welfare policies over the last two decades, but social welfare legislation has not been fully implemented.

Only a few major welfare laws have been enacted, including the *Government Employee Insurance Law* and the *Labor Insurance Law* adopted in 1958, and the *Insurance Law for Retired Employees* adopted in 1964. Most of the legislation of the ROC's social welfare laws, however, did not take place until the 1970s, a decade in which the ROC's welfare measures were gradually institutionalized.

The development of social welfare in Taiwan during the past forty years can be characterized by three major features. First, the legislation of welfare policies is nearing completion and social welfare is in-

454

creasingly institutionalized. Second, social welfare services are meeting the needs of different groups by providing diverse services, and, third, government expenditures on social welfare have risen rapidly.

The legal foundation for the promotion of social welfare in Taiwan is based on (1) the Republic of China Constitution, Chapter XIII: Fundamental National Policies, Section 4 Social Security; (2) the *Social Policies for People's Livelihood at the Present Stage* (adopted in 1965 by the Executive Yuan); and, (3) the *Social Development Outline for the Present Stage* (1969). The other related laws as indicated in Table 1 were mostly drafted or amended after 1970. In order to meet social changes and public demand, the related laws governing social welfare in Taiwan were revised considerably after 1990. For example, in 1990, temporary health insurance plans were drafted for low-income families, and the *Welfare Law for the Handicapped and Disabled*, the *Group Insurance Law for Students in the Taiwan Province*, and the *Health Insurance Law for Retired Government Employees* were all revised. In 1991, the *Health Insurance Plan for the Disabled* was put into effect. In 1992, the *Employment Service Act* was promulgated and the *Temporary Health Insurance Plan for Low-Income Families* was amended. The *Children's Welfare Act* was amended in 1993.

Table 1
The Development of Social Welfare Legislation
in Taiwan

| Year Enacted | Year Revised |
|---|---|
| 1950 Taiwan Province Labor Insurance Plan and Enforcement Regulations | |
| 1950 Servicemen Insurance Plan | |
| 1951 Taiwan Province Occupational Labor Insurance Plan | |
| 1953 Fishermen's Insurance Plan | |

| | | |
|---|---|---|
| 1953 | Insurance Program for Army, Navy, and Air Force Servicemen (An amendment of the 1950 Servicemen Insurance Plan) | 1956 |
| 1958 | Government Employees' Insurance Law | 1974 |
| 1958 | Labor Insurance Act | 1968,'73,'79,'88 |
| 1964 | Insurance Plan for Retired Employees (Insurance extensions terminated in July, 1985) | 1964, 1975 |
| 1970 | Servicemen Insurance Provisions | |
| 1973 | Children's Welfare Law | 1993 |
| 1975 | Comprehensive Safety Insurance for Students in the Taiwan Province | 1979, 1980 |
| 1980 | Insurance Provisions for Teachers and Employees of Private Schools | |
| 1980 | Insurance Law for Senior Citizens | |
| 1980 | Insurance Law for the Disabled | 1990 |
| 1980 | Social Aid Act | |
| 1982 | Health Insurance Plan for Family Members of Government Employees | |
| 1982 | The Taiwan Province Students' Comprehensive Accident Insurance Provisions (revision of the 1975 plan) | 1990 |
| 1984 | Labor Standards Law | |
| 1985 | Health Insurance for Retired Government Employees | 1988, 1990 |
| 1985 | Health Insurance for Spouses of Retired Government Employees | 1988, 1990 |
| 1985 | Health Insurance for Spouses of Retired Private School Teachers, Employees and their Spouses (Purviewed by the Ministry of Personnel in December 1985, put into effect in July 1985) | |
| 1985 | Temporary Provisions for Farmers' Insurance | |
| 1989 | Farmers' Health Insurance | |
| 1989 | Youth Welfare Act | |
| 1989 | Temporary Provisions for the Health Insurance for Local Representatives Heads of Villages, Li里 and Lin鄰 at All Levels of Provincial Government (The same regulations also apply for the municipalities of Taipei and Kaohsiung) | |
| 1989 | Health Insurance for the Family Members of Teachers and Employees of Private Schools | 1992 |
| 1990 | Temporary Provisions for Low-Income Family Health Insurance | 1992 |
| 1991 | Health Insurance for the Disabled and Handicapped | |
| 1992 | Employment Services Act | |

## Table 2
## Welfare Laws Being Drafted or Revised by the Government

| Being Drafted | Being Revised | | Year Enacted | Year Revised | Administrative Authority |
|:---:|:---:|---|:---:|:---:|---|
| * | | Enforcement Regulations of the Children's Welfare Law | 1973 | — | Dept. of Social Affairs, MOI |
| | * | Social Aid Law | 1980 | — | Dept. of Social Affairs, MOI |
| | * | Senior Citizens' Welfare Law | 1980 | — | Dept. of Social Affairs, MOI |
| | * | Labor Standards Law | 1984 | — | Council of Labor Affairs |
| | * | Labor Insurance Provisions | 1950 | 1988 | Council of Labor Affairs |
| | * | Farmers' Health Insurance Provisions | 1989 | — | Council of Agriculture |
| | | National Health Plan (or Provisions) | | | Dept. of Health |
| * | | Equal Rights Employment Law | | | Council of Labor Affairs |
| * | | Labor Welfare Promotion Act (A revision of the Occupational Labor Welfare Fund) | 1948 | | Council of Labor Affairs |
| | | Social Workers' Act | | | |
| * | | Citizens' Annuity Act | | | Dept. of Social Affairs, MOI |
| * | | Laborers' Added Annuity Provisions (A revision of the Labor Standard Law's Pension Allocation Act) | | | Council of Labor Affairs |
| * | | Laborers' Basic Annuity Provisions (A revision of the Labor Insurance Pension Plan) | | | Council of Labor Affairs |
| * | | Farmers' Annuity Act | | | Council of Agriculture |
| * | | Women's Welfare Law | | | Dept. of Social Affairs, MOI |

From Table 1 above, one can see that legislation for social welfare programs in the ROC is gradually nearing completion. In addition to the regulations that have been enacted or revised, the government is also drafting many welfare related regulation to better meet the present needs of the people.

In the course of its development, the ROC's social welfare system has expanded the scope of available services and the types of recipients covered. Statistics for 1986, 1989, and 1992 indicate that the number of people covered by social welfare programs increased greatly, and the number of people covered by each individual program also grew rapidly, as indicated in Table 3.

If we continue to do a cross-section analysis of the people covered by each social welfare service program, we will see that by the year 1992, social service programs for senior citizens, children, youth, and disabled people in Taiwan Province, Taipei City, and Kaohsiung City had become more diverse. Please refer to Tables 4 to 7.

# Table 3
# Number of People Covered by Social Welfare Programs in the Taiwan Area

| Program | 1986 | 1989 | 1992 |
|---|---|---|---|
| Labor Insurance | 4,711,969 | 5,980,157 | 7,708,868 |
| Farmers' Health Insurance | 113,365 | 676,461 | 1,695,167 |
| Government Employees' Insurance | 483,473 | 496,175 | 560,127 |
| Insurance for Government Employees' Family Members | 180,739 | 176,749 | 950,307 |
| Insurance for Retired Employees | 4,222 | 3,352 | 2,579 |
| Insurance for Retired Government Employees | 49,976 | 73,877 | 70,490 |
| Insurance for Spouses of Retired Government Employees | 32,241 | 53,045 | 50,880 |
| Insurance for Teachers and Employees of Private Schools | 26,974 | 28,110 | 36,075 |
| Insurance for Family Members of Teachers and Employees of Private Schools | | | 35,690 |
| Insurance for Retired Teachers and Employees of Private Schools | 310 | 550 | 821 |
| Insurance for Spouses of Teachers and Employees of Private Schools | 131 | 240 | 332 |
| Health Insurance for Local Representatives at all levels | | | 28,343 |
| Health Insurance for Low-Income Families | | | 112,815 |
| Students' Comprehensive Insurance | | | 4,998,249 |
| Senior Citizens' Welfare Law (Number of people in old-age homes) | 10,483 | 10,747 | 10,707 |
| Children's Welfare Law (Number of children in orphanages) | 3,289 | 3,145 | 2,777 |
| Welfare Law for the Disabled and Handicapped (Number of people in homes for the disabled) | 3,477 | 4,740 | 5,679 |
| Social Aid Law (Number of households receiving aid) | 21,975 | 20,711 | 24,307 |

Sources: 1. *Statistics by the Ministry of the Interior, 1992.*
2. Ko Mu-hsing. *Social Insurance: 1993.*

# Table 4
# Senior Citizens' Welfare Services and
# Number of Recipients (December, 1992)

| Program/Area | Taiwan Province | Taipei | Kaohsiung | Notes |
|---|---|---|---|---|
| Government expenses | 6,196 | 1,997 | 467 | |
| Own expenses | 1,616 | 455 | 193 | |
| Treatments and care | 647 | 122 | | |
| Home care | 45,321 | | | |
| Day care | 50,104 | 40 | 150 | |
| Free physical examination for the old | 541,196 | 23,100 | | |
| Medical care subsidies for low and middle income senior citizens | | | | Total budget for the Taiwan Province is NT $60,263,800. |
| Evergreen College | 112,065 | 4,179 | | |
| Old Age Human Resources Bank | 3,643 | | | |
| Recreation centers for senior citizens | | | | There are 119 recreation centers for senior citizens in Taiwan Province and 22 in Kaohsiung. |
| Volunteer services for senior citizens | | 57,964 | | |

# Table 5
# Children's Welfare Services and
# Number of Recipients (December, 1992)

| Program | Taiwan Province | Taipei | Kaohsiung | Notes |
|---|---|---|---|---|
| Day care | 208,411 | 14,029 | 11,451 | |
| Aid for children living in poverty | 1,518 | 808 | 54 | |
| Children placed in foster care | 1,617 | 1,180 | 212 | |
| Consultation for children | | 2,306 cases | | Taiwan Province has three consultation centers for children. |
| Child protection | | 110 cases | 106 cases | Taiwan Province has three emergency centers for victims of child abuse. |
| Medical care subsidies for children | | 457 | | |
| Free lunch for children of low income families | | 220 | | |

# Table 6
# Youth Welfare Services and Number of Recipients (December, 1992)

| Program | Taiwan Province | Taipei | Kaohsiung | Notes |
|---|---|---|---|---|
| Welfare Centers for Teenagers | 42 centers | | 5 centers | |
| Youth Shelters | 20 centers | | 3 people | |
| Youth Protection | | 25 cases | 20 people | |
| Care and place-ment of youths in need | | 144 people | 46 people | |
| Medical care subsidies | | 63 people | 16 people | The maximum subsidy in Taiwan Province is NT$300,000. |
| Living subsidies | | 1,189 people | | |
| Schooling subsidies for orphaned youths | | 95 people | | |
| Counseling for teen-age prostitutes | | 40 people | | |

# Table 7
# Welfare Services for the Disabled and Number of Recipients (December, 1992)

| Program | Taiwan Province | Taipei | Kaohsiung | Notes |
|---|---|---|---|---|
| Full-time car and training for disabled people | 3,094 | 913 | 99 | |
| Day care for the mentally retarded | 1,394 | | 27 | |
| Care for severely disabled people | 500 | | | Full-time care will be available in the future in Taiwan Province. |
| Living subsidies for severely disabled people | | 3,070 | 4,348 | Taiwan Province provides NT$6,800,000 in subsidies. |
| Rehabilitation for disabled people | 1,052 | | | |
| Medical care subsidies for disabled people | | | | |
| Health insurance | | | 688 | |
| Subsidies for living aids (e.g. wheelchairs, artificial limbs, etc.) | | | 564 | |
| Vocational training for disabled people | 791 | | 82 | |
| Welfare factories | 110 | | 8 | |
| Employment quota for disabled people | 8,144 | 4,000 | 1,368 | |
| Venture capital for disabled people | | 25 | 9 | |
| Dormitory rooms for disabled single women | | 10 | | |

In addition to the welfare programs for children, youths, and disabled people covered by the tables above, social aid programs in the ROC also include living subsidies, medical care subsidies, emergency relief subsidies, and subsidies for disaster relief. From Table 8 below, we can see that by the end of 1992, a total of 43,411 households, composed of 114,499 persons, had been listed in the registry of social aid recipients in the Taiwan area. A total of 15,158 persons were categorized as living in low-income households of the first degree, accounting for 13.24 percent of the total of low-income households. Another 46,818 persons were listed living in low-income households of the second degree, accounting for 40.89 percent. And, 52,524 persons were considered to be living in low-income households of the third degree, accounting for 45.87 percent.

Precisely 11,922 households were classified as low-income households of the first degree, accounting for 27.46 percent of all 43,411 low-income households. Another 14,579 households were classified as second degree low-income households, accounting for 33.58 percent of the total. And, 16,910 households were classified as low-income households of the third degree, accounting for 38.95 percent. Compared to the 1990 figures, these statistics indicate that while the number of low-income households has increased slightly, the discrepancy in number of people is very small. Evidently, the ratio of low-income households to population indicates that a large number of the low-income households of the first degree consists of persons living alone.

# Table 8
## The Number of Low-Income Households and People in the Taiwan Area

|  |  | Total | Class 1 | Class 2 | Class 3 |
|---|---|---|---|---|---|
| End of 1992 | **Total Population** | 114,499 | 15,158 | 46,818 | 52,524 |
|  | Taiwan Province | 94,374 | 12,007 | 38,452 | 42,915 |
|  | Taipei | 12,456 | 2,565 | 5,498 | 4,393 |
|  | Kaohsiung | 7,669 | 586 | 2,868 | 4,216 |
| End of 1992 | **Total Number of Households** | 43,411 | 11,922 | 14,579 | 16,910 |
|  | Taiwan Province | 34,407 | 9,556 | 11,424 | 13,427 |
|  | Taipei | 5,445 | 1,875 | 1,825 | 1,745 |
|  | Kaohsiung | 3,559 | 491 | 1,330 | 1,738 |
| End of 1991 | **Total Population** | 116,142 | 15,123 | 48,147 | 52,872 |
|  | Taiwan Province | 94,708 | 11,885 | 38,731 | 44,092 |
|  | Taipei | 13,490 | 2,672 | 6,529 | 4,289 |
|  | Kaohsiung | 7,944 | 566 | 2,887 | 4,491 |
| End of 1991 | **Total Number of Households** | 42,511 | 11,807 | 14,835 | 15,869 |
|  | Taiwan Province | 33,520 | 9,414 | 11,522 | 12,584 |
|  | Taipei | 5,523 | 1,923 | 2,030 | 1,570 |
|  | Kaohsiung | 3,468 | 470 | 1,283 | 1,715 |
| End of 1990 | **Total Population** | 114,031 | 15,187 | 48,916 | 49,928 |
|  | Taiwan Province | 92,658 | 11,792 | 39,275 | 41,591 |
|  | Taipei | 13,768 | 2,842 | 6,822 | 4,104 |
|  | Kaohsiung | 7,605 | 553 | 2,819 | 4,233 |
| End of 1990 | **Total Number of Households** | 40,805 | 11,824 | 14,965 | 14,013 |
|  | Taiwan Province | 32,114 | 9,339 | 11,728 | 11,047 |
|  | Taipei | 5,464 | 2,033 | 2,032 | 1,399 |
|  | Kaohsiung | 3,227 | 452 | 1,208 | 1,567 |

## Table 9
## Percentage of Low-Income Households and People in the Taiwan Area (From 1990 to 1992)

|  |  | Total | Class 1 | Class 2 | Class 3 |
|---|---|---|---|---|---|
| End | **Total Population** | 114,499 | 13.24% | 40.89% | 45.87% |
| of | Taiwan Province | 94,374 | 12.72% | 40.75% | 45.47% |
| 1992 | Taipei | 12,456 | 20.59% | 44.07% | 35.27% |
|  | Kaohsiung | 7,669 | 7.64% | 37.40% | 54.97% |
| End | **Total Number of** | 43,411 | 27.46% | 33.58% | 38.95% |
| of | **Households** |  |  |  |  |
| 1992 | Taiwan Province | 34,407 | 27.77% | 33.20% | 39.02% |
|  | Taipei | 5,445 | 34.44% | 33.52% | 32.05% |
|  | Kaohsiung | 3,559 | 13.80% | 37.37% | 48.83% |
| End | **Total Population** | 116,142 | 13.02% | 41.46% | 45.52% |
| of | Taiwan Province | 94,708 | 12.55% | 40.90% | 46.56% |
| 1991 | Taipei | 13,490 | 19.81% | 48.40% | 31.79% |
|  | Kaohsiung | 7,944 | 7.12% | 36.34% | 56.53% |
| End | **Total Number of** | 42,511 | 27.77% | 34.90% | 37.33% |
| of | **Households** |  |  |  |  |
| 1991 | Taiwan Province | 33,520 | 28.08% | 34.37% | 37.54% |
|  | Taipei | 5,523 | 34.82% | 36.76% | 28.43% |
|  | Kaohsiung | 3,468 | 13.55% | 37.00% | 49.45% |
| End | **Total Population** | 114,031 | 13.32% | 42.90% | 43.78% |
| of | Taiwan Province | 92,658 | 12.72% | 42.39% | 44.89% |
| 1990 | Taipei | 13,768 | 20.64% | 49.55% | 29.81% |
|  | Kaohsiung | 7,605 | 7.27% | 37.07% | 55.66% |
| End | **Total Number of** | 40,805 | 28.98% | 36.67% | 34.34% |
| of | **Households** |  |  |  |  |
| 1990 | Taiwan Province | 32,114 | 29.08% | 36.52% | 34.40% |
|  | Taipei | 5,464 | 37.21% | 37.19% | 25.60% |
|  | Kaohsiung | 3,227 | 14.01% | 37.43% | 48.56% |

A survey of the ratio of the central government's budget allocated to social welfare in recent years indicates a marked increase of government expenditure on social welfare. For example, the central government's budget for social welfare in 1981 was more than NT$34.27 billion, accounting for 12 percent of all government expenditures (See Table 10). In 1989, the central government's budget for social welfare increased to NT$101.33 billion. By 1991 the welfare budget had risen to NT$155.36 billion and in 1993 it was increased again to NT$210.54 billion. Since 1990, the central government's budget for social welfare has accounted for 19 percent to 20 percent of the central government's total expenditures (See Table 10).

The ROC's welfare budget covers two major categories, social security expenditures and pension expenditures. The social security expenditure for 1991 was NT$8.0619 billion, accounting for 9.75 percent of the total budget that year. In 1992, social security expenditures increased to NT$11.9 billion, accounting for 11 percent of the total budget for welfare. The expenditure for welfare services was the highest, accounting for 35.82 percent of the central government's total budget for social security; the expenditure for vocational assistance was the lowest, accounting for only 1.74 percent (See Table 11). The ROC's welfare expenditures are comparable to those of other nations with similar economic strength (e.g. South Korea and Singapore). The ROC, however, faces a special situation—a considerable part of its welfare expenditures are spent on pensions for retired veterans. Viewed from a social security perspective, more budget should be allocated to social welfare.

We can tell from the statistics above that the government's welfare services have been directed mostly toward servicemen, government employees, and Chinese mainland compatriots, respectively. The proportion of welfare funds going to disadvantaged groups, such as low-income households, blue-collar laborers, farmers, senior citizens, children, and the disabled, has been rather limited.

### Table 10
### Central Government Social Welfare Expenditures

Unit: NT$1,000

| Fiscal Year | Government Budget | Social Welfare Expenditures | Percentage of Government Budget |
|---|---|---|---|
| 1981 | 275,054,175 | 34,279,486 | 12.00 |
| 1982 | 318,092,114 | 43,971,930 | 14.00 |
| 1983 | 338,299,591 | 55,147,006 | 16.00 |
| 1984 | 323,144,574 | 55,723,980 | 17.00 |
| 1985 | 359,279,880 | 57,953,786 | 16.00 |
| 1986 | 412,324,363 | 67,256,860 | 16.00 |
| 1987 | 432,056,982 | 71,755,780 | 17.00 |
| 1988 | 467,613,687 | 85,074,130 | 18.00 |
| 1989 | 561,570,448 | 101,332,492 | 18.00 |
| 1990 | 680,444,396 | 125,951,350 | 19.00 |
| 1991 | 827,190,123 | 155,360,060 | 19.00 |
| 1992 | 981,219,175 | 196,340,059 | 20.00 |
| 1993 | 1,086,004,944 | 210,547,406 | 19.39 |

Sources: Ministry of Finance, provincial/city governments.

# Table 11
## Comparative Analysis of Central Government Annual Expenditures on Social Security (1991-1993)

### NT$ Amount

| Year | 1991 | 1992 | 1993 |
|---|---|---|---|
| Total government budget | 827,190,123 | 981,219,108 | 1,086,004,944 |
| Social Security Expenditures | 80,619,243 | 107,311,175 | 119,001,580 |
| Social Insurance | 18,687,579 | 29,513,936 | 33,016,475 |
| Social Relief | 3,811,484 | 6,033,270 | 2,496,094 |
| Social Services | 33,272,453 | 39,187,101 | 42,627,330 |
| Vocational Assistance | 1,231,902 | 1,828,120 | 2,069,254 |
| Housing and Community Development | 4,489,478 | 6,977,657 | 8,263,910 |
| Health Care | 6,383,665 | 11,620,269 | 11,557,138 |
| Environmental Protection | 6,502,788 | 12,150,822 | 18,971,379 |
| Retirement Found Expenditures | 74,740,817 | 89,028,884 | 91,545,826 |

### Percentage Breakdown of Social Security Budget

| Year | 1991 | 1992 | 1993 |
|---|---|---|---|
| Social Security Expenditures | 100.00 | 100.00 | 100.00 |
| Social Insurance | 23.18 | 27.50 | 27.75 |
| Social Relief | 4.73 | 5.62 | 2.10 |
| Social Services | 41.27 | 36.52 | 35.82 |
| Vocational Assistance | 1.53 | 1.70 | 1.74 |
| Housing and Community Development | 5.57 | 6.50 | 6.94 |
| Health Care | 7.92 | 10.83 | 9.71 |
| Environmental Protection | 8.07 | 11.32 | 15.94 |

### Percentage of Total Government Budget

| Year | 1991 | 1992 | 1993 |
|---|---|---|---|
| Social Security Expenditures | 9.75 | 10.94 | 11.00 |
| Social Insurance | 2.26 | 3.01 | 3.00 |
| Social Relief | 0.46 | 0.61 | 0.20 |
| Social Services | 4.02 | 3.99 | 3.90 |
| Vocational Assistance | 0.15 | 0.19 | 0.20 |
| Housing and Community Development | 0.54 | 0.71 | 0.80 |
| Health Care | 0.77 | 1.18 | 1.10 |
| Environmental Protection | 0.79 | 1.24 | 1.80 |
| Retirement Fund Expenditures | 9.04 | 9.00 | 8.40 |

Source: Directorate General of Budget, Accounting, and Statistics.

Under ROC policy, social relief has been tantamount to social welfare. Further observation of the ROC Government's allocation of welfare funds therefore reveals that the ROC's welfare budget is nominal, and that uniform and reliable statistics are not available. Furthermore, different groups have different views about what services social welfare should cover. The data collected by these groups do not conform to the same range. As a result, accurate statistics on social welfare expenditures are very difficult to obtain. The statistics on budget allocation cited in this paper are based on the statistics released by the Ministry of the Interior's Department of Social Affairs. According to the Department of Social Affairs' *Briefing on Social Welfare*, the central government's budget for welfare services directed towards senior citizens, children, youth, disabled people, and social relief has grown substantially in the past three years, as indicated by Table 12.

## Table 12
## A Breakdown of the Department of Social Welfare's Annual Budget for Welfare Services

Unit: NT$

| Year | Children's Welfare | Youth Welfare | Women's Welfare | Senior Citizens' Welfare | Welfare for Disabled People | Social Relief |
|------|------|------|------|------|------|------|
| 1991 | 1,016,100 | 268,842 | 35,050 | 1,263,620 | 1,280,310 | 652;634 |
| 1992 | 728,230 | 361,280 | 77,440 | 1,061,620 | 3,257,627 | 819,563 |
| 1993 | 478,776 | 397,202 | 104,622 | 1,630,956 | 3,477,225 | 1,319,004 |
| 1994* | 828,000 | 430,000 | 137,200 | 1,964,600 | 3,742,340 | 2,346,534 |

*Preliminary assessments by the Executive Yuan.
Source: *Briefing on Social Welfare* 1993, Department of Social Affairs, MOI.

Furthermore, the expenditure for social welfare is related to Gross National Product and taxable capacity. The percentage of a government's GNP directed towards social welfare is an objective indicator of that nation's progress in social welfare. In 1967, taxes accounted for 14.5 percent of the ROC's GNP, and in

1991, this figure grew to 17.8 percent. During the same period of time, the percentage of the total budget directed towards social welfare grew from 7.2 percent to 19.6 percent (including social security expenditures and retirement funds expenditures); and the percentage of GNP spent on social welfare grew from 1.6 percent to 6.3 percent (See Table 13).

Table 13
The Government's Social Welfare Expenditures:
Scale and Taxable Capacity

Units: NT$ Million

| Year | Social Security Expenditures | % of Total Budget | GNP | % of GNP | % of Tax Income to GNP |
|------|------|------|------|------|------|
| 1967 | 2,198 | 7.2 | 135,063 | 1.6 | 14.5 |
| 1968 | 2,581 | 7.8 | 156,199 | 1.6 | 15.6 |
| 1969 | 3,752 | 8.9 | 184,620 | 2.0 | 17.8 |
| 1970 | 4,712 | 9.6 | 210,508 | 2.2 | 17.4 |
| 1971 | 5,683 | 10.4 | 245,813 | 2.3 | 16.6 |
| 1972 | 8,102 | 12.7 | 289,234 | 2.8 | 16.6 |
| 1973 | 8,663 | 10.9 | 349,689 | 2.5 | 17.4 |
| 1974 | 9,719 | 10.8 | 499,653 | 1.9 | 17.8 |
| 1975 | 12,657 | 10.0 | 555,094 | 2.3 | 17.6 |
| 1976 | 16,940 | 11.3 | 647,466 | 2.6 | 19.0 |
| 1977 | 20,428 | 10.6 | 764,179 | 2.7 | 18.3 |
| 1978 | 24,489 | 10.8 | 900,455 | 2.7 | 18.8 |
| 1979 | 29,118 | 11.4 | 1,092,653 | 2.7 | 20.2 |
| 1980 | 38,224 | 11.1 | 1,335,794 | 2.9 | 19.6 |
| 1981 | 51,143 | 11.8 | 1,639,753 | 3.1 | 19.3 |
| 1982 | 71,542 | 14.5 | 1,845,436 | 3.9 | 18.4 |
| 1983 | 75,501 | 15.2 | 1,985,319 | 3.8 | 17.2 |
| 1984 | 81,714 | 15.8 | 2,235,514 | 3.7 | 17.1 |
| 1985 | 88,400 | 15.7 | 2,412,326 | 3.7 | 16.1 |
| 1986 | 98,728 | 15.6 | 2,265,217 | 3.8 | 15.0 |
| 1987 | 102,482 | 15.5 | 3,055,465 | 3.4 | 14.7 |
| 1988 | 131,457 | 17.5 | 3,344,972 | 3.9 | 16.3 |
| 1989 | 151,567 | 12.2 | 3,684,970 | 4.1 | 18.0 |
| 1990 | 199,769 | 17.1 | 4,045,588 | 4.9 | 20.4 |
| 1991 | 277,370 | 19.6 | 4,434,831 | 6.3 | 17.8 |

Source: 1991 *Annual Financial Report*, Ministry of Finance.

# Conclusion

Based on an analysis of the three indices of social welfare development in Taiwan from a macro perspective, from the 1950s to the 1970s, the government's distribution of welfare resources (in terms of both the structure of welfare expenditure and the recipients of welfare services), has evidently been based on an authoritative hierarchy. The policy-making concerns were to consolidate two government functions: the accumulation of capital and legitimacy. Before the rapid industrialization of the Taiwan area in the 1970s, social alienation and turbulence brought about by industrialization and urbanization were not yet apparent, and on the other hand, democratic government was still based on the foundation of traditional authority, therefore, at that stage, the beneficiaries of social welfare were essentially military servicemen and government employees. The aim was to consolidate the legitimacy of the government's political status. The function of the pilot labor insurance program implemented by the government in 1950 was more economic than social, because it accumulated capital (including human resources) more than it protected the rights of laborers. The budget for the labor insurance program mostly came from the 80 percent premium shouldered by the employers. The government only took care of the administrative expenses and subsidized the premium payments of guild members.

Let us now reconsider the situation from John Saville's point of view. Why did employers consent to shoulder the costs of the ROC's labor or social insurance system? The answer involves the interaction of three factors. Capitalist society demanded a more efficient environment for production, and the industrial sector especially required a highly productive labor force. The labor class was struggling against exploitation and insisted on certain benefits. The bourgeoisie agreed that providing these benefits was the price that had to be paid in order to maintain political stability and to protect their interests.

In more specific terms, the influence of unions was relatively weak at the time. Especially if we take into consideration the political ecology in Taiwan during the 1950s, the unions had no chance whatsoever to develop, much less fight for labor rights. The government became involved with social welfare and provided labor insurance for two major reasons: to meet the demand for a productive labor force and to ensure political stability. While the government played a relatively active role in the development of social welfare development in the Taiwan area before the 1970s by providing welfare services for military personnel and civil servants and offering labor insurance, the government's role was still limited to that of a regulator. In the legislation and distribution of wealth for welfare services for the disadvantaged, the government played only a marginal role. This type of welfare development mode is similar to the preliminary development of welfare systems in the West.

The situation changed towards the latter half of the 1970s, due to the emergence of pressure groups. After 1980, when the government passed the "three laws" of social welfare (for senior citizens, the disabled, and social relief, respectively), the development of social welfare entered a new phase in the Taiwan area. The government began enacting welfare laws for the disadvantaged and promoting a system of professional social workers. The annual increases in the government's social welfare budget reflected this change in the government's role. The government's involvement in social welfare has transformed from a marginal and hands-off role to a "liberal" or "provider" one.

The government's increasing concern for the social welfare of the disadvantaged can be explained by citing several phenomena. Rapid industrialization and urbanization during the 1970s gave rise to welfare needs of the new city-dwellers, such as employment security, income security, and occupational safety for minors and women. With the emergence of nuclear families, the ability of extended families to care for family members dwindled, calling attention to the problem of caring for the elderly and disabled. Growing political opposition forces threatened the legitimacy of the ruling party's political authority. This prompted the government to adopt social welfare policies as a tangible form of political propaganda. And, finally, the people became increasingly conscious of their rights, and demanded that the government safeguard them.

For all these reasons, the government adjusted its role in providing social welfare towards the end of the 1970s. On the one hand, it was a functional response to industrialization and urbanization. On the other hand, it was a strategic response to the political opposition movements. With the termination of the *Emergency Decree*, effectively ending martial law on July 15, 1987, a new milestone was reached in the democratization of Taiwan. This event, along with subsequent democratic developments, has had a tremendous impact on the development of social welfare in Taiwan.

With the advent of multiparty politics, opposition parties have based their party platforms on social welfare issues in a bid to win votes. In response, the ruling party has had to adjust its welfare policies to safeguard its political status and legitimacy. Democratization has thus expanded the voting power of the people. For example, the number of elected representatives at all levels of government have increased, and mayors of municipalities are to be elected by popular vote.

The emergence of private organizations and spokespersons serving as advocates for the disadvantaged, such as the Alliance for the Disabled, the Women's Rescue Foundation, the Children's Welfare Fund, and secondary political groups formed by elected officials, such as the Hou-sheng Foundation, have made forceful demands for increased social welfare. The activities of these advocates have aroused public concern for the disadvantaged, which, in turn, has pressured the government to speed up social welfare measures.

The growing power of labor unions has also had an impact on the development of social welfare in Taiwan. Complicated labor movements and tension between labor and management in post-martial-law Taiwan have directly called the foundations of the government's political legitimacy into question. The ruling party was forced to adjust its labor welfare policies in order to mitigate the threat to its legitimacy posed by labor movements and labor-management conflicts.

Recent years have also seen the emergence of various foundations and policy research centers that focus on social welfare. Examples include the 21st Century Foundation, the Evergreen Foundation, the National Policy Research Center, the Hou-sheng Foundation, the Democracy Foundation, and the Taiwan Research Foundation. The reports or policies introduced by these organizations concerning government-instituted social welfare policies have been very influential.

To sum up, democratization, diversified competition for political power, the expansion of the people's political rights, and the emergence of pressure groups have all contributed to pressure on the government to improve its social welfare policies. Increased income insecurity, employment insecurity, and the question of economic security for the disadvantaged, as well as higher levels of education and better flow of information have increased expectations for social welfare.

Democratization has, however, also had some negative influence on social welfare. The pluralization of political power has given rise to different views on how to implement welfare programs, making it difficult to reach a consensus. This lack of consensus has presented a major obstacle to the overall development of social welfare programs. The National Health Insurance Plan presently being drafted is one good example. The different views held by the general public, the government, different political groups, and different pressure groups in terms of the structure of the program, the principles of payment and the distribution of costs have consistently thwarted the planning of the National Health Insurance Plan.

Political democratization can have a positive impact on the development of social welfare. This is evident from the experiences of developed welfare states in the West. A look at the development of social welfare in Taiwan over the past forty years reveals similar developmental experiences. With the pluralization of political groups, the emergence of more pressure groups, and the rise of public awareness for social welfare, the government should plan accordingly to meet the new demands in the future development of its welfare policies.

Five points will have to be observed. First, the government and public must do away with the concepts of social welfare being tantamount to social relief, and accept the concept of social welfare as a social right. Second, social welfare organizations, national or local, must effectively distribute welfare resources, and adopt comprehensive plans. Third, limited welfare resources must be distributed according to need and in a fair and just manner. Fourth, the government's involvement in social welfare should focus on care of the disadvantaged. The welfare of the economically sound population should be based on a system of mutual aid. And, fifth, the private sector should be encouraged to pitch in and participate in social welfare, and to push for the diversification of welfare development.

# Freedom of Expression and Development of the Media

Jason C. Hu

*Jason C. Hu is director-general of the Government Information Office, Executive Yuan.*

## Foreword

The political reforms undertaken by the Republic of China have confirmed the principle of freedom of expression as an essential prerequisite of a democratic society. A growing freedom of expression in the ROC on Taiwan has brought about revolutionary changes in its communications culture, and it is quite evident that the ROC allows the broadest scope of free expression and boasts the most diverse communications environment ever witnessed in 5,000 years of Chinese history. This accomplishment undoubtedly constitutes a key element of the Republic of China's "quiet revolutions."

As the authority responsible for overseeing mass media and broadcasting in the ROC, the Government Information Office has set forth three major policy goals:

■ To establish a fair and reasonable communications system and to create a diverse, democratic and deregulated communications environment.

■ To provide information to the public and convey public views and opinions back to policymakers to ensure that government policies accurately reflect popular sentiment.

■ To gather information from abroad, strengthen international exchanges, and disseminate information about freedom, democracy, and progress in the Republic of China.

The GIO is also promoting informational exchanges with the Chinese mainland which do not conflict with the ROC's overall mainland policy. Such exchanges can foster mutual trust and friendly interaction, thereby reducing hostilities between the two sides and contributing to the eventual reunification of China.

The various media within the ROC have changed more in the past seven years than in the preceding three decades. This article discusses the most significant of these changes as they occurred in four areas— newspapers, books and periodicals, radio broadcasting, and television broadcasting.

## Newspapers

The lifting of the *Emergency Decree* on July 15, 1987, paved the way for the GIO's announcement five months later that applications for registration of new newspapers could be submitted as of January 1, 1988. In effect, the lifting of the *Emergency Decree* removed restrictions on licensing, number of pages, and printing sites. Prior to this development, Taiwan had only 31 newspapers islandwide. In the six years since, this figure has multiplied nine-fold to 286 by early 1994.

The licensing restrictions on newspaper and news agencies had been ordered by the Executive Yuan on June 10, 1951, thus precluding new entrants into the newspaper industry. A page restriction on the dailies was imposed shortly after the ROC government's relocation to Taiwan, at a time when newsprint was extremely scarce. In 1955, newspapers were limited to six pages per issue. This was expanded to eight in 1958, ten in April 1967, and 12 in February 1974. The 12-page limitation remained in effect for nearly 14 years. Now that this restriction has been completely removed, some newspapers publish as many as 48 pages per issue. The Ministry of the Interior, in 1970, also placed a restriction on the printing sites. Thereafter, newspapers were required to be printed and distributed in the city of origin designated on their registration. This stipulation was designed to facilitate government regulation of the newspaper industry, but it had negligible impact upon the development of the newspaper industry and drew little attention.

These three restrictions set by the ROC government, which was on a wartime footing during the Cold War era, reflected the realities of military confrontation between Taiwan and the Chinese mainland. Nevertheless, such restrictions hampered the development of the newspaper industry. Only 31 newspapers were in print on Taiwan between 1949 and 1988.

Social progress, economic development, universal education, and political reform set the trend for media deregulation. The government is profoundly aware that the mass media are an important source of news and information for the public. The more accessible information is, the more stable, advanced and democratic a society will be. Deregulation of news communications was a necessity for the democratization of the ROC on Taiwan. The lifting of the ban on new newspaper registrations produced immediate and obvious results in the form of increased expression of public views, political and social pluralism, growing freedom of expression, a thriving marketplace of opinion, and a more progressive society.

Deregulation of the newspaper industry also put an end to the exorbitant cost of newspaper licenses, which were once regarded as rare commodities. When the *Emergency Decree* was in effect, newspaper owners often made enormous profits by selling their licenses. Newspaper publishing proved inaccessible to individuals without substantial financial resources. The opening of newspaper registration has drawn more publishers into the media market, resulting in a more pluralistic and competitive newspaper industry.

The current requirements for newspaper registration are simple. Applications can be filed by submitting the following particulars: the title of the newspaper; the purpose of publication; the frequency of issue; the organizational structure of the publishing establishment; the name and location of the publishing and printing establishment; and the names, ages, and places of birth of the publisher and chief editor. The minimum required capital is NT$3 million. By early 1994, the ROC government had issued licenses to 286 newspapers, including 156 dailies, 16 that are published every other day, and 18, 17, 35, and 44 newspapers that are published once every three, four, five and six days, respectively. However, only 30 to 40 of these newspapers are widely read, enjoy a stable market share, and are available on the newsstands. Most of these are either morning or afternoon dailies. A distinct market order where survival is determined by free competition has emerged.

Taiwan enjoys the highest possible degree of press freedom. The government realizes that the "fourth estate" is absolutely essential to democratic operations. Press censorship is neither necessary nor practicable.

But the exercise of press freedom has also brought complaints of its misuse. The most important concern has been that news reports are often based on hearsay and have even been libelous. The *Criminal Code* carries provisions pertaining to libel, and Article 15 of the *Publication Law* stipulates that the parties concerned have the right to demand in writing that inaccuracies be corrected by the media. According to this article:

> In case the person or persons or organization (s) involved in a certain article appearing in a newspaper or magazine should demand corrections or publication of rebuttals, the daily newspaper concerned shall make the corrections accordingly or publish the rebuttals within three days after the demands are received; the newspaper which is not published daily or the magazine so concerned shall do the same in its next issue immediately following the receipt of the demands. However, the newspaper or magazine shall not be bound to make corrections or publish rebuttals if the said corrections or rebuttals should obviously violate current laws and ordinances, if the person or persons making the demands fail to indicate their names and addresses, or if the demand or demands are made after six months from the date the article in question is published.

If an aggrieved party lodges a complaint with the government stating that a medium has either not run a correction or has published a correction or rebuttal that differs from the aggrieved party's demands, the authorities may impose a fine on that medium according to Article 38 of the *Publication Law*.

The government, as a matter of principle, guarantees rather than restricts media freedom. It encourages self-discipline rather than imposes order. Because of the high regard in which the government holds press freedom, it refrains from interfering in media operations and has removed as many legal restrictions as possible. Especially as the newspaper market in Taiwan is nearly saturated (one newspaper is printed for every four ROC citizens), the media cannot afford to ignore their readership. The government therefore encourages private citizens with complaints about press quality to present their grievances to their newspaper's editorial board. This is surely a more effective and appropriate approach than government interference.

The National Press Council of the ROC plays an important role in protecting press freedom and preventing its abuse. The NPC, which was formed by eight news groups on September 1, 1974, is a national organization that advocates self-discipline in the media. The NPC's goals are to safeguard press freedom, promote press discipline, raise the ethical standards of the media, promote the development of media enterprises, and thereby fulfill the media's social responsibilities. The NPC reviews news reports, commentaries, programming, and advertisements appearing in the Taiwan media. The NPC review board comprises senior members of the press, media scholars, legal experts, and prominent civic figures. The panel reviews complaints raised by the public or other concerned parties, and announces its conclusions only after exhaustive investigation and hearings. Thus, its decisions are highly objective and authoritative. The government also takes the NPC's opinion into consideration when handling related issues. To raise journalistic standards, the NPC offers awards and programs for advanced studies. It produces a news evaluation program called "News Bridge" to propagate the ideal of press freedom and social responsibility.

Foreign-language newspapers are imported freely into the Taiwan area, where the domestic papers are supplemented by 152,000 copies of 116 imported foreign-language papers each month. As in the case of local newspapers, free-market mechanisms determine the sales and distribution patterns of foreign-language newspapers.

Despite the gradual growth in information exchanges between Taiwan and the Chinese mainland, a breakthrough has been difficult to achieve. The people of both areas share the same ethnic background and speak a common language, but four decades of armed confrontation and separate development have created an ideological gulf between the two sides. The exchange of information between Taiwan and the Chinese mainland is, therefore, significant for three reasons. First, news professionals and media scholars are trained intellectuals and are more capable of criticism, judgment and reflection. These individuals are the vanguard of social change. Second, news media, which serve as channels for the exchange of information, are far more influential than other enterprises. Third, the communication of comprehensive and diverse kinds of information would eliminate misunderstanding and bridge the gap between Taiwan and the Chinese mainland. From the reunification of East and West Germany, we have seen the tremendous positive forces that can be generated through such communication.

The Government Information Office has drawn up plans to promote the exchange of information between the two sides of the Taiwan Straits pursuant to the *Guidelines for National Unification*. Following Premier Lien's directive in December 1993 to "reject zero-sum approaches and proceed towards win-win solutions," we hope to end the opposition between the official media on the two sides; foster information, film, television, videotape and publication exchanges across the Straits; and hold consultations on mutual copyrights. Such exchanges must, however, be carried out on the basis of equality and reciprocity. We also look forward to developing cooperative relations between newspapers in the two areas, opening avenues for information exchange, allowing newspapers to station journalists or set up bureaus in each other's area, and eventually leading to a mutual agreement on the exchange of newspapers. Although these specific proposals may not be completely feasible at the moment, they do indicate the direction we would like to take in promoting cross-Straits exchanges.

The GIO has begun reorganizing laws and regulations pertinent to information exchanges with the Chinese mainland and is gradually easing related restrictions. We are reasonably and pragmatically promoting exchanges of information between the two sides based on the principles of equality and reciprocity and the provisions of the short-term phase outlined in the *Guidelines for National Unification* and the *Statute Governing Relations Between the People of the Taiwan Area and the Mainland Area*. Visits across the Straits by media professionals have increased tremendously in recent years but few mainland reporters have visited Taiwan. Almost all our newspapers devote a major section to mainland news which includes coverage of the Chinese Communist Party, the mainland government, and military and economic affairs. Such reporting is highly beneficial to fostering understanding of the mainland among Taiwan residents.The mainland media, however, provides little coverage of news from Taiwan.

## Books and Periodicals

The long-term objectives of the ROC's publishing industry are defined by the themes of the last two Taipei international book exhibitions — "Sharing Our Heritage and Broadening Global Horizons" and "Building a More Literate Society and a More Vigorous Publishing Industry."

The past several years have seen major improvements in the quality and quantity of Taiwan's books and periodicals. Taiwan's 4,151 publishing houses release as many as 13,500 titles annually and the number of audio publishing companies now totals 1,076. Taiwan's 4,658 periodicals include 304 weeklies, 25 ten-day periodicals, 63 biweeklies, 132 semimonthlies, 2,234 monthlies, 685 bimonthlies, and 1,415 quarterlies. These numbers point to a flourishing book and-magazine industry in Taiwan.

Neither books nor periodicals are subject to government examination. As part of an attempt to build a well-read society, the ROC government sponsors a number of activities including the Golden Tripod Award for outstanding publications. In 1990, the GIO published the first issue of the monthly magazine *Bibliogony* to provide more information on Taiwan's book market. With a circulation of eight thousand copies, *Bibliogony* is distributed to libraries, information centers, publishers, and major bookstores. Over a thousand publishing houses now provide information on new books to *Bibliogony*, which carries reviews of some 900 books (including government publications) each month. The number of domestic and overseas agencies asking for *Bibliogony* is also on the rise.

On September 1, 1993, the GIO set up a *Bibliogony* bulletin board system, allowing users direct access to bibliographic information through computer terminals, modems, and telephone lines. The input of the title, author, title of the series, publisher, ISBN code, or classification number of a Chinese book sets off a computerized search through a database at the rate of one thousand entries per second. Only 10 to 20 seconds are required to locate the full bibliographic entry. The electronic bulletin contains 20,000 entries of books published in the past two years and provides on-line service with *Bibliogony*. The bulletin board system saves much time for authors, publishers, sellers, exhibitors, collectors, buyers, and readers who need to locate information about a particular book. The system also allows viewers to form a comprehensive understanding of Taiwan's progress in publication distribution and library management.

One of the GIO's important functions is to assist publishers develop overseas markets and participate in or sponsor book exhibitions. Beginning in 1987, the GIO has helped publishers participate in about ten international book fairs each year. In 1989, Taiwan publishers made a successful return to the world's largest book exhibition in Frankfurt. In 1993, Taiwan's publishers scored another hit at the Bologna Children's Book Fair, often referred to as the "United Nations of children's publications." The ROC's own Taipei International Book Exhibition was successfully held in January 1994. A total of 922 booths in the exhibition hall were rented by 872 publishers from the ROC and 21 other countries and areas.

The biennial Taipei International Book Exhibition was first held in 1987 and has become the largest book fair in Asia and one of the five largest in the world. Its well-designed thematic display added a distinctive flavor to the event. The theme, "From Bud to Bloom: Taiwan's Booming Publishing Industry," was a sequel to the theme for the 1992 exhibition, "History of Chinese Publications." The display highlighted the breadth and depth of Chinese culture and presented a complete picture of the Chinese publishing industry.

A total of 120,000 titles were on display at the Taipei International Book Exhibition, which drew more than 400,000 visitors. A series of seven lectures on the development of a well-read society was held during the exhibition, attracting large audiences. Both President Lee Teng-hui and Premier Lien Chan visited the exhibition.

This grand exhibition carried a threefold significance for the ROC publishing industry. First, it
marked the entry of the ROC's publishing sector into
the international market. Second, it indicated growing
respect for intellectual property rights in the ROC's
publication market, thereby generating the interest of
foreign publishers seeking cooperation and investment
opportunities in Taiwan. Third, it demonstrated the
leading role of the ROC in developing the Chinese-
language book market.

As Peter Weidhaas, organizer of the Frankfurt
Book Fair and distinguished guest at the Taipei International Book Exhibition, has noted: "Book exhibitions do not only mean copyright transactions. They
allow more in-depth understanding into the quality
of the local publishing sector and the potential for
regional development, which would greatly benefit the
establishment of a world liaison network." The success
of the fourth Taipei International Book Exhibition is
even more significant in terms of the ROC's ties to the
international community. At a time when the Chinese
communists seek to isolate and suppress the ROC in
the international arena, this exhibition attended by
668 foreign publishers from 21 countries testifies to
the ROC's status, prosperity, and strength.

As the ROC endeavors to become an international publishing center, we are also erasing the
old image of being a "pirating haven." We have worked
very hard to promote intellectual property rights,
protect copyrights, crack down on book piracy, and
encourage international copyright transactions to expand the market for legal publications.

As part of our program to build a well-read society, we have also encouraged publishers to publish
quality books and to improve publishing standards. In
the present information boom, we are using electronic

media to strengthen information exchange on new books and to map out a national publication network. We hope that the ROC will become the center of both the Chinese-language and international book markets in the not-too-distant future.

Before the lifting of the *Emergency Decree*, the import of mainland publications into Taiwan was strictly controlled. Only a few government agencies were permitted to import mainland publications for research or other purposes. After the abolition of the *Emergency Decree* in July 1987, the GIO was placed in charge of overseeing publication exchanges between Taiwan and the Chinese mainland. In November 1987, the GIO responded to public demand for more information about the mainland by allowing mainland publications set in simplified characters to be printed in traditional Chinese characters and distributed in Taiwan. In July 1988, the ban on the import of mainland publications was lifted for governmental, academic and mass media institutions. Individuals were permitted, in principle, to bring as part of their luggage a small quantity of mainland works for personal use, so long as such works did not propagate communism. This regulation accommodated the needs of agencies conducting specialized research into the mainland, and it also satisfied the requirements of private individuals who wished to read publications from the Chinese mainland.

On March 3, 1993, the GIO responded to the growing information and publication exchanges with the Chinese mainland by expanding the scope of professional applications. Individuals were permitted to bring in a greater number of mainland publications in their luggage. As a result, there has been an annual increase in the number of mainland publications brought into Taiwan. The figure stood at 310,000 in 1991, rising to 490,000 in 1992, and then to 1.45 million in 1993. In April 1994, the National Central Library sponsored the first-ever mainland book exhibition to foster publication exchanges and mutual study. Ninety-nine members of the mainland's publishing sector participated in seminars in Taiwan, casting a positive light upon publication exchanges and strengthening mutual understanding between the publishing sectors on the two sides of the Taiwan Straits.

## Radio Broadcasting

The Republic of China's radio broadcasting industry began in 1918 with the inception of the Central Broadcasting Station, which was later renamed the Broadcasting Corporation of China (BCC). After the ROC government moved to Taiwan in 1949, radio stations improved their facilities and coverage. Local and relay stations were established and transmitters were distributed across Taiwan, even on the tops of high mountains. Despite Taiwan's complicated topography, the radio broadcasting sector has succeeded in filling all gaps in the coverage area. Today, the extensive distribution of broadcast frequencies has created a dense network of radio stations around Taiwan. New facilities and techniques have been introduced and the programming content is far richer than before.

The early radio programs were mostly unidirectional broadcasts with little interaction between listeners and broadcasters. Today, the stations have developed into pluralistic stereo broadcast networks, most of which provide round-the-clock service. Much attention is devoted to how programs are presented. News programs, for example, often employ two broadcasters instead of one and include feature stories, recorded interviews, live broadcasts, telephone interviews, and even overseas interviews. Instead of having a single commentator, informal and dramatic dialogue between two or more people is commonly employed.

Military hostilities with the Chinese mainland inevitably turned radio broadcasting into a weapon for psychological warfare. Both Taiwan and the mainland once broadcast large volumes of special programs to the opposite side for political purposes. The requirements of the military and the telecommunication sector, therefore, left only a limited number of frequencies available for commercial broadcasting. As a result, Taiwan had only 33 frequencies, leading to a lack of new competition for over four decades and to compla cency among a number of radio stations.

In response to social developments and public demands for higher broadcasting standards, the government invited scholars and experts to assess the radio broadcasting sector. In 1990, an evaluation committee was formed to assess the modes of operation, standards in program and advertisement production and broadcasting, and hardware facilities. Stations which failed to meet set criteria were notified to make improvements within a prescribed time limit according to law. Those stations unable to make the corrections or to do so within the time limit could not have their operating licenses renewed.

The government has been considering the release of more broadcast frequencies to the private sector since July 1987. In the first phase of liberalization, the government announced on December 11, 1993, the approval of 13 applications for the establishment of FM stations. A second phase of liberalization is to be implemented in two stages in 1994. In the first stage, the government announced on January 29, 1994, that frequencies within the range of FM 96 and 98 MHz would be released. The results of the review will be announced at the end of 1994. In the second stage, the release of AM frequencies is expected to be announced by February 1995. The Ministry of Transportation and Communications is in charge of deciding the number of AM frequencies to be released.

In addition, domestic political transformations have been accompanied by a vigorous marketplace of ideas. People are earnestly interested in communicating directly with government leaders during the formulation and execution of policy. At the same time, government officials have an obligation within a political democracy to explain and promote their policy positions. While the media often invite government officials to their programs, the GIO also arranges for the heads of government ministries and agencies to appear on radio and television programs to directly explain or defend their policies. Beginning in October 1993, the Broadcasting Corporation of China, in cooperation with the GIO, set up the "Minister's Hotline" as a new segment in its popular program, the "Joint Broadcast Hotline." Government leaders appear on the live broadcast to answer questions called in by listeners concerning pertinent administrative affairs. This program has been well received by the public.

## Television Broadcasting

The history of the ROC's television industry goes back some 30 years to the inception of the experimental National Education Television and to the inauguration of the Taiwan Television Enterprise (TTV) in 1962. During the 1960s, TTV faced little competition from the educational channel, which could be received only in some areas of Taipei. In 1969, the China Television Company (CTV) was established. Two years later, a third commercial television station, the Chinese Television System began operations. As the China Television Company and the Chinese Television System gathered strength, TTV faced intense competition throughout the 1970s.

The following decade saw the rapid diversification of televised media. Chinese Public Television (CPTV) programs were first broadcast on the three commercial stations in May 1984. In November 1986, a UHF channel was especially allocated for School-of-the-Air programs. Videocassette recorders/players and laser disc players also carved a niche for themselves in the home recreation market. Rooftop satellite dishes for the reception of KU-band and C-band satellite transmissions became quite common, and community antennas were erected on higher elevations to improve TV reception in some areas. Underground "fourth channels" became so active that government efforts to cut illegal cable operations were mostly in vain.

Democracy, spurred by deregulation of the newspaper industry, also spread to the television industry, which had not yet been deregulated. "Democracy TV" stations openly challenged governmental authority either through cable or over-the-air telecasts.

The diversification of televised media over the last ten years has pressured the three legal television stations to become more competitive. They have replaced old facilities, eliminated poor reception, provided more information and improved programming. Affiliated enterprises have been set up, greater emphasis is being placed on local news, and foreign markets are being developed for their programs.

Nevertheless, due to the commercial orientation of the three private television networks, there has been a constant demand for public television programming that would provide increased balance, refinement, public service messages, and educational content. In 1984, the government invested in a public television unit to produce programs for broadcast on airtime allocated by the three commercial channels. Then, in 1990, the government resolved to set up a public television station. In January 1991, the GIO formed a preparatory task force for the establishment of Chinese Public Television . The task force was assigned to draw up a *Public Television Bill* and blueprints for CPTV hardware facilities.

In June, a preparatory committee for the estab-lishment of the CPTV was formally set up. The 22-member committee included scholars and representa-tives of the mass communications sector, arts circles, and the fields of economics, foreign relations, science and technology, education, law and sports. The com-mittee was responsible for drafting a public television bill and for mapping out the allocation of CPTV's financial resources over the long term. Furthermore, the committee was put in charge of determining pro-gramming content and operational policies, not to mention the procurement of suitable facilities and hiring qualified personnel. A resolution was reached that the government would in principle allocate a budget for the establishment of CPTV. Recently, some parties have suggested that the three commercial stations should shoulder a major portion of CPTV's expenditures. The ROC government, however, is determined that CPTV should enjoy complete auton-omy in its operations and that it should be owned and shared by the public.

In response to growing demands for liberaliza-tion of the electronic media, the government has made it an important policy measure to allocate TV broad-cast frequencies previously reserved for military use. The GIO has met several times with the Ministry of Transportation and Communications and the Ministry of National Defense to study this issue. The MND has decided to release the 76-88 MHz frequency band for television broadcasting by a fourth commercial TV channel. Interested parties may apply for the right to broadcast on this channel.

The GIO has also asked the provincial and municipal governments to survey local demand for broadcast frequencies. When the survey is completed, the GIO will meet with the Ministry of Transportation and Communications to discuss a comprehensive plan for allocating TV frequencies and to study the feasibility of setting up local over-the-air TV stations.

The Ministry of National Defense plans to further release in June 1994 the 524-542 MHz and 554-560 MHz frequency bands (this range could accommodate four TV channels). A study by the MOTC has concluded that the frequencies could be used for television broadcasting but the 524-530 MHz band would be reserved for stationary and mobile telecommunications.

Community antenna television systems were developed as a means to overcome poor reception for many rural households and high-rise neighborhoods. CATV was technologically and economically more practical than UHF transmissions for improving reception. In communities where reception of television signals is hindered, operators have set up community antennas on higher ground for direct or indirect reception of over-the-air TV signals. These signals are boosted and then transmitted to subscribers via coaxial cables. Subscribers pay a service charge for cable hookup and a monthly fee to operators who are responsible for cable installation and maintenance.

On February 28, 1979, the Ministry of Transportation and Communications and the GIO announced the *Measures for the Installation of Boosters, Converters, and Community Antennas* to define the criteria for the establishment of CATV systems and other details concerning their regulation. Since then, numerous operators have filed applications to legalize their CATV operations. On May 5, 1988, the ROC Association of Community Antenna Television Systems was established with the long-term objective of developing CATV operations into cable television systems.

In addition to CATV, "fourth channels" gradually emerged, transmitting programs from videocassette players through cables to neighborhood subscribers for a fee. Because of the absence of a call-number on transmissions from these illegal operations, they became commonly known as "fourth channels," i.e., not one of the three commercial stations—TTV, CTV, and CTS.

Since fourth channel operations were never legalized or regulated, no reliable information on their history is available. It is generally believed that the first fourth channel appeared in 1976 in hilly Keelung, where TV signal reception was poor. Nearly two decades later, it is said that hundreds of fourth channels are operating in Taiwan, but the figures cannot be verified. These operations generally offer foreign entertainment programs, some of which are pirated copies, and adult programs that are relayed after midnight. Satellite TV programs were included in the fourth channel programming menu after KU-band receivers were legalized.

Fourth channel operations violate a number of laws, the main ones being the *Broadcasting and Television Law*, the *Telecommunications Law*, the *Copyright Law*, the *Income Tax Law*, and during elections for public officials, the *Public Officials Election and Recall Law*. The government regularly cracks down on the fourth channels by cutting cables and confiscating equipment. After a particularly vigorous crackdown by the authorities in early 1988, fourth channels did indeed begin to fade out. However, after the registration of new newspapers and new political parties was permitted in 1988, the public began to express its views more vigorously and fourth channels organized themselves for a resurgence. Their subsequent proliferation has defied repeated government crackdowns.

The GIO has effectively dealt with the problem of regulating fourth channels by promulgating the *Tem-*

*porary Regulations Governing the Transmission of Cable Television Programs* on November 9, 1993. The new legislation provides for the legalization of fourth channel operations that respect intellectual property rights and eliminate pornographic programs. This measure has effectively reduced copyright infringements and pornographic programs and has encouraged fourth channel operators to formally apply to become legitimate cable TV operations. It has also put an end to the rapid growth in the number of illegal fourth channels.

Legal cable TV systems are integral to Taiwan's transformation into an information-based society. As a solution to the lack of broadcast frequencies in a limited electromagnetic spectrum, cable TV provides diversified and professional entertainment and informational services to the public and satisfies local demand. Immediately after the ROC Executive Yuan affirmed its policy on cable television in 1990, the GIO formed a task force to address the issue.

The task force spent two years formulating the *Cable Television Law*, which was promulgated by President Lee Teng-hui on August 11, 1993. Explanatory sessions on pertinent laws and regulations were held around Taiwan for interested parties and the cable TV sector was urged to establish a rational and legal operational order. On January 26, 1994, the Government Information Office formally announced the demarcation of 51 cable service areas in 25 counties and cities in the Taiwan area. Those who wish to operate a cable TV system within one of these areas must file an application that includes a cable network plan drawn up and submitted in accordance with provisions of the pertinent law.

As the ROC government has deregulated electronic media operating in the Taiwan area, TV programs broadcast from outside the Taiwan area via satellite have become pervasive. The government, recognizing that satellite broadcasts are an inevitable feature of the global village, is now drawing up plans to develop and regulate satellite transmissions. In October 1993, the GIO established a satellite TV consultative committee, in which scholars and experts were invited to study the following issues: satellite TV transmissions to Taiwan by the Chinese communists; the spillover effect, copyright issues, cultural encroachment, programming and advertisement management of satellite TV; the Asia-Pacific satellite TV market and development; the related policies and laws of the ROC and other nations, and how the ROC could express its stand in satellite TV organizations.

The spillover effect in particular has become an issue of major concern in countries that are affected in varying degrees in terms of culture, politics and religion. Unfortunately, the ROC is not a member of the International Telecommunications Union, and it is difficult for us to arrange discussions with transmitting countries through diplomatic channels. Under the premise of allowing the free flow of information while preserving the ROC's national sovereignty, the GIO will conduct a comprehensive review of the spillover issue when drafting the satellite television bill. The GIO will study satellite TV in terms of legal applicability, openness and fairness. Legal applicability means that satellite programs will not be accorded privileges outside the law. The openness factor is intended to give people as much access to satellite programming as possible, and fairness, of course, means maintaining fair competition among the different electronic media.

## Conclusion

This article provides an overview of the growing freedom of expression and the development of communications in the Taiwan area over the last six years in terms of policy and actual conditions, while also touching on information exchanges between Taiwan and the Chinese mainland. The ROC's political reforms have reinforced the public consensus on the importance of press freedom. Without press freedom, there cannot be freedom of speech, and without freedom of speech, there cannot be true democracy. Of course, the abuse of press freedom brings adverse effects. Nevertheless, we must cherish press freedom as one of the most valuable components of our society as we forge along on the path of democracy.

The advanced telecommunications technology of the 20th century has completely transformed the old pattern of mass media development. Constant innovation and technical breakthroughs have made communications more sophisticated, faster, and less prone to limitations in content, form, and scope. The mass media have become an integral part of social operations, and yet, developments in communications technology are just beginning. The production of high-resolution television sets, the emergence of electronic news, and the universality of picture transmission and cable television have repeatedly proven that communications development is boundless. The immeasurable influence of information exchange has shortened the distances between people, countries, and continents. The global village is no longer a dream.

Moreover, the development of communications technology is not limited to innovations in communications equipment. The rapid flow of vast quantities of information has, in practice, built the fourth estate into a formidable institution. The flow of information is more than just a commercial process. It transmits knowledge about civilization, serves as a gauge for social assessment, and promotes social justice. For these reasons, the unimpeded flow of information has confirmed the media's role as an effective instrument of social change.

Indeed, the unfettered flow of information is a prerequisite for democratic development. Deregulating the news media allows media professionals to handle information according to the best of their ability and free judgment. It is extremely important for the media to make information available, serve as a government watchdog, make social assessments and resolve conflicts. Therefore, the government as well as the public should respect and safeguard the independence of the media in their role as a fair and impartial fourth estate that checks and balances the executive, legislative and judicial branches of the government.

The ROC has laid a sound foundation for the freedom of expression and communications development, and we are justifiably proud of our success in promoting a quiet revolution in communications. We now hope that increased information exchanges across the Taiwan Straits will strengthen mutual understanding and trust, and thus lay the foundations for national unification under a free and democratic system. Such a peaceful solution to the China problem would contribute substantially to world peace and the welfare of mankind.

This is the true value of the freedom of expression and the real contribution of the ROC's quiet revolutions.

# Appendices

Previous page: The Chiang Kai-shek Memorial Hall and adjoining gardens are an oasis of serenity in the heart of bustling Taipei.

# Free China's Lee Looks Ahead

**Claudia Rosett**
*Wall Street Journal*
September 25, 1990

TAIPEI — In a reception room of red and gold — the Chinese colors for luck and prosperity — President Lee Teng-hui comes across as relaxed and thoughtful; a tall, smiling, professorial type in a blue suit and bifocals. But this unassuming man has taken on a large job. In an interview Friday with three *Journal* reporters, he describes his goal of achieving on Taiwan the world's first enduringly democratic Chinese society. He hopes this might help lead to freedom for the Communist mainland.

"We hope China will be reunited soon," says Mr. Lee, speaking through an interpreter. "But it has to be under the principle of free economics, democracy and free elections."

It wasn't so long ago that many saw the Nationalist claim to mainland China as fiction. But with the world lauding the Cold War's end, that claim deserves a closer look. Taiwan has become a model of economic and political progress, while the mainland Communists have wrought poverty, repression and last year's suppression of the democracy movement.

Though Communist China today enjoys the diplomatic recognition stripped from the Republic of China in the 1970s, Taiwan is quantum leaps worthier of world esteem. Mr. Lee is delivering the kind of free society that mainland demonstrators last year were demanding in Tiananmen Square. At Saturday's opening in Beijing of the 1990 Asian Games, the delegation that along with Kuwait drew the greatest applause was Taiwan — a crowd reaction surely meant as a snub to Beijing.

## Tempting Parallels

The fall of communism in Europe has inspired hope of a similar collapse among the creaking holdouts of Asia, including

503

those aging leaders of the People's Republic of China. The rapid reunification of Germany, for example, makes it tempting to seek parallels in the two Chinas.

It all starts to look like precisely the kind of opening for which the Nationalist government has been waiting since Mao Tse-tung's Communist forces seized the mainland in 1949, and Chiang Kai-shek retreated with two million mainlanders to Taiwan and set up the Republic of China's capital in Taipei. Chiang and his Kuomintang followers vowed they or their successors would return to free the mainland.

So began one of the most impressive postwar flowerings in the Far East. Though Chiang Kai-shek ruled on Taiwan as a dictator, he did respect some basic institutions of a free society, such as private property. He also opened the island more and more to trade. This produced decades of double-digit economic growth, and rising demand for a more open political process. When Chiang died in 1975, leadership passed to his son Chiang Ching-kuo. The younger Chiang turned out to be a reformer. In 1987, the year before he died, he lifted martial law, allowed opposition parties to organize, began opening up travel to the mainland and ended what was becoming a Chiang dynasty.

Chiang Ching-kuo's hand-picked vice president and successor was Mr. Lee, now 67, who was born on Taiwan. This has helped gain him support from citizens of Taiwanese descent, who make up some 85% of the island's 20 million people. Mr. Lee was educated in Japan and the U.S. as an agricultural economist, and taught at Taiwan's leading university before going into government.

It's a background in keeping with the softer approach toward the mainland that Taipei has been evolving for some time. Mr. Lee does not think that China will take the German fast track to reunification. Nor does he speak of retaking the mainland by force. Instead, he looks to "long-term gradual communication" to help bring about reunification on Taiwan's terms.

The main task Mr. Lee faces for the rest of his term, which expires in 1996, is bringing government policies into line with the freedoms that people on Taiwan have already seized for themselves. This involves a balancing act among the Kuomintang old guard, a younger, more liberal generation of Kuomintang members, and a vigorous opposition that in some cases has been pushing for Taiwan independence. That position is still officially considered seditious on Taiwan, though now it is often discussed. The mainland doesn't like the idea of Taiwanese independence either, and has repeatedly threatened to invade should Taiwan try it.

"Whatever we do, we have to respect our constitution," says Mr. Lee, who several times during the interview stresses the importance of the rule of law. The stickiest problem is how to reconcile local democracy with the 1947 Nationalist constitution, which provides for representation of all China. Mr. Lee himself was elected this year to his current term by the National Assembly, a branch of government whose job is to elect the president. It is still made up of old deputies who have held office since before the 1949 loss of the mainland. This setup provoked protests, including a student hunger strike at Taipei's Chiang Kai-shek memorial.

Mr. Lee's response was to call a constitutional reform conference in June, to which he invited outspoken members of the opposition as well as members of the ruling Kuomintang. The proposals that emerged were vague, but Mr. Lee suggests that what might prove workable would be a body "similar to the electoral college of America." The idea would be to hold the mainland seats in trust, with mainland deputies temporarily bound to follow the Taiwan popular vote.

A similar problem of aging mainlanders in the legislature has been heading toward a gradual resolution, with an increasing proportion of seats going to legislators elected on Taiwan. Some 60% of all government spending is done by the central government, 40% by the Taiwan provincial and local authorities. This balance will continue to shift away from the central government, according to the finance minister, Wang Chien-shien.

In mainland affairs, Taipei is also scrambing to square its rules with reality. A few years ago, the strict government policy was the three nos: "No contact, no negotiation, no compromise" with the mainland. These days, Taiwan's finance minister freely acknowledges that businessmen from Taiwan have become big unofficial investors in Communist China. It's even easy to direct-dial Beijing. To start catching up with the traffic, Taiwan's Board of Foreign Trade last week announced it will officially permit the importation from China of dozens of goods, including badger hair, bamboo and coal.

The difficulty is judging at what point contact with the mainland might backfire into subversion on Taiwan. Since the U.S. withdrew recognition in 1978, Taipei has been keenly aware that it lacks firm allies. Mr. Lee hopes that should a mainland attack ever come, the U.S. might provide some military aid. But "we don't think we should count on America or the Japanese." Indeed, for all the business ties with Japan today, he's not yet ready to trust the Japanese in a clinch: "Most of the Asian people cannot forget what Japan did in World War II." He hopes the U.S. will continue to police the Asian Pacific.

There have been some recent setbacks, mainly Saudi Arabia's decision this year to switch recognition to Beijing from Taipei. Increasingly, however, Taiwan has been shoring up its ties abroad by claiming its place at international events, such as this year's Asian Games.

In 1988 Taiwan ended its boycott of Asian Development Bank meetings, which it had begun when the ADB admitted mainland China as a member in 1986. Last year the Republic of China even sent its finance minister to an ADB meeting in Beijing — although the ADB imposes the craven requirement that it attend under the name "Taipei, China," so as not to offend the Chinese Communists. Taiwan has also been hoping to join the General Agreement on Tariffs and Trade, for which it is well qualified. The only reason GATT won't make the offer is the usual fear of offending mainland China, which wants in first, and is still far from qualified.

Taiwan's lingering insecurities are further evident in Mr. Lee's asking one of his interviewers, Dow Jones Vice President Karen Elliott House, whether she expects war over the Iraqi invasion of Kuwait. The interview runs half an hour over the allotted 40 minutes as he discusses the fine points of large military powers invading small neighbors.

## A Faster Opening

One defense Mr. Lee might usefully pursue is a faster opening of Taiwan's markets to the world in general. Economic ties are Taipei's most promising form of diplomacy. Mr. Lee worries about U.S. protectionism, and notes that "we have to expand our markets and depend on the international community." He also predicts that "Taiwan will be able to become a hub for Asian markets and a financial center." But the government can't seem to work itself up to the serious deregulation still needed. For example, Federal Express has been considering setting up Taipei as a regional hub. So far, however, the bureaucratic obstacles have been too great.

Or, to take a more visible problem, by keeping out direct foreign investors — who tend to know something about developing markets — the government probably contributed to the wild boom and more than 70% recent free fall of the Taiwan stock market. This month's decision to let in big pension funds still doesn't go far enough.

Import controls and tariffs have been coming down for years, but in slow steps that have kept domestic prices high. As the world's 12th-largest trading power, Taiwan deserves respect. But its economic controls can only hinder the adjustments any economy must make to keep growing. By now, they are driving away business.

Nonetheless, the main impression after a meeting with President Lee is that the Republic of China is steering a worthy course. Other governments may lack the courage to flout Beijing's claim to represent the Chinese people. Lee Teng-hui reminds his visitors that Asian countries can move forward only "with a free economy, democratic rule and pluralistic society."

Reprinted by Permission of the *Wall Street Journal*
1990 Dow Jones & Company, Inc., All Rights Reserved

# Taiwan: Too Big to Ignore

An editorial in the
*New York Times*
November 10, 1990

Taiwan is now one of Asia's most powerful industrial and trading economies. It is America's sixth-largest trading partner, doing more business with this country than France or Saudi Arabia and twice as much as mainland China. Taiwan has become a major global investor; its companies now buy out American businesses.

Yet in the eyes of official Washington, and of most other governments, Taipei scarcely exists.

When Washington belatedly recognized the People's Republic 12 years ago, it accepted the proposition then put forth by both Beijing and Taipei that there could be only one China. But in reality, there remain two Chinas. America's traditional one-China policy is ripe for critical review.

The one-China fiction grows increasingly hard to justify as Taiwan deepens its economic relations with the outside world and China turns its back on market reforms. After last year's blood-bath in Tiananmen Square, no one imagines an easy fusion of the two Chinese states any time soon.

Taipei's application to rejoin the capitalist world's main trade organization, the General Agreement on Tariffs and Trade, has already set off a debate within the Bush administration. Carla Hills, the Trade Representative, supports Taipei's bid. But the State Department, reluctant to upset Beijing and perhaps endanger its cooperation against Iraq, resists.

Taiwan was a founding member of the Trade Agreement in 1947 but was forced out in 1971 when the People's Republic assumed China's seat in the United Nations. Its return would automatically subject Taiwanese trade to the world's agreed trading ground rules. That can also be done, as now, by a network of bilateral agreements.

Ultimately, GATT membership is symbolic and political. But it is just for symbolic and political reasons that the U.S. should now look with favor on Taiwan's readmission. There is no doubt about Taiwan's commitment to a market economy, a standard condition for GATT membership. And, unlike mainland China, Taiwan is now committed to democracy.

There are obvious problems. Beijing insists on subordinating Taiwan's application to its own membership bid. But that may not prove insuperable. Both Chinas now participate in the Asian Development Bank, with Taiwan accepting the designation "Taipei, China." That formula honors the fiction of one China while acknowledging the reality of two regimes. Taipei would reenter GATT as the "Customs Territory of Taiwan, Penghu, Kinmen and Matsu."

Washington is not obliged to humor Beijing's desire to deny the reality of two Chinas. Especially on economic matters, the U.S. holds far more cards than the People's Republic, and can afford to put American interests first. Those interests are served by maintaining normal diplomatic and economic relations with mainland China. But they are also served by dealing with the reality of Taipei.

Copyright (c) 1990 by the *New York Times*, Reprinted by Permission

# Taiwan, in Historic Gesture, Says It Recognizes Leadership of China

Jeremy Mark
*Wall Street Journal*
May 1, 1991

TAIPEI — After more than 60 years, China's civil war has officially ended — at least in Taiwan's eyes.

Taiwan President Lee Teng-hui, speaking at a news conference yesterday, declared the termination of a period of emergency rule imposed just before the Communists took control of China in the late 1940s. That emergency froze in place a state of war with the Communists that, despite some periods of cooperation, extended back to the late 1920s. Until now, the Kuomintang government in Taipei has officially viewed the Beijing government as rebels who had usurped the KMT's rightful authority to rule mainland China.

President Lee's proclamation, which came as a quasi-official Taiwan delegation visited Beijing for the first wide-ranging talks ever held with mainland officials, represents another important step in the gradual relaxation of tensions across the Taiwan Straits. With Taiwan investments on the mainland exceeding $2.5 billion last year and indirect trade totaling some $4 billion, many Taiwanese have been awaiting such a shift in policy to confirm the normalization of informal relations that has taken place since the late 1980s.

## Facing Facts

"The mainland now is under the control of the Chinese Communists, and this is a fact we must face," the president said in answer to a question. "We'll regard the Chinese Communists as a political entity that controls the mainland, and we'll call them the 'mainland authorities' or the 'Chinese Communist authorities,' " he added. In the past, Taipei called the Beijing government "bandits" or "a seditious organization."

The president reiterated his government's position that Taiwan won't attempt to regain the mainland by force — a stance that was a cornerstone of policy for years after the Kuomintang was ejected from mainland China. But he also called on China to renounce the use of force in pursuing reunification with Taiwan, something that the Beijing government refuses to do.

"If the Chinese Communist regime won't give up using force in the Taiwan Straits and keeps isolating us in the international community, then we can only believe them to be a hostile political entity," President Lee said. The president called for Taiwan to "strengthen its defense capability."

The proclamation ending the Period of Mobilization for Suppression of the Communist Rebellion was accompanied by the implementation of constitutional amendments passed last month by a special session of the National Assembly. The assembly approved a series of amendments that abrogated an emergency decree attached to the constitution when the period of mobilization was declared. Other amendments set the stage for elections for a new National Assembly later this year, and inserted in the constitution certain emergency presidential powers originally embedded in the emergency decree.

## Beijing Talks

As the president spoke, a delegation from Taiwan's Straits Exchange Foundation was holding initial discussions in Beijing on a range of practical issues that have arisen as business, family and tourism ties between Taiwan and China have increased. The foundation is a nongovernmental organization that is supervised by a cabinet-level council and has no power to discuss political issues.

But with the Beijing talks attracting headlines, the president appeared to go out of his way to damp speculation of any imminent breakthrough in the political relationship. He restated the government's position that official talks between Taipei and Beijing must wait for a later stage after the Communist authorities have demonstrated their peaceful intentions. "We could wait for 10 years or 20 years," he said.

Business leaders in Taiwan had mixed reactions to the president's proclamation, which had been expected since his election last May. Many businessmen view most government initiatives toward the mainland skeptically, because they believe the Taiwan authorities aren't willing to address their practical needs in such areas as shipping, finance and legal protection.

"This really has no significance beyond the fact that the government can't any longer call someone a traitor" simply for doing business with the mainland, one business leader said.

But some scholars say the end of mobilization does represent an important step in fostering a new relationship with Beijing. "This is significant in the sense that we will renounce the fiction we clung to before that we represent the whole of China," says Chi Su, deputy director of the Institute of International Relations, Taiwan's main China-watching institution. "This is pretty important both for developing our foreign relations and for developing relations with China."

Reprinted by Permission of the
*Wall Street Journal*, Copyright 1991,
Dow Jones & Company, Inc.
All Rights Reserved

# The Eyes of the Chinese Dragon

Adapted from a translation of an article by
Paul Walder in Chile's *Hoy*
May 1991

In Taipei's great luxurious hotels, western businessmen and women begin to make their first trade contacts. Right there in the hotel lobby they receive their partners from the east, who carry, in their shiny black briefcases, samples of their latest inventions, marvels that in a few months' time will be in the shop windows in Paris, California, or Madrid. Here everything is negotiated, everything is manufactured; there are no limits on the imagination. The Chinese who once invented the printing press, writing, the abacus and complicated water clocks, have no trouble in making — for a convenient price — any gadget asked for by businessmen from western markets.

The Chinese, who will pass into the 21st century, heirs to traditions of meticulous work, to love of things in miniature, to tiny ivory work, and with craftsmen capable of engraving the history of the universe on a nutshell, have brought this talent to the manufacture of microchips and a vast array collection of technological tools, much to the delight of the west.

They know their markets, and that is the direction they are heading. They have invaded the world with toys, computers, radios and objects which are difficult to classify, yet bear the label, "Made in Taiwan." From first plastic flowers, calculating machines and cotton clothes, they are now jumping towards high quality. Neighbouring states like Malaysia or Singapore have learned the trick, can count on cheaper labour, and are also disciplined oriental workers who are meticulous and creative. Taiwan wants to advance quickly, with the Japanese as an example to follow, from making products of doubtful quality. Due to the rise in labour costs, and in Taiwanese living standards, they will have to leave their new neighbours who have joined the rapidly developing nation club to worry about such products. To achieve this rapid advance, Taiwan will have to create its own trademarks, and seek the market acceptance. That is the challenge: either Taiwan stays in the backwater of manufacturing cheap articles, or if makes the leap and converts to high technology.

Taipei is long and narrow. Most of the island's seven million motorbikes scurry round its streets, and during rush hour, the queues of cars are like a great Chinese dragon brought to a standstill. The city seems to have been built at the same pace as Taiwan's economic development as an Asian tiger, without time for carefully worked out architectural or urban planning. Long elevated expressways cross the city, which is composed of drab and densely populated buildings. Next to a temple you may see a polarized glass business tower rise, and next to a street food stall a department store displays a video wall with Australian surfers. Parked motorbikes form an impenetrable barrier on the sidewalks.

**Young and elegant**

Deep oriental mystery is diluted on Chunghsiao Road in Taipei. Here the young people follow European tastes. Somewhat androgenic, they dress elegantly in wide suits and silk shirts — an oriental version of a David Bowie. Their gestures are gentle, and their taste exquisite, and they seem to have integrated into the new modernness of this island with the codes and fashions of the great cities of Europe.

The drab and austere architecture of Taipei comes alive at night. Humble though a shop may be, however local a street, the exuberant lighting of night-time trading is a permanent carnival of capitalism. In these places everything is sold, from haircuts with body massage included, nightclubs served by sweet young Chinese girls dressed in silk, Japanese television sets and cameras, locally made motor scooters, to hamburgers with a slight taste of soya and ginger.

If Taipei is Taiwan's shop window, where you can see new generations of satisfied Chinese rushing down the highways in their modern Japanese cars, with per capita income nearing eight thousand dollars, in the south, in the port of Kaohsiung, you will find the engines of this powerful industrial aircraft carrier. In a country without natural resources, enormous ships coming from mines overseas bring tons of material for steel-making, while a few hectares away from the steelworks, the shipyards have already launched hundreds of ships into the Straits. These state-owned factories, where the presence of human beings is insignificant beneath the chimneys and the metal muscle of the machines, also form the turbine which once drove the small- and medium-sized industries of Taiwan. This aircraft carrier island today has departed from port and has spread its products as far as the little markets of the cities of Latin America.

Likewise in Kaohsiung these light industries have been installed in special economic development zones, sponges which absorb workers, and which produce a large part of the 67 thousand-million green dollars which arrived last year for the exports. From these zones, poles of attraction for investors, the kaleidoscope of articles and garments keeps coming out, to keep the North American people happy.

The true Chinese of the 21st century are no longer in the steelworks nor in light industries. They have moved to the outskirts of Taipei, to an industrial park of information technology. Here the executives, with their doctors' degrees from the universities of California and their eyes on the next decade, drink their green tea and think up strategies to get ahead of their Japanese and American competitors; the researchers create new applications for semiconductors; while the working girls in their uniforms and miniskirts solder integrated circuits in aseptic rooms. This generation, with its children in primary school learning English and information technology, photography for a hobby, and a walkman with them whenever they go for a walk, has already decided that it will embrace high technology.

### Austere and savers

Old oriental luxury has given way to a new generation with austere habits. Although they do consume, and are fond of all the latest technological advances, of all kinds of computer entertainment, and they like Japanese cars with automatic transmissions and air-conditioning, they do not talk about this.

They are introverted, family men, and silent, and they keep the signs of their economic prosperity at home. In Taiwan you will not find the mansions of Hollywood, nor the palaces of western businessmen. The Chinese with money prefer to pass unnoticed, and to exercise their power through their work.

This hard-working and austere spirit, so similar to that of the primitive Calvinist, and quite the opposite of the way North Americans see life, has been the fuel for the Taiwanese aircraft carrier. In the Republic of China's forty years of history, the savings rate has not fallen below 30 percent, and this has permitted private investment to keep the mythical oriental tiger in full stride: an average growth of ten percent in the decade of the 1970s, and an average of more than eight percent for the 1980s.

It is that strange love of working which makes them different. It is eight hours a day, with only seven days' vacation a year, and a disciplined spirit that respects all norms, conventions and traditions. In a few decades they have discovered capitalism, the great bulwark of the west, and they have recycled it, developed it and refined it.

## Tradition versus technology

Management strategies, production techniques, trade talk and state of the art technology exist alogside the customs and religions of the East. In industry, the administrative staff leave their computerized office to lunch on sweet and sour pork and duck with rice, aided by a pair of chopsticks. During working breakfasts, Chinese executives eat fish and pasta opposite their western colleagues with their croissant and coffee with milk. In public places, video screens are integrated with soft drinks and tea machines and traditional Chinese cooking is dispensed as fast food in polystyrene boxes and chopsticks, both disposable, and from a thousand temples the odor of incense rises, reaching as far as the export offices.

It is a cultured people, with all children in school, and a high proportion of bilingual citizens. Their language, which they know is an obstacle for communication with the west, has been extended to include English, which they handle cleverly and naturally. To hear them with their North American accent, the eastern enigma with its customs, the smell of ginger and the Chinese characters disappear.

There is nothing exotic about these people; rather they are at the epicenter of world happenings, in a generator hidden in an area of the Pacific called East Asia, which emits energy throughout the whole planet, in a space where the technological and commercial directions in which the human race will march in the next century are being hatched.

The economic accelerator, which has been pressed to the floorboard for decades has been let up in the last year. The figures no longer impress us, and one of the reasons is the great leap forward in the Taiwanese standard of living. Chinese investors based in the United States no longer put their money in Taiwan, and they prefer to put it into Malaysia or mainland China, where the costs are lower, the same way the capitalists who are dismantling their offices in Hong Kong are doing. If the manufacture of cheap articles is going to remain in the new countries of the club of newly industrialized nations, Taiwan will be left with the challenge of meeting a technological future and with fostering innovation. For that reason every year the state invests more than seven thousand million dollars in education.

Changes have also reached public affairs. This island, which for nearly forty years lived in a state of emergency and which is anti-communist, as laid down in the Constitution, and which has regarded the People's Republic of China as its worst enemy, has decided to draw nearer to the continent. Last week Chiang Kai-shek's historic government party, the Kuomintang, approved an amendment to the Constitution in parliament to recognize the government of mainland China as legitimate, and to begin a diplomatic rapprochement. And if Germany could do it, will it be possible, too, for the great Chinese dragon?

# Taiwan's Rosy Future

**Caspar W. Weinberger,** *Publisher*
*Forbes*
October 28, 1991

It was 1979 when the U.S. cut its formal ties with Taiwan as part of our establishing diplomatic relations with mainland China. It seems clear now, with the benefit of 12 year's hindsight, that that was a serious policy error. President Carter's goal was of course to open a dialog with the People's Republic of China after President Nixon had made the first overtures some years earlier.

No one can quarrel with the idea of our improving what was a nonexistent relationship with one of the largest countries on earth. But we paid an unnecessarily heavy price: We did not have to give in to the PRC's demand that we so weaken our ties with Taiwan. Many in Congress agreed, and the Taiwan Relations Act, passed later, was an attempt to define how we could keep on speaking to Taiwan even though we had formally recognized the PRC and its claim to be the only China.

We did downgrade all meetings and discussions with the Republic of China, all with the idea of not offending the mainland. Thus American cabinet officers were prohibited from visiting Taiwan, and official meetings in this country with Taiwan could be attended only by medium and lower-level officials.

The rationale for all of these artificial restrictions collapsed with Tiananmen Square. It became evident then that all of our careful work both with the mainland military and officials, designed to help Deng Xiaoping move China away from its fierce ideological attachment to doctrinaire Marxism, had come to naught.

Meanwhile, unofficial organizations whose goal has been to help Taiwan and its people, such as the USA-ROC Economic Council (the requirement of full disclosure leads me to state that I am the U.S. chairman of this group), engaged in active trade discussions and supported the interests of Americans seeking to do business in Taiwan. But they were always limited by the rules that forbade upper-level government participation.

Last month in Salt Lake City, when the Joint Councils of the USA-ROC met, a major breakthrough was achieved. Two American cabinet officers attended, publicly and visibly, and made excellent presentations. And not a moment too soon either. For Taiwan is embarking on one of the largest civil projects in modern times, a $300 billion six-year development plan.

Other countries such as France, Germany and England have long sent cabinet officers to visit Taiwan without impairing their relations with the PRC. Now that contracts are about to be awarded for vast amounts of work, it's only logical for the U.S. to become as actively involved with Taiwanese officials as any other country, and to make major efforts to help them complete this huge development plan. About $100 billion in work will be open to foreign bidding, which will make Taiwan the world's largest market for major construction projects.

In the first year, rapid transit, highways and a high-speed railway will be started, and in subsequent years some 775 other economic and cultural projects will begin or be completed. These include nine power plants and Taiwan's fourth nuclear plant, housing and urban development and an extensive medicare network. Taiwan will also purchase pollution control equipment, computers, laboratory and scientific instruments, telecommunications, medical equipment, autos and parts, and aerospace and aviation equipment.

Both officials and the people of Taiwan are very kindly disposed to the U.S. and desire a closer and warmer relationship. We have a great deal to lose if we do not abandon our outmoded and artificial restraints on our relations with the ROC. It seems clearly impossible to get a kinder, gentler PRC until the present generation of elderly leadership is changed.

In any event, we should recognize Taiwan for what it is: a strong society that never looked back and has never had a lower GNP from one year to the next since the island was transformed by Chiang Kai-shek from a sleepy agricultural economy. This new development plan will raise the per capita GNP from $8,000 in 1990 to $14,000 in 1996. That and the other vital statistics place Taiwan far ahead of its gigantic neighbor — a nation condemned to economic failure by its slavish adherence to rigid ideological communism and socialist economics.

Reprinted by Permission of *Forbes* Magazine
(c) Forbes Inc., 1991

# Taiwan's Democratic Example

*Washington Post*
December 30, 1991

As China settles further into repression, Taiwan settles further into democracy. The progress in the latter place is one of the more cheering and less remarked political developments anywhere. It confounds glib pronouncements that Chinese people don't know how to handle democracy and sets up a clear yardstick by which to measure Beijing's laggard pace.

For decades, the Republic of China, representing the Nationalist faction that lost China's civil war to the Communists and retreated to an offshore redoubt, was rigidly anti-communist in an authoritarian style. It met its patron Washington's opening to Beijing in the 1970s with a prolonged sulk. But in the 1980s Taiwan got smart and adopted a strategy of controlled democratization, by this one stroke setting itself clearly off from Beijing in the world's eyes and responding to its own maturing population's demands.

The key move was to admit into political life an opposition party speaking for the island's 80 percent native Taiwanese majority. It posed a risk of encouraging Taiwanese separatism, but it paid off the other day when, in the closest thing to free elections in 40 years, Taiwanese voted in a landslide for a Nationalist legislature. The vote was a reward for the liberalization, prosperity and stability delivered by the Nationalist government. The new legislature is meant to amend the constitution in order to plant Taiwan institutionally, and not just by leadership choice (which can change), in the democratic column.

Were voters influenced by China's threats to invade if Taiwan, forsaking the one-China platform on which mainland Communists and island Nationalists agree, turned to independence? Beijing's threats are not what they used to be. Twenty million people to the mainland's billion-plus, Taiwan has drawn China into a web of personal contacts measured in the millions of visits and of business transactions measured in the billions of dollars. These new ties amount to a serious effort by both Chinas to take their mutual destiny as Chinese into their own hands.

"Peace by pieces" is what people on Taiwan like to call it. It exposes China to a way of life prosperous and democratic beyond imagining now on the mainland. In this way does Taiwan's progress serve China's people as well as its own.

Reprinted by Permission of the *Washington Post*

# Taiwan: Once-Shunned Ally Getting Respect

**Paul Gonzales**

*Los Angeles Times*

July 28, 1992

## Key Dates in U.S.-Taiwanese Relations
### 1949-50

Chiang Kai-shek's Nationalist Party loses civil war and flees from China to Taiwan. Chinese Communist Party declares founding of People's Republic of China, but United States refuses to recognize it. At outbreak of Korean War, Truman administration deploys 7th Fleet in Taiwan Straits between Taiwan and China.

### 1972

President Nixon travels to China and signs Shanghai Communique. It says United States does not challenge belief of both Communist and Nationalist governments that there is only one China and Taiwan is part of China.

### 1978-79

In second communique, President Carter establishes diplomatic relations with China, breaks off mutual defense treaty with Taiwan and agrees to withdraw forces from the island. Congress passes Taiwan Relations Act promising the United States will provide Taiwan with defensive arms and resist any use of force or coercion jeopardizing Taiwan's security.

### 1982

President Reagan issues new communique with China pledging to limit amount and quality of American arms sales to Taiwan and eventually to end them; no date is given for final phaseout of arms sales.

Copyright (c) 1992 by the *Los Angeles Times*,
Reprinted by Permission

# Taiwan to U.S. — We're Back!

**Jim Mann**
*Los Angeles Times*
July 28, 1992

Taipei's wealth is forcing the White House to re-evaluate its once-shunned ally. The carrot: a $300-billion public works program.

TAIPEI, Taiwan — Last January, James Soong, the secretary-general of Taiwan's ruling Kuomintang (Nationalist Party), flew into Washington for a private breakfast chat at the home of Vice President Dan Quayle in a session that barely skirted the 13-year ban on official U.S. contacts with Taiwan.

"I think they talked about golf," says Kuomintang spokesman Johnny Sand, who accompanied Soong to Washington. While Bush administration officials point out that Soong is a party leader, not a government official, Kuomintang officials crow that it was the highest-level contact between Taipei and the United States since 1979, when the United States broke off diplomatic relations with Taiwan.

Party officials say Soong will attend the Republican National Convention in Houston next month, and his deputy, a former Taiwan finance minister, was at the Democratic Convention in New York two weeks ago — marking in each case the first time in more than a decade for such appearances, Kuomintang officials say.

Their presence is more than symbolic. After a decade on the sidelines, long-shunned but ever-richer Taiwan is once again moving toward center stage as a major problem for U.S. foreign policy.

The next occupant of the White House, whether George Bush or Bill Clinton, will have to make some important decisions about future U.S. ties with Taiwan.

Washington, Beijing and Taipei all quietly put off resolving the problem of Taiwan's ambiguous status throughout the 1980s, a decade of tranquil prosperity and increasing democratization on the island. But a series of new developments — political, economic and military — suggest that some decisions cannot be delayed much longer. The status quo may not hold.

Whatever the next American president does concerning Taiwan could provoke a new crisis in relations with China, and it could have profound implications for the future of Asia.

"We've got to do some hard thinking about Taiwan," says one Bush administration official. "The situation has changed, and we've got to look out for our interests. . . . The downside to it is the question of whether, if the United States changes its policy. Beijing will downgrade the relationship [with the United States]."

One of the big decisions confronting the United States is whether to change current policy by stepping up arms sales to Taiwan.

Pointing to an increasing threat from China, Taiwan is making a concerted push to get advanced new U.S. military equipment, especially the F-16 fighter planes that the United States has been refusing to sell it for more than a decade. China already has acquired Russian Sukhoi 27 fighter planes and is engaged in an extensive campaign to buy other hardware and technology from Russia.

"The Chinese People's Liberation Army is modernizing their military forces," says Andrew N.D. Yang of Taiwan's Chinese Council of Advanced Policy Studies. " . . . China is acquiring modern planes, tanks and even maybe an aircraft carrier. It arouses a lot of anxieties in this country."

The second major question is whether the United States should give a degree of official recognition to Taiwan, which now leads the world with $80 billion in foreign exchange reserves and is in the early stages of a six-year, $300-billion public works program.

Arguing that Taiwan's spending plans could mean big contracts for American companies, some U.S. officials, especially in the Commerce Department, are urging the administration to send a Cabinet-rank official to Taiwan. No American official at that level has visited the island since 1979.

"We are the 13th-largest trading nation in the world. The world can't ignore this simple fact," Taiwan Vice Foreign Minister C.J. Chen said in a recent interview.

Over the past decade, U.S. policy toward Taiwan has been fixed by the three official communiques that were worked out between Washington and Beijing as part of the process of U.S. recognition of China.

Under these, the United States has agreed not to give official recognition to Taiwan as an independent nation. It also vaguely promised, in a 1982 agreement negotiated by the Ronald Reagan administration, to limit and eventually to phase out U.S. arms sales to Taiwan.

But many factors have changed since the last of these three communiques was signed 10 years ago:

• In 1982, Taiwan was diplomatically isolated, and the United States was virtually the only major power willing to deal with it. Now, French, German and other European government leaders — some of them of Cabinet rank — have been flocking to Taipei, looking for commercial contracts and even offering to sell planes and other weapons.

• Ten years ago, China was, in effect, the United States' partner in strategic cooperation against the Soviet Union, and the United States was just beginning to sell military equipment to Beijing. Now, the Soviet Union has collapsed, U.S.-Chinese cooperation has been frozen and American officials are beginning to eye China itself warily as a possible future threat.

• In 1982, Taiwan was still an extremely authoritarian state. In political terms, China seemed back then to be different more in degree than in kind. Since then, Taiwan has moved quickly toward a functioning democracy, while the Chinese regime maintains a severe political repression.

Now, pointing to Taiwan's increasing wealth, the end of the Cold War and China's Tian An Men upheavals of 1989, some critics are arguing that the basic American policies toward Taiwan should be changed.

Former U.S. Ambassador to China James R. Lilley said last year that the United States has been "locked for too long into the three communiques" and that China's claims to sovereignty over Taiwan are "anachronistic."

"You can't just stand still. You've got to move forward," said Lilley, who was a private citizen at the time but has since rejoined the Bush administration as an assistant secretary of defense.

Many in the U.S. business community here agree. American exports to Taiwan last year were $13.2 billion, $2.1 billion more than exports to China — even though China has more than 50 times as many people.

"Times have changed, and the world has changed....There aren't many countries in the world with plans to spend $300 billion," says James O'Hearn, president of the American Chamber of Commerce in Taiwan.

Some experts say Taiwan's $300-billion public works program is little more than a public relations gimmick, a clever repackaging for overseas consumption of a number of existing plans. But it still adds up to a lot of public spending. Experts estimate that about $50 billion to $60 billion of the $300 billion will go to foreign companies.

What is emerging is a rush by foreign companies and governments to help Taiwan spend its money. And the foreign competition extends not only to commercial contracts, but to military sales.

France has led the way. This year, French officials and executives have been trying to arrange a groundbreaking deal to sell Mirage 2000-5 jet fighters to Taiwan. The French Mirages are advanced warplanes, much more sophisticated than any flown by Taiwan's air force. If the sale goes through, it will mark a dramatic departure from Taiwan's four-decade pattern of relying upon the United States for most of its advanced military supplies.

"My government is too dependent on the United States," explains Ding Shou-chung, a leading Kuomintang member. "The U.S. government values mainland China more heavily than its friends on Taiwan."

For more than a decade, Taiwan's air force has been flying much older American planes, F-5Es and F-104s. With the help of American technology, Taiwan has also been producing its own new warplane.

But there have been problems in the development of Taiwan's indigenous jet fighter, which one U.S. defense official admits is "an underpowered, Mattel version of the F-16."

Yang and several other defense experts here suggested that Taiwan is using the proposed Mirage deal as, in effect, a bargaining chip aimed at putting pressure on the United States to sell its F-16s.

A Taiwan military delegation visited Washington in June with its annual request for military equipment, including F-16s. Interviewed after the meetings, Chen said glumly, "Up to now, we haven't been given any positive signal" that Taiwan will get the long-denied aircraft.

Indeed, some U.S. officials who strongly oppose any major change in American policy toward Taiwan argue that it will be good for the United States if the Nationalist government buys the French planes.

"Let the French sell Taiwan the planes, and let them [France] take the heat from Beijing," quipped one of these American officials, who refused to speak for the record.

But O'Hearn says he is afraid that if France wins Taiwan's favor by selling Mirages, it may also land the huge commercial contract that will be awarded this year for Taiwan's fourth nuclear power plant. The French firm Framatome is competing for the work with American companies such as Westinghouse, General Electric and Combustion Engineering, he points out.

For more than a decade, European governments have shunned Taiwan for fear of offending authorities in Beijing. But this year, European officials, particularly those involved in trade and industry, have been streaming to Taiwan full of smiles and contract bids.

"More than 28 Cabinet or sub-Cabinet-level officials from Western European countries have visited Taipei," boasted Chen last month. The French, Germans, Italians, Dutch and other Europeans are all joining the parade.

In the most surprising foreign visit of all, and the clearest sign yet of Taiwan's eagerness to reduce its dependence on the United States, two Russian admirals went to Taipei in June, the first top-level military officials from Russia to visit there since 1949.

Chen said in the interview that "we have no plan to purchase any military hardware from Russia." But his boss, Foreign Minister Fredrick Chien, was later quoted as saying he had learned "never to say never."

Yet while other nations rush to upgrade their ties with Taiwan, the U.S. response has been low-key.

At the beginning of the year, Assistant Secretary of Commerce Thomas J. Duestenberg visited Taipei as part of a U.S. trade mission, the highest-level U.S. official to visit Taiwan since 1979. But even that visit demonstrated how nervous the Bush administration is about upsetting Beijing.

Duestenberg created a stir by saying before his trip that he would be meeting with Taiwan's economic minister "on a government-to-government basis," thus suggesting a degree of official recognition. The State Department quickly disavowed Duestenberg, saying his comments were made "in error."

Administration officials have gone through similar contortions to make sure that Soong's meeting with Quayle last January does not offend Beijing. An aide to the vice president told *The Times* that Quayle saw Soong only "in his capacity as president of the Senate," and that the session was "just a courtesy call."

Two decades ago, overcoming political and diplomatic pressure from Taiwan was one of the key elements in the successful drive by President Richard M. Nixon and then-Secretary of State Henry Kissinger to normalize relations with China.

Now, some of the veterans of that earlier era, within both the Bush administration and the career foreign service, are privately resisting any major change in policy toward Taiwan that would upset the agreements they worked out with Beijing.

Pointing to Taiwan's $5-billion-a-year trade with mainland China and the ever-growing stream of contacts between Beijing and Taipei, they argue that the U.S. policies of the 1970s have brought prosperity to the island and have worked out better than even Kissinger had hoped.

And they say Taiwan will realize it needs the United States far more than it needs the Europeans. "They [Taiwan officials] can't screw around too much with an old, vital friend, to make new friends who don't care about the Pacific," says one old American China hand.

Here in Taiwan, however, some elected officials say they now mistrust these assurances of American support and urgently need new military supplies from abroad to bolster Taipei's hand in dealing or bargaining with Beijing.

"Our American friends have been neglecting our security needs for so long," said Ding. "Compared with the mainland, Taiwan is not that important. . . ."

"People [in Taiwan] are scared of China," he continued. "These days, Taiwan businessmen say they invest in China in order to buy insurance. If we have a greater defense capability, China will look more seriously at our demands. And we may help bring about a more democratic China."

Copyright (c) 1992 by the *Los Angeles Times*, Reprinted by Permission

# Taiwan Has Means to Solve Woes

**Mark Memmott**
*USA Today*
December 18, 1992

TAIPEI, Taiwan — Much like Japan in the late '70s, this tiny island nation of crowded, smoggy cities and lush green mountains is poised to move up the ranks of economic powerhouses. And its climb will jostle the superpower at the top.

Everywhere U.S. businesses look the next decade, they will see competitors from Taiwan:

• "Made in Taiwan" doesn't just show up on toys and T-shirts anymore. It appears on personal computers and televisions. Competitors can't dismiss Taiwan as just another source of cheap labor.

• In mainland China, Taiwanese business executives are re-establishing ties severed more than 40 years ago. Their ventures will be running when most U.S. businesses arrive.

• In financial markets, Taiwan's investors already are giants. In 1991, Taiwan's government and private investors — not Japan's — were the biggest foreign purchasers of U.S. Treasury securities. Their net investment in Treasuries totaled $10 billion. Japanese investors, hard hit by their economy's slump, sold $4 billion more in U.S. Treasury securities than they bought last year.

As an economic power, Taiwan has arrived, and its track record is amazing. If the U.S. economy had averaged 8.8% real growth over the past 40 years, as Taiwan's economy has, U.S. businesses would be producing $38 trillion worth of goods and services annually — $7\frac{1}{2}$ times their current $5 trillion.

As Taiwan's economy grows, however, the nation also is struggling with serious problems. A tour of Taipei reveals a clanking honking exhaust-spewing definition of the term growing pains.

Try crossing a street: Either you can't, because workers are ripping up the concrete to rebuild the roadbed, or you have to weave through a crush of cars, buses and scooters waiting for the light to turn green.

Look at housing costs: Homes are scarce and expensive because of heavy demand from a growing middle class. A two- or three-bedroom house in the suburbs an hour's drive from central Taipei can easily cost $600,000 in U.S. dollars. Sky-high costs, and tradition, are two reasons most families, including grandparents, share small apartments.

Read the newspapers: There are daily reports on the government's $360 billion Six-Year National Development Plan, begun last year. There's no escaping the glowing accounts of future apartment complexes, superhighways and water-treatment plants. And there's no escaping the feeling that the government wouldn't be spending that money if a lot of work didn't need to be done. Only 600,000 of the country's 21 million people live in homes connected to sewage-treatment plants.

Taipei is the rapidly expanding and modernizing center of the Republic of China, or Taiwan. That realization is startling since most Western visitors only vaguely know Taiwan as an island 120 miles east of mainland China where Gen. Chiang Kai-shek and 2 million others moved in 1949 to escape the communists.

It's easy to see the problems and challenges facing Taipei and Taiwan. Fortunately, thanks to booming exports, the newly acquired wealth that comes with rapid economic growth is giving people here a chance to conquer those challenges. Exports, worth $76 billion last year, amounted to almost 45% of Taiwan's $170 billion gross domestic product.

Where does Taiwan's economy get the strength to boost the real value of its goods and services 7.3% last year and an expected 6.1% this year while the U.S. economy pokes along at less than half that pace? The strength increasingly comes from sophisticated, high-technology companies such as Acer, a personal computer manufacturer that has 5,200 employees and had 1991 worldwide revenue of nearly $1 billion. Or Tatung, which makes home appliances, computers, videocassette recorders and other products. Tatung last year reported revenue of $2 billion.

Those companies and others like them have spurred Taiwan's growth. Tatung, which in 1949 changed from an engineering and construction company to a manufacturer of electric fans, now sells computer workstations around the world and has 21,000 workers. Acer, founded in 1976, markets its ACROS computers in stores across the USA.

Taiwan also has enjoyed strong growth at its 82,000 small to medium-size factories. "They are small enough to be very flexible and very quick to change when it's necessary," says Mary-Yueh Ho, a division director at the Ministry of Economic Affairs' Industrial Development Bureau. Taiwan's businesses also are blessed with an educated workforce. "Everyone at this factory is at least a high-school graduate," says Steve Huang, human resources manager at AT&T Taiwan's suburban factory, where switching equipment is made.

But Taiwan's businesses aren't immune from forces affecting other nations. Economic growth is slowing as the global economy cools and because Taiwan's businesses find it hard to boost production when streets and highways in and around Taipei are constantly crowded — making it difficult to receive and ship goods.

The third quarter, gross domestic product growth cooled to its slowest pace in two years — a 5.2% annual rate, torrid by current U.S. or European standards.

This year's expected 6.1% growth far outpaces even Japan, where GDP will likely expand just 2% for the year. Also making other countries envious: Through the first half of this year, Taiwan's exports were up 10.5% over first-half 1991 — a slowdown because exports grew 13% last year. And Taiwan's unemployment rate remains under 2%.

While the global slowdown will cause minor changes in Taiwan this year, and possibly next, the nation's outlook remains upbeat. Government economists expect real GDP growth of 5% to 7% annually the next five years. Most private economists agree.

"Over the next decade we'll have growth rates of 6% or 7% a year," predicts Tzong-shian Yu, president of the Chung-Hua Institution for Economic Research.

One major source of growth will likely be mainland China, even though Taiwan's government still bans most direct business contacts. That policy has led many Taiwan businesses to set up joint ventures with firms from Japan or elsewhere to do businesses on the mainland. Even with such obstacles, business between Taiwan and the mainland is growing quickly. Last year, trade totaled $5.8 billion — up 43% over 1990. Exports from Taiwan to the mainland totaled $4.7 billion, 6% of Taiwan's total.

Taiwan's economy also will continue to expand because there's so much work to do.

The cranes and construction sites all over Taipei make clear that unless there is a dramatic economic bust or drastic over-building demand for improved services, better homes and more offices will help fuel the economy through the rest of the decade and beyond.

"There is much we need," says Albert Yeh, deputy director general of the Government Information Office. "But I think in even two years it will be much better. We have no choice, we have to do this to keep growing."

Copyright (C) 1992 by
USA Today Intl.

# Giant Stride towards Democracy

Adapted from a translation of an article by Gebhard
Hielscher in Germany's *Süddeutsche Zeitung*
December 18, 1992

While a change of government is still inconceivable, the
parliamentary elections on Saturday will nevertheless put the
government in Taipei on a completely new, democratic footing.
For the first time since 1949, when the Nationalist Chinese Generalissimo Chiang Kai-shek fled with his defeated troops to Taiwan and turned the island into the last bastion of the "Republic of
China," the over 20 million inhabitants of an island approximately the size of Baden-Württemberg are free to choose their
government themselves with no restrictions.

It is the final step in the transformation, originally initiated
by Chiang's oldest son Ching-kuo, of the authoritarian Kuomintang regime into a parliamentary democracy. The younger
Chiang, who served as premier under his father and was later
president for ten years, appointed a Taiwanese citizen, the current
President Lee Teng-hui, as his deputy. Then in 1987, under pressure from an increasingly confident opposition, Chiang Ching-
kuo ended martial law, which had been in force since 1948.

The head of state and leader of the ruling national party
(Kuomintang, KMT) since 1988, Lee has slowly but surely
pressed on with the reform process. In 1988, the formation of new
parties was allowed and press censorship abolished (television is
however still under the direct or indirect control of the KMT).
This was followed by a law that provided generous compensation
payments to ease the transition of the aged members of parliament ("old pirates" in the terminology of the opposition) into
long overdue retirement. These elderly men, most of them from
mainland China, had been "elected" in the areas of China controlled by Chiang Kai-shek's troops before his flight to Taiwan.
For four decades they had blocked almost all democratic reforms
in the three "national" elected bodies of Taiwan.

Lee's 1991 constitutional reform involved a complete reorganization of the elections for the National Assembly, Legislative Yuan, and Control Yuan, and the abolition of various emergency rights of the president. Only bona fide citizens of the Republic of China, in other words primarily the inhabitants of Taiwan, are now entitled to vote. With this move, the myth that Nationalist China also represented the huge mainland was virtually abandoned. In December, the 13 million members of the electorate in Taiwan elected a new National Assembly as the first step in the transformation of the three bodies into democratically legitimate bodies.

Much more important is the re-election of the Legislative Yuan on Saturday. This body will then fulfill all the functions of a normal parliament, with the exception of amending the constitution and electing the president and vice president, which are normally the functions of the National Assembly.

A total of 14 parties and over 400 candidates — many of them independent — are competing in the election for 161 seats. Some 125 members of parliament will be elected directly in the 29 constituencies of the provinces, which have from one to nine members each depending on the size of the constituency, while the rest of the seats will be distributed between the parties that garner at least 5 percent of the valid votes.

Based on the results of the election for the National Assembly a year ago, only two parties will qualify for the seats distributed on a proportional basis, the Kuomintang and the opposition DPP (Democratic Progressive Party, Minchintang) under its leader Hsu Hsin-liang. In December 1991, the DPP won 24 percent of the votes and the KMT 71 percent. The opposition party hopes to get over 30 percent this time. However, even if the DPP did succeed against all probability in getting all of its 78 candidates elected (the KMT has 157 candidates) it would still not enjoy a parliamentary majority. On the other hand, KMT Premier Hau Pei-tsun is evidently prepared, in spite of his party's expected victory, to resign with his entire cabinet at the first session of the new parliament in order to create a "democratic precedent" and give President Lee a free hand.

# One China, Plus Democracy

*New York Times*
December 30, 1992

Two-party democracy arrived on Chinese soil this month, following Taiwan's first fully democratic legislative election. While Chiang Kai-shek's old Nationalist Party won a majority of seats, the Democratic Progressive Party will now offer significant organized opposition. That's a historic breakthrough not only for Taiwan, but also for the larger China of which it remains a format part.

The incoming Clinton administration, promising a democracy-oriented foreign policy, will want to take positive note of Taiwan's encouraging political evolution. The trick is to do so without needlessly provoking Beijing.

Taipei, Beijing and Washington all agree to the diplomatic convention that there is only one China. But since defeated Nationalist armies fled to Taiwan four decades ago, a distinctive Chinese society has emerged there, far richer and freer than its mainland counterpart. Mainland China now welcomes Taiwanese investment, while Taiwan has eased its own curbs on people-to-people ties.

On both sides, dreams of rapid reunification have receded. But Beijing still explicitly reserves the right to achieve unification by force. And it reacts sharply to any overt challenge of the One China formula.

Tensions rose last summer when the Bush administration violated American diplomatic commitments and sold new fighter jets to Taiwan. Meanwhile, Taiwan's ascendant opposition party openly calls for an independent Taiwan.

That leaves the Clinton administration a narrow tightrope to walk. It can praise Taiwan's democratic advances, encourage freer commerce and increased cultural and educational inter-change. And it can urge Beijing to refrain from military threats.

But it also needs to recognize explicitly that the unification issue is for the Chinese on either side of the Taiwan Straits to work out. On the Taiwan side, at least, they'll now be able to make a democratic choice.

Copyright (c) 1992 by the *New York Times*, Reprinted by Permission

# Frigates Not Enough for "Little China"

Adapted from a translation of an article by
Joachim Penner in Germany's *Saarbrücker Zeitung*
January 2-3, 1993

Frigates and submarines are not the only subject requiring a decision by the Federal Security Council. The Republic of China, also known as Taiwan or Formosa, has become an important economic power in East Asia.

Tawian's trade with the Federal Republic amounts to around seven billion marks a year, almost as much as communist China's trade with Germany. And this is in spite of the fact that the Republic of China with its population of approximately 20 million is much smaller than the population of China, which is still ruled by the communists.

In 1991, Taiwan ranked 14th in the world as a trading nation. For five years it has occupied fifth place with respect to foreign investment, and it now has the largest currency reserves in the world. The gross national product (GNP) of the "little tiger" is already one-third that of communist China, but 20 times higher per capita in Taiwan than on the mainland.

Economically, "little China" is extremely interesting, even for a reunified Germany, particularly since the Taiwanese are themselves consciously seeking contact with the Germans, whom they hold in high esteem — the quality of the latter's products, their systematic thinking and their long-term economic commitment being just some of the attractions.

What we are seeing at present is not just the sale of a few warships, but rather the start of long-term, extensive cooperation between the countries, which even in the medium term may bring large orders. Areas under discussion are the ICE (inter-city ex-

539

press), undergrounds and in particular sewage plants, for which the Taiwanese will gladly pay more to Germany than elsewhere, since they have a high opinion of German environmental technology.

Germany is also seen as an alternative to Japan, which is still overshadowed by its history in the eyes of many Chinese. Taiwan does not want to become dependent on this world economic power, but is seeking contact with Europe to escape renewed dominance by the Japanese.

The Taiwanese do not feel that German business with communist China will suffer if economic relationships with their country continue to expand. On the contrary, the opinion is being voiced that in the long term it would even be better for the Germans to open up the mainland market in cooperation with the Taiwanese, since the latter have already got a firm foothold in the rapidly developing southern Chinese coastal region. The leadership of the Republic of China is convinced that, in any case, the western nations have no chance of making it alone on the mainland.

Any comparisons with Germany with respect to reunification are treated with scepticism by the Taiwanese, given the political situation in China. For this communist China is too large and Taiwan too small. Formosa cannot swallow the mainland (as happened in Germany) or impose its system upon it. However, German reunification does serve as a model for communist China, and this will be even more the case if the latter decentralizes in the future.

Taiwan feels it is being proved right by the developments in the British colony of Hong Kong. It is now widely accepted that Hong Kong will be unable to remain as it is today. It is not for nothing that many firms are emigrating from Hong Kong to the USA, to the Philippines, and, last but not least, to Taiwan.

An additional factor is that the Republic of China has now become much more democratic. Although the ruling Kuomintang suffered heavy losses in the latest parliamentary elections, it still has a solid majority in the country. A democratically legitimate government, which western powers value so highly, is no longer a missing feature in Taiwan.

# Starting to Build Their First Bridge, China and Taiwan Sign 4 Pacts

**Nicholas D. Kristof**

*New York Times*

April 30, 1993

SINGAPORE, April 29 — Delegates from China and Taiwan today concluded the first high-level meeting they have ever held by signing four agreements, including one providing for a regular dialogue between the two former adversaries.

As dozens of strobe lights flashed, the septuagenarians who head the two delegations slowly signed copies of the agreements, which call for increased exchanges across the Taiwan Straits and closer cooperation in areas like fighting crime. For the first time, the two sides will have a formal channel for communication, instead of the informal method used until the end of the 1970's — pounding the other side with artillery shells.

"This is a historic meeting in relations between the two sides," said Wang Daohan, the beaming head of the Chinese delegation. "It is a crucial step for the future development of our relations."

His Taiwan counterpart, C.F. Koo, said, "Both sides have won."

## Different Versions

Still, a few details suggested the huge gap that remains between the two sides. The Taiwan and China texts of each document were not even identical, for Taiwan's copy was written in traditional Chinese characters while China's was in the simplified characters used by the Communists.

Likewise, the year was left out for each side to fill in later. To China, this is 1993; to Taiwan, this is the year 82, for Taiwan's calendar begins with the establishment of the Nationalist Government upon the collapse of the Qing Dynasty. Nor did the two sides manage to hold a joint news conference: instead they held simultaneous and competing sessions.

The meeting was the first high-level encounter between the two sides since the Chinese civil war ended in 1949, and the Nationalist Government was forced to flee to Taiwan. While almost everyone regards the talks as a milestone, it is still unclear where the process now under way will lead.

One possibility is that the dialogue will hasten economic integration and will lead sometime in the next century to reunification. A rival interpretation is that these talks effectively confirm and consolidate a separate identity for Taiwan, which would lead ultimately to a proclamation by Taiwan that it is an independent country.

### Mail, and Other Exchanges

Two of the agreements signed today were technical, concerning cross-delivery of registered letters and verification of official documents issued by the other side.

## For Taiwan and the mainland, a gulf remains

A third outlined a schedule for contacts between the organizations that each side has set up to act as a liaison to the other. The heads of the two organizations, Mr. Wang and Mr. Koo, will meet "as needed," while the deputy heads will meet every six months, and other officials at least every three months. Meetings will take place in China, Taiwan or a third location.

The two sides also approved a statement setting forth the topics they would like to address in the future. These include crime, illegal immigrants, protection of intellectual property, fisheries disputes, judicial cooperation and the exchanges across the Taiwan Straits. In particular, the delegates discussed making it easier for journalists and young people from China to visit Taiwan.

The principal negotiating difficulty was in economic areas. Taiwan wanted some kind of formal protection for Taiwan investors on the Chinese mainland, while China urged Taipei to permit direct shipping across the Taiwan Straits.

For now, Taiwan does not permit direct trade, so all shipping and passenger flights are supposed to be routed through Hong Kong or a third country. Nevertheless, Taiwan's exports to the mainland are booming. In just the first two months of this year, indirect two-way trade totaled $1.17 billion, up 30 percent from a year ago.

Cheyne J.Y. Chiu, a spokesman for the Taiwan side, said the talks were tough but generally cordial. He acknowledged, however, that the heads of the delegations relied mostly on formal presentations.

Some unanticipated give and take occurred this morning when a mainland official, Tang Shubei, arrived for the signing ceremony. Several Taiwan legislators from the opposition party unfurled a banner proclaiming Taiwan's independence.

"Taiwan is Taiwan!" they shouted, as Singapore police officers tussled with them and confiscated the banner "Oppose unification!"

For Beijing officials like Mr. Tang — unused to such protests — the Taiwan opposition has been a more frightening presence in Singapore than the Nationalist officials who run Taiwan. The mainland officials, used to the docile Communist press, have also been a bit overwhelmed by the boisterous and often chaotic Taiwan press corps.

Copyright (c) 1993 by the *New York Times*,
Reprinted by Permission

# Taiwan Wants to Enter U.N. without Forcing the Expulsion of Beijing

Adapted from a translation of an article by Fernando Pastrano in Spain's *ABC*
May 22, 1993

For the first time in the forty-four years since the division of China, Taiwan is willing to enter the U.N. without this move entailing the exclusion of the Communist representatives of mainland China. This decision implies an important change in Taiwan's diplomatic strategy and follows the first direct talks held between Beijing and Taipei last April, the prelude to reunification negotiations.

In 1971, after having been represented by Taipei for twenty-one years, the Chinese delegation at the U.N. was taken over by the communists. This step signalled the triumph of the Nixon-Kissinger "ping-pong" policy and foreshadowed the imminent macroeconomic development of the mainland and the fall out of favour of nationalist China. The reasoning at the time was that if, as both Governments maintained and still maintain, there was only one China, then the country could be represented by only one delegation.

In the twenty-two years that have passed since then, the Republic of China has not disappeared, been absorbed, annexed or conquered by the other part. On the contrary, it has reasserted itself and has reinforced the validity of the model of a modern China based on the "Taiwan economic miracle." This is emphasized by the fact that Taiwan currently has the second-highest level of foreign reserves in the world, is the seventh leading country in terms of foreign investment, the fourteenth in trading volume and the twentieth with regard to Gross National Product, with a per capita income of around $10,000.

Since the end of the civil war in 1949, the Chinese process had involved the development and deepening of a division. The path towards reunification has only just begun to be glimpsed in the wake of the discussions held last month in Singapore. In the diplomatic arena, Ministries of Foreign Affairs all over the world have had to choose between Beijing and Taipei. In this tug-of-war, the diplomatic presence of nationalist China — the smaller of the two — has been significantly curtailed.

Taiwan, however, has never thrown in the towel. It claims another factor to be taken into account: while the People's Republic of China was founded by Mao Tse-tung on the 1st of October 1949 in the aftermath of triumph of communism on the mainland, the Republic of China in Taiwan is the natural continuation of the Republic established in 1912 by Doctor Sun Yat-sen: forty-two years of existence compared to eighty-one.

The two governments believe there is only one China and that reunification should be peaceful and negotiated. Both also accept the existence of two independent political entities, without one being subordinate to the other. The theory of "one country, two systems" has been made famous the world over by Deng Xiaoping, with the aim of justifying the absorption of the island while simultaneously maintaining its political-social system. Taiwan bases its strategy on attempting to use its opponent's strength to its own advantage, as if skillfully engaged in martial arts manoeuvres. Beijing, however, plays its trump card in the arena of international public opinion by refusing to allow Taipei to be represented in the U.N.

To support its argument, the Republic of China in Taiwan points to the examples of the two Koreas, both with permanent delegations in the United Nations, and of the two now successfully reunited Germanies. Nine countries have so far supported the Taiwanese proposal, as was made evident at the XLVIII General Assembly of the U.N. held recently, and it is expected that others will join this list.

Until reunification is achieved, which it is hoped will be before the year 2000, a developed, democratic country called Taiwan, with a population of 21 million, deserves appropriate international status.

Reprinted by Permission of Spain's *ABC*     *545*

# Peaceful Revolution in Little China

Adapted from a translation of an article by Matthias
Nass in Germany's *Die Zeit*
August 6, 1993

The demonstrators have pulled their straw hats down over
their faces to protect themselves from the steamy midday heat.
They are perhaps two hundred in number, most of them old men
and women, all wearing yellow headbands. After marching into
the center of Taipei they are now squatting in front of the Parliament steps applauding the words that their leader, dripping with
sweat, is bawling into his megaphone.

The entrance into the building is blocked by two dozen
young policemen who are unarmed and wearing open-necked,
short-sleeved shirts. The parliament building on this island,
where six years ago all demonstrations that did not support the
politics of the ruling Kuomintang were broken up, is not even
surrounded by inviolable precincts.

The angry farmers from the Taichung area in central Taiwan are after the Kuomintang's blood. The route for the
highspeed railway planned between Taipei and the harbor city of
Kaohsiung will run right through the middle of their land, for
which the government is prepared to pay a mere seventh of the
market price. "The Kuomintang won't help us!" grumbles a gaunt
old man, flashing a double row of silver teeth. Only the members
of the DPP, the Democratic Progressive Party, can be relied upon.
Everyone standing round nods in agreement.

In Taiwan today no one is afraid of the authorities of the
past. Members of parliament such as Chen Chien-jen from the
Kuomintang and Chen "Mark" Tan Sun from the DPP debate as
fairly and wittily with one another as if the "Legislative Yuan" had
been imbued for generations with the spirit of Westminster. In
fact the DPP was only founded in 1986 — illegally when Taiwan
was still under martial law.

One of the Chens had a career at the university and in the diplomatic service, and rose to become deputy foreign minister. The official biography of the other Chen is only half as long: for years he lived as a dissident in exile in America.

"Some people worked within the system," says the first Chen, justifying his own position. "I was one of those who pressed for Mark's return to Taiwan." Other government opponents however had no such prominent advocates, and if they did, it was not much help to them. Shih Ming-teh, for example, was imprisoned for 25 years because of his demand for independence. Today Shih is a member of parliament representing the DPP. Such steadfastness, says Mark Chen, has "put the government under an awful lot of pressure."

It was probably a combination of pressure from below and the gradual dawning of understanding at the top that instigated Taiwan's "peaceful revolution." It was in the mid-eighties that President Chiang Ching-kuo, son of Generalissimo Chiang Kai-shek who fled from the communists to Taiwan in 1949, began to push ahead with political liberalization. After martial law was ended in 1987 it was permissible to form political parties; the press also came into its own. The Kuomintang had realized that the era of autocratic rule was over, and the DPP has now become an opponent to be reckoned with. In the parliamentary elections in December 1992, the DPP won 32 percent of the votes and 51 of the 161 seats.

For those once persecuted under the dictatorship, the state has lost its terror. "We are not afraid of the military or the police," says the DPP chairman Hsu Hsin-liang. "Our only concern is the dominance of the Kuomintang. It still controls television. And, its funds are seven times the size of ours."

## Parliament is now the scene of wild chases over benches and tables and flying fists

The 52-year-old party leader talks animatedly about his first experience with politics, when he worked at the party headquarters of the Kuomintang, on which however he turned his back after three years. The young rebel edited magazines critical of the government such as the *Formosa Magazine* and won a seat in the provincial assembly as an independent candidate. In the year of unrest, 1979, he finally left the island. ("I was in the middle of this conflict.")

Hsu spent ten years in the United States. In September 1989, he finally returned to Taiwan aboard a smuggler's boat that brought him across from the Chinese mainland at night — only to be caught by the coastguard, taken to court and sentenced to ten years' imprisonment for rebellion. Eight months later he was free again. Upon taking office, Taiwan's new president Lee Teng-hui ordered an amnesty for all political prisoners. The following year Hsu stood for the chairmanship of the DPP — and won.

Everyone in Taiwan knows the man with the bald pate and sparse ring of black hair. In the hotel restaurant the staff hover obsequiously round the famous former dissident. "Why do we seem so strong, even though we only have a third of the seats in parliament?" asks Hsu Hsin-liang, and answers the question himself: "Because the Kuomintang is split. We are united and are hence the strongest political force." He laughs, typically sounding a little nervous and embarrassed, but nevertheless light-hearted.

People no longer look cautiously over their shoulders when talking in a restaurant. Taiwan is the second Asian country, after South Korea, to make giant strides from dictatorship to democracy. Taipei likes to be complimented on this. Never before in all the five thousand years of Chinese history has there been a democracy.

The small island of Taiwan is now also teaching its big neighbor a lesson in politics. For a long time now Taiwan has been leading the way in economic matters. The per capita income — a meagre 70 dollars in 1945 — rose to 10,215 dollars last year. And the People's Republic? Their citizens today make a mere 300 dollars. As the Kuomintang sees it, this means that "we are thirty times better than the communists."

Unfortunately they have not yet been able to make much political capital out of this economic success. There are still only 29 nations that have diplomatic relations with Taipei. China has a population of 1.2 thousand million, atomic weapons and a permanent seat in the Security Council. Taiwan has a population of 20 million and was excluded from the U.N. in 1971. Most nations have no difficulty choosing between the two.

548

Taiwan is not however going to put up with the political isolation pursued with cold deliberation by Peking for much longer. The island now ranks 20th in the world in terms of economic power and occupies 14th place as a trading nation, points out Foreign Minister Fredrick Chien. "I think we have a role to play in the international organizations."

The government's campaign for the country to be allowed back into the United Nations is also supported by the opposition. All the politicians find it "unjust and unfair" that their country has been cut off from the rest of the world in this way.

The way back to the U.N. is of course disputed after twenty years of isolation. The DPP wants an independent "Republic of Taiwan," while the Kuomintang is still clinging on to the idea of national unity. It is however no longer dreaming of the "liberation of the mainland," but has settled for the formula "one China, two governments." "We have become completely realistic and pragmatic," says Foreign Minister Chien. "We do not pretend to lay claim to things that are outside our control."

And thus relationships between the two sides of the Taiwan Straits are gradually normalizing. Since 1987 five million Taiwanese have visited the mainland, and Taiwanese businessmen have invested 10 thousand million dollars in the People's Republic.

It certainly did no harm to peaceful coexistence when two years ago the government in Taipei officially ended the *Period of Mobilization for Suppression of the Communist Rebellion.* Since then the communist rulers in Peking are no longer "rebels" but "political authorities" who can be negotiated with.

For the first time, at the end of April, there was a meeting in Singapore between high-ranking representatives of two semi-official organizations. They signed four agreements, involving for example the mutual recognition of documents and the reliable delivery of registered letters — not exactly a spectacular start to change through a rapprochement of the two Chinas. How deep the divisions really are is revealed by a glance at the documents. Taiwan's copy is in the classic Chinese characters, while Peking's diplomats use the simplified characters introduced by the communists.

However, the fact that they are talking to each other is by no means an indication that Peking intends to formally renounce the use of force. As recently as October 1992, Politburo member Li Ruibuan warned against a declaration of independence. "We would not hesitate to shed blood." In the opinion of the Taiwan opposition this is the roaring of a paper tiger. Why then, they ask slyly, did Peking never send over the troops all those years when the Kuomintang was still blustering about the military reconquest of the mainland and the expulsion of the "rebels" from power?

The good thing is that in Taiwan today all this can be argued in public. There is no longer any need for anyone to be afraid of being locked up for demanding independence, and the subject is even raised in parliament.

This is now the scene of wild chases over benches and tables and flying fists in front of the lectern. As in guerrilla warfare, the political opponent is tricked — by the switching off of microphones, late-night votes, filibustering and occupation of the parliamentary president's chair. In all there is a splendid lack of inhibition after the rigidity of dictatorship. If only a hint of this were to be detected in the National People's Congress on Tiananmen Square in Peking.

# The Real Chinese Revolution
## It's Taiwan where radical change looks permanent

*Far Eastern Economic Review*
September 2, 1993

When Sun Yat-sen reorganised his fledgling band of Chinese into the National People's Party, or Kuomintang (KMT), the movement described itself as a "revolutionary democratic party." And that is how it continued to define itself until recently. At the 14th Party Congress, delegates voted to purge the word "revolutionary."

In a way we are sorry to see this reaction against revolution. Although we certainly understand why the KMT would want to rid itself of its Leninist inspirations, it's sad to think that the word "revolutionary" must forever remain the provenance of those whose lasting achievement is the ruination of their respective countries. For what the KMT has achieved on Taiwan — a prosperous, self-ruling Chinese society advancing rapidly towards liberal democracy — merits a much greater claim to the word "revolutionary" than anything accomplished by the communists on the mainland.

The real revolution was on exhibit at the just-ended party congress. The 1,310 delegates spent most of their time haggling over party structure, especially who would get what job. At times this presented an unsavoury spectacle, as disputes over power usually do. Doubtless stakes are especially high when one party has long been accustomed to ruling. Doubtless too, the formation of the New Party by a group of KMT rebels and the election of a surprising number of younger, more progressive members to the Central Committee — not to mention the threat to President Lee Teng-hui's own job — suggest that the KMT may face the same problems that ended the decades-long, one-party rule of Japan's Liberal Democrats.

Yet this in itself represents great progress. What is often described as the crack-up of KMT unity can also be seen as the maturation of the country's political system into something more in line with its much-envied economic achievements. Although the process has its growing pains, it has at least been peaceful, and there are sufficiently few precedents that it might be called remarkable. On one of our visits to Taipei, the government spokesman, Jason Hu, put it this way: "It used to be that when a reporter came to see me, it meant he was in trouble. Now when a reporter comes to see me, it means I am in trouble."

For all their penchant for upheavals — the Great Leap Forward, the Cultural Revolution, the Open Door — China's aging Long Marchers have yet to leave anything of similar magnitude in place. Indeed, there is evidence that even Mao understood this. In Richard Nixon's 1972 visit to Peking, he paid homage to his host's stature: "The Chairman's writings have moved a nation and changed the world." But Mao was quick to respond that he had changed nothing save for "a few places in the vicinity of Peking." Today we can see that a revolution did indeed take hold in China. But to find it we need to look on the other side of the Taiwan Straits.

Reprinted by Permission of
the *Far Eastern Economic Review*

# Taiwan — A Mature Tiger

**Caspar W. Weinberger,** *Chairman*
*Forbes*
December 6, 1993

The Republic of China continues to offer evidence that delights proponents of a free-market economy and political democracy. Paradoxically, the elements of Taiwan's growing movement toward full democracy — a multiparty, pluralistic society with guaranteed human rights and a free press — may make the transition more difficult. Taiwan will need more time in order to implement the next phase of its development. By the same token, this democratic progress should undergird and make more lasting the astonishing growth and development Taiwan has already experienced.

The recent visit Steve and Christopher Forbes and I had with President Lee Teng-hui, Premier Lien Chan, Minister of Foreign Affairs Fredrick Chien and other top officials confirmed that Taiwan, having completed a period of unparalleled growth, is now on the threshold of a slightly slower but more solid economic surge. Per capita income will approach $20,000 at the beginning of the 21st century. For several years Taiwan has maintained an annual growth rate of 6% or higher with low inflation and low unemployment. The contrast of this with the socialist, repressive mainland that has a per capita income still measured in the very low hundreds cannot be more marked.

As wages rise and the Legislative Yuan — Taiwan's congress — becomes more recalcitrant, i.e. more democratic, and mainland China appears to be acquiring more weapons designed for offensive operations, it is clear Taiwan will have no lack of challenges in the years ahead.

Taiwan's National Development Plan, a six-year program to strengthen and modernize infrastructure and transportation and to improve conservation, health and environmental conditions, has been slowed by legislative alarm at the size of the $240 billion program, at the difficulties and costs of land acquisition, and at labor shortages (Taiwan does not import labor on a large scale). Even so, the plan is a gigantic set of projects that offers potential benefits to U.S. business. Our government could be of great help to our own economy by giving up foolish rules born of the fear of offending communist China: The U.S. generally permits only low-level U.S.-Taiwan official visits.

Currently, Taiwan's high wage scale ("the price of democracy," one businessman calls it) causes many ROC manufacturers seeking cheap labor to export some of their operations to mainland China, India, Malaysia, Thailand and the Philippines. There are wildly varying estimates, from $10 billion to $30 billion, as to the dollar amount of Taiwan's investments in China. Some concern about confiscation by the People's Republic of China has been expressed, but most Taiwan companies are large enough so that possible loss of their PRC investment is an acceptable risk.

Taiwan would like to be a member of the United Nations, but an almost certain PRC veto has led it to consider other routes to full membership. Actually, Taiwan, by every economic or quality-of-life measure, is far more qualified to be a member than a great many present members — including the PRC. Irreverent observers have begun asking why Taiwan would want U.N. membership after the U.N.'s performance under the hapless Boutros Boutros-Ghali in Europe and Africa during the past few months. Taiwan officials point out that 20 million Chinese are denied membership in GATT as well.

The immediate challenge Taiwan faces is whether the present government will continue in office. The next election is for local posts and will be closely watched. The ruling Kuomintang (KMT) party won 14 of 21 posts three years ago, and in 1991 it won 70% of the popular vote for the National Assembly. Now, however, there are two other parties, the opposition Democratic Progressive Party and the New Party, a breakaway from the KMT.

If next time the voters should turn against the KMT, many of the confident predictions for Taiwan's future would be off. There would be delays and stagnation while the victors' policies and actions were being assessed. And if a wholly new government direction were taken, Taiwan's future could be determined only by consulting a very cloudy crystal ball.

Reprinted by Permission of *Forbes* Magazine
(c) Forbes Inc. 1993